Women in Pacific Northwest History

Women in Pacific Northwest History

Revised Edition

EDITED BY KAREN J. BLAIR

A McLellan Book

UNIVERSITY OF WASHINGTON PRESS
Seattle and London

This book is published with the assistance of a grant from the McLellan Endowed Series Fund, established through the generosity of Mary McCleary McLellan and Mary McLellan Williams.

Second Printing (paperback), 1990

Printed in the United States of America

Library of Congress Cataloging-in-Publication Data

Women in Pacific Northwest history : an anthology / edited by Karen J. Blair.—Rev. ed.

p. cm.

Includes bibliographical references and index.

ISBN 0-295-98046-X (alk. paper)

1. Women—Northwest, Pacific—History—19th century. 2. Women—Northwest, Pacific—History—20th century. I. Blair, Karen J.

HQ1438.A19 W65 2001

305.4'09795—DC21 00-049755

The paper used in this publication is acid free and recycled from 10 percent post-consumer and at least 50 percent pre-consumer waste. It meets the minimum requirements of the American National Standard for Information Sciences—Permanence of Paper for Printed Library Materials, ANSI Z39.48-1984. ♾♲

To my grandmothers,

Margaret Stilson LeVanda
and
Hedwig Harevich Bunoski

CONTENTS

ACKNOWLEDGMENTS

I am grateful for the help of several individuals in revising the 1989 edition of this anthology to create this updated version. Susan Armitage of Washington State University, Chris Friday of Western Washington University, and Merle Kunz of Central Washington University, all professors of Northwest history, advised me on selections for inclusion. I also appreciate that Graduate Studies and Research awards from Central Washington University provided funding for some of my expenses, including the reproduction and permission rights for the photographs that illustrate these essays. Antoinette Wills assisted me with editing. Cindy Roberts did valiant service as a student assistant, and Kathy Sala aided me with typing. My crackerjack proofreading team included Cindy Emmans, Merle Kunz, Sue Litchfield, Shawne Melvin, Susan Peterchik, and Tom Wellock, whose x-ray vision caught many typos. At the University of Washington Press, I have relied on the advice of Julidta Tarver for this and the former edition.

The completion of the previous edition, as well as my own development as an historian of Pacific Northwest women, owes much to the members of the now-defunct Seattle's Women's History Discussion Group. I wish to thank Audra Adelberger, Jean Coberly, Margaret Hall, Nan Hughes, Kathy Friedman Kasaba, Doris Pieroth, Laura Shapiro, Paula Shields, Nancy Slote, Susan Strasser, Antoinette Wills, and most especially Susan Starbuck for their scholarly companionship, rigorous criticism, unfailing inquisitiveness, seriousness of purpose, and unflagging good humor. I would also like to express my appreciation to Judy Hodgson, who, as director of the University of Washington Women's Information Center, long ago sponsored the conference that inspired the original anthology.

PART 1

NEW DIRECTIONS FOR RESEARCH

More than ten years ago, I introduced the first edition of this anthology with these words:

> When we visualize the history of the Pacific Northwest, we can quickly reconstruct the roles that men played. Early explorers, trappers, missionaries, traders, the Indian chiefs, loggers, sailors, pioneer farmers, miners, businessmen, and aeronautical engineers—all these leap easily to mind. Women are conspicuously absent from the colorful pictures that rise before us. Yet how considerably this omission distorts the truth. The bias that has dismissed women's varied and critical contributions to Washington and Oregon history begs for correction.

The 1988 edition of *Women in Pacific Northwest History* attempted to rectify the imbalance. Yet in the course of the '90s, new research emerged to broaden and deepen our knowledge and analysis of women's historical experience in Washington and Oregon. I am delighted to include new essays by Susan Armitage on historiography, Mary Cross on quilts, and Jerry García on Chicanas and to reprint here material by David Peterson del Mar on domestic violence, Maurine Weiner Greenwald on women and unions, Sylvia Van Kirk on Native American wives of fur traders, and my own case study of a Seattle music club. This edition spans a much wider spectrum of history, from late-eighteenth-century traders to the modern Chicana experience.

I am sorry that it is not possible to include many other fine contributions, including the work of Lillian Schlissel on the Mallek family, Lorraine McConaghy on conservative women of the Seattle suburbs in the 1950s, Mildred Andrews on women's places in King County, Washington, Ron Fields on the painter Abby Williams Hill, Mary Dodds Schlick on Columbia River women's basketry, Sandra Haarsager on women's voluntary organizations and on Mayor Bertha Landes, Julie Roy Jeffrey on the missionary Narcissa Whitman, G. Thomas Edwards on the fight for woman suffrage, Dana Frank on union activists, Jacqueline Williams on pioneer cooking, Nancy Woloch on the landmark Supreme Court case *Muller v. Oregon* (ushering in protective legislation for women), Wayne Carp on adoption, Amy Kesselman on defense workers during World War II, Catherine Parsons Smith and Cynthia Richardson on the composer Mary Carr Moore, Linda Di Biase on the Seattle years of the writer Sui Sin Far, Marilyn Watkins on rural women, and Vicki Halprin on women painters. The scope and strength of recent scholarship makes for a delightful dilemma: rather than offer a comprehensive overview of the literature, I have identified five areas for consideration: New Directions for Research, Politics and Law, Work, Race and Ethnicity, and the Arts.

The following bibliographical essay by Susan Armitage, with dozens of useful suggestions for further study, catalogs the growing sophistication of recent scholarship in the field of Northwest women's history. Scholars are no longer content to embellish traditional histories of the accomplishments of Northwest men with biographies of a few unusual women who mastered skills generally acquired by men, such as the cowgirls, the Roman Catholic missionary and architect Mother Joseph, and the Socialist Anna Louise Strong.

Nor are they willing to flag a few exemplary exponents of "women's work" in such arenas as volunteerism, motherhood, or teaching, the traditional roles for women. Instead, Armitage pushes us to note the viewpoints of new research, especially in the context of women's relationships to others, observing the nuances that gender as well as race and class effect. She reminds us that women are employees of bosses, employers of workers, wives to husbands, mothers to children. They are farmers of the land, missionaries to the Native Americans, trappers for the fur traders, authors to readers, teachers to students, nurses to patients, mayors to constituents, neighbors to neighbors. They manage convents, households, farms, and missions. By surveying new scholarship for women's relationships in six categories, Armitage enables us to embrace the complexity of women's interactions with their world and assess the impact they have made in history.

Happily, even as they are printed, her suggestions grow outdated. New scholarship emerges daily to address topics deserving exploration. Several new studies on neglected subjects will become available in the future to students of Northwest women's history. Among those will be Frances Sneed-Jones's research on African American women's clubs, Susan Starbuck's study of the environmentalist Hazel Wolf, Doris Pieroth's study of mid-twentieth-century women educators, and Gail Dubrow's program to map the spaces utilized by Washington's minority women. We can look forward to a twenty-first century in which women's history continues to enjoy exploration as a vital part of Northwest scholarship.

Tied To Other Lives: Women in Pacific Northwest History

SUSAN ARMITAGE

I never set out to deliberately de-mythologize the West, but . . . when you try to make your characters real and layered and tied to other lives in other places—your work has the inevitable effect of dismantling the myth of the West as the home of heroic, loner white guys moving through an unpeopled and uncomplicated place.

Deirdre McNamer

Some facts are so obvious that we tend to forget them, and one is that the Pacific Northwest could not have been a site of continued human habitation without women. Women are *essential* in all societies: they assure continuity physically by birthing the next generation and psychologically by raising the children who claim the land and build lasting communities on it.[1] Once we understand how basic the presence of women has been to the Pacific Northwest, we can begin to see history through their eyes. As we do that we will find, as the Montana author Dierdre McNamer did, that women's lives are "real and layered and tied to other lives in other places."[2] That realization requires us to think of Pacific Northwest history in new ways. This essay begins with a background sketch showing how women's historians have come to understand the significance of gender relationships. Building on that knowledge, the essay shows the importance of gender relationships in six different areas: the lives of American Indian women, intercultural relations, Euro-American migration and settlement, social reform, labor, and community building. The larger goal of the essay is to demonstrate the way in which the focus on relationships provides a basic conceptual framework for the study of Pacific Northwest history.

As women's history has developed over the past thirty years into a major field within American history, ways of thinking about women in historical terms have changed. At first, in the 1970s, women's historians concentrated on recovering the lives of overlooked women—first the famous ones, and then lesser-known ones—and adding them to the historical record.[3] As the historical details of women's lives were recovered, it became obvious that appropriate female behavior (often summed up in the term *womanhood*) was not an unchanging ideal but a concept that changed from one historical period to the next. Sometimes the changes were abrupt, as in the 1920s when the cigarette-smoking flapper with her short skirts and bobbed hair repudiated her mother's long skirts, long hair, and modest behavior. Sometimes the changes were slower, as in the long struggle for woman suffrage. It took almost a century for women to convince men that females should vote.[4] As women's historians were working to put women into history, feminist cultural anthropologists were discovering that there was wide variety in the meanings that different cultures have given to sexual difference.[5] Building on this insight, the historian Joan Scott's influential 1986 article, "Gender: A Useful Category of Historical Analysis," proposed gender as a basic analytic category, as important as other commonly used historical concepts like race and class. Scott observed that the way a particular society defines the difference between the sexes—gender—is the key to understanding other relationships of difference and power within that society.[6]

Women's historians now believe that gender relationships are what hold a culture together. You might say that it all begins at home. The way a particular culture views the difference between the sexes shapes relationships between husband and wife and between parents and children and establishes a gendered division of labor within the family and in its wider kinship network. The gender relationships that operate at a personal and individual level structure people's expectations about the connections between private and public power and their understanding of how those power relationships operate. For example, in the highly patriarchal world of colonial America, women were defined as inferior and dependent upon men. Women did not expect to play leadership roles in public matters such as politics or formal religious observances. With the exception of a few famous rebels like Anne Hutchinson, colonial women knew that their roles were subordinate and private. But in differently organized groups, such as American Indian societies where the kinship network was paramount, power was often so diffused as to be hard to locate, the difference between public and private was small, and women assumed a wide variety of roles. As these brief examples show, attention to gender relationships offers historians a new and powerful way to understand the power relationships within a given society.

At a more personal level, individuals rarely think to question the family relationships, work roles, and public power structures of their own society, and they are surprised when they discover different gender relationships in other cultural groups. For example, when Phoebe Judson pioneered the

Nooksack Valley with her family in the 1880s, she felt a strong "bond of womanhood" with the Lummi woman she knew as "Old Sally," arising out of their common concerns for their children and family. But for all their commonalities, the two women were, as Phoebe realized, very different. She thought it was because she and her family had progressed to a "higher stage of civilization" than Sally and her fellow Lummis.[7] We, however, can see that each woman was embedded in a different gender relationship. They inhabited different networks of power relationships, beginning with marriage and kinship ties and patterns of economic livelihood, widening outward to relationships among different races and access to economic opportunities and political power. Their expectations about how people should interact were based on their own gender relationships, specific to their own societies. Given these unarticulated differences, it is no wonder that cultural misunderstandings and conflicts were so prevalent when white pioneers interacted with American Indian peoples.

By focusing on the gender relationships of different cultural groups, historians can link the life of an individual woman or man to larger generalizations about the public issues with which regional history is concerned. Family and kinship relationships are replicated in the ways communities are organized, and that organization in turn shapes politics at the nonlocal level. Gender thus gives us a way to understand the link between the lives of ordinary people and great national events, such as, for example, the role shifts that occurred during World War II when many young men went off to war and their wives took new and unaccustomed jobs in Pacific Northwest shipyards and airplane factories. Above all, we now have a way to think about how relationships of gender, race, and class interact when peoples of different races and cultures, such as Phoebe and Sally, and Euro-American pioneers and indigenous peoples, met in the Pacific Northwest.

There is much about the history of Pacific Northwest Indian societies before contact with Europeans that we will never know, but gender analysis gives us a place to start. Women's history has taught us that for most women work and kinship have been intimately related. In Pacific Northwest Indian societies, the tribal unit was a kinship network that cooperated to gather, hunt, fish, and grow the food necessary for life. We can easily see how work and kinship interacted in the lives of Indian women. Or we would, if the male anthropologists who did the early studies of Pacific Northwest Indian groups had paid more attention to women's work!

From scanty sources, we can begin to piece together an outline of women's lives before white contact. The Plateau tribes (so called because of their location in the interior Pacific Northwest) followed a seasonal round of gather-

A woman from the mid-Columbia region weaves a storage bag, 1907
(courtesy Maryhill Museum of Art, 1991.06.01)

ing, hunting, and fishing activities. Women provided about half the food supply, a finding that is consistent with worldwide reconsideration of the importance of women's activities in so-called hunter-gatherer societies. All tribal work was strictly gender-divided, but there was no indication that men's work was regarded more highly than women's work. Nor in the ceremonial and religious aspects of life did there appear to be much gender difference. It is difficult to fully grasp the worldview that life in such tight-knit, traditional societies produced, but one route is through serious appreciation of Indian art. A book such as Mary Schlick's *Columbia River Basketry: Gift of the Ancestors, Gift of the Earth* shows us the ways in which all aspects of life—work, religion, and kinship—came together in the baskets that women wove.[8] Baskets were practical implements of daily life and work, but the skill with which women wove them, their decoration, and their wider uses had important religious and symbolic meaning to the native peoples of the Columbia River. Another splendid example of the connection between culture and women's arts is offered in *A Song to the Creator: Traditional Arts of*

Native American Women of the Plateau. One of the most important contributions of this book is its recognition of cultural continuity: women's traditional arts are still practiced today.[9]

The lesson of cultural continuity is also a major theme of Margaret Blackman's life history of Florence Edenshaw Davidson, a Haida woman. This study provides a useful model. Blackman, an anthropologist, interviewed Davidson many times, drawing from her not only recollections of family and tribal history but also a clear sense of the ways that Davidson adapted traditional customs and attitudes to contemporary life. Other anthropologists, working carefully with material gathered early in the century, have begun to tease out a better understanding of women's lives and of their important roles in their societies.[10]

One unusual regional source is the writings of Christine Quintasket (Mourning Dove) of the Colville Confederated Tribes of eastern Washington. Generally acknowledged as the first female American Indian novelist, Mourning Dove had a life better documented than most of her contemporaries. Both her life and her writings shed light on the difficulties of Indian life in the early twentieth century. A mixed-race woman who spent much of her life as a migrant worker, Quintasket was grateful for the friendship and literary support provided by Lucullus McWhorter, a serious student of American Indian life. With his help, she published her novel, *Cogewea, the Half-Blood*, in 1927. But, as was often true in such patronage relationships, McWhorter's efforts to make Quintasket's writings acceptable to a white audience partially robbed her of her own voice, and critical opinion of her novel was lukewarm. Today, we recognize her novel (reprinted in 1981), her volume of tribal stories, and her recently discovered autobiography as important sources for understanding the history of Pacific Northwest Indian women. Her writings remind us that many northwestern women have written fictionalized autobiographies. Using their fiction carefully, historians can learn much about the emotional realities of women's lives.[11]

The lives of American Indian women who lived on the edges of the Plateau region differed in many respects from those of Plateau women, reminding us that *Indian* is a designation applied by Euro-Americans to cultures that perceived themselves as very different from one other. The Nez Perce, who lived in what is now Idaho, acquired horses in the 1730s. They quickly developed an obsession with them and an attraction to Plains Indian customs such as buffalo hunting. These changes probably adversely affected Nez Perce women, as they did the women of the Plains tribes. As men began to claim status depending on the number of horses they owned, women's work came to seem more menial and their personal status lower, for only men owned horses. Still another pattern is evident in the rich and complex coastal tribes from the Makah and the Quileute-Hoh in the south to the Tlingit in the north. These groups are usually described as warring, trading, captive-taking, slave-owning, hierarchical, and status-proud. As was the case with the Nez Perce, the existence of private wealth may have made coastal women subordinate, but it seems also to have encouraged special roles and skills among them, such as trading.[12]

Certainly the first Europeans to visit the Pacific Northwest were impressed by coastal Indian women's prowess as traders. Chinook women traded sea otter furs to the British and American sailors engaged in the China trade that began in the 1780s. Chinook women also traded sex, a relationship that the Europeans viewed as prostitution but that had a different meaning for the Indian women themselves. While the Europeans understood sexual intercourse with native women as an immoral transaction (sex for money or trade goods), the Chinook women, who did not share restrictive European sexual notions, regarded it as simply another kind of barter.[13] This is an early example of the misunderstandings that different cultural ideas about gender roles produced.

Still another aspect of cross-cultural gender relationships can be seen in the history of the Hudson's Bay Company post at Fort Vancouver, center of the land-based Pacific Northwest fur trade. Many of the Indian women associated with Fort Vancouver were traders of furs, sex, or other services.[14] Some, such as Margaret McLoughlin, were married to Euro-American men, in Margaret's case to John McLoughlin, the chief official of the Hudson's Bay Company for the Columbia District. In western Canada, the original home of the Hudson's Bay Company, a distinct population, known as the *métis* ("mixed" in French) emerged as a result of several centuries of sexual encounters between fur-trading Europeans and native women. The history of the *métis*, and especially *métis* women, has been studied by Sylvia Van Kirk, Jennifer Brown, and Jacqueline Peterson. *Métis* women were highly sought as wives by Hudson's Bay Company officials until 1830, when British settlement (as opposed to trading) was allowed in the Canadian West and white women became available as marriage partners. In the Pacific Northwest, the mixed-race children that Margaret McLoughlin and other women bore were living evidence of intercultural contacts, but the Americans who claimed the region from the British in the 1840s did not acknowledge the *métis* as a distinct people. Janet Campbell Hale, herself a *métis* descendant of Margaret and John McLoughlin, recounts in her memoir *Bloodlines* the pain of this unacknowledged ancestry. In American eyes, she is simply "Indian."[15]

Compared to what happened in many other regions of the West, American occupation of the Pacific Northwest occurred with relatively little open warfare between Euro-Americans and Indian peoples. But there are other forms of violence that we have failed to fully recognize. Even before they claimed land, Euro-American traders and settlers disrupted native life by drawing Indians into the commercial economy and by spreading disease that devastated indigenous peoples throughout the Americas. Furthermore, recent studies that focus on private lives and the experience of women seem to indicate that domestic violence was a more than occasional aspect of intercultural sexual relationships.[16] Indeed, when viewed from the perspective of Indian women, it appears that the peaceful settlement of the Pacific Northwest by Euro-Americans was as much an act of conquest as open warfare would have been.

Euro-American women played a critical role in the intercultural interactions of the settlement period. The advance wave of settlement included three Euro-American missionary women, Narcissa Whitman, Eliza Spalding, and Mary Richardson Walker, who are among the best-known women in Pacific Northwest history.[17] As Julie Jeffrey so poignantly shows in *Converting the West,* Narcissa Whitman genuinely felt a mission to "civilize" the Indians, but she neither understood nor liked the Cayuse peoples she had come to save. Women missionaries and their successors such as the schoolteachers and field matrons who worked on Indian reservations later in the nineteenth century were employed to work with native women, but, like Whitman, many had great difficulty bridging the cultural gap between themselves and their pupils. Because their purpose was to encourage Indian women to adopt Euro-American gender roles, missionary women and teachers distrusted and disparaged Indian gender relationships. They disapproved of Indian attitudes toward sexuality, they urged the adoption of European styles of clothing, they discouraged native religion, and they wanted to confine American Indian women's work to domestic tasks. We need to look carefully at both sides of these "civilizing" missions to understand how Pacific Northwest Indian women resisted or adapted to the pressures to change their traditional beliefs and adopt new roles. It is too simplistic to see the white women as naïve, misguided, or evil, although the effects of their efforts may have been all three. Similarly, it is equally simplistic to view Indian women as resistant traditionalists. Rather, they doubtless sought to make their own choices between old and new behaviors and attitudes.

The attraction of paying close attention to these meetings among women of different cultures is precisely that they do not yield simple answers. The places where women of different racial ethnic groups met and disagreed are some of the most fruitful locations for study of cultural differences. As the historian Peggy Pascoe has pointed out, these "cultural crossroads" are the places where the interconnections (and misunderstandings) among gender, class, and culture are most clear.[18]

Large-scale American settlement of the Pacific Northwest began in the 1840s. The most celebrated pioneers migrated via the Oregon Trail, and the story of their journeys still holds great popular appeal today. However, as women's historians have rediscovered many women's trail diaries, the trail experience that used to be regarded as a dramatic male adventure now has a more somber tone. John Mack Faragher's *Women and Men on the Overland Trail* (1979) was one of the first efforts to study systematically patterns of daily life on the four-to-six-month trip. Faragher gave us a clear sense of the ways in which men's and women's work on the overland journey differed and how those differences shaped expectations. While never denying the adventure and excitement of the journey, Faragher found that women's diaries revealed the reserves of endurance on which overlanders had to draw to counteract the general exhaustion of the long trip. Lillian Schlissel, in *Women's Diaries of the Westward Journey* (1971), found that women's reactions varied by age and maternal status, but generally women were less eager pioneers than men because they more strongly felt (or at least expressed) the pain of parting with their kin who remained behind.[19]

This gender difference in trail diaries gives us a glimpse of Euro-American gender relationships at an important moment of transition. As Mary Ryan has shown in *The Cradle of the Middle Class* (1981), early-nineteenth-century Americans in the first throes of industrialization were breaking away from extended kin networks and tight-knit communities in favor of more autonomous nuclear families that fostered individualism in their children.[20] One of the ways to read the gendered difference in trail diaries is to suggest that men were further along in this transition toward individualism than were women. Men perceived the overland journey as a challenge and adventure, while their wives, still deeply embedded in kin networks, experienced it as painful separation.

Unfortunately, many trail diaries cease at the trail's end. Even a well-known memoir like *A Pioneer's Search for an Ideal Home* by Phoebe Judson tells us more about the six months of her trail experience than of the sixty subsequent years she lived in Washington. We need to know more about what women did once they got here, and writers like Shannon Applegate—who wrote *Skookum* (1988), an engaging history of the pioneer Applegate family—are beginning to fill in the blanks. Ironically, one of the most prolific pioneer-era historians was a woman, but although Frances Fuller Victor was an enthusiastic recorder of contemporary events, she seemed to believe that only what men did was important. One of her best-known books, *The River of the*

Harvest cook and crew in Eastern Washington wheat fields, 1916
(courtesy Washington State University Archives, 79–150)

West (1870), glorified the life of the mountain man Joe Meek. Another early writer, Margaret Jewett Bailey, wrote such a candid account of domestic violence within the Oregon missionary community that her lightly fictionalized novel, *The Grains* (1854), was shunned as scandalous.[21] Women's historians have tended to rely heavily on Abigail Scott Duniway's autobiography, *Path Breaking* (1914) and Ruth Moynihan's biography of her, *Rebel for Rights* (1983), for insight into the female pioneer experience. Duniway offered a famous catalog of a farm woman's work:

> To bear two children in two and a half years from my marriage day, to make thousands of pounds of butter every year for market, . . . to sew and cook, and wash and iron; to bake and clean and stew and fry; to be, in short, a general pioneer drudge, with never a penny of my own.[22]

Duniway's reference to her economic contribution underlines the immense importance of women's efforts in the establishment of the region's farms. Later generations of farm women continued to perform the same productive activities on the family farm until after World War II. Their activities represent an interesting and still inadequately understood intersection of gender with regional history. The farms themselves—wheat farms in the eastern part of the region, dairy and mixed farming in the west—were commercial farms almost from their beginnings, yet well into the twentieth century farm women performed the same range of activities as had their grandmothers. Long after manufactured products were available, farm women continued their home production of food, clothing, and items for family use. Clearly, on poor and marginal farms, home production by women freed up scarce cash for farm equipment and supplies rather than for family subsistence.[23] But the persistence of women's domestic work patterns even on wealthier farms suggests that their motivation went beyond economic explanations. Perhaps, just as the women on the Oregon Trail struggled to hold onto kinship networks, Pacific Northwest farm women tried through their own domestic work to demonstrate their commitment to the gender relationships that were a key part of family farm enterprises. In a world where individual wage work has long been the norm, farm women remained committed to a family work ideal.[24]

Aside from her candid description of her life as a farm woman, Abigail Scott Duniway remains a fascinating and controversial regional figure. After they lost their farm in 1862, the Duniways moved to Portland, where she began her own newspaper, *The New Northwest*, in 1871 and became the Pacific Northwest's best-known and most persistent advocate for women's rights. Duniway's outspoken feminism was unusual in an age when few women freely voiced their opinions. Her campaign for woman suffrage, which she began in 1871 and continued until success in Oregon in 1912, clearly sprang from her personal sense of the discrepancy between women's essential economic role and their political voicelessness.

In her career as an activist, Duniway experienced a generation gap between members of the pioneer generation like herself and younger, more urban and genteel women who came to the Pacific Northwest in the 1880s, when the transcontinental railroad made travel to the region relatively easy. The attitudes and activities of these post-pioneer women indicated the extent to which the Pacific Northwest was becoming part of the national and international economy. The new urban women were building a middle class and becoming much more like their East Coast counterparts than had been true of Duniway's contemporaries. The difference that their presence and attitudes made can be traced in G. Thomas Edwards's *Sowing Good Seeds*, which examines changing attitudes of regional newspapers toward the veteran suffragist

Susan B. Anthony when she toured the Pacific Northwest in 1871, 1896, and 1905. Beginning with unbridled hostility toward woman suffrage and the "unnatural" Anthony in the 1870s, most newspapermen by the turn of the century were resigned (if not reconciled) not only to suffrage but to the notion of women's participation in public affairs.[25] These changing attitudes reflect a significant shift in gender relationships. The active reform efforts of middle-class women, while falling short of a direct political challenge to men, indicate the development of middle-class gender relationships that made women more confident and assertive in public activities than had been earlier generations of women. As an essential part of their new understanding of gender roles, many women entered the public arena with reform agendas on behalf of women and children of all economic classes. To these reformers, gender was such a strong tie among women that class (and sometimes even racial) differences paled in comparison.

Beginning in the 1880s, middle-class women in Seattle, Portland, Boise, and many smaller towns formed women's clubs with serious civic agendas, just like their eastern counterparts. In *Seattle Women: A Legacy of Community Development* and *Washington Women as Path Breakers*, the historian Mildred Andrews documents a mind-boggling array of women's organizations devoted to health care, hospitals, orphan homes, libraries, YWCAs, settlement houses, education, arts, and preservation, in addition to more conventionally "political" crusades for temperance and woman suffrage.[26] Suffrage was successful in Idaho in 1896, probably because of its links with Populism, and was enacted in Washington in 1910 and Oregon in 1912. The reason why suffrage succeeded in the West while failing in the East probably lies with the effectiveness of western women's organizing. The relative recency of settlement in the Pacific Northwest gave women opportunity for institution-building that eastern women, in longer-established regions, did not have. Club members who began by founding libraries and other uncontroversial institutions often turned to more activist sorts of social reform such as children's health and moral reforms like campaigns against prostitution and alcohol. These were all gendered issues. Certainly temperance was defined in gendered terms: alcohol posed a threat to the home, for men who drank too much threatened their wives and children with economic ruin as well as domestic abuse. For these reasons, temperance was an issue on which many women (although not Abigail Scott Duniway) agreed.[27]

Indeed, gender solidarity was such a compelling cause in the Pacific Northwest that Oregon led the nation in a key issue in women's rights. In 1903, the state passed a law that limited the work of women and children in commercial laundries to no more than ten hours a day. When a Portland laundry owner, Curt Muller, challenged the law, the case made its way to the Supreme Court, where in a landmark 1908 decision (*Muller vs. Oregon*) the Court decided in favor of Oregon. This gendered ruling, which was specifically argued on the basis of the need to protect the reproductive health of women, formed the basis for protective labor laws, which were pioneering state interventions in private enterprise.[28]

The strong current of social reform that carried so many middle-class Pacific Northwest women into public affairs peaked in the 1920s. The career of Bertha Knight Landes, briefly mayor of Seattle in that decade (the first woman mayor of a major American city), epitomized the trajectory of the reform impulse. Landes, an active suffragist and social "housekeeper," was elected mayor in 1926 on a reform platform to clean up bootlegging and prostitution in the city. As Sandra Haarsager showed in her thoughtful biography, Landes's defeat just two years later had no single cause, but suddenly her linkage of women's domestic role and social reform seemed out of date. The 1920s roared on, and Landes faded from the political scene. Yet another shift in gender relationships had occurred, causing younger women to scorn their mothers' reforming zeal.[29]

The 1920s were also a culmination point for the labor radicalism that had distinguished the Pacific Northwest since the 1890s. Several famous women played parts in this labor militancy. Elizabeth Gurley Flynn, the famous "Rebel Girl," was an organizer for the Industrial Workers of the World (the IWW) in the Spokane Free Speech fight of 1909. When she was jailed for her militancy, the Spokane Women's Club successfully argued that a pregnant woman, regardless of her politics, ought not to be jailed. Flynn, four months pregnant, was released. A few years later, Anna Louise Strong, a Socialist journalist, played a role in fomenting the Seattle General Strike of 1919 by making sure that Seattle workers knew about the triumph of communism in Russia.[30] Dana Frank's impressive study *Purchasing Power* examines the role of women in the decline of militancy in Seattle following the general strike. During the 1920s, Seattle's labor unions turned away from strikes and workplace confrontations to consumer organizing, emphasizing cooperative buying, boycotts, and union label purchasing. This moved union tactics into women's terrain, for, as Frank points out, working-class women's task was consumption: "Women's assigned *job* within the working-class family was to stretch the family budget." What happened in the 1920s, Frank demonstrates, was that male unionists adopted new tactics without adjusting their ideas about gender relations. "Without a willingness to share power with women, without a willingness to ask how women might choose to politicize consumption, and without an equal commitment of women's concerns at the waged workplace as well, consumer organizing could only partially succeed."[31]

Meanwhile, as the economy of the region grew, the population diversified and increasing numbers of women entered the work force. The opportunities they found were very limited. Although in the earliest days of Pacific Northwest settlement there had been greater opportunity for professional women—doctors like Bethinia Owens-Adair in Oregon and lawyers like Ella Knowles in Montana—than on the East Coast, by the turn of the century this western differential had disappeared.[32] Women's choices were restricted because there were few large cities with diverse industries and because the work forces in large regional occupations like logging, fishing, and mining were male.[33] Women continued to work on family farms, as noted earlier, but in popular stereotype the man was the farmer and the woman the farm wife. Off the farm, wage work for women was largely confined to domestic service and restaurant work or to teaching and nursing.

The topic of women's work in the Pacific Northwest has yet to be investigated in a systematic way. Our few scraps of information have come largely from oral history interviews. One Euro-American woman recalled that she reluctantly chose nursing because "in reality, I couldn't even dream of becoming a doctor. The nearest thing I could ever be was a nurse." An African American woman recalled her mother's work as a domestic: "She did x and y and all that for 25 cents a day. Can you beat it?" Another woman recalled, "I was in the ninth grade when my mother took me out of school to help her in the restaurant because she couldn't find a girl that could turn out work like I could. She and I would sit up until 12 o'clock at night picking those chickens and getting them ready."[34]

These brief oral history excerpts alert us to a significant aspect of women's labor: as limited as the choices were, there were further restrictions depending on one's race, ethnicity, and social class. We do not yet fully understand how this sorting process worked. The restriction of African American women to domestic work was a well-known national phenomenon, but we cannot explain the different participation rates of Scandinavian women in domestic service that Janice Reiff found in late-nineteenth-century Seattle: 90 percent of Norwegian women were domestics and 60 percent of Swedish women, compared to 25 percent of the women in other ethnic groups.[35] Another study, of hop picking in the Yakima Valley, showed constant female participation in a rapidly changing work force: within a forty-year period, the pickers changed from Indian families to local Euro-American women and children who were encouraged by the farmers to regard picking as a semiholiday to Mexican migrant families.[36] Furthermore, much of women's work remained hidden, as this oral history reminds us: "[My mother] did a little dressmaking at home, much against my father's better judgement. It was in the days when women weren't supposed to work outside the home. He felt that he would be embarrassed if she worked for money. He didn't object to her working but he didn't like people to know it."[37] These complex labor patterns deserve our careful attention. Drawing on studies of East Coast immigrant women, we infer that the work roles of women of different races and ethnicities were determined partly by their culture's understanding of gender relationships and partly by the available niches in the Pacific Northwest economy, but we cannot yet say with precision what those were.[38]

Whatever the prewar patterns of women's work may have been, there is no doubt that World War II was a turning point for the region's economy and for women personally. Work in shipyards and munitions factories—so much of it that it even pulled Native American women off the reservations where they had been struggling to survive—the migration of African Americans to Seattle and Portland, the efforts of Japanese and Japanese American women to hold their families together under the onslaught of internment, the accelerated push toward farm mechanization caused by the war—all meant changes for the region and its women. Of all of these dramatic changes, the employment of women in the Kaiser shipyards in Portland has drawn the most attention. In the 1970s, the Northwest Women's Oral History Project conducted many interviews with former shipyard women and distilled the findings in a slide/tape show, "Good Work, Sister!" A few years later, Amy Kesselman, a project member, provided further documentation in *Fleeting Opportunities*, based in part on the oral histories. Other historians have written on women's wartime work in Portland and Seattle.[39] Wartime work attracts attention in part because it is so unlike traditional women's work. The war plants gave women their first chance to prove that they could do "men's work" at (almost) men's wages. For the majority of women, when the war ended, their jobs ended. But the effects were long-lasting, for historians believe that the brief wartime accomplishment fueled the substantial and permanent entry of women into the work force that began in the 1950s and continues today.[40]

Following World War II, the Pacific Northwest was changed by the effects of the great dam-building projects of the 1930s and continued migration to the region from other parts of the United States, from Mexico, and from Asia. The irrigated farmlands of central Washington and southern Idaho created by the dams were sites of new community-building beginning in the 1950s by Euro-Americans and Mexicans alike. The cities, Seattle in particular, experienced major suburban growth, while within the city the Japanese community dispersed but the Chinese community was revitalized by the lifting of restrictions on Asian immigration.

The story of women's activities in the building of these new urban, suburban, and ethnic communities is an important part of post-World War II regional history. There are lessons to be learned from the ways in which ethnic studies scholars have approached community studies. Although some scholars have ignored gender, preferring to concentrate on issues of race and economic class, ethnic studies scholars have always understood the importance of community to *everyone,* female and male alike. There is valuable information in studies like Quintard Taylor's *Forging of a Black Community,* Erasmo Gamboa's *Mexican Labor and World War II: Braceros in the Pacific Northwest* and the essays gathered in *Peoples of Washington.* There are exceptionally valuable community oral history projects, especially Esther Mumford's on African Americans and Dorothy Cordova's on Filipinos. Gail Nomura's beautiful essay "*Tsugiki,* a Grafting" and her forthcoming study both focus on the Japanese farming community in Yakima.[41] In Oregon, there are similar studies of Portland's racial and ethnic communities and particularly rich studies of the Japanese in Oregon's Hood River Valley. Lauren Kessler's *Stubborn Twig* tells the moving story of three generations of the Matsui family, while Linda Tamura's collection of oral histories, *The Hood River Issei,* is another rich source.[42] These studies serve as a useful corrective to the strong tendency in all of western history to see only the individual and not the networks of family, work, and ethnicity in which we are all embedded.

There is still another reason to read community studies: they help us avoid the error of treating one particular author as representative of her entire ethnic or racial group. This was the fate of Seattle's Monica Sone, whose fine autobiography, *Nisei Daughter,* was for a long time the only book by a Japanese woman on Seattle and the wartime internment experience. Now that other books and articles have appeared, we can more fully appreciate the individuality of Sone's account.[43]

Historians have been slow to treat the past fifty years of regional events as history, yet the same processes of migration and community formation go on today as they did a century ago. As is so often the case, regional writers have done more to illuminate the lives of women, and the connections in which they are embedded, than have historians. Contemporary novelists build on a tradition of community-based regional novels, often autobiographical, that was established early in the century and that has been explored in Jean M. Ward and Elaine Maveety's collection, *Pacific Northwest Women, 1815–1925: Lives, Memories, and Writings* (1995).[44] Perhaps the best-recognized of these early novelists was Carol Ryrie Brink, who in the 1930s wrote several novels set in and around Moscow, Idaho, her family home. Marilyn Robinson's memorable novel about the 1950s, *Housekeeping*, pits Sylvie, a quintessential western adventurer, against the demands of domesticity in a haunting western setting, Lake Pend d'Oreille in northern Idaho. Recently, western women's writing has enriched our understanding of many different women. To mention but three examples, Mary Clearman Blew's *All But the Waltz* and *Balsamroot* follow three generations of women as they move from the changing ranch life of Montana to Puget Sound and Lewiston, Idaho. Ursula LeGuin imagines an entire Oregon seacoast community, its women, their families, and their histories, in *Searoad*, while in *Bloodlines* Janet Campbell Hale tells an often-searing family story that links the lives of residents of the early-eighteenth-century Hudson's Bay post of Fort Vancouver with today's Coeur d'Alene Indians of northern Idaho. Many other fine writers, poets, and artists are also currently exploring women's lives.[45]

For all of the previous pages' insights into the lives of Pacific Northwest women, we are still a long way from a full understanding of regional women's history. Until we have that history, the knowledge of the Pacific Northwest will remain incomplete. Women's history has given us the tools to fully map the webs of relationships that have tied the lives of the diverse women of the Pacific Northwest to other lives. Only when we have followed those ties will we be able to write the real, layered, complicated, and densely peopled history of our region.

NOTES

1. Carolyn Merchant explains the central role of women in biological and cultural reproduction in *Ecological Revolutions: Nature, Gender, and Science in New England* (Chapel Hill: University of North Carolina Press, 1989).

2. Dierdre McNamer, quoted in *Auntie's Newsletter* (Spokane, Wash.), 1996.

3. Among the early works were Nancy Cott, *Root of Bitterness* (New York: Dutton, 1972); Eleanor Flexner, *Century of Struggle: The Woman's Rights Movement in the United States* (Cambridge: Belknap Press of Harvard University Press, 1959); Gerda Lerner, *The Grimke Sisters from South Carolina: Pioneers for Woman's Rights and Abolition* (New York: Houghton Mifflin, 1969); Ann D. Gordon, Mari Jo Buhle, and Nancy Schrom, "Women in Society," *Radical America* 5 (1971): 4–5.

4. See, for example, Mary Ryan, *Womanhood in America* (New York: Franklin Watts, 1983).

5. See, for example, Gayle Rubin, "The Traffic in Women: Notes on the 'Political Economy' of Sex," in Rayna Reiter, ed., *Toward an Anthropology of Women* (New York: Monthly Review Press, 1975).

6. Joan Scott, "Gender: A Useful Category of Historical Analysis," *American Historical Review* 91, no. 5 (December 1986).

7. Phoebe Judson, *A Pioneer's Search for an Ideal Home* (1925; rpt. Lincoln: University of Nebraska Press, 1984), pp. 225, 245–48.

8. Mary Schlick, *Columbia River Basketry: Gift of the Ancestors, Gift of the Earth* (Seattle: University of Washington Press, 1994).

9. Lillian Ackerman, ed., *A Song to the Creator: Traditional Arts of Native American Women of the Plateau* (Norman: University of Oklahoma Press, 1997).

10. Margaret Blackman, *During My Time: The Life of Florence Edenshaw Davidson, a Haida Woman* (Seattle: University of Washington Press, 1982); Laura F. Klein and Lillian Ackerman, eds., *Women and Power in Native North America* (Norman: University of Oklahoma Press, 1995).

11. Christine Quintasket, *Cogewea, the Half-Blood* (Lincoln: University of Nebraska Press, 1981); *Tales of the Okanogans* (Fairfield, Wash.: Ye Galleon Press, 1976); Jay Miller, ed., *Mourning Dove: A Salishan Autobiography* (Lincoln: University of Nebraska Press, 1990).

12. Alan M. Klein, "The Political-Economy of Gender: A 19th Century Plains Indian Case Study," in Patricia Albers and Beatrice Medicine, eds., *The Hidden Half: Studies of Plains Indian Women* (Washington, D.C.: University Press of America, 1983), pp. 143–74; Margot Liberty, "Hell Came with Horses: Plains Indian Women in the Equestrian Era," *Montana, the Magazine of Western History* 32, no. 3 (Summer 1982): 10–19.

13. James Rhonda, *Lewis and Clark Among the Indians* (Lincoln: University of Nebraska Press, 1984), p. 208.

14. John Hussey, "The Women of Fort Vancouver," *Oregon Historical Quarterly* 92, no. 3 (1991): 265–308.

15. Sylvia Van Kirk, *Many Tender Ties: Women in Fur Trade Society, 1670–1870* (Norman: University of Oklahoma Press, 1983); Jennifer Brown, *Strangers in Blood* (Vancouver, B.C.: University of British Columbia Press, 1980); Jacqueline Peterson and Jennifer Brown, eds., *The New Peoples: Being and Becoming Métis in North America* (Lincoln: University of Nebraska Press, 1985); Janet Campbell Hale, *Bloodlines: The Odyssey of a Native Daughter* (New York: Random House, 1993).

16. Coll Peter Thrush and Robert Keller, "'I See What I Have Done': The Life and Murder Trial of Xwelas, a S'Klallam Woman," *Western Historical Quarterly* 26, no. 2 (1995): 169–83; David Peterson del Mar, *What Trouble I Have Seen: A History of Violence Against Wives* (Cambridge: Harvard University Press, 1996).

17. Julie Roy Jeffrey, *Converting the West: A Biography of Narcissa Whitman* (Norman: University of Oklahoma Press, 1991); see also Clifford Drury, *First White Women Over the Rockies* (Glendale, Calif.: Arthur H. Clark, 1983), 3 vols. Although Drury's interpretation is dated, his volumes include almost complete texts of diaries kept by these early missionary women.

18. E. Jane Gay, *With the Nez Perces: Alice Fletcher in the Field, 1889–92* (Lincoln: University of Nebraska Press, 1981); Peggy Pascoe, "Western Women at the Cultural Crossroads," in Patricia Nelson Limerick, Clyde Milner, and Charles Rankin, eds., *Trails: Towards a New Western History* (Lawrence: University of Kansas Press, 1991), pp. 40–58; Peggy Pascoe, *Relations of Rescue: The Search for Female Moral Authority in the American West, 1874–1939* (New York: Oxford University Press, 1990).

19. John Mack Faragher, *Women and Men on the Overland Trail* (New Haven: Yale University Press, 1979); Lillian Schlissel, *Women's Diaries of the Westward Journey* (New York: Schocken Books, 1971).

20. Mary Ryan, *The Cradle of the Middle Class: The Family in Oneida County, New York, 1790–1865* (New York: Oxford University Press, 1981).

21. Shannon Applegate, *Skookum: An Oregon Pioneer Family's History and Lore* (New York: William Morrow, 1988). Frances Fuller Victor, *River of the West* (1870; rpt. Boise: Tamarack Books, 1984); Jim Martin, *A Bit of a Blue: The Life and Work of Frances Fuller Victor* (Salem, Ore.: Deep Well Publishing Co., 1992); Margaret Jewett Bailey, *The Grains* (1854; rpt., Corvallis: Oregon State University Press, 1986).

22. Abigail Scott Duniway, *Path Breaking* (New York: Schocken Books, 1971), pp. 9–10; Ruth Barnes Moynihan, *Rebel for Rights: Abigail Scott Duniway* (New Haven: Yale University Press, 1983).

23. Corky Bush, "'He Isn't Half So Cranky As He Used to Be!': Agricultural Mechanization, Comparable Worth, and the Changing Farm Family," in Carol Groneman and Mary Beth Norton, eds., *"To Toil the Livelong Day": America's Women at Work, 1780–1980* (Ithaca, N.Y.: Cornell University Press, 1987).

24. I am indebted to Crystal Cambron, Ph.D. candidate in American Studies at Washington State University, for this insight.

25. G. Thomas Edwards, *Sowing Good Seeds* (Portland: Oregon Historical Society Press, 1990).

26. Mildred Andrews, *Seattle Women: A Legacy of Community Development* (Seattle: YWCA of Seattle-King County, 1984); Mildred Tanner Andrews, *Washington Women as Path Breakers* (Dubuque, Iowa: Kendall/Hunt Publishing, 1989); see also a forthcoming work by Sandra Haarsager on women's clubs in Washington, Oregon, and Idaho.

27. Sandra Haarsager, *Organized Womanhood: Cultural Politics in the Pacific Northwest, 1840–1920* (Norman: University of Oklahoma Press, 1997).

28. Nancy Woloch, *Muller vs. Oregon: A Brief History with Documents* (New York: Bedford/St. Martin's, 1996).

29. Sandra Haarsager, *Bertha Knight Landes of Seattle, Big-City Mayor* (Norman: University of Oklahoma Press, 1994); Doris H. Pieroth, "Bertha Knight Landes: The Woman Who Was Mayor," in this volume. For the wider 1920s role shift and the failure of women's reforms, see Rosalind Rosenberg, *Divided Lives: American Women in the Twentieth Century* (New York: Hill and Wang, 1992), pp. 63–101.

30. Helen C. Camp, *Iron in Her Soul: A Biography of Elizabeth Gurley Flynn* (Pullman: Washington State University Press, 1995), pp. 22–25; Anna Louise Strong, *I Change Worlds* (1935; rpt., Seattle: Seal Press, 1979).

31. Dana Frank, "Gender, Consumer Organizing, and the Seattle Labor Movement, 1919–1929," in Ava Baron, ed., *Work Engendered: Toward a New History of American Labor* (Ithaca: Cornell University Press, 1991), pp. 291, 295; Dana Frank, *Purchasing Power: Consumer Organizing, Gender, and the Seattle Labor Movement, 1919–1929* (New York: Oxford University Press, 1994).

32. There are several biographies of Bethinia Owens-Adair. One appears in Kathy Luchetti, *Women of the West* (St. George, Utah: Antelope Island Press, 1982); Richard Roeder, "Crossing the Gender Line: Ella L. Knowles, Montana's First Woman Lawyer," *Montana, the Magazine of Western History* 32, no. 3 (1982): 64–75.

33. For women in the logging industry, see Katherine Morrissey, "Engendering the West," in William Cronon, George Miles, and Jay Gitlin, eds., *Under an Open Sky: Rethinking America's Western Past* (New York: W.W. Norton, 1992), pp. 132–44.

34. Oral history from the Washington Women's Heritage Project collections are located at the libraries of Western Washington University, University of Washington, and Washington State University.

35. Janice L. Reiff, "Scandinavian Women in Seattle, 1888–1900: Domestication and Americanization," in Blair, *Women in Pacific Northwest History*, 1st ed., pp. 170–84.

36. Joan Jensen and Susan Armitage, "Women in the Hop Harvest from New York to Washington," in Joan Jensen, ed., *Promise to the Land* (Albuquerque: University of New Mexico Press, 1991), pp. 97–109.

37. Washington Women's Heritage Project collection.

38. Virginia Yans-McLaughlin, *Family and Community* (Ithaca: Cornell University Press, 1977); Donna Gabaccia, *From the Other Side: Women, Gender, and Immigrant Life in the U.S., 1820–1990* (Bloomington: Indiana University Press, 1994).

39. "Good Work, Sister!" Northwest Women's Oral History Project, Portland, Ore.; Amy Kesselman, *Fleeting Opportunities: Women Shipyard Workers in Portland and Vancouver during World War II and Reconversion* (Albany: State University of New York Press, 1990); Karen Beck Skold, "The Job He Left Behind: Women in the Shipyards During World War II," in this volume; Karen Anderson, *Wartime Women* (Westport, Conn.: Greenwood Press, 1981).

40. William Chafe, *The American Woman: Her Changing Social, Economic, and Political Role* (New York: Oxford University Press, 1974).

41. Quintard Taylor, *The Forging of a Black Community* (Seattle: University of Washington Press, 1994); Erasmo Gamboa, *Mexican Labor and World War II: Braceros in the Pacific Northwest, 1942–1947* (Austin: University of Texas Press, 1990); Sid White and S. E. Solberg, eds., *Peoples of Washington: Perspectives on Cultural Diversity* (Pullman: Washington State University Press, 1989); Esther Mumford, "King County

Black Oral History Project"; Dorothy Cordova, "King County Filipino Oral History Project"; Gail Nomura, "*Tsugiki*, a Grafting," in this volume.

42. Lauren Kessler, *Stubborn Twig: Three Generations in the Life of a Japanese American Family* (New York: Random House, 1993); Linda Tamura, *The Hood River Issei* (Urbana: University of Illinois Press, 1993).

43. Monica Sone, *Nisei Daughter* (Seattle: University of Washington Press, 1953); Valerie Matsumoto, "Japanese American Women During World War II," in Vicki Ruiz and Ellen Carol DuBois, eds., *Unequal Sisters*, 2d ed. (New York: Routledge, 1994).

44. Jean M. Ward and Elaine Maveety, *Pacific Northwest Women, 1815–1925: Lives, Memories, and Writings* (Corvallis: Oregon State University Press, 1995).

45. Carol Ryrie Brink's major Idaho novels, *Snow on the River, Strangers in the Forest*, and *Buffalo Coat*, were reprinted by the Washington State University Press in 1993; Marilyn Robinson, *Housekeeping* (New York: Farrar, Straus, Giroux, 1980); Mary Clearman Blew, *All But the Waltz* (New York: Penguin, 1991) and *Balsamroot* (1994); Ursula K. LeGuin, *Searoad* (New York: Harper, 1994); Janet Campbell Hale, *Bloodlines*. Regional women's presses and publications include Seal Press in Seattle and *Calyx: A Journal of Art and Literature by Women* (Corvallis, Ore.).

PART 2
POLITICS AND LAW

The age-old maxim that "woman's place is in the home" came under increasing attack by suffragists in the mid-nineteenth century. Arguing that women were fully capable of making intelligent election-day decisions, the suffragists agitated from 1848 to 1920 to win female representation in the most nondomestic or public location—at the polling place. The Northwest produced a good share of strong-minded American reformers who worked to overcome popular resistance to a woman's full rights to citizenship. Abigail Scott Duniway along with Emma Smith DeVoe and May Arkwright Hutton were among those who devoted themselves to correcting the injustices and inequities that impeded women.

The rabble-rouser Abigail Scott Duniway (1834–1915), as Ruth Barnes Moynihan informs us in her article, lived a life typical of mid-nineteenth-century rural women before her family made the two-thousand-mile overland journey from Illinois to Oregon. Eventually Duniway was able to draw on her early experiences when she became a spokesperson for the need to redress the inequities and hardships in all women's lives. She had assisted her mother at a multitude of tedious household routines—cleaning, sewing, weaving, churning butter, tending chickens, rearing children, preparing fruit for winter drying, chopping wood, and planting. She was, however, prepared to assume similar responsibilities when she married a farmer at the age of eighteen and bore him six children. She remembered the hardships that she faced not only on the farm but also on her 1852 migration on the Oregon Trail, an experience that brought danger, sickness and death, shortages of necessities, and remoteness from friends and culture rather than the glory, adventure, and fortune celebrated in popular legend. She collected further experiences as a teacher and a writer. With the foreclosure of the family farm and a wagon accident that disabled her husband, the role of family breadwinner fell totally to Duniway. She gained further insights into the difficulties women faced in making a living, as she tried her hand at supporting her loved ones as a millinery shopkeeper and a journalist.

Keenly aware of the special hardships and injustices she suffered as a woman, Duniway generalized her difficulties to those faced by all women. Thus inspired, she applied her considerable talents to seeking full citizenship rights for women. She toured the region widely, lecturing, debating, reporting, and involving herself in the suffrage campaigns of several states. She wrote seventeen novels on women's issues and edited and published a weekly women's rights newspaper, the *New Northwest*. Having apprenticed herself to Susan B. Anthony, on the latter's 1871 tour of the Pacific states, Duniway made herself a presence throughout the West by rallying women to organize as clubwomen and suffragists. True to her own principles, she not only defied conventions of society by devoting herself to the suffrage cause but she also ensured the ire of her sister suffragists by refusing to endorse prohibition. The movement to outlaw the production and sale of alcoholic beverages raised no less controversy in the late nineteenth century than does the contemporary effort to balance the dangers of narcotics against the preservation of the individual's freedom of choice. Duniway remained adamant in her support of wide freedoms, and practical in her refusal to alienate the antiprohibition forces from the campaign for women's rights. Probably no figure better exemplifies the most venerated qualities of western womanhood—hard-working, strong, and unshakably determined in the face of adversity.

Duniway and other women's rights activists throughout Washington and Oregon tapped a wide range of techniques to persuade the public of the need for woman suffrage. How to win access to the public ear was a crucial question to the advocates of reform. Some subscribed to the "still hunt" or quiet, ladylike approach, such as formation of women's discussion groups to support change. Others endorsed more boisterous "hurrah campaigns" with fanfare, parades, and "Votes for Women" banners flying atop the mountains of the region. Regardless of style, however, coverage by major newspapers was unarguably an expeditious way to call attention to the cause. Lauren Kessler's piece, "The Fight for Woman Suffrage and the Oregon Press," demonstrates the difficulties the suffrage movement faced in its attempts to get fair—or any—press coverage. Kessler examines thirteen major Oregon newspapers in twelve cities, in the months just prior to the 1884, 1900, 1906, 1908, 1910, and 1912 statewide referenda on woman suffrage. She finds an unfailing dearth of news stories, feature stories, editorials, and letters to the editor in most of them. A few noteworthy exceptions emerged in 1906. At that time, the National American Woman Suffrage Association bigwigs brought much ballyhoo to the campaign, winning Northwest as well as national headlines. Simultaneously, the established *Oregonian* found itself competing with the upstart *Oregon Journal* and felt obliged to cover local issues more fully than it had previously done. In 1912, the year Oregon voters finally endorsed woman suffrage, the drama of whether the elderly fighter Abigail Scott Duniway would live to vote captured some headlines. On balance, coverage was remarkably poor.

Ultimately, Kessler blames the sexism of members of the press—particularly the powerful *Oregonian* editor Harvey Scott (brother of Abigail Scott Duniway)—for the failure to give exposure to women's arguments for the vote. If informal networks of debate—for instance around the stoves of Oregon general stores—had arisen, these might have made up for the deficiency of coverage. Kessler found that no such systems did emerge. Consequently, press neglect was especially serious and hurtful to the women's cause.

Virtually ignored by the press, turn-of-the-century women developed an array of alternate techniques to ensure that the suffrage question remained before northwestern citizens. Conferences, rallies, speeches, debates, club meetings, guest sermons, their own publications, broadsides on fences, buttons, and banners flying from mountaintops—these were among the tactics the suffragists used. Their resourcefulness and the courage and resilience of their leaders, as seen in Duniway and Hutton, may well be admired by feminists today.

David del Mar presents another campaign to win women protection under law. Del Mar uses court testimony from five hundred early-twentieth-century divorce cases to provide a window on domestic violence in Portland, Oregon, and surrounding Multnomah County. He documents widespread abuse of wives by husbands in income brackets of every level. He also argues the ineffectuality of a 1905–11 law that penalized four wife beaters with an anachronistic punishment, the whipping post. Del Mar points out that women's rights groups like the Women's Christian Temperance Union took little interest in the law's passage, favoring other remedies for gender inequity. On the other hand, the law appealed to male legislators, attracted by the notion of "protecting" dependent wives from unmanly and un-American men, particularly foreigners, alcoholics, and husbands who did not provide adequate economic support to wife and family. The difficulty of reframing social roles for women persists as a theme throughout these essays and invites modern reformers to find compatriots in the distant past.

Of Women's Rights and Freedom: Abigail Scott Duniway

RUTH BARNES MOYNIHAN

"When women go for their own rights they generally get them," said Abigail Scott Duniway of Oregon in January 1871. She was announcing the establishment of her weekly *New Northwest* "upon the rock of Eternal Liberty, Universal Emancipation and Untrammeled Progression."[1] Such was the enthusiasm, determination, and optimism with which thirty-six-year-old Mrs. Duniway joined thousands of other post-Civil War Americans in the demand for woman suffrage. The nation had finally achieved universal suffrage for men—both white and black. Those voters included newly freed slaves, recent immigrants, illiterates, and criminals, as well as gentlemen of property and educated scholars. Could women be far behind?

Almost forty-two years later, in 1912 when she was seventy-eight, Abigail Scott Duniway finally became the first woman voter in Oregon. In Idaho and Washington, where she had also campaigned, women had become voters in 1896 and 1910 respectively, but most American women could not vote until the ratification of the Nineteenth Amendment in 1920.[2]

Abigail Scott Duniway spent almost half a lifetime writing, lecturing, traveling, and debating—throughout the Pacific Northwest and often elsewhere. She was an indomitable publicist for women's rights on the frontier and the foremost representative of western women in the national movement. For sixteen years she published her widely read weekly *New Northwest,* founded state and local suffrage societies in Oregon, Washington, and Idaho, and lobbied almost every session of the legislatures of those states. She held a vice-presidency in the National Woman Suffrage Association, founded and

Abigail Scott Duniway, editor of *New Northwest*, in 1871 *(courtesy David C. Duniway and the Oregon Historical Society, OrHi37312)*

presided over the Oregon Federation of Women's Clubs, and was even nominated for governor of Washington Territory in 1884. By personal example and determined leadership, she inspired thousands of women to seek the autonomy she claimed for herself.

Despite enthusiastic support and widespread admiration among many men and women, Abigail Duniway also experienced personal loss, hatred, and slander. She lived in a time when American society was changing profoundly, and so was the woman's movement. The hegemony of pioneer free-thinking egalitarianism among first-generation suffragists, like herself and Elizabeth Cady Stanton and others, had virtually ended when Abigail Duniway died in 1915. As she wrote her autobiography at the age of eighty, Duniway reveled in the pathbreaking heritage of her log-cabin pioneer progenitors, and in her pathbreaking career on behalf of women, but she also attacked what she saw as dangerous fanaticism and religiosity among some new-generation suffragists who opposed her leadership. Her significance obscured by that controversy and acrimony, she has had to be rediscovered as a courageous pioneer feminist and as a worthy representative of frontier womanhood.

Born in 1834 in a log cabin in Tazewell County, Illinois, not far from Fort

Peoria, on the northern edge of the sparsely settled frontier, young Jenny Scott (as she was called by her family) was the third child and second daughter among the twelve children born to her Kentucky-born parents. Five living sisters provided a supportive peer group of equally strong-minded future suffragists, while three younger brothers (the firstborn had died as a baby) completed the household.

Two of those brothers died young, but Harvey Scott, just three years younger than Abigail, became her lifelong rival in brilliance and influence. Harvey spent more than forty years as powerful editor of the *Oregonian*—and powerful opponent of woman suffrage. Although he appeared to condone and encourage his sister's editorship of the *New Northwest,* he may also have encouraged the demise of the paper when its political influence began to seem too dangerous. Certainly his paper's editorials against women voters were major causes of suffrage defeats in Oregon in 1884, 1900, 1906, 1908, and 1910. Only after Harvey Scott's death did Abigail Scott Duniway finally share the forbidden fruit of political equality in Oregon.[3]

Life was not easy for little girls, or their mothers, on frontier farms in the early nineteenth century. No one worried about requiring young Jenny Scott to work with her brother on such "unfeminine" chores as planting ten-acre cornfields or hoeing potatoes or chopping wood, in addition to the "abominable," "feminine" tasks of picking wool to prepare it for yarn-making, peeling bushels of apples to dry for winter eating, or caring for all the younger children while her mother spent hours at the weaving loom. The physical labor of milking cows and churning butter and tending chickens was also assigned to farmers' wives and daughters, while almost all frontier women deplored the debilitating job of carrying water and washing heavy dirty clothes by hand. Relieving women of such work—by means of hired labor or new technology—later became one of Abigail Scott Duniway's primary concerns.

Although she learned to read by the age of three or four, Abigail Jane Scott had only a few months of formal education. She suffered from frequent illnesses, developed an intense dislike for domestic drudgery, and delighted in all available books and newspapers. These included Horace Greeley's *New York Tribune,* filled with information about the reform issues of the era, and Amelia Bloomer's *Lily,* a temperance paper that frequently printed essays by one of the nineteenth century's most eloquent women activists, Elizabeth Cady Stanton. Charles Dickens's polemical novels became Duniway's model of literary excellence, and righting the world's wrongs her life's major goal. Her younger sister later called Abigail Scott Duniway "the burden-bearer of our childhood."[4]

In 1852, when Abigail Jane was seventeen, the Scott family took the overland trail to Oregon. Following the large Neill Johnson family, relatives who had left the previous year, the Scotts joined thousands of others in ox-drawn covered wagons on the six-month, two-thousand-mile search for the so-called Eden of the West, where the climate was bountiful and the land was free. Jenny Scott had orders from her father to keep the family's daily journal of the trip. That duty became the foundation of her future journalistic career.

Unfortunately, cholera and other unforeseen troubles stalked everyone on the trail that year. Not far from Fort Laramie, Wyoming, three months after leaving home, Mrs. Scott—who had been an "invalid" ever since the stillbirth of her twelfth child in September—came down with cholera one night and was dead a few hours later. Jenny Scott never forgot that her overworked mother had always feared and suffered through her many pregnancies and had only reluctantly obeyed her husband's traveling orders. For the rest of her life Abigail Duniway argued against involuntary motherhood and religious prescriptions for wifely obedience.

There were more deaths in the Scott party before they arrived in Oregon, including three-year-old brother Willie, a recently married cousin, a "worthy young man" who was Jenny's "sweetheart," and several others. The rest of the Scotts barely survived. With their property destroyed, their hearts broken, and their father quickly remarried, the Scott children found that self-sufficiency had become a necessity. Toughness and resilience learned from such overland trail experiences shaped the lives of most mid-nineteenth-century western pioneers before the amenities of railroad and commercial development. Abigail Duniway was one of the most vocal of those "unrefined" pathbreakers. She believed that one should "Trust in God and keep your powder dry" and that "self-preservation" was the "primary law" of existence—as applicable to women as to men. "Ladies" were likely to be parasites on society; it was working women who constituted true womanhood, and who deserved legal rights with which to protect themselves.

Abigail Jane Scott left her family to become a schoolteacher soon after they arrived in Oregon. A few months later, while she was still eighteen, she became Mrs. Benjamin Duniway, a frontier farmer's wife. Within a few years she had survived a destructive tornado, a disastrous fire, and near-fatal hemorrhaging during her second child's birth. Then, at twenty-five, she published a novel, *Captain Gray's Company, or Crossing the Plains and Living in Oregon.*[5] It was full of arguments about the necessity of improvements in women's health and personal autonomy, though Duniway did not yet advocate political equality. Critics objected to its "fool love stories," and even claimed her husband must be henpecked. She was devastated, but not for long.

Abigail Scott Duniway became a regular contributor to the radical new

Republican *Oregon City Argus* and the *Oregon Farmer,* along with her farm work and child-rearing duties. Then another tragedy struck. Her husband, having mortgaged their farm without her permission in order to help out a friend, suddenly faced foreclosure because of financial depression and disastrous floods in 1861. No laws protected a wife's right to the value of her contribution in the property, an inequity that became one of Duniway's major public concerns. Then in 1862, Ben Duniway was run over by a heavily loaded teamster's wagon. His injury left him with lifelong pain, too disabled to return to farming.

The Duniways lost their farm, and Abigail Scott Duniway had to become the family breadwinner, first as a schoolteacher, then as a millinery shopkeeper—virtually the only kinds of work a respectable nineteenth-century woman could undertake. She also had two more children (six altogether). The last childbirth, when she was thirty-five, left her forever "crippled," she later said, with chronic pain and bladder problems and justifiable fear of further involuntary motherhood. Such a condition was not unusual, but many other women of Duniway's era became semi-invalids because of it. Abigail Duniway, however, certainly did not.

For one thing, Abigail Scott Duniway's business activities had ended her domestic isolation. She met other women and learned about their troubles. Her shopping expeditions to San Francisco introduced her to other suffragists and activists, while the money she made gave her self-confidence. She had long dreamed of editing a newspaper. Now she saw its necessity for publicizing injustices and arguing the cause of women's rights. Abigail Scott Duniway moved her family to Portland in May 1871, bought type and a printing press, set up an office in the upstairs bedroom, and began publishing her *New Northwest.*

Even if she had done little else, Duniway's weekly newspaper would have been a major accomplishment. Packed with information about national or international events and attitudes related to women in her era, the paper also printed sixteen of Duniway's own serial novels and the detailed descriptions of her extensive travels. From the columns of *New Northwest* one may derive an extraordinarily rich picture of frontier women and of the passions involved for and against the voting rights we now take for granted. We can also learn a great deal about Duniway herself.

Abigail Scott Duniway combined zeal for the feminist cause with keen powers of observation and prodigious physical energy. Despite the terrible transportation facilities of her time, especially in the sparsely settled Pacific Northwest, she made frequent lecture tours throughout the Willamette Valley, among the Northwest's coastal villages, and to central and eastern Oregon, Washington, and Idaho. In regular newspaper columns, she reported details about her trips and the people she met, building up a wide-ranging network of concern about women's rights among both men and women. She also represented western women at several national suffrage conventions, traveling in 1872 by train from San Francisco, in 1876 and 1880 by stagecoach from Walla Walla eastward, and in both 1884 and 1885 by Pullman car on the newly completed railroad from Portland. Although her editor brother, Harvey Scott of the *Oregonian*, often provided her with free passes, she managed most of the costs by giving lectures wherever she could along the way, averaging more than two hundred every year. She also canvassed for *New Northwest* subscribers and organized suffrage associations wherever possible. Hers was a full-time commitment—and a grueling schedule.

Abigail Duniway argued that giving women social, financial, and political autonomy would benefit intellectual and economic development in the region as well as among individuals. She was an unabashed "booster" of the whole Pacific Northwest, promoting new settlements and new business possibilities just as enthusiastically as she promoted improved conditions for women. In fact, she was the one who constantly assured her listeners, and perhaps created the myth, that western women already had more freedom than eastern women because enlightened western men would *surely* grant woman suffrage very soon.

The rhetoric of Abigail Scott Duniway's suffrage campaign derived from the same Jeffersonian tradition as that of Elizabeth Cady Stanton and other first-generation suffragists. Her pioneer farmer heritage gave her an admiration for entrepreneurial pragmatism and a firm disdain for aristocracy and inequality. Like Stanton, she proclaimed the injustice of an "aristocracy of sex" or the denial of equal political and economic opportunity to the wives, mothers, and sisters of enfranchised men. The "radicalism" of her feminist goals did not preclude a defense of property rights, small-scale land speculation, and railroad building, along with support for Knights of Labor union organization and various joint-stock cooperatives. Duniway's politics were evolutionary rather than revolutionary. Her attitudes were shared by many who were to become the Populists of the 1890s.

Duniway was, in fact, a member in the 1890s of a small populist study group made up of prominent Oregonians. The group developed and promoted the so-called Oregon system of reforms—legislation by initiative and referendum, provisions for public petitions, and the secret ballot. She also became a founder of the Oregon woman's club movement, hoping that it would be a means of educating women in parliamentary procedures and the necessity of women's rights.

Abigail Duniway made her first connection to the National Woman

Suffrage Association as manager of an extensive two-month lecture tour by the famous and controversial Susan B. Anthony. In the fall of 1871 Duniway invited Anthony to the Pacific Northwest, much to the horror of some post-Civil War conservatives, especially those of southern background like Seattle's editor Beriah Brown. After Anthony's Seattle speech, Brown denounced both women as dangerous revolutionaries, "aiming at nothing less than the breaking up of the very foundations of society, and the overthrow of every social institution." Their "licentious social theories," he said, would destroy home, marriage, and nation, for the female character was much too delicate to be exposed to politics and public issues. An anti-feminist by the name of Mrs. J. Blakesley Frost followed Anthony and Duniway throughout their tour, giving antisuffrage lectures. (The *New Northwest* reported that Frost's audiences were much smaller.)[6]

There are many stories from the columns of the *New Northwest* that illustrate the vicissitudes of Abigail Duniway's career. One of her favorites was about "Old Footsie Toaster." She was traveling by stagecoach to Yakima in eastern Washington when an inebriated fellow traveler remarked belligerently: "Madam! you ought to be at home, enjoying yourself, like my wife is doing. I want to bear all the hardship of life myself, and let her sit by the fire, toasting her footsies." When the stage finally reached his house, however, they saw "his protected wife, busy with an ax, chopping away at a pile of snow-covered cord wood." Abigail Duniway had the last laugh. "I see, my friend, that your wife is toasting her footsies!" she said. The man's new nickname stuck with him for life.[7]

On another occasion, "Mother" Duniway went to newly settled eastern Oregon and northern Idaho in late November, traveling for hours in an open carriage in bitter cold and rain. In the tiny hamlet of Moscow, Idaho, now the thriving location of the University of Idaho, she encountered the reality of frontier housewifery, which she and her mother and relatives had once experienced. It was a scene like many in Duniway's novels:

> We had had a tedious way. The roads were bad in places, worse in some, and worst in others, and we were not sorry when a blacksmith shop, a post office, and two or three single-roomed box-houses greeted our longing eyes. . . . The woman of the house where we halted was in bed with a new baby, a bouncing boy of a dozen pounds. There were other children running about, and a young girl was busy at the house-work. The one room was at once parlor, bed-room, kitchen, store-room, dining-room, and pantry. The invalid mother felt the privations of her pioneer life most keenly, and expressed her opinion freely. God bless her.[8]

One can imagine what that woman's comments must have been with a distinguished guest from Portland under such circumstances. Duniway's account continued with one of her many eloquent polemics about the virtues and unjust hardships of frontier women and their right to voluntary motherhood and equal opportunity.

During this same trip, Duniway also lectured in Palouse, Washington, where her bed was located in a roofless unfinished hotel "upstairs among the stars." She spoke to a large crowd in the hotel's dining room:

> [A]nd the speech was fairly begun when *crack* went the floor, and *smash* went the benches, and *down* went the people into the cellar below, leaving the undersigned well-braced against a tottering partition to prevent it knocking her on the head. Luckily nobody was hurt, but the confusion was indescribable. The fallen and frightened crowd after a while emerged from the cellar through the *debris,* somebody lifted the partition from the burdened shoulders of the speaker, and we all repaired to another room, where the lecture was resumed amid a general feeling of thankfulness that nobody had been injured. By morning the break was repaired and everybody was happy.[9]

Other Duniway adventures did not always conclude so pleasantly. Opponents sometimes accused her of practicing free love and holding "bacchanalian revelries" in her rooms as she traveled. Rumors circulated that her husband and children were neglected. (They were actually hard at work printing, managing, and selling her newspaper.) Political "dirty tricks" plagued her publishing company and her travel itinerary. In Jacksonville, in the southern part of Oregon in 1879, she even achieved a minor martyrdom. "The 'militia's' been out and egged us!" she reported. "And they've burnt us in effigy, the image being a fair likeness of George Washington, so we're told, though we didn't see it. . . . Only one egg hit us, and that was fresh and sweet, and it took us square on the scalp and saved a shampooing bill."[10]

Nevertheless, Abigail Scott Duniway had an enthusiastic constituency of farmers' wives and other pioneers. Among her supporters were many men as well as women, like such city founders as the Sylvesters of Olympia and the Yeslers of Seattle. Leading Portland businessmen and politicians—Mayer, Reed, Ainsworth, Denny, Hirsch, Mitchell, and others—all Republicans, helped her cause with interest-free loans. She was regularly invited to speak at legislative assemblies where suffrage bills received significant support. Despite the harsh opposition she encountered, there seemed to be good reasons for Duniway's confidence that her cause would soon succeed.

In 1872, for example, Oregon's legislature voted twenty-one for suffrage and twenty-two opposed, almost making it the first state in the union to have women voters. (Wyoming and Utah, which had approved woman suffrage in 1869 and 1870, were still territories at that time.) Washington Territory legislators, who had first acted on a suffrage bill as early as 1854, defeated suffrage by only eighteen to twelve in 1873 and fifteen to eleven in 1875. Washington's Constitutional Convention of 1878 came within one vote of approval. Duniway claimed a great victory when the Territory's women did become voters in 1883. No one yet knew (as we shall see below) that their victory was only temporary, that they would be cheated out of the privilege for another generation.

A younger generation of women, many of them inspired by the Washington Territory victory, became newly active suffragists around this time. National Woman's Christian Temperance Union leader Frances Willard lectured in Portland that winter, sharing a platform with Abigail Scott Duniway. To the latter's delight, Willard urged WCTU members to change their antisuffrage stance. The woman's vote, she said, was essential in order to achieve the Union's goal of liquor prohibition throughout the country.[11]

Both Washington and Oregon already had long-active state woman suffrage associations, both founded in 1871, and usually opposed by more conservative WCTU women. Duniway considered herself leader of both Oregon's and Washington's fight for suffrage legislation, hoping and expecting any new suffragists to follow her lead in regard to tactics and arguments. She did not approve of making prohibition "the tail to the suffrage kite," but she hoped to persuade new suffragists of the wisdom of her view.

The campaigns of 1883 and 1884 in Washington and Oregon, respectively, proved her hopes mistaken. Prohibitionists, both men and women, now convinced of the value of political power for their cause, rallied behind the issue of woman suffrage and then insisted that Abigail Scott Duniway was a *hindrance.* That fall, as the Washington legislature prepared to consider an act removing the word *male* from the territory's suffrage law, Duniway arrived in Olympia as usual to lobby for women. But several Washington women were in a "panic," she was told. Certain prosuffrage legislators, who were also Democrats and prohibitionists (Duniway was always a Republican), warned them to keep Duniway away. "It makes the members mad to see you on the streets! . . . Your very presence will kill the bill!" they claimed.[12]

Reluctantly, she returned to Portland. Other longtime Washington suffragists begged her to return. A week before the November fifteenth vote she did. After detailing the whole legislative battle to *New Northwest* readers, foretelling the exact vote and designating beforehand which two Council members were secretly "pledged to whiskey," Duniway presided joyfully at the ratification

Abigail Scott Duniway at the end of her life
(courtesy Oregon Historical Society, OrHi78930)

banquet to celebrate the victory. Washington women were *voters.* Oregon was sure to follow.[13]

Oregon's state constitutional amendment on woman suffrage was to come before the voters in June 1884. The Republican-controlled legislature had approved it twice as required, in 1880 and 1882. Promises of support were widespread, even from editor Harvey Scott. Abigail Scott Duniway was even nominated for governor of Washington Territory, which she immediately declined.[14] And she was named one of five vice-presidents of the National Woman Suffrage Association. When Duniway crossed the country to attend the April 1884 convention, she was jubilant with expectation.

Unfortunately, she was wrong. While she was gone, the prohibitionist women of Washington launched an ambitious local option campaign. In places like Seattle, newly elected Democrats toppled the ruling Republicans. In Oregon the WCTU suddenly organized its own suffrage campaign, with the prohibitionist Mary Clement Leavitt hired from the East to lecture throughout the state, and white-ribboned women urging woman suffrage as a means of fighting whiskey. Thousands of new male voters, unemployed since the completion of the transcontinental railroad the previous fall, thronged into Portland. Harvey Scott's *Oregonian,* while he was "out of town," launched a three-month antisuffrage editorial campaign. Faulty ballots were printed, and ward bosses recruited unemployed voters at $2.50 a vote. Abigail Scott Duniway returned from the East to unforeseen disaster.[15]

Duniway immediately blamed the WCTU women. She also blamed her brother's *Oregonian,* and other betrayers, but she felt that they had been influenced by the apparent strength of prohibitionists who should have followed her advice to keep quiet. Duniway's WCTU opponents obviously did not agree, and were furious at her criticism. They were ideologists; Abigail Duniway was always a pragmatist.

The situation deteriorated as Duniway campaigned vigorously against the local option movement in Washington, finally rejoicing in its defeat in 1886. She knew that hop growing and breweries were major industries in both the Willamette and Puyallup valleys of the Pacific Northwest in the mid-1880s. Profits were huge, and some farms were hiring more than twelve hundred workers in their hop fields each year.[16] Duniway was convinced that Washington women might lose their voting rights if they were not careful how they used those rights.

WCTU women were rightly afraid of the political power of whiskey, as well as of its often devastating effects in individual households. But Abigail Duniway was also rightly afraid of the political power that could prevent woman suffrage everywhere. There was "but one cure for intemperance," she said, "and that was not the ballot *per se,* but the independence, liberty, and financial and political standing that the ballot represents."[17] The *New Northwest* reported that women laborers were being employed at the new Oregon City textile mills at half the pay of men. It documented the way current laws of marriage and divorce prevented women's financial freedom. And it deplored the lack of education or opportunity that restricted women's personal autonomy. Drunkenness, said Duniway, was a disease that required personal moral reform and medical cures, not legal measures that would stir up opposition to all other necessary reforms. If women had political and economic rights, they would not marry drunken husbands or tolerate abusive behavior, she explained. For Abigail Duniway the right to vote was the key to all other issues.

In January 1886, Abigail Scott Duniway's daughter died of consumption. She herself was exhausted and depressed. Friends suggested she step aside for a while to "let the prohibition fever quiet down." Her husband and sons urged her to give up her newspaper and buy a ranch in Idaho. The "boys" were eager to move on to new fields and did not want to continue their work for the *New Northwest.* They claimed that the paper was not sufficiently profitable, although the record books show that it was doing better than in 1880.[18] Since they were equal partners in the Duniway Publishing Company, Abigail Duniway had to accede to their opinions.

Accusations that Duniway had "sold out to whiskey" were widely circulated, and even published in WCTU papers. As far away as Boston the women of the Massachusetts Woman's Christian Prohibitory League accused her of bringing "disgrace on the Woman Suffrage cause." Abigail Duniway never quite recovered from her hurt and anger. Reflecting their totally different approach to the entire woman's rights campaign, they censured her for "attempting to conciliate the liquor power" and continued, "We feel that we voice the sentiment of every true woman in America when we say: God grant that the ballot may never be given to women if, in order to obtain it, we must conciliate men."[19]

That fall of 1886, Abigail Scott Duniway reluctantly sold her beloved *New Northwest* "at a good profit" to a close friend of Harvey Scott's. She agreed that others should take over the suffrage organization leadership if they would. All her own funds were now tied up in the Idaho land. The new publisher promised to print all her contributions, but—oddly enough—the newspaper went out of business within two months.

Shortly afterward Washington women lost their right to vote. Duniway's worst fears had proved accurate. Washington's Territorial Supreme Court in February 1887 set free a convicted murderer because he had been tried by a jury that included women. The judges were all Democrats named by President Grover Cleveland after he came to office in 1885. (Most first-generation Washington pioneers and women voters were Republicans.) They claimed that a technical error in the 1883 woman suffrage law effectively nullified the legality of mixed juries. Washington's 1888 legislature passed a corrected suffrage law. Then a saloonkeeper's wife, Mrs. Nevada Bloomer, brought a damage suit about being refused the right to vote. She lost the suit and did not appeal, thus negating the suffrage law once again. Her status and failure to appeal clearly suggest that hers was a test case engineered by the opponents of suffrage. With Duniway's *New Northwest* silenced, there was no way to publicize the details or mobilize reaction in the Territory's scattered frontier communities. Washington became a state in 1889, but its women had to wait another generation before they could vote for prohibition—or anything else.[20]

Abigail Scott Duniway never stopped her work for woman suffrage. She continued to lecture and write and to organize women's clubs and suffrage campaigns for the rest of her life. Always she argued that women must work *with* men, rather than as antagonists, in order to achieve their equal rights goal. Even after Oregon's victory in 1912, when she herself was badly crippled from arthritis and approaching eighty, she insisted that she had not "retired." She wanted the vote for *all* American women. Having been bitterly slandered by President Anna Howard Shaw and others in the National American Woman Suffrage Association, Duniway allied herself with women like Laura Clay, Jane Addams, and Alice Paul.[21] The latter eventually started the campaign for an Equal Rights Amendment.

As Abigail Scott Duniway suspected, the men who threw eggs at her in Jacksonville, Oregon, in 1879, or who refused to allow their wives to speak to her or read her newspaper, or who wrote slanderous editorials against her on numerous occasions saw much more at stake than the ballot's supposed danger to female virtue. For example, it was an expensive and complicated enterprise for enemies to establish in 1882 a *pro*whiskey newspaper misleadingly entitled *Northwest News.* It was mailed to all of Duniway's *New Northwest* subscribers, undermining her credibility and causing endless legal and financial complications for the Duniway Publishing Company. Then, just after winning a court suit to keep its name, the rogue newspaper went out of business—two weeks after the 1884 Oregon suffrage amendment was defeated.[22]

Why did it take so long to get votes for women in Washington and Oregon, not to speak of the rest of the country? Clearly, the answer is complicated. Powerful political and financial interests were threatened by the potential of women voters. It was the status quo of "polite" society, the financial prerogatives of those already in power, the hegemony of corrupt politicians that were threatened by doubling the voting populace. People opposed a woman's right to vote, as they still do her equal rights, for many reasons that have nothing to do with sex.

Abigail Scott Duniway told young women of her time that new freedoms had been "bought for them at a great price." She knew what kind of a price it was. But she believed that "the debt that each generation owes to the past it must pay to the future." And she did her best to prove that "when women go for their own rights, they generally get them," sooner or later.[23]

NOTES

Some portions of this chapter have previously appeared in another version as part of "Abigail Scott Duniway: Pioneer Suffragist of the Pacific Northwest," Linfield College *Casements* 4, no. 1 (Spring 1984).

1. *New Northwest,* May 5, 1871. Further biographical information and documentation appear in Ruth Barnes Moynihan, *Rebel for Rights: Abigail Scott Duniway* (New Haven: Yale University Press, 1983). See also Duniway's *Path Breaking: An Autobiographical History of the Equal Suffrage Movement in Pacific Coast States* (1914; rpt. New York: Schocken Books, 1971). See Duniway Papers, Special Collections, University of Oregon Library, Eugene.

2. A basic history of America's woman suffrage movement is contained in Mari Jo and Paul Buhle, eds. (Urbana: University of Illinois Press, 1978). It consists of selections from the six-volume *History of Woman Suffrage,* edited by Elizabeth Cady Stanton, Susan B. Anthony, and Matilda Joslyn Gage (vols. 1–3, 1881, 1886) and the National American Woman Suffrage Association (vols. 5–6, 1922).

3. According to David Duniway, Abigail's grandson (and longtime State Archivist of Oregon), all family members were well aware of the heated confrontations between Abigail and Harvey, especially after Oregon's 1900 referendum defeat. The two did not speak for many years. An apparently deliberate error on printed ballots contributed to the defeat in 1910, as did other "dirty deeds" in the other elections. It is an irony of ironies that the NAWSA's *History of Woman Suffrage,* in an article written by Clara Colby, a prohibitionist who led the opposition to Duniway's leadership in 1905, later claimed that Abigail Duniway's tactics were the cause of the six defeats in Oregon. This was repeated by Eleanor Flexner in the first major history of the suffrage movement, and then echoed by many writers since. See *History of Woman Suffrage,* vol. 6, chap. 36, and Flexner, *Century of Struggle* (1959; rpt., New York: Atheneum, 1974), pp. 159, 255.

4. Catherine Scott Coburn to Duniway, Oct. 12, 1912, in ASD Scrapbook II, Duniway Papers.

5. Abigail Scott Duniway, *Captain Gray's Company, or Crossing the Plains and Living in Oregon* (Portland: S. J. McCormick, 1859).

6. "Editorial Correspondence," *New Northwest,* September-November 1871.

7. Duniway, *Path Breaking,* pp. 89–90.

8. "Editorial Correspondence," *New Northwest,* Dec. 7, 1877.

9. "Editorial Correspondence," *New Northwest,* Nov. 30, 1877.

10. "Editorial Correspondence," *New Northwest,* July 17, 1879.

11. "Frances Willard's Visit to Portland," *New Northwest,* Jan. 21, 1883.

12. *New Northwest,* Nov. 1, 1883.

13. *New Northwest,* Nov. 15, 1883.

14. *Washington* (D.C.) *Post,* Jan. 24, 1884. Clipping in ASD Scrapbook, Duniway Papers.

15. Joseph Gaston, *Portland, Oregon: Its History and Builders,* vol. 1 (Chicago and Portland: S. J. Clarke Publishing Co., 1911), p. 562.

16. *New Northwest,* March 22, 1883; Gaston, *Portland, Oregon,* 1:334–35; Ezra

Meeker, *The Busy Life of Eighty-five Years* (Seattle: The author, 1916), pp. 225–29; John E. Caswell, "The Prohibition Movement in Oregon," *Oregon Historical Quarterly* 40 (1939): 79.

17. "Editorial," *New Northwest,* June 10, 1886.

18. The Duniway Publishing Company Ledgers are at the Oregon Historical Society, Portland.

19. Reprinted in "Editorial Correspondence," *New Northwest,* Sept. 30, 1886.

20. See T. A. Larson, "The Woman Suffrage Movement in Washington," *Pacific Northwest Quarterly* 67 (April 1976): 54; Norman H. Clark, *The Dry Years: Prohibition and Social Change in Washington* (Seattle: University of Washington Press, 1965), p. 37.

21. Letters from these women, and others, are in the Duniway Papers; the collection also contains extensive correspondence with Anna Howard Shaw.

22. See *Rebel for Rights,* pp. 179–80, notes 30–33, p. 250; details of the Duniway court case against the *Northwest News* were reported in *New Northwest,* Oct. 5, 1882, to June 26, 1884.

23. Duniway, *Path Breaking,* p. 297.

The Fight for Woman Suffrage and the Oregon Press

LAUREN KESSLER

"The press," said Rabbi Stephen Wise of Portland, "is a people's university that never shuts its doors." But the Oregon press of the late nineteenth and early twentieth centuries did not function as a university—a purveyor of ideas, a forum for serious discussion—and did indeed shut its doors to one of the most significant political questions of the day: the enfranchisement of women. The ideas, arguments, and goals of Oregon woman suffragists were consistently excluded from the mainstream press.

To determine if Oregon suffragists were able to gain access for their ideas in the pages of the state's newspapers,[1] this study looked for the presence of specific suffrage ideas in news stories, feature stories, editorials, and letters to the editor in thirteen Oregon newspapers[2] during the two months prior to each of the six votes on the amendment.[3] The six suffrage ideas were: (1) men and women were created equal; therefore, if suffrage is the natural right of men, it is also the natural right of women; (2) women's lack of the franchise subverts the egalitarian principles on which the United States was founded; (3) granting suffrage would correct the inequities (in occupational opportunities, education, and wages, for example) between the sexes; (4) women need the ballot for their own economic protection; (5) enfranchised women will benefit society; (6) the ballot will enhance the traditional values of women.[4]

Out of all the newspapers reviewed for each of the six time periods, only two granted all six suffrage ideas access. Both papers—the *Oregonian* and the *Oregon Journal*—served the state's most populous city, Portland, and both papers granted access only once, during the same period—the two months prior to the 1906 election.

It is essential to note that the campaign of 1906 presented a special case.[5] Twice before, in 1884 and 1900, suffrage advocates had succeeded in placing their amendment on the ballot. But in these days before the initiative and referendum, this was a lengthy and enervating process. It was necessary for both houses of the legislature to approve a ballot measure in two successive sessions (the legislature met every other year) before the measure could be put to a general vote. Thus suffragists expended enormous amounts of time and energy persuading legislators merely to allow the amendment to reach the voters. By 1906 this had changed. The initiative and referendum permitted suffragists to place their amendment on the ballot after simply securing the required number of signatures. It could be argued that the suffragists had more energy to devote to the actual campaign now that they did not have to spend years lobbying in Salem. But speculation such as this is unnecessary, for the very nature of the 1906 campaign was different from the two that preceded it.

Under Abigail Scott Duniway's leadership, Oregon suffragists had worked quietly and, for the most part, out of the public eye. Duniway called her campaign style the "still hunt" because it shunned demonstrations, mass rallies, and other public displays, which she felt would serve only to "rouse the rabble" and motivate the opposition.[6] But the 1906 campaign was, in the parlance of the day, a "hurrah campaign." This public style of campaigning, the antithesis of Duniway's "still hunt," was the method used by the National American Woman Suffrage Association (NAWSA), and the Nationals were in charge of Oregon's 1906 campaign. In the summer of 1905, NAWSA held its annual convention in Portland, the first time in thirty-seven years that the organization had met west of the Mississippi. When the convention ended, many of the Nationals stayed in Oregon to organize the next year's campaign. They were hungry for a state victory and were convinced that Oregon would be next.[7] During the two months prior to the June 1906 election, the Nationals organized numerous meetings, rallies, conferences, and conventions, many of them held in Portland. Never before had the movement been so visible. Never before—and not again until 1912—had suffragists given journalists so much to report on.

In Portland, the 1906 campaign was unique in another way that deserves at least passing mention. Harvey Scott's *Oregonian*, long the undisputed leader of Oregon journalism, was then being seriously challenged by C. S. "Sam" Jackson's *Oregon Journal*. The *Oregonian* was almost a half-century old when the *Journal* began publishing in 1902. At first, the *Journal* posed no real threat to the venerable, politically omnipotent *Oregonian*, but by 1906 Jackson's upstart publication boasted a circulation in excess of 25,000 and was rivaling the *Oregonian* for advertising linage.[8] The two papers thus competed to outdo each other in covering the local political scene.

The access of woman suffrage ideas to these two newspapers must be seen in light of the special circumstances of the 1906 campaign and within the context of two competitors battling each other for readers in the state's most populous city. Although both newspapers did grant access to all six suffrage ideas, the *Oregonian* was, in fact, far less open to these ideas than the *Journal.* Not only did the *Oregonian* print less than one-third the total number of ideas the *Journal* did, but the *Oregonian*'s suffrage stories were shorter, more uniform (primarily news briefs and announcements compared with the *Journal*'s lengthy news and feature stories), and less prominently placed.

Two other papers took advantage of the high visibility campaign of 1906, although neither granted full access. Both the *Eugene Guard* and the *Pendleton East Oregonian* carried stories that included five of the six suffrage ideas during the campaign coverage. But none of the remaining nine discussed the issue of woman suffrage in any depth. Even during this most highly visible campaign run by experienced professionals who traveled throughout the state giving public lectures and organizing local groups, full access was denied suffrage ideas by all but the two Portland papers (see Table 1).

In only one other election campaign did suffrage ideas fare relatively well in terms of their access to the press—the final and victorious campaign of 1912. The coverage by both the *Oregon Journal* and the *Salem Statesman* during the two-month period made mention of all six suffrage ideas. In fact, the *Journal* gave the suffrage movement its most extensive coverage during the 1912 campaign. The *Oregonian,* the *Medford Mail-Tribune,* and the *Eugene Guard* all granted access to five of the six suffrage ideas, while the *Pendleton East Oregonian*—the only newspaper to consistently support suffrage since 1906—included at least a moderate number of suffrage stories and ideas. Access to the remaining newspapers was poor. The *Coos Bay Times* and the *Daily Astorian,* for example, published no suffrage stories during the two months. The *Albany Democrat* and the *Corvallis Gazette-Times* published one story apiece.

Although press coverage of the 1912 campaign did contain some bright spots, the majority of newspapers refrained from publishing or discussing the ideas of woman suffrage. This is not surprising in light of the press's history of excluding suffrage ideas, but it is surprising when one considers that the 1912 campaign presented, once again, a special case. The campaign was not as energetic or quite as public as that of 1906, but national leaders did tour Oregon and mass rallies were held in Portland and other cities. Suffrage clubs were in abundance, with most areas boasting at least one organized and

TABLE I

Selected Oregon Newspapers[a] and Access of Suffrage Ideas, 1906 Campaign

Newspaper	Suffrage Stories	Suffrage Ideas	Diversity of Ideas[b]	Diversity of Sources[c]
Albany Democrat	7	0	0	0
Daily Astorian	1	2	1	2
Corvallis Gazette	0	0	0	0
Coos Bay News	4	3	3	2
Eugene Guard	10	9	5	4
Medford Mail	4	0	0	0
Oregon City Enterprise	3	2	2	1
Pendleton East Oregonian	18	14	5	3
Portland Oregon Journal	67	62	6	5
Portland Oregonian	37	21	6	5
Roseburg Review	5	3	1	1
Salem Statesman	9	4	3	3

[a]Microfilm for the *Baker Democrat* was unavailable for this period.

[b]Diversity of ideas is the measurement of the variety of ideas mentioned in newspaper coverage of the campaign. The highest possible score would be six, indicating that all six suffrage ideas were mentioned at least once during the two-month period.

[c]Diversity of sources is the measurement of the variety of sources linked to the suffrage ideas stated in the stories. Source categories were (1) Oregon State Equal Suffrage Association spokeswomen and members and suffrage "insiders" (those formally allied with the suffrage movement both in and outside the state); (2) government and public officials (including, but not limited to, mayors, governors, legislators, and other elected and appointed officials); (3) newspapers (any of the thirteen newspapers or any of their editors, reporters, or representatives); (4) nonsuffrage groups (organized local, state, and national groups not allied with the suffrage movement); and (5) individual commentators. The highest possible score would be five, indicating a diversity of sources.

active group. There were, in other words, "news pegs" on which reporters could hang their suffrage stories. Aside from such obvious pegs as a speaking tour made by automobile through downtown Portland by the national suffrage leader Dr. Anna Howard Shaw, the 1912 campaign presented reporters and editors with at least two additional reasons—unique to this campaign—to cover the suffrage issue in some depth.

TABLE 2

Oregon Newspapers and Access of Suffrage Ideas, 1912 Campaign

Newspaper	Total Suffrage Stories	Total Suffrage Ideas	Diversity of Ideas	Diversity of Sources
Albany Democrat	1	1	1	1
Daily Astorian	0	0	0	0
Baker Democrat	7	1	1	1
Corvallis Gazette-Times	1	0	0	0
Coos Bay Times	0	0	0	0
Eugene Guard	13	8	5	3
Medford Mail-Tribune	15	13	5	5
Oregon City Enterprise	10	7	3	3
Pendleton East Oregonian	18	12	4	3
Portland Oregon Journal	33	28	6	4
Portland Oregonian	27	27	5	5
Roseburg News	11	12	4	3
Salem Statesman	21	10	6	3

First, Oregon's two neighbors, Washington (1910) and California (1911), had each recently enfranchised their women. This gave the issue regional importance. Oregon, the state that had taken pride in championing such democratic measures as the initiative and referendum and the direct election of U.S. senators, was not lagging behind its western neighbors. Second, Abigail Scott Duniway, grande dame of the Oregon suffrage movement, was seventy-eight years old in 1912. Her enthusiasm remained, but her health was failing.[9] As a symbol, if not as an active leader, Duniway was a potent factor in 1912. She was an Oregon pioneer and a member of one of the first families of the state. She had almost singlehandedly organized the state suffrage movement in 1870. She had traveled by horseback, stagecoach, and riverboat throughout the Northwest, delivering speeches and organizing local clubs. Now she was old and ill. She might die, after forty-two years of tireless work, an unenfranchised woman. Surely this is the stuff of journalism. But even with a reasonably public campaign to report on, a salient regional issue to discuss, and a powerful symbol to evoke, the Oregon press denied access to the ideas of woman suffrage during the 1912 campaign (see Table 2).

If the Oregon press, by and large, granted little access to woman suffrage

TABLE 3
Oregon Newspapers and Total Suffrage Ideas Gaining Access, 1884, 1900, 1908, and 1910 Campaigns
Total Suffrage Ideas Mentioned

Newspaper	1884	1900	1908	1910
Albany Democrat	0	0	3	0
Daily Astorian	3	1	0	0
Baker Democrat	*	0	1	0
Corvallis Gazette (Gazette-Times)	*	0	2	0
Coos Bay Times (News)	3	0	0	0
Eugene Guard	0	0	8	0
Medford Mail (Mail-Tribune)	a	0	0	1
Oregon City Enterprise	a	0	6	0
Pendleton East Oregonian	a	0	11	1
Portland Oregon Journal	b	b	9	3
Portland Oregonian	9	20	3	1
Roseburg Review (News)	0	0	9	0
Salem Statesman	9	7	0	4

[a]Microfilm unavailable for issues during these periods.
[b]*Oregon Journal* began publication in 1902.

ideas during the "special case" campaigns of 1906 and 1912, when journalists had unusually good opportunities to deal with the issue in a substantive manner, how then did suffrage fare in the less-than-spectacular campaigns of 1884, 1900, 1908, and 1910? The picture here is bleak. Even in the absence of "reportable" events, the press should have felt the responsibility to discuss the suffrage issue in some depth. The equal suffrage amendment was on the ballot and of some concern to every Oregon voter. Certainly there is evidence to suggest that the press discussed other ballot issues during these election years (see discussion at end of chapter). Woman suffrage, however, was almost universally ignored (see Table 3).

A reader of the *Albany Democrat,* for example, who had read every issue of that newspaper in the two months prior to the 1884, 1900, 1908, and 1910 elections would have been exposed to a total of four suffrage stories and three suffrage ideas. A *Coos Bay Times* reader would have had the same experience. The *Corvallis Gazette* (*Gazette-Times*) published a total of two stories containing two ideas during all four election campaigns. *Baker Democrat* readers would have found only one story with one idea. In Oregon City, readers of the *Enterprise* fared slightly better: their paper published four stories with six ideas. Readers in Medford, Roseburg, and Astoria would also have had a difficult time learning about woman suffrage through the pages of their newspapers.

It cannot be argued that Oregon voters were ignorant of the ideas of woman suffrage because their newspapers failed to discuss the issue. Certainly discussion could have taken place through less formal channels of communication. But regardless of the existence of other channels, it can be argued that it is the responsibility of a constitutionally protected press in a democratic society to inform voters of the issues they must vote on and to offer substantive discussion of these issues. On the issue of the enfranchisement of women, the Oregon press neglected this duty.

The question is why. The answers are complex and, in certain cases, speculative. They range from specific characteristics of the Oregon press to the general status of women in late-nineteenth-century America.

Certain characteristics of the Oregon press during this period appear to have had a direct bearing on the lack of access afforded the ideas of woman suffrage. First, most of the newspapers were published in and designed to serve small communities. For the most part, small population correlated with limited access. Except for Salem and Portland, all cities of publication during the twenty-eight years studied had populations under ten thousand, with the bulk under five thousand. Newspapers serving the smaller cities gave far less access to the ideas of woman suffrage than those few serving larger audiences. It may have been that in the small towns of Oregon the lack of a rigid social structure allowed for informal discussion and debate among groups. That is, the issue of woman suffrage may have been discussed at the local dry goods store or at private social gatherings. Perhaps because an interpersonal, nonstructured forum for the exchange of ideas existed in small communities, the local newspaper did not feel compelled to offer itself as a public forum. In larger communities where the population was both diffused and segmented into distinct neighborhoods, informal discussion may have been more difficult and the press may have taken on the responsibility of presenting issues of importance to the community. While this explanation has some validity, it is probably more likely that the opposite situation existed: small towns, attracting and reinforcing a relatively homogeneous population, may have functioned as closed enclaves resistant to change and to nonconforming ideas. It is possible that discussion of woman suffrage ideas did not take place either formally or informally in these small communities. The cities of Portland and Salem, with their rapidly increasing populations, their cultural and economic diversity, and their regular exposure to new ideas via itinerant lecturers and visiting politicians, were necessarily less resistant to change. It is logical that the ideas of woman suffrage received their fullest discussion in the few newspapers that served the most diverse urban audiences.

A second characteristic of the Oregon press linked to access was the taking of an editorial stand either for or against woman suffrage. By endorsing or opposing the suffrage amendment, a paper at the very least signaled its recognition of the issue. This editorial recognition often meant that the paper included woman suffrage in its agenda of issues to be covered. In addition, editorials frequently stimulated letters to the editor, which in turn stimulated more letters to the editor, thus opening the way for a discussion of enfranchisement. The nine newspapers that editorially endorsed the suffrage amendment during one or more campaigns published an average of 9.81 ideas within any two-month period. The three papers editorially opposing suffrage published an average of 8.83 ideas. But the majority of newspapers took no editorial stand. In fact, every one of the papers studied failed to mention the suffrage amendment in the editorial columns during at least one, and as many as all six, campaigns. Those papers taking no editorial stand on the suffrage issue published an average of 3.04 ideas during any two-month period. Clearly, access would have been enhanced had the newspapers broached the issue in their editorial columns.

A third characteristic of the Oregon press of the late nineteenth century was the power of Harvey Whitefield Scott. Scott was more than just the editor of the state's largest and most influential newspaper. He was a molder of public opinion and a model for small town editors. And he was a staunch and vocal opponent of woman suffrage. The suffrage leader Abigail Scott Duniway called him "the meanest enemy of woman suffrage that the state possesses today."[10] Her vision was probably clouded by the fact that Scott was not only a virulent opponent but also her brother. Scott's opposition was not "mean"; in fact, within the intellectual context of the late-nineteenth-century West, his arguments were well reasoned. Although he may not have been the meanest enemy of woman suffrage, he was almost certainly its most powerful opponent. As editor of the *Oregonian*, Scott communicated with the largest newspaper audience in the state. His editorials were almost certainly read by hinterland editors. Small town editors of Republican newspapers looked to the *Oregonian* for guidance on political issues of the day and often modeled their thinking after Scott's. He was, in the press historian George Turnbull's words, "the schoolmaster of the Oregon press."[11] He not only educated his readers, he helped educate an entire generation of Oregon editors.

It is clear that Scott had power beyond his editorship of the *Oregonian*.

The *Corvallis Times,* a Democratic newspaper, grudgingly credited him with transforming Oregon from a Democratic to a Republican state in twenty-five years.[12] He has been credited with delivering Oregon to McKinley in 1896, a year when Bryanism was a powerful force in the West.[13] The *Providence Journal* (Rhode Island) called him "the leading figure of the Pacific Coast." The *New York Tribune* said he was "a force to be reckoned with in Oregon life." The *Salt Lake Telegram* commented that "his voice has been the most potent ever raised within [Oregon's] borders."[14] "Oregonians," wrote one historian, "drank deeply of Mr. Scott's intelligence."[15] Scott himself was well aware of his position of influence. As one of his *Oregonian* colleagues wrote: "Mr. Scott often remarked, when efforts were made to stimulate in him the spirit of political ambition, that he would not 'step down' from the editorship of the *Oregonian* into the United States Senate. And this was no boast; for the editorship of the *Oregonian,* as carried by Mr. Scott, was truly a higher place, a place of wider responsibilities and of larger powers than any official place possibly attainable by a man geographically placed as Mr. Scott was."[16]

Scott's journalistic and political influence in Oregon is a fact. The extent to which this man may have hindered the access of woman suffrage ideas not only to his own newspaper but to other Oregon journals as well is not and can never be known. It is, however, reasonable to assume that Scott played an important role in the denial of access.

The more general explanations for lack of access have to do with definitions of news. It is, for example, possible that newspapers are—and have always been—event oriented rather than issue oriented. It would follow that, because Oregon suffragists did not organize a sufficient number of reportable events, they and their ideas were denied access to the press. It is true that during the 1906 campaign, which abounded with demonstrations and public lectures, more attention was paid to woman suffrage and more suffrage ideas were communicated in the press than during any other campaign. But even during this most highly visible statewide campaign, only two of the thirteen newspapers granted complete access. During the energetic, event-filled campaign of 1912, the Oregon press did no better. Although the other four campaigns were reasonably quiet, following Duniway's "still hunt" strategy, it is clear that suffragists planned and executed a wide variety of public events, including lecture tours, conventions, and banquets. But even in the absence of *any* planned suffrage activities, each newspaper was presented with six events of irrefutable statewide importance: the six votes on the suffrage amendment.

Another possibility is that, in the words of one historian of the Oregon movement, "woman suffrage arguments, either for or against, had after a while ceased to be news."[17] In other words, news is what is new. Certainly one can see how reporters, readers, and even the suffragists themselves would have tired of presenting the same ideas and arguments for forty-two years. But, if ideas were excluded because they became old and shopworn, one might reasonably expect access for the ideas when they were new or at least relatively "young"—that is, during the first campaign of 1884. But in fact far more ideas can be found in the press coverage of the last campaign of 1912—when the ideas were four decades old—than in coverage of the first.

If suffrage ideas were excluded from the press even when these ideas could have reasonably been considered newsworthy and even when suffragists presented the press with a variety of reportable events, perhaps a more satisfactory explanation for lack of access lies with who was making the news rather than with what was considered newsworthy. One contemporary critic of the mass media suggests that "what is or is not news on any occasion depends on who is talking to whom."[18] When those with power and influence talk, the press listens. The activities and ideas of those with power are news. The activities and the ideas of nineteenth-century women—as a group denied political power, economic influence, and legitimate status outside the home—are not news. This may be particularly true when the powerless address their remarks to the powerless (when women talk to women). Two specific observations lend credence to this explanation.

First, the state press, even when it did report on suffrage activities, did not listen to what Oregon suffragists were saying. The "enfranchised women will benefit society" idea, which dominated the coverage of all six campaigns, was precisely the argument Oregon suffragists avoided mentioning in their speeches and campaign literature. The link between enfranchisement and prohibition had hurt the Oregon movement in its early years and had caused trouble in Washington as well. Duniway's battle with the WCTU wing of the state suffrage association in the late 1880s and her run-in with the antisuffrage liquor lobby prior to the 1906 election made her wary of using an argument that linked women's enfranchisement to a particular reform. In fact, Oregon suffragists were not the source for most of the mentions of this "expediency" idea. State suffragists were talking about natural rights and the equality of the sexes while the press was talking about woman's role as a purifier of society. The image of the enfranchised woman as the nation's housekeeper may have been in keeping with some conception of "true womanhood," but it was decidedly not what Oregon suffragists were trying to communicate.

Second, the access afforded suffrage ideas during the campaigns of 1906 and 1912, when the largest number of ideas were included, can be attributed not to the activities of Oregon woman suffragists but rather to influential outsiders. In 1906 it was the presence of the eastern NAWSA workers that stimulated newspaper coverage of the movement. Although female, NAWSA members like Dr. Anna Howard Shaw had both national reputations and male friends in high places. In 1912, suffrage ideas were catapulted into view when politicians, businessmen, and clergy finally allied themselves with the movement and began mouthing the arguments woman suffragists had been expounding upon for four decades. It took outsiders to make the woman suffrage movement worthy of substantial coverage by the press. For the most part, the activities of insiders—Oregon woman suffragists—were perceived by the press as less newsworthy.

Although both specific characteristics of the Oregon press and operational definitions of news played a part in the denial of access, another larger concern must be examined: the role of the newspaper in late-nineteenth-century Oregon. One cannot criticize the press for failing to present "a representative picture of the constituent groups in society"[19] if editors did not see this as their function. If newspapers of the time were not concerned with monitoring their respective environments and reporting on the activities and issues within their readership areas, then to fault them for failing to do so would be an error of "presentism."[20] Running what were essentially one-man operations, most small town editors did not have the time, or perhaps lacked the perspective, to comment on what they saw as the responsibilities of a newspaper. But the *Oregonian* editor Harvey Scott, the *Oregon Journal* editor Sam Jackson, and the *East Oregonian* editor Bert Huffman did leave behind statements, and it appears from this limited evidence that they saw the press as having wide responsibilities.

"A great journal," wrote Harvey Scott, "is a universal newsgatherer and a universal truth-teller. It cannot afford to have any aims which are inconsistent with its telling the truth."[21] Scott further defined the responsibility of a newspaper by saying that its excellence "depends on it being an expert, efficient purveyor of each day's occurrences."[22] Clearly, Scott defined a "free and responsible press" in terms consistent with the Hutchins Commission guidelines proposed almost one hundred years later (see note 19). Sam Jackson, editor of the *Pendleton East Oregonian* and later of the *Oregon Journal,* wrote: "A newspaper must be public spirited[;] . . . it must ever diffuse knowledge."[23] Jackson, then, was not only concerned with "show[ing] all the life and activity possible,"[24] but with what Harold Lasswell called "equivalent enlightenment"—passing on knowledge to the reading public. Bert Huffman, Jackson's handpicked successor at the *East Oregonian,* went a step further when he wrote: "The newspaper, like the torchbearer exploring the cave, should walk a step in advance of the crowd following."[25] While it is true that the remarks of three editors cannot be generalized into a statement of how all Oregon editors perceived the role of their newspapers, there is other evidence suggesting that editors were concerned with monitoring their environments. For example, all the newspapers studied reported on a variety of issues of statewide and local concern: government corruption, the initiative and referendum, the direct election of senators, local option, civic improvements, education, and sanitation, to name a few. In addition, most newspapers granted access to a variety of local groups involved in the political, cultural, and social life of their communities. But these same newspapers excluded suffragists and suffrage ideas from their pages. It appears that most editors were interested in discussing significant issues and reporting on the activities and concerns of local groups, and their denial of access to the suffragists must be seen in this light.

Although the Oregon press can be faulted for shirking its responsibility regarding a full and substantive treatment of the issue of woman suffrage, the denial of access can also be evaluated in terms of the larger societal context. If the press is a mirror of society, then perhaps the exclusion of woman suffrage ideas reflected the norms and values of the society. On the most fundamental level, the political scientist John Roche argues persuasively that the concepts of individual liberty and the marketplace of ideas are and have always been myths.[26] American society and the American press have never been open to a diversity of ideas. Ideas and beliefs inconsistent with those held by community leaders have rarely been tolerated. If, as Roche believes, American society operated as a series of closed enclaves from which divergent ideas and nonconformists were routinely excluded, then perhaps Oregon society of the late nineteenth and early twentieth centuries can be seen as a closed enclave and the exclusion of woman suffrage ideas as merely part of a larger intolerance. While this explanation is enticing, it ignores the fact that a number of ideas threatening to the status quo were tolerated, as least to the extent that they were included in the press, during this time. Both the direct election of senators and the initiative and referendum amendments to the Oregon constitution were direct threats to the dominance of political party "regulars"—men who were often powerful community leaders and even newspaper editors—yet these ideas were discussed fully in the Oregon press. Local option, a threat not only to the powerful state liquor wholesalers association but also to the hundreds of hop growers in Marion, Polk, Linn, and Benton counties, was discussed fully in the press. Seen in this context, the exclusion of woman suffrage ideas becomes, if not unique, at least unusual, forcing one to look beyond Roche's "myth of libertarianism" explanation.

For it was this most vital of women's issues, enfranchisement, that was excluded from the press, not just any divergent idea. It was not merely antilibertarianism at work, but sexism. Lasswell writes that "the most serious threat to effective communication stems from community values like power, wealth and respect."[27] Those with power and wealth, those who commanded respect, were men.[28] Men controlled the government and men controlled the newspapers. Woman suffrage posed a powerful and immediate threat to one overwhelming community value: male dominance. It is entirely possible that male editors purposefully excluded substantive discussion of woman suffrage—that is, stood in the way of effective communication—simply because they were men threatened by the idea of female equality.[29] If representation in the media signifies social existence, then exclusion signifies nonexistence or, as one contemporary critic put it, "symbolic annihilation."[30] Although Oregon women were, in a political sense, "nonpersons," they did exist and they did fight long and hard for their rights. By trivializing their concerns, by excluding their ideas, male editors denied the social existence of woman suffragists just as the Oregon constitution denied their political existence.

But denial of access is not only "symbolic annihilation," it is an ultimate form of social control. Those who have the power to define reality and set the social agenda—those in control of the media of communication—hold the key to social control. One critic has argued that the media purposefully promote passivity, which precludes widespread participation and ensures maintenance of the status quo.[31] But it is more subtle than that. The media need not promote passivity; they need only exclude certain ideas—ideas that threaten to change the status quo. If "equivalent enlightenment"—the sharing of knowledge between expert and layman—is the key to informed participation as Lasswell believes, then denial of access, a barrier to equivalent enlightenment, may result in uninformed participation or no participation at all. More simply put, the Wobblies (Industrial Workers of the World) believed that "the power to transmit ideas is the power to change the world." Is not, then, the power to *omit* ideas the power to keep the world the same? In the interests of preserving male hegemony and maintaining the status quo, Oregon editors symbolically annihilated woman suffragists by denying their ideas access to the press. Whether this denial was purposeful and vindictive or merely an unconscious reflection of the way men perceived women, the result was the same: the Oregon press created a barrier to social change by restricting the flow of ideas.

NOTES

This chapter was published under the title "The Ideas of Woman Suffrage and the Mainstream Press" in the *Oregon Historical Quarterly* 84, no. 3 (1983): 257–75.

1. For a full discussion of the concept of access—the openness of the press to the ideas of constituent groups—see Lauren Kessler, "A Siege of the Citadels: Access of Woman Suffrage Ideas to the Oregon Press, 1884–1912," Ph.D. diss. (University of Washington, 1980), chap. 1. For the purpose of this study, *access* was operationally defined as the simultaneous achievement of three conditions: (1) the mentioning of woman suffrage ideas with relative frequency within any two-month period; (2) the presence of all six suffrage ideas in press coverage within any two-month period; and (3) the linking of suffrage ideas to a variety of sources outside the suffrage movement, suggesting that woman suffrage had become an acceptable and legitimate topic for debate and discussion.

2. The thirteen Oregon newspapers selected were the largest circulation newspapers that existed in the most populous Oregon towns of the time. All parts of the state were represented: the north and south coasts, mid and lower Willamette Valley, southern Oregon, and eastern Oregon. The selected papers were the *Albany Democrat,* the *Daily Astorian,* the *Baker Democrat,* the *Corvallis Gazette* (after 1909, the *Gazette-Times*), the *Eugene Guard,* the *Coos Bay Times* (when unavailable, the *Coos Bay News*), the *Medford Mail* (after 1909, the *Mail-Tribune*), the *Oregon City Enterprise,* the *Pendleton East Oregonian,* the Portland *Oregonian* and *Oregon Journal,* the *Roseburg Review* (when unavailable, the *Roseburg Evening News*), and the *Salem Statesman.* The University of Oregon library has the most complete microfilm collection of state newspapers and most of those listed above can be found there. The Oregon Historical Society, Portland, and the State Library, Salem, both have scattered holdings.

3. From Abigail Scott Duniway's correspondence with her son Clyde and with national suffrage leaders and from the details concerning the suffrage campaigns found in her *Path Breaking: An Autobiographical History of the Equal Suffrage Movement in Pacific Coast States* (Portland: James, Kerns and Abbott Company, 1914), it was clear that Oregon suffragists began their campaigns in earnest from six to eight weeks prior to each election. Duniway, when she had control of the campaigns, attempted to keep them quiet until the last possible moment in order not to arouse and antagonize antisuffragists and other special interest groups opposing women's enfranchisement. For this reason, the selected newspapers were analyzed for a period of eight weeks prior to each election.

4. The ideas were culled from manuscript sources including the Abigail Scott Duniway Papers, held by David C. Duniway, Salem, Oregon; the Eva Emery Dye Papers, the Bethenia Owens-Adair Papers, and the Oregon State Equal Suffrage Association Records, all at the Oregon Historical Society, Portland; editorials in Duniway's prosuffrage weekly *New Northwest* and two other Portland-based prosuffrage newspapers, *Pacific Empire* and *Woman's Tribune* (microfilm and scattered hard copies available at Oregon Historical Society); and suffrage campaign literature and several general histories of the movement.

5. For a discussion of the 1906 campaign and its coverage by the *Oregonian* and *Oregon Journal,* see Lauren Kessler, "Sam Jackson, Harvey Scott, and the 1906 Campaign for Woman Suffrage in Oregon: A Study of Newspaper Bias," paper presented to the West Coast Journalism Historians Conference, Berkeley, California, March 1980.

6. Duniway, *Path Breaking,* p. 106.

7. National American Woman Suffrage Association, *Proceedings of the 37th Annual Convention of NAWSA* (Warren, Ohio: The Tribune Co., 1905), pp. 89–90.

8. *American Newspaper Annual Directory* (Philadelphia: N. W. Ayer and Son, 1907), p. 727.

9. According to her own account in *Path Breaking,* Duniway was bedridden during most of the 1912 campaign work.

10. *New Northwest,* June 12, 1874.

11. George Turnbull, *History of Oregon Newspapers* (Portland: Binfords and Mort, 1939), p. 133.

12. *Corvallis Times,* March 9, 1903, quoted in *Portrait and Bibliographic Record of the Willamette Valley, Oregon* (Chicago: Chapman Publishing Co., 1903), p. 72.

13. One of Scott's major editorial battles was against the free coinage of silver. His efforts began in 1877 and culminated in 1896 when it was "universally admitted that Republicans then carried the gold standard issue in Oregon through the efforts of Mr. Scott." See Alfred Holman, "Harvey Scott, Editor," *Oregon Historical Quarterly* 14, no. 2 (1913): 111–13.

14. All are excerpts from obituaries quoted in Leslie M. Scott, "Tributes to Mr. Scott's Achievements in Journalism," in Harvey W. Scott, *History of the Oregon Country,* 6 vols. (Cambridge, Mass.: Riverside Press, 1924), 1: 110–12.

15. Lee M. Nash, "Scott of the Oregonian: The Editor as Historian," *Oregon Historical Quarterly* 70, no. 3 (1969): 202.

16. Holman, "Scott, Editor," p. 130.

17. Martha Francis Montague, "The Woman Suffrage Movement in Oregon," M.A. thesis (University of Oregon, 1930), p. 97.

18. Harvey L. Molotch, "The News of Women and the Work of Men," in Gaye Tuchman, Arlene Kaplan Daniels, and James Benet, eds., *Hearth and Home: Images of Women in the Mass Media* (New York: Oxford University Press, 1978), p. 178.

19. This is one of several guidelines for press responsibility proposed by the Commission on Freedom of the Press, *A Free and Responsible Press* (Chicago: University of Chicago Press, 1947), pp. 21–28.

20. David Hackett Fischer, *Historians' Fallacies* (New York: Harper and Row, 1970), pp. 135–40.

21. From a March 15, 1879, editorial by Scott quoted in Leslie M. Scott, "Review of the Writings of Mr. Scott," introduction in vol. 1 of Scott, *History,* p. 107.

22. From one of Scott's editorials quoted in William Swing, "Combative Oregonian Editor Harvey Scott," *Sunday Oregonian,* Dec. 4, 1960, p. 44.

23. From a Nov. 23, 1897, editorial by Jackson quoted by Gordon Macnab, *A Century of News and People in the East Oregonian* (Pendleton: East Oregonian Publishing Co., 1975), p. 92.

24. C. S. Jackson to Fred Lockley, July 31, 1902, C. S. Jackson Correspondence, Special Collections, University of Oregon. Lockley, a young reporter at the *East Oregonian,* took over some editorial responsibilities at the paper when Jackson became editor of the *Oregon Journal.* Lockley later moved to Portland and wrote a regular column for the *Journal* for many years.

25. Macnab, *Century of News,* p. 120.

26. John P. Roche, "American Liberty: An Examination of the Tradition of Freedom," in *Shadow and Substance* (New York: Macmillan, 1964).

27. Harold D. Lasswell, "The Structure and Function of Communications in Society," in Wilbur Schramm and Donald Roberts, eds., *The Process and Effects of Mass Communication* (Urbana: University of Illinois Press, 1972), p. 95.

28. Women were respected for their piety, purity, and domesticity and not as citizens of and contributors to public life according to Barbara Welter, "The Cult of True Womanhood: 1820–1860," in Thomas R. Frazier, ed., *The Underside of American History* (New York: Harcourt Brace Jovanovich, 1971), pp. 206–28. Julie Roy Jeffrey makes essentially the same point in *Frontier Women: The Trans-Mississippi West, 1840–1880* (New York: Hill and Wang, 1979).

29. One thoughtful historian has speculated that turn-of-the-century men were threatened by female equality because men's own roles were uncertain and they "depended on women to mask the ambiguities in their definitions of manliness" at a time when the "strenuous life" was disappearing and cooperation, not individualism, was being stressed. See Peter G. Filene, *Him/Her/Self* (New York: Harcourt Brace Jovanovich, 1974), p. 123.

30. The media critic Gaye Tuchman contends that the media's condemnation of, trivialization of, or lack of attention to a certain group means the symbolic annihilation of that group; that is, the group ceases to exist (or never exists at all) in the minds of the audience. See Gaye Tuchman, "The Symbolic Annihilation of Women by the Mass Media," in Tuchman et al., eds., *Hearth and Home,* pp. 3–38.

31. Herbert I. Schiller, *The Mind Managers* (Boston: Beacon Press, 1973), p. 29.

"His Face Is Weak and Sensual": Portland and the Whipping Post Law

DAVID PETERSON DEL MAR

The decade or so before the outbreak of World War I was Portland's greatest period of growth and expansion. The Lewis and Clark Centennial Exposition of 1905 drew over one million visitors to Portland and helped establish it as a modern city. These years also saw a vigorous and often successful challenge to political corruption that brought Oregon national attention, a movement that culminated in a series of progressive laws, including legislation establishing the initiative, the referendum, and the direct election and possible recall of U.S. senators. The whipping post law for wife beaters was a much-discussed part of Oregon politics at this time, although it has attracted very little attention since.[1]

The whipping post law ostensibly protected women from brutal husbands. On closer examination, however, it is clear that it served a cluster of other, less worthy purposes. The law in large part constituted a reaction by well-to-do Portlanders to shifts in class, ethnicity, and gender that seemed to be transforming their city. It offered them an opportunity both to define the problem of wife beating and to identify its perpetrators.

By 1900 Portland was very different from the rest of Oregon. Sheer size accounted for much of that difference; by the century's turn the city at the mouth of the Willamette River had more than 90,000 residents. Astoria, the state's second largest city, did not have even 10,000. Salem, the state capital, had barely 4,000. Portland's population boomed in the next decade. In 1910 it had more than 207,000 people, 31 percent of the state's total.[2]

Portland also had a much more varied population than the rest of Oregon.

In 1910 about one-quarter of its residents originated from outside the United States—45 percent of the state's foreign born. This was a highly heterogeneous group, hailing predominantly from Germany, China, Great Britain, Canada, Sweden, Russia, Norway, and Italy. Well-to-do Portlanders had their misgivings over the new immigrants. The *Oregonian* observed that "most of the material at hand is partly Americanized, but with a steadily increasing number of foreign laboring people, particularly from Southern Europe."[3] Another editorial, addressing the need for "more competent physical inspection of aliens," made specific reference to "the Italian, Hebrew, Polish, Slavak, and Magyar races."[4] Portland also had a different occupational mix from the rest of Oregon. Its number of factory workers even outpaced its sharp population increase, growing from more than 5,000 in 1899 to more than 12,000 in 1909.[5]

Women participated in the city's social and cultural transformation. Portland's Abigail Scott Duniway, a longtime advocate of women's rights, recalled in a 1902 address to the Oregon Federation of Women's Clubs "the time, thirty years ago, when, of the many silver-haired women now present, few, if any, imagined that the time would come when any Oregon woman, save only my foolhardy self, would ever be guilty of such a supposed-to-be unwomanly act as to assist in forming, much less in addressing, a public assembly of this character."[6] Large numbers of Portland women participated in the Federation of Women's Clubs, the Woman's Christian Temperance Union, and other organizations dedicated to improving society and reforming men's habits. Suffrage was of course the most powerful symbol of women's growing power. Oregon advocates for a woman's right to vote waged a vigorous grass-roots campaign in 1906 and less public ones in 1908 and 1910. In 1912 they returned to an open campaign. Their victory gave Oregon women the vote nearly a decade before the passage of the Nineteenth Amendment to the U.S. Constitution.[7]

Portland women gained power and independence more rapidly than their rural and small town counterparts. In 1900 they constituted about 15 percent of the city's wage earners, but just 9 percent for the rest of the state. Ten years later the census showed only 56.5 percent of Portland women age fifteen or over as married, this despite a sex ratio of 134.5 men to 100 women. Portland women also divorced more frequently than their sisters elsewhere, a trend that the *Oregonian* properly linked to women's "developing individuality."[8]

Increasing numbers of Portland women sought autonomy. One "working woman," attempting to explain why many of her peers shunned a boarding home run by the Portland Women's Union, asserted that "the very fact of having to live under restrictions makes it appear as if we are in need of surveillance and incapable of taking care of ourselves, and no girl likes to admit that." She identified "liberty" as "the fundamental principle underlying all successful American institutions."[9] Married women evinced similar desires for independence. John Illk's answer to his wife's divorce petition asserted that she often neglected to prepare his meals, wasted her money on theaters and other amusements, and went out drinking with men. Two times she had gotten abortions, saying that "if she was burdened with children she would be deprived of her good times and that children . . . were too much trouble."[10] "I like to go out; any lady will," asserted another divorce-seeking woman to a judge.[11] To be sure, the early twentieth century did not see a revolution in gender roles—not in Portland, not in the rest of the nation. But a broad if subtle shift was occurring, one that was already straining the nineteenth-century paradigm of separate spheres and the self-sacrificing wife.

Portland men noted and often criticized women's expanding roles. Some complained that their wives worked instead of, in the words of one legal reply, "remaining at home and caring for their home, as a wife should."[12] Woman suffrage elicited much less negative press than it had in the nineteenth century, but Oregon editors more often ignored the movement than supported it. Other men asked women to retain their traditional roles. The Presbyterian minister Henry Marcotte, preaching in Portland in 1911, spoke against the city's fashionable dress, admonishing women that "the fight of the vast majority of men, to keep clean, to be worthy to ask some good woman to be our wife, is hard, harder than you good women know."[13]

Marcotte asked women to be touchstones of purity and selflessness in a society in great flux: "Our men are in danger of being materialized. You women can prevent it. You can be the idealists, priestesses of true culture, knowing the best of literature, art, music, and yet true home makers, realizing that your highest honor is to be the companions of great & good men, the mothers of the more glorious men of the future."[14] Another Portland-area Presbyterian cleric, Andrew Carrick, preached that "*the greatest heroine in the world is the self sacrificing mother*" and quoted a line that read, "O, spotless woman in world of shame!"[15] "When the old-fashioned mother ceases to be in this land," preached Marcotte in 1911, "the end is not far off."[16] Carrick in 1909 praised the woman who "will endure more suffering and hardship uncomplainingly than any other person," the mother who "literally yielded her life to her worthless husband and her increasing family until before she was fifty," leaving nothing "but the shell of former beauty and attractiveness."[17] That fewer women seemed to be willing to undertake such sacrifices was of course cause for alarm. The ministers expected women to counterbalance modernity, not to spearhead it.

Several trends troubled well-to-do, native-born Portland men early in the twentieth century. Portland had always been more stable than most western cities. Now it was growing quickly, and its foreign born and working class seemed particularly salient. Women, too, were demanding and assuming a greater role in public affairs. These demographic and social shifts were accompanied by what James McGovern has described as "a vast dissolution of moral authority."[18] For prosperous Portland men, who had long enjoyed a highly disproportionate amount of power and authority, this erosion of authority probably seemed quite personal.[19] It was in this context that Oregon legislators considered a law that would punish wife beaters with a whipping.

Elizabeth Pleck characterizes Oregon's passage of the measure as "unusual," since the only other two states to make wife beating punishable by whipping, Maryland and Delaware, were located in the upper South and had passed the laws well before the turn of the century. T. J. Jackson Lears identifies the whipping post movement as part of a backward-looking shift to a more martial culture among the well-to-do, and Pleck asserts that "in Progressive era America, the whipping post was an anachronism."[20] Yet Oregon, certainly on the Progressive movement's leading edge, became the third and last state to adopt it. Portland-area legislators played a large role in the law's passage. The law, the debates over male violence and women's behavior that accompanied it, and the way in which Oregon judges enforced it reveal a great deal about how well-to-do Portland men understood wife beating.

Governor George Chamberlain, a progressive Democrat born and raised in Mississippi, recommended the whipping post for wife beaters in his January 12, 1905, message to the Oregon state legislature. Chamberlain opened his discussion of family legislation by arguing that husbands who had deserted their families should be extradited from other states and given a choice between supporting their wives and children or going to jail. "But criminal statutes will not reach the brute who strikes and beats a defenseless woman," the governor remarked. Imprisonment would simply punish "the helpless wife and children who are dependent upon him for their daily bread. For such inhuman creatures the public whipping-post has been proven to be the most effective punishment."[21] Although the conservative Portland *Oregonian*, no friend to Chamberlain, remarked that the governor's call for the whipping post "struck a popular chord," neither the governor's remarks nor subsequent debates of the bill identified it as the child of popular agitation.[22]

On the same day that Chamberlain addressed the legislature, Senator Sigmund Sichel, a freshman Republican from Portland, introduced a bill stipulating that wife beaters receive up to forty lashes within the walls of county prisons. Nearly thirteen years later one of Sichel's many obituaries explained that the gregarious Jewish merchant "had listened to so many pitiful stories about brute husbands who had beaten their wives that he determined to try and put a stop to this."[23] A member of Portland's police commission and many benevolent organizations, Sichel had a strong interest in both criminology and civic reform.

The state senate's judicial committee drew some of the teeth from Sichel's bill. It strongly opposed whipping as a mandatory punishment, and Sichel agreed to make the bill part of the existing statute on assault and battery, which imposed penalties of three to twelve months in jail or a $50 to $500 fine. The committee also changed the bill so that local justices of the peace could not sentence a wife beater to be whipped, and it reduced the maximum penalty to twenty lashes. As amended, the bill stipulated that a man must be tried and found guilty in circuit court before being flogged, and it gave judges the option of imposing a jail term or fine rather than a whipping. The amended bill won the judiciary committee's "hearty approval" and passed the senate by a vote of twenty-three to zero on February 3, 1905.[24]

The legislation faced much stiffer opposition in Oregon's House of Representatives. Robert S. Smith, a southern Oregon progressive, objected to judges having discretion over whether to sentence a wife beater to flogging since, as one reporter paraphrased him, "a poor man would feel the whip, while a richer man would escape with a fine."[25] Smith also argued that twentieth-century Oregon was neither the time nor the place for corporal punishment: "They do not have such a law in England, they do not have it in Germany, and they do not have it in France, but they do have it in Maryland and Delaware, down close to the line where they burn niggers for [a] pastime."[26] Representatives Linthicum and Mears of Portland's Multnomah County countered Smith's arguments. One asserted that Maryland's whipping post law had nearly eradicated wife beating; the other cited an instance in which a man had stamped upon his wife's face with spiked logging boots, a brutal act that, he argued, deserved a whipping. The whipping post law carried the day by a comfortable margin.[27]

Portland's editors were divided on the new law. The conservative *Oregonian* readily agreed that "the brutal creature miscalled a man who beats his wife deserves forty lashes well laid on," but it blamed wife beating largely on wives' reluctance to fight or prosecute violent husbands: "She is a moral coward—he a physical coward. . . . The simple truth, tersely stated, is that if a woman won't be whipped she doesn't have to be."[28] No law could make good the moral defect of women who allowed themselves to be beaten. Portland's other major conservative newspaper, the *Evening Telegram*, was much more sanguine about the bill. It predicted that the whipping post "would eventually lead to" wife beating's "extirpation."[29] The progressive, Democratic *Oregon Daily Journal* agreed that the wife beater deserved the lash, but noted "a popular prejudice against this form of punishment." It instead recommended that a violent husband be forced to work and that "for a considerable time his wages shall be given to his wife."[30] This system, the editor concluded, made much more sense than simply jailing the wife beater and thereby depriving his family of his income.

Just a few years later the law faced determined legislative criticism, led by John Buchanon, a freshman representative from southern Oregon. Reporters identified the Roseburg attorney as a key leader of Oregon's conservative machine, a man who backed corporations at the expense of progressive legislation. Yet Buchanon, conservative credentials notwithstanding, cited progressive reasons for repealing the corporal punishment of wife beaters. He called the measure an "emblem of the Dark Ages" that did not belong in "enlightened Oregon."[31] He asserted, in the words of a reporter, "that the whipping post was an institution of revenge rather than of punishment; that its use does not serve to reform the inhumanity of the man punished."[32]

Most representatives disagreed. Several Portland legislators asserted that the law had deterred wife beating, and most of their rural counterparts also stood by the whipping post. The repeal effort failed decisively.

The whipping post law proved to be much more vulnerable during the next legislative session, in 1911. In 1909 the *Oregon Daily Journal* had editorialized that "the whipping post law, good or bad, might as well be repealed; it is not enforced."[33] In 1911 Buchanon, again attempting to repeal the whipping post, claimed that it had been employed only twice, and not at all since 1909. He termed the law "a dead letter on our statutes" and remarked that "the officers in Multnomah county will not enforce this law."[34] Indeed, each of the nine Multnomah County representatives who voted on Buchanon's bill joined him in calling for its repeal, a strong reversal from 1905 and 1909.

Buchanon opposed the whipping post on both moral and practical grounds. "I remember the last time I saw a man whipped and when the process was over there were a dozen gaping wounds on his bare back," he asserted. "Is that civilization?"[35] Reading from a report by the Prison Reform League, he argued that such treatment "deprives a man of self respect without reforming him."[36] The whipping post contradicted the Constitution's guarantee of freedom from cruel and unusual punishment. It was "a relic of slavery days retained only by Maryland and Delaware," a "blot on the good name of Oregon."[37] According to Buchanon, the whipping post law was an inefficient, inhumane, ineffective, and anachronistic embarrassment.

The law's proponents apparently had difficulty countering Buchanon's arguments. An eastern Oregon representative argued that the whipping post, unlike prison, cured wife beaters. A Clackamas County legislator from just outside Portland recalled a bloodied woman who had fled to his home for protection: "Gentlemen, I tell you that if that drunken brute had come to my house and attempted to take that woman away I would have committed murder. I believe in humiliating such men."[38] But Buchanon's bill passed easily. Five days later, on February 2, 1911, it passed the senate, apparently after little or no debate.

But newly elected Governor Oswald West vetoed Buchanon's bill to repeal the whipping post. His official veto letter allowed that whipping criminals might be "a barbarous practice," but asserted that "the wife-beater is also a relic of barbarism." It was only fitting, then, to "retain upon our statute books at least one such barbarous punishment for these barbarians." Because West attributed his life's successes to "my mother, my wife, and other good women," he could not "see my way clear to give my approval to any measure framed in favor of their common enemy."[39] West also argued for the law's efficacy, contending that men who had been lashed stopped battering their wives.[40]

Governor West's veto changed few votes. The Democrat had just won a hotly contested election from conservative Republicans, who had hoped to gain back some of the power that the reformers had distributed to the electorate. He remained at loggerheads with old-guard politicians such as Buchanon throughout the legislative session and vetoed many bills. Buchanon tried to exploit this issue: "I don't believe that the members of this Legislature are going to let the Governor do their thinking, that every time he coughs, they will cough, that every time he speaks they will applaud."[41] The governor, he continued, had apparently not given the question much thought and did not realize that one could oppose both wife beating and the whipping post. Most of Buchanon's colleagues apparently concurred; only three members changed their votes, and two of these went against the governor. The house overrode West's veto, and the senate did so without debate. "We have no more whipping post for the cowardly brutes who beat their wives," lamented an *Evening Telegram* editorial.[42]

Buchanon's arguments suggest why Oregon's whipping post lasted for only six years. He asserted that corporal punishment was inhumane and that he had decided to oppose the bill after reading a firsthand account of a flogging. Even the conservative *Evening Telegram* allowed that "the whipping of a human being . . . excites involuntary repulsion in the average person, however vigorously we may tell and repeat to ourselves that it is right, proper, meet and expedient that cowardly, brutish wifebeaters should be so treated."[43] By 1911, furthermore, Buchanon could describe the law as "a dead letter."[44] For legislators, the law's efficacy was something of a moot point if judges refused to use it. In late 1906 a Portland judge had remarked that "two years is not enough for a proper test" of the law.[45] By 1911, though, Buchanon could make a strong case that six years had shown the law to be unworkable.

Indeed, Oregon's whipping post had not made much of an impact. It did not last long, and at the time of its repeal the *Oregonian* could recall its being employed only four times, three in Portland and once in isolated Baker County. Oregon's short-lived whipping post law directly affected only a handful of men.[46]

Yet many influential Oregonians clearly felt strongly about the whipping post law. Most of the state's major newspapers wrote editorials on the bill's passage in 1905 and repeal in 1911, and they devoted more space to it than to most bills. The legislators themselves often warmed to the topic. A reporter wrote that the 1909 debate over the bill "was the most animated discussion of the present session."[47]

A desire for social control united many of the whipping post's supporters. Portland legislators, living among the state's major working-class and ethnic populations, supported the bill in disproportionate numbers in 1905 and 1909. Indeed, they so vocally backed the law during the 1909 debate that a coastal legislator quipped that "it appears from this discussion that all of the wifebeaters come from Multnomah County."[48] Sichel, the bill's author, was a Portland merchant and police commissioner. Others hinted strongly at links between violence and class. Two legislators who cited personal experiences with wife beaters indicated that the violent husband had been a logger or a drunk. "The trouble for this wife-beating is whisky," asserted another.[49] The superintendent of Portland's Boys and Girls Aid Society, addressing a related issue, called for stringent immigration restriction, asserting that "the manner in which foreigners, especially those of Russia, Italy and other European countries have raised their children is not permissable in this country, as we do not allow them to cruelly beat or punish their children."[50] Such comments represented violent husbands or fathers as men who had not achieved a white, native-born Protestant level of civilization and self-control.

The three Portland husbands who felt the lash were precisely the sort of men for whom middle- and upper-class Oregonians had little use. Portland arrest books for the six years that the whipping post law existed reveal little if any bias in the sentencing of men who assaulted their wives with the exception of the three men who were whipped. Charles McGinty, the first, was an unemployed waiter at the time of his trial in June 1905. McGinty's wife, a waitress, testified, "I wouldn't give him money that I had earned and he blackened my eye and bruised my body."[51] A few weeks later Clem Bieker, an immigrant blacksmith from Russia, received ten lashes for beating his spouse. He reportedly drank up much of his own earnings and then "would demand coin from his wife, who took in washing to provide clothes for herself and the children." "When this money was refused," the article continued, "he would beat his wife."[52] Some two years later the *Oregonian* reported on a third whipping, this time of Henry Schaefer, a laborer. The story identified Schaefer as a "Slavonian" in its first line, and it included quotations from him that underlined his poor command of English. Another reporter referred to him as "the gigantic Russian wife-beater."[53] These men drank, took money from their spouses instead of supporting them, or could barely speak English. They not only hit their wives, they were failures as men, failures as Americans.

The identification of wife beaters as anti-American was most intense with Schaefer. One newspaper quoted his remarks after being whipped: "For seven years I break my back for my womens, in the old countries black bread an plow enough for woman, here you make a Saint Maria of 'em and de black whip hits my back for woman."[54] The whipping post's proponents could hardly have scripted a more edifying testimonial, the lesson of which was not lost on Portland women. One who identified herself as foreign born castigated Shaefer for perceiving a wife as "the husband's property, his chattel and his slave." "What mercy can a woman expect from a man with such ideas or from a [foreign] government that makes it possible for these men to have such ideas?" she asked rhetorically.[55] A year earlier, another woman had declared her "pardonable feeling of pride . . . that it is generally men of mixed nationality, and generally, too, drunken or otherwise morally degraded" men who beat their wives.[56] Strongly identifying the wife beater as a debased foreigner served to affirm his counterpart, the upright, native-born husband.

Wife beaters were not truly men. A reporter described McGinty as "the type of man one might have looked for in a search for wife-beaters. His face is weak and sensual."[57] Corporal punishment was a suitable punishment for this monstrosity, this "brutal creature miscalled a man" who beat his wife, for the act of whipping served to reveal these husbands' unmanliness.[58] A reporter happily noted that Shaefer, though determined not to flinch while being beaten, in fact cried out. Robert Cecil of eastern Oregon, apparently the only non-Portlander to be whipped, reportedly spent the night before his punishment "crying and blubbering in a disgusting manner." While being whipped he "blubbered like a baby."[59]

At best, the whipping post law reflected Oregon men's paternalism. Several legislators or editors emphasized battered women's helplessness, as did newspaper accounts of the three Portland cases. The same writer who referred to Schaefer as "the gigantic Russian wife-beater" described his wife as "a little, frail woman."[60] Governor West accompanied his veto of the law's repeal with a tribute to his mother and wife. In a much later reminiscence, he dated his support of woman suffrage to a summer day in 1883 when he heard Abigail Scott Duniway speak on women's rights. The words that "struck home and never left me all down through the years" were "Don't you consider your mother as good, if not better, than an ordinary Salem saloon bum?"[61] In locating women's antagonists among boozy loafers rather than the male sex as a whole, progressives like West could favor woman suffrage and temperance without forfeiting masculinity's more substantial prerogatives. Historians have pointed out that much of progressivism was shot through with masculinist rhetoric, that a more muscular type of reform seemed to be shouldering aside the feminine variety of the late nineteenth century. The whipping post well fit this model. Legislated, imposed, and enforced completely by men for women's benefit, it reached back beyond the nineteenth century's sentimentalism to a time when justice was more retributive, bloody, and manly. Hence a male reader of the *Oregonian* referred to it as "that good old whipping post law."[62]

Oregon's legislators and judges seldom exhibited much respect for women as they argued over a measure ostensibly for women's benefit. Accounts of legislative debate did not indicate that the participants had consulted women. Judges, too, drew their own conclusions on what wives needed. Judge H. L. Benson of southern Oregon asserted that wives who accused their husbands of physical brutality changed their stories once the case reached court and might even refuse to testify. "Such women need beating," claimed the judge. "They have got to have it in order to respect and admire the man they swore to love, honor and obey."[63] If battered women truly wished to escape their husbands, argued Benson, they should get a divorce. Two Portland-area judges also pointed to divorce as a better recourse than the whipping post for battered women, though they expressed much more empathy for such wives than Benson did. The Portland district attorney John Manning, however, identified "loose ideas of marriage and divorce" as wife beating's "primal cause."[64] Only one of the judges interviewed by the *Oregonian* pointed out that the law's effects were hard to gauge because wives might "remain silent, as she hesitates at having her husband lashed."[65]

Oregon newspapers often assumed a lighthearted, highly misogynist tone while speaking of the whipping post law. The reporter who asserted that twenty lashes were too few for McGinty, that the man "should have been made to scream and plead for mercy," closed his article by assuring readers that he

Smith, as Husband and Father. Smith, as Citizen.

This image suggests that husbands could be powerful only outside the home. Cartoon by Henry Murphy, *Portland Oregonian,* 25 July 1909, p. 1 *(courtesy Oregon Historical Society, OrHi98925)*

This cartoon from the *Portland Evening Telegram* (28 February 1911, p. 6) represents women as being capable of beating men, although their violence does not seem potent *(courtesy Oregon Historical Society, OhHi98923)*

A SHELL GAME—By Will B. Johnstone

would not "interfere with the ancient and honorable custom of wifebeating if practiced privately and in moderation."[66] Likewise, a rambling editorial in the *Oregonian* entitled "Women and Dogs" remarked that woman, "while refusing to be licked by any stranger that comes along, recognizes the prescriptive right of her husband to administer a thrashing." With the cost of marrying a wife going up "and Sichel flogging a man for beating one after he has got her, who is going to marry in Multnomah County?" wondered the editor. Several other newspapers also offered editorials making light of the law.[67] Indeed, spousal violence was something of a staple of newspaper humor. Just before the law's repeal, the conservative *Oregonian* published a mock conversation between a judge and a woman who wanted her husband arrested for assaulting her. When the judge expressed surprise that the wife would not need the warrant for a month, she explained that her husband would be incapacitated for that long because after "he slapped my face I took my rolling pin and hit him on the head, so that he had to be removed to the hospital."[68] A few weeks later another conservative Portland paper printed a cartoon showing a prissy young wife thrashing her drunken husband before calling her mother to complain, "I just can't stand this abuse!"[69] Cartoons of women favoring suffrage pictured them hitting or threatening to hit men with umbrellas or rolling pins.[70] Many of the whipping post's supporters, as well as its opponents, no doubt felt a strong and sincere opposition to wife beating. But men on both sides of the issue not uncommonly found it difficult to take the problem seriously.

Women, for their part, expressed much less interest in the whipping post law than did men. An account of the state suffrage association's February 1905 meeting noted a discussion on forming a Travelers' Protective Association to safeguard women visiting Portland during the Lewis and Clark Exposition but made no mention of the whipping post law then being passed. Perhaps these women agreed with a suffragist in California who attributed violence against women to political and legal inequality and asserted that once women received a "square deal" they could "manage the wife-beater without the whipping-post."[71] Oregon's Woman's Christian Temperance Union also apparently ignored the law. In 1909, the year of Buchanon's unsuccessful repeal attempt, the WCTU's legislative report indicated that it had worked for bills to establish a Sunday law, discourage cigarettes, suppress the sale of liquor in dry counties, and prohibit liquor from being shipped into dry states. It had also lobbied to get a bill introduced to establish a girls reform school. In 1911, the year that the legislature overturned the whipping post, the legislative report of Oregon's WCTU expressed concern over prostitution, and its resolutions praised Governor West's prison reforms. But, as in 1909, it was silent on the whipping post, the law West had identified so strongly with women's interests. The measure captured the attention and support of some of Oregon's leading male progressives, but not their female counterparts.[72]

Oregon's women reformers may well have expressed so little interest in the whipping post because it was of so little utility. In the first place, the law could only be employed against husbands who had been charged with and convicted of assault and battery against their wives in circuit court. The court for the city of Portland referred only about seventeen wife beaters to the circuit court during the law's six years on the books, three of whom were then sentenced to a whipping. Only one man faced assault and battery charges for hitting his wife in the circuit court of Marion County, the second largest county in the state. Moreover, the few women whose husbands were whipped may well have regretted it. Such men could return straight home after being flogged rather than spending some months in jail, a fact that perhaps accounted for why McGinty's wife was reportedly "nearly overcome" when the judge announced that her husband would be whipped.[73] A columnist who followed the case no doubt compounded her difficulties when he wrote that only "bad women" would fall in love with a man like her husband, who "looks as if he had lived comfortably off the earnings of those whose ways take hold on hell."[74] Henry Schaefer's wife apparently suffered less calumny for being beaten, though the *Oregonian* quoted her husband at some length on her alleged behavior: "She spit in me face, and called me names of a vileness; she go places no womens should go."[75] Wives who read or heard of such accounts could not have been much encouraged to avail themselves of Oregon's new law.

Clem Bieker's whipping and subsequent behavior vividly illustrated the law's problems. An editorial quoted or paraphrased him as saying that "the punishment did him good."[76] Katherine Bieker's attorney noted that Clem then "went to one of the clergymen here and was very penitent and whined around being sorry . . . and there was some sort of a compromise between them, and they went back to live together." Three months later Katherine returned to her lawyer and related that "as soon as he got to drinking he seemed to feel that she was responsible for him being whipped," that he was "mad all the time . . . and strike me all the time." "We hoped the whipping post would have been a blessing in his particular case," her attorney noted, "but after a while he went back to the old life again." Indeed, Katherine's complaint described Clem as being "a frenzied monomaniac on the subject of the whipping post" who, when drunk, "has sought vengeance on plaintiff for being publicly disgraced by being whipped at the whipping post."[77]

Oregon's whipping post law probably better served Oregon's men than its women. The focus on brutal, barbaric husbands may have reassured politicians beleaguered by women's repeated demands for suffrage and other reforms that they were looking out for women's best interests. The law passed only a few months before the National American Woman Suffrage Association held its annual convention in Portland. In welcoming delegates from across the United States, Governor Chamberlain asserted that, although Oregon had not passed suffrage, "it had given women more rights in other public matters than any other state" and cited the newly passed whipping post law.[78] A 1906 pamphlet from Oregon's antisuffrage organization offered the whipping post law as evidence that Oregon men could be trusted to protect disenfranchised women.[79]

Respectable Oregon men used the whipping post law to define themselves as women's proper guardians at a time when women's demands for equality and autonomy were becoming increasingly determined. Discussions of wife beating and the whipping post commonly stressed women's helplessness and the need for men's paternalism, themes that reassured men who objected to women's growing independence. Even the reporter who implied that McGinty's wife was a prostitute referred to her as a "frail little woman."[80] The conservative *Oregonian* happily paired women's vulnerability and inferiority in a 1908 editorial on the Supreme Court's decision on *Muller v. Oregon*, the landmark case affirming protective laws for women wage earners. It praised the Court's observation that women and men differed "in the amount of physical strength, in the capacity for long-continued labor" and noted that such differences justified laws "designed to compensate her for some of the burdens that rest upon her." The editorial then quickly moved on to Milton on sexual inequality: "He for God only, she for God in him."[81] This was quite a leap, from acknowledging women's vulnerability to asserting their subservience, but the editorialist made it look easy. Men who began a discussion of women's issues with seeming empathy often closed with a reassertion of male dominance.

The public discourse around the whipping post law was a male discourse, with men assessing the law's purpose and efficacy. Women had no seats in the state legislature. They wrote no editorials for major Portland newspapers. The powerful men in these positions assured the public that the law had served women well. A representative from Pennsylvania asserted in Congressional debate that by 1906 wife beating had "almost disappeared" in Oregon due to the whipping post.[82] The *Oregonian* editorialized in early 1911 that since the law's passage "there had been very little wife-beating."[83] Sichel, shortly before his death, stated that his law had reduced the frequency of wife beating by 75 percent.[84] Such assertions reflected a remarkable confidence in men's ability to solve quickly such an intractable and widespread women's dilemma.

Despite Sichel's assertion, wife beating remained common in early-twentieth-century Portland, and it rested on a set of broadly shared masculine ideas that the men who debated the whipping post law often articulated themselves. Oregon newspapers attributed wife beating to wives' cowardice, repeatedly treated the practice as funny or improbable, and implied that the wife of a man punished at the whipping post was a loose woman.

The whipping post law did not prompt men to search their own souls. The reporter who noted that Charles McGinty "slunk out of sight, a thing ashamed" after his whipping wrote from the perspective of a guiltless bystander.[85] When the managers of the Southern Pacific shops greeted Clem Bieker on the day after his whipping with the news that "wifebeaters were not wanted, and that he would have to look elsewhere for work," they could watch him leave feeling better about themselves as men and as husbands. Bieker carried on his shoulders the guilt of many men as he "hung his head and left the shops."[86]

The whipping post law offered men troubled by the discomforting relationships among wife abuse, male dominance, and misogyny a simple and painless solution. The handful of wife beaters who suffered a flogging were classic scapegoats, marginal men selected by community leaders to bear the larger group's mostly unacknowledged flaws. McGinty was ideal for this role, a contemptible, grotesquely abusive man whose bloodied back served to cleanse the consciences of more powerful and respectable husbands. He distracted attention from the more stubborn and widely shared causes of wife beating.[87]

In actuality, of course, many different sorts of men hit their wives. Evidence from nearly 500 Multnomah County divorce petitions indicates that husbands' propensity toward violence varied little by class. Seventy percent of working-class women seeking divorces described their husbands as violent, compared to 74 percent of the wives of proprietors, white-collar workers, and professionals. The frequency of violence for the two categories was nearly identical.[88] Qualitative evidence underscores this quantitative evidence. Bertha Sproat, married to Dr. James Sproat, a surgeon, asserted that he subjected her to personal violence on her slightest remonstrance to his ungovernable temper when he was intoxicated. Edwin Mayor, a manager in an investment company, reportedly gave his wife an extensive beating with his fists.[89]

Immigrant status was somewhat more likely to predict physical cruelty. The proportion of abusive spouses who used violence stood at 83 percent for first-generation immigrants, 73 percent for second-generation immigrants, and 72 percent for those with native-born parents. The frequency of violence for the foreign born versus the other two groups was virtually the same, however. Measuring use of wife beating by particular social groups is notoriously difficult, even among contemporary populations. But the evidence offers scant support for whipping post proponents' connecting foreign birth and low socioeconomic status with wife beating.[90]

Proponents of Oregon's whipping post law identified and punished a handful of wife beaters and claimed great success in assisting abused wives. Yet such women more often looked to neighbors and friends for help than to the law.

The city court tended to handle assaults against wives differently from other assaults. Only 21 percent of men arrested for assaulting their wives received a fine or jail sentence compared to 45 percent for the other assaults. The wife beaters who were fined tended to get stiffer penalties. They were much more likely to receive a continued or suspended sentence, presumably so the police and the court could keep an eye on them, and to be sent on to the circuit court, where they might receive a harsher penalty than the lower court could impose. The court, then, punished wife assault less commonly than other types of assault, but the punishments for wife assault it did mete out were relatively stiff.[91]

Only small numbers of Portland wife beaters encountered the police. Out of nearly 500 divorce cases describing wife abuse, only 34 reported intervention by the police. Intervention did not necessarily result in arrest. The city's arrest books indicate only 157 arrests of husbands for assaulting their wives during the whipping post law's six-year life, or barely 2 per month. African American, foreign-born, and working-class husbands were arrested in disproportionate numbers. But the police commonly hesitated to arrest all types of husbands. Mary Glaze, who had just recently left Russia with her husband, asked them to arrest Minon for threatening her life. They chose not to, for he assured them that no further disturbances would occur. Later that day Minon was dead from a gunshot wound, apparently inflicted by his wife in self-defense.[92]

Neighbors were often more helpful than police were. Portland wives apparently enjoyed more assistance from third parties early in the twentieth century than had their more rural counterparts late in the nineteenth. The boarders or servants with whom so many Portland couples lived could be particularly useful. G. W. Phelps resided at Zerildea Pershin's boarding house and on at least two occasions "interfered" when her husband tried to assault her.[93] A boarder at the Clifton House, kept by Eliza and Thomas Dodson, said that when Thomas shook his fist at Eliza "I thought he was going to slap her and I stepped between them."[94] Charles and Harriet Carlson's housekeeper acted similarly:

> At one time I was in the kitchen doing something and I knew when he went into the other room that he was angry and I heard her scream. I did not want to go near them at all but I had to. I did not want to interfere. I heard Mrs. Carlson scream, I went in and he had a great long butcher knife, he had it in one hand and the other hand he had raised as if he was going to strike her, he was using hard words. I said, "Mr. Carlson what do you mean by this," and I separated them and Mrs. Carlson went over and laid on the lounge and fainted.[95]

Even a servant, employed for less than a month, felt obligated to interfere with a knife-wielding husband.

Neighbors in densely packed neighborhoods often felt a similar obligation. Mrs. Slatton, neighbor to Ada and Frederick Diez, literally rescued Ada from the upstairs window that she had climbed through as the drunken and threatening Frederick searched the home's interior: "I got the ladder and took her down into my room in her night clothes; in the pouring rain and she was wet and hanging with her finger tips."[96] Male neighbors ran similar risks. S. C. Hilton recalled an evening when he and a friend were sitting out on his front porch:

> We saw quite a gathering over in front of Mr. Pederson's place, and I sat there and didn't pay much attention to it, but directly the crowd got a little larger, so I proposed to the other fellow we go over and see what the trouble is; so we came down and he was out there on the sidewalk talking very loud, and she was standing there with her clothes bursted open down as low as my vest or a little lower, and he asked some one to go and get a doctor; he tried to leave the impression on the crowd that she was out of her head. I could tell that the man had been drinking some which I had heard that he had right along before; and then he wanted her to go back into the house with him and she says, "No, I will never go back in the house again with you for you to beat me and tear my clothes off." Shortly afterwards he seemed to get ashamed and he goes back in the house by himself. I asked the plaintiff to go over to the house with me, my wife and I were living in the next block, and she asked me to go in and get her child, but I refused to go in and get the child, but I told her I would go into the door with her, and she could go in and get the child, which she did, and she went in and went over to my place, and stayed probably a couple of days; something like that.

Hilton asserted that "I didn't know them at the time . . . my wife had never been over there," though he had heard from "the general talk of the neighbors" that Pederson was a poor provider. He concluded his testimony by remarking, "I would have done the same with any one as I did that evening. I thought it was every man's duty."[97]

Portland men often exercised this duty cautiously, however. C. W. Peckham recalled being awakened by "some hollowing" one night and looking out his window to see a couple arguing and struggling. Peckham then "opened my front door and stood in the door and watched them" and "waited until I was called" rather than rushing to the woman's assistance.[98] Likewise, Fred Bauer recalled a day when "I mistrusted something" about his neighbor, Peter Sitta. Hence "in the evening when I saw him going down to the saloon, thinks I, I better kind of look after him and see what he does." Bauer watched Sitta "fill up pretty well on beer," and noted that when Sitta returned home "he didn't blow out the light but he walked back and forth, storming around" and kicking chairs.[99] Bauer eventually left his post at the window and went to bed. At about 1:00 A.M. a noise from the Sittas' home awakened Bauer, and as it grew louder he dressed himself. But the tumult ceased, and Bauer again retired. Some two hours later Rose Sitta, an invalid, sent her foster daughter to the Bauers' for help, and Fred Bauer awoke to see his son carrying the bloodied Rose to safety. Fred Bauer took considerable pains to monitor Peter Sitta's behavior, but he hesitated to intervene without strong evidence of a physical assault.

Not all neighbors were so attentive. Maud Logan recalled becoming "so angry that I had to go away" from her neighbors. "He was striking her," she explained, "and I didn't want to get into the fight myself."[100] Some Portland wives found themselves expelled from their homes along with their violent spouses. Docia Stevens recalled a landlady telling her and her husband to move: "She could not stand it; she was afraid he would do something to me."[101] T. Hammersly, a landlord and police officer, recounted hearing a quarrel between his tenants late at night: "I says, 'What is this trouble about?' And she says, 'This man is trying to kill me, and I want to show you where he has beaten me,' and I says, 'No, I want you folks to get your clothes on and get out of here as soon as you can.'"[102] Yet Hammersly testified that he had believed the woman's claim of physical abuse.

Violent husbands fiercely contested the rights of others to interfere in their domestic affairs. H. F. Cuthill recalled awaking to the sound of his sister, Marjorie Coles, screaming as her husband, James, tried to wrench some money from her. Cuthill separated the couple, an action that prompted James to threaten "trouble" if Cuthill went "between me and my wife." "I don't care for law, heaven, hell nor God," he explained, for "I will kill the first man that interferes between me and my family."[103] B. Phelps witnessed an especially explicit assertion of absolute patriarchy when she heard a gunshot and ran to her daughter's apartment to find her prostrate and the son-in-law in the act of fatally shooting their fleeing child. "Get out of here," he told her. "Everything here belongs to me."[104]

Homicidal Portland husbands might refuse to draw a distinction between their wives and their wives' families. In 1902 A. Lester Belding shot and killed his wife and mother-in-law and seriously wounded his father-in-law. After the shootings he reportedly rejoiced, "I have got three of them," and asserted, "I would have liked to kill everybody by the name McCroskey." E. P. McCroskey, the slain wife's brother, explained that another sister "often urged Mrs. Belding to leave her brutal husband, and for this reason the fiend wished to slay the whole family."[105] In 1907 Portland's Fred Martin, formerly a salesman for the Pacific Biscuit Company, fatally shot himself after wounding his wife and murdering her sister, whom he held responsible for the end of his marriage. In a letter written just before the shootings he explained to his wife that his sister-in-law "stands between us" and "has put us both where we will soon be."[106] Martha Dickerson's 1907 divorce complaint noted that her husband had said, "I mean to kill you, your child and your father and wipe out the whole race."[107] In early-twentieth-century Portland, a time and place poised between the traditional public family and the emergent private one, a wife and her family could appear to be one.

A sense of shame could inhibit wives' reaction to violence. Minnie Tweed recalled telling a sister who inquired about her swollen face that "I bruised it on the sewing machine" since "I was ashamed" of her husband's blow.[108] Clara Young remarked, "I ought to be ashamed to tell it," before describing to the court how her husband, A. G., had threatened her with a revolver and slapped her.[109] Portland's large size did not keep divorce cases from being something of a public spectacle. Newspapers routinely summarized the most lurid cases, and curiosity seekers attended court cases. In one instance a judge "cleared the courtroom of a curious crowd of men" before a divorce-seeking wife testified.[110]

Yet divorce became increasingly attractive to Portland's wives. Even the *Oregonian,* one of the state's most conservative papers, editorialized in 1910 that divorces, though "doubtless regrettable," were "not so deplorable as they are depicted sometimes."[111] The court apparently agreed. In a sample of more than 240 wives who cited abuse in suits filed from 1905 to 1907, it awarded 82 divorces for every suit it dismissed.[112] Oregon courts also ordered long-term payments to divorced wives more commonly than they had during the nineteenth century. In 1905 the Oregon Supreme Court established that a man owed his former wife child support, even though he had been the one to obtain the divorce.[113] Such decisions, though by no means common, combined with

Portland's growing economic opportunities to take some of the economic sting out of divorce.

Nonetheless, the decision to leave a violent husband still brought many financial risks and hardships, particularly for wives with children. A 1913 survey of Oregon's women workers found that three-fifths of the women employed in Portland industries made less than $10 per week. "A larger majority of self-supporting women in the state are earning less than it costs them to live decently," the report concluded.[114] Pauline Gray left her husband and had to board her six-year-old boy out while she earned a living. "After I worked myself down," she recalled, "I could not keep the boy and I sent him back to his father.... My health would not permit me to support myself and the boy any longer."[115] Carrie Rees said that her husband, Park, had left her and that she gave up custody of their two children to him because "he would not support them and have them with me."[116] Portland's separated or single mothers might also lose their children to institutions like the Boys and Girls Aid Society, which grew increasingly common and powerful around the turn of the century. In one case the court ordered that organization to turn over the children to their father, who had recently won a divorce from his wife on grounds of adultery. A couple of years later the woman learned from a newspaper report that her ex-husband had been accused of sexually abusing their oldest daughter, not yet a teenager: "I can't express my feeling when I heard... and must say that it is why I fought so hard for my children and I think that peeple will begin to realize what I have had to contend with but it seems as it mite be to late."[117] Leslie Tentler, in her survey of wage-earning women, concludes that "regardless of how unsatisfactory she felt her marriage to be—no matter how genuinely she resented the restrictions of her life—the working-class wife could not help but learn . . . that, in the real world, women needed men."[118] Working-class women on the West Coast, less apt to belong to conservative ethnic groups and living in states with more liberal divorce laws, probably felt these restrictions less keenly than those in the East did. But in Portland, too, divorce continued to bring many risks and hardships.

Much of that hardship consisted of threats, assaults, and even murders by estranged or former husbands. O. C. Ogden reportedly tricked his way into the home that his wife had fled to by saying that their infant daughter was dying. He then beat his wife unconscious. Bertha Highfield said that her estranged husband waited outside her place of employment "and when the girls would start out from work he would stand out and abuse me." She consequently had to quit the job, since "the firm wouldn't stand anything like that."[119] A witness in another suit recalled a conversation between Eliza and

Thomas Dodson: "They would have difficulty some time and he would seem to be very angry and mean to her and she says to him 'If you don't treat me better I will leave you,' he says, 'If you do . . . I will kill you and every one that helps you.'"[120] Such threats were not always empty. From 1900 to 1910 at least five Multnomah County wives died at their husband's hands.[121]

Class and immigrant status, apparently of little import in predicting husbands' violence, more strongly conditioned how wives reacted to it. Fifty-one divorce cases citing physical violence that described one of the spouses as leaving could be uncovered in the 1900 manuscript census. Foreign-born women left in only 38 percent of the cases, second-generation women in 54 percent, and women born to native-born parents in 77 percent.[122] Class also influenced whether or not a woman left a violent husband, although less dramatically. Only 50 percent of women married to white-collar men left, compared to 62 percent of women married to working-class husbands. This same pattern emerged from accounts of third-party interventions. Some 38 percent of the wives with working-class husbands described such interventions, while only 28 percent of women wed to proprietors or white-collar men did.[123] Women married to men with high-status occupations and immigrant women left violent husbands more rarely than did other women, and well-to-do women benefited from direct interventions more rarely than other women did.

Staying with a violent husband did not necessarily mean submitting to him. Portland women seemed to resist their violent husbands more directly than their rural and small-town counterparts of the 1890s had. Zerildea Pershin testified that her husband had "choked me so many times that I learned the habit of standing perfectly still, allowing my body to relax." In another instance she resisted more overtly: "I grabbed him by the whiskers, he kept trying to get nearer and kept gnawing at my hand with his teeth, I kept close to his face so he could not eat me, he kept kicking me, I thought he was trying to kill me."[124] Other women successfully fought their husbands off. Jennie Fine recalled how her husband returned home at 3:00 A.M. one morning, hit her, and declared: "Now, God damn you, I am going to kill you." "But he did not amount to anything anyhow," remarked Jennie, "and I finally got loose from him," went to a friend's house, and "have not lived with him since."[125] Eva Hazel described how her husband, Edwin, attempted in vain to terrorize and intimidate her:

> I had dinner waiting for two or three hours, and there was word about dinner being cold, and I said, "I have waited since 12 o'clock for you, and now it is nearly three," and we had some words, and he says, "I will fix you" and he made a dive at me and tore my waist off, and then he says, "I know a better way," so

> he went right to my canary bird and tore its head off of it and threw it out into the yard and then he made another dive at me, and I told him I wasn't afraid of him, and then he said he would skin my dog, and I got the dog away.[126]

One woman reportedly hit her husband over the head with a shoe to repulse forcible attempts at sex; another knocked her spouse downstairs with a broomstick to keep him out of the house.[127]

Elsie Siedow recounted a particularly harrowing struggle with her ex-husband, Fred, when he accosted her on the street with a revolver. She later recalled that she "looked him in the eye, like you would an animal . . . and I got up close and jumped at him." Fred fired and missed, then tried again to shoot her, "but I threw all my strength on him, caught his wrist and began tearing at it to make him let go of the revolver." The weapon eventually fell from Fred's hand, and Elsie picked it up and ran to a neighbor's home. "This is the third time he has tried to kill me," she concluded, "and I think he ought to get about six years this time."[128]

Ida Carlisle's ex-husband, John, accosted her on the street, fired into her head from only four feet away and then, believing her dead, shot and killed himself. The bullet, deflected by Ida's teeth, passed through her cheek, leaving her only slightly wounded. "I could not make up with him," Ida explained to a reporter. "I had suffered for 30 years through him and I did not intend to go back to that terrible life."[129] Increasing numbers of wives married to violent men exhibited that resolution in early-twentieth-century Portland, even at the risk of horrible cruelties, even at the risk of death.

The resources that women such as Ida Carlisle actually used against their violent husbands contrasted sharply with the images painted of them by proponents of Oregon's whipping post law. Rather than acknowledging and abetting women's power, the law was a unilateral male solution. It was also an attempt by prominent men to define and ultimately to minimize this problem by representing the wife beater as a highly deviant and unusual type.

In Portland's homes and streets wife beating assumed a much different form than it did in debates carried on at the state capital or in the columns of leading newspapers. Physical violence occurred commonly among all types of Portlanders, including the well-to-do and the native born. A wife's best defense against a violent spouse was not the threat of twenty lashes, but the help of neighbors, together with her own courage and skill.

More than six decades would pass between the repeal of the whipping post law in 1911 and renewed public and legislative concern for the safety of Oregon wives. Yet those six decades were hardly safe ones for these women. Sigmund

Sichel died in 1917, apparently believing that his law had brought a dramatic decrease in wife beating. He was mistaken. Violence against wives would in fact grow during the twentieth century, abetted by a cultural transformation that had already begun in Portland and that would soon spread even to the state's most remote hamlets.

NOTES

This essay originally appeared in *What Trouble I Have Seen: A History of Violence against Wives* (Cambridge: Harvard University Press, 1996); reprinted with permission of Harvard University Press.

1. Robert Douglas Johnston, "Middle-Class Political Ideology in a Corporate Society: The Persistence of Small-Propertied Radicalism in Portland, Oregon, 1883–1926," Ph.D. diss. (Rutgers University, 1993); Carl Abbott, *Portland: Planning, Politics, and Growth in a Twentieth-Century City* (Lincoln: University of Nebraska Press, 1983), pp. 49–57.

2. U.S. Bureau of the Census, *Thirteenth Census of the United States, 1910: Population by Counties and Minor Civil Divisions, 1910, 1900, 1890* (Washington, D.C.: Government Printing Office, 1912), pp. 436–44.

3. *Portland Oregonian,* Nov. 13, 1904, p. 4. Paul G. Merriam, "The 'Other Portland': A Statistical Note on Foreign Born, 1860–1910," *Oregon Historical Quarterly* 80 (Fall 1979): 258–68.

4. *Portland Oregonian,* Dec. 13, 1904, p. 6.

5. U.S. Bureau of the Census, *Thirteenth Census of the United States Taken in the Year 1910, Abstract of the Census: Statistics of Population, Agriculture, Manufactures, and Mining for the United States, the States, and Principal Cities with Supplement for Oregon* (Washington, D.C.: Government Printing Office, 1913), p. 665. See also William Toll, *Women, Men, and Ethnicity: Essays on the Structure and Thought of American Jewry* (Lanham, Md.: University Press of America and American Jewish Archives, 1991), pp. 85–106. Many of Portland's Russian immigrants were Jewish, as were some of its German newcomers.

6. Abigail Scott Duniway, "Response to Address of Welcome," *The Club Journal* 2 (June 1902): 12.

7. G. Thomas Edwards, *Sowing Good Seeds: The Northwest Suffrage Campaigns of Susan B. Anthony* (Portland: Oregon Historical Society Press, 1990), pp. 212–300; Lauren Kessler, "A Siege of the Citadels: Search for a Public Forum for the Ideas of Oregon Woman Suffrage," *Oregon Historical Quarterly* 84 (Summer 1983): 116–49.

8. *Portland Oregonian,* Feb. 9, 1910, p. 10; U.S. Bureau of the Census, *Occupations at the Twelfth Census* (Washington, D.C.: Government Printing Office, 1904), pp. 368,

370, 686, 688; *Thirteenth Census of the United States, Population, Agriculture, Manufactures, and Mining,* pp. 587, 593; Elaine Tyler May, *Great Expectations: Marriage and Divorce in Post-Victorian America* (Chicago: University of Chicago Press, 1980).

9. Newspaper clipping from 1899 in scrapbook, Portland's Women's Union Papers, box 3, mss. 1443, Oregon Historical Society (OHS), Portland.

10. Multnomah County Circuit Court records, no. 45606, Portland, Oregon. On changes in wives' roles during the early twentieth century, see Steven Mintz and Susan Kellogg, *Domestic Revolutions: A Social History of American Family Life* (New York: Free Press, 1988), pp. 107–31; Alice Echols, *The Demise of Female Intimacy in the Twentieth Century* (Ann Arbor: Women's Studies Program, University of Michigan, 1978).

11. Mult. Co. no. 30837. On shifts in pre-World War I Portland women's morality, see Gloria Elizabeth Myers, "Lola G. Baldwin and the Professionalization of Women's Police Work, 1905–1922," M.A. thesis (Portland State University, 1993), pp. 19–39. See also Kathy Peiss, *Cheap Amusements: Working Women and Leisure in Turn-of-the-Century New York* (Philadelphia: Temple University Press, 1986); Joanne Meyerowitz, "Sexual Geography and Gender Economy: The Furnished Room Districts of Chicago, 1890–1930," *Gender and History* 2 (Autumn 1990): 274–96; James R. McGovern, "American Woman's Pre–World War I Freedom in Manners and Morals," *Journal of American History* 55 (September 1968): 315–33.

12. Mult. Co. no. 45471.

13. "Is the Young Man Safe," Henry Marcotte collection, box 7, University of Oregon Special Collections, Eugene. Kessler, "Siege of the Citadels," Edwards, *Sowing Good Seeds,* p. 242. On men's reaction to women's growing sphere in the early twentieth century, see Ava Baron, "Another Side of Gender Antagonism at Work: Men, Boys, and the Remasculinization of Printer's Work, 1830–1920," in idem, ed., *Work Engendered: Towards a New History of American Labor* (Ithaca, N.Y.: Cornell University Press, 1991), pp. 47–69; Gail Bederman, "'The Women Have Had Charge of the Church Work Long Enough': The Men and Religion Forward Movement of 1911–1912 and the Masculinization of Middle-Class Protestantism," *American Quarterly* 41 (September 1989): 432–65; Victoria Bissel Brown, "The Fear of Feminization: Los Angeles High Schools in the Progressive Era," *Feminist Studies* 16 (Fall 1990): 493–518; Peter Filene, *Him/Her/Self: Sex Roles in Modern America,* 2d ed. (Baltimore: Johns Hopkins University Press, 1986), pp. 72–101; Clyde Griffen, "Reconstructing Masculinity from the Evangelical Revival to the Waning of Progressivism: A Speculative Synthesis," in Mark C. Carnes and Clyde Griffen, eds., *Meanings for Manhood: Constructions of Masculinity in Victorian America* (Chicago: University of Chicago Press, 1990), pp. 183–204; Jeffrey P. Hantover, "The Boy Scouts and the Validation of Masculinity," *Journal of Social Issues* 34 (Winter 1978): 184–95; Michael S. Kimmel, "Men's Responses to Feminism at the Turn of the Century," *Gender and Society* 1 (September 1987): 261–83;

Angel Kwolek-Folland, "Gender, Self, and Work in the Life Insurance Industry, 1880–1930," in Baron, ed., *Work Engendered*, pp. 168–90.

14. "Mothers Old & New," box 6, Henry Marcotte collection.

15. Sermon no. 767, box 1, Andrew Carrick collection, University of Oregon Special Collections (emphasis in original).

16. "Mothers," box 6, Henry Marcotte collection.

17. Sermon no. 767.

18. McGovern, "American Woman's Pre–World War I Freedom," pp. 318–20. See also T. J. Jackson Lears, *No Place of Grace: Antimodernism and the Transformation of American Culture, 1880–1920* (New York: Pantheon, 1981); John Higham, "The Reorientation of American Culture in the 1890s," in John Weiss, ed., *The Origins of Modern Consciousness* (Detroit: Wayne State University Press, 1965), pp. 25–48.

19. Johnston, "Middle-Class Political Ideology in a Corporate Society," pp. 62–69.

20. Elizabeth Pleck, *Domestic Tyranny: The Making of Social Policy against Family Violence from Colonial Times to the Present* (New York: Oxford University Press, 1987), p. 120; Lears, *No Place of Grace*, 97–139. The whipping post is also treated in Pleck, "The Whipping Post for Wife Beaters, 1876–1906," in Leslie Page Moch and Gary D. Stark, eds., *Essays on the Family and Historical Change* (College Station: Texas A&M University Press, 1983), pp. 127–49; Robert Graham Caldwell, *Red Hannah: Delaware's Whipping Post* (Philadelphia: University of Pennsylvania Press; and London: Geoffrey Camberlege, Oxford University Press, 1947).

21. *Portland Oregonian*, Jan. 13, 1905, p. 8.

22. *Portland Oregonian*, Jan. 12, 1905, p. 10.

23. *Portland Evening Telegram*, Dec. 10, 1917, pp. 1–2.

24. *Portland Evening Telegram*, Jan. 26, 1905, p. 6; *The Journal of the Senate of the State of Oregon, Twenty-Third Legislative Assembly, Regular Session, 1905* (Salem: J. R. Whitney, State Publisher, 1905), pp. 548–72; *Laws Enacted by the People upon Initiative Petition at the General Election June 6, 1904* (Salem: J. R. Whitney, 1905), pp. 335–36.

25. *Portland Oregonian*, Feb. 16, 1905, p. 4.

26. *Portland Evening Telegram*, Feb. 16, 1905, p. 6.

27. (Portland) *Oregon Daily Journal*, Feb. 16, 1905, p. 3.

28. *Portland Oregonian*, Jan. 22, 1905, p. 4.

29. *Portland Evening Telegram*, Jan. 13, 1905, p. 16.

30. (Portland) *Oregon Daily Journal*, Jan. 28, 1905, p. 4.

31. *Portland Evening Telegram*, Jan. 27, 1909, p. 2. Carl Smith and H. P. Edward, *Behind the Scenes at Salem* (n.p., 1911), pp. 34–36, 72. [Joseph Gaston], *The Centennial History of Oregon, 1811–1912* (Chicago: S. J. Clarke, 1912), 4: 27–28.

32. *Portland Oregonian*, Jan. 27, 1909, p. 7.

33. (Portland) *Oregon Daily Journal*, Jan. 25, 1909, p. 6.

34. *Portland Oregonian,* Jan. 18, 1911, p. 6; (Salem) *Daily Capital Journal,* Feb. 14, 1911, p. 8.

35. *Roseburg Review,* Feb. 15, 1911, p. 1.

36. (Portland) *Oregon Daily Journal,* Jan. 28, 1911, p. 3.

37. (Salem) *Daily Capital Journal,* Feb. 14, 1911, p. 8.

38. *Roseburg Review,* Jan. 15, 1911, p. 1; *Ashland Tidings,* Feb. 2, 1911, p. 6.

39. *Journal of the House of the Twenty-Sixth Legislative Assembly of the State of Oregon, Regular Session, 1911* (Salem, Ore.: Willis S. Duniway, 1911), pp. 536–37.

40. *Portland Evening Telegram,* Feb. 11, 1911, p. 9.

41. Ibid., Feb. 14, 1911, p. 10.

42. Ibid., Feb. 18, 1911, p. 6.

43. *Portland Evening Telegram,* June 8, 1905, p. 8. Negative reactions to whipping appeared in another editorial and in a letter to the editor: (Portland) *Daily News,* Aug. 5, 1907, p. 2; *Portland Oregonian,* June 9, 1905, p. 9.

44. *Portland Oregonian,* Jan. 18, 1911, p. 6.

45. *Portland Oregonian,* Nov. 27, 1906, p. 11; *Oregon City Courier,* Aug. 25, 1905, p. 8.

46. *Portland Oregonian,* Feb. 13, 1911, p. 6. Even the state's most influential newspaper may have missed some instances. But circuit court records for Marion and Clatsop counties, which contained Oregon's second and third largest cities in 1910, indicated that neither area employed the punishment from 1905 to 1910, although a Clatsop County judge sentenced a wife beater to a whipping and then suspended the sentence. I also examined Portland's arrest books for 1905 to 1911 and Multnomah County Circuit Court records for 1905 to late 1907 and for 1910 and found only the three whippings cited by the *Oregonian.*

47. *Portland Oregonian,* Jan. 27, 1909, p. 7.

48. Ibid.

49. Ibid.; *Roseburg Review,* Feb. 15, 1911, p. 1; (Portland) *Oregon Daily Journal,* Feb. 16, 1905, p. 3.

50. W. T. Gardner, Portland, to Prescott F. Hall, Boston, June 22, 1903, outgoing letter book, Boys and Girls Aid Society, Portland, Oregon.

51. (Portland) *Oregon Daily Journal,* June 7, 1905, p. 1; newspaper clipping, June 1905, scrapbook no. 73, p. 198, OHS.

52. *Portland Evening Telegram,* July 19, 1905, pp. 1, 11.

53. (Portland) *Daily News,* Aug. 1, 1907, p. 1; *Portland Oregonian,* Aug. 2, 1907, p. 9.

54. *Portland Evening Telegram,* Aug. 1, 1907, p. 13.

55. (Portland) *Oregon Daily Journal,* Aug. 14, 1907, p. 8.

56. *Portland Evening Telegram,* June 29, 1906, p. 6.

57. Newspaper clipping, June 1905, scrapbook no. 73, p. 198, OHS.

58. *Portland Oregonian,* Jan. 22, 1905, p. 4.

59. (Portland) *Oregon Daily Journal,* Sept. 16, 1905, p. 8; (Portland) *Oregon Daily Journal,* Aug. 1, 1907, pp. 1, 12.

60. (Portland) *Daily News,* Aug. 1, 1907, p. 1.

61. Oswald West, "Reminiscences and Anecdotes: Political History," *Oregon Historical Quarterly* 50 (December 1949): 249.

62. *Portland Oregonian,* Feb. 20, 1911, p. 6; James R. McGovern, "David Graham Phillips and the Virility Impulse of the Progressives," *New England Quarterly* 39 (September 1966): 334–55; Joe L. Dubbert, "Progressivism and the Masculinity Crisis," in Elizabeth H. Pleck and Joseph H. Pleck, eds., *The American Man* (Englewood Cliffs, N.J.: Prentice-Hall, 1980), pp. 305–20; Pleck, "Whipping Post"; E. Anthony Rotundo, *American Manhood: Transformations in Masculinity from the Revolution to the Modern Era* (New York: Basic Books, 1993), pp. 262–74.

63. *Portland Oregonian,* Nov. 26, 1906, p. 9. Pleck, "Whipping Post," points out that legislative debates on the whipping post often featured light-hearted discussions of wife beating.

64. *San Francisco Sunday Call,* clipping, ca. 1906, scrapbook no. 88, p. 88, OHS.

65. *Portland Oregonian,* Nov. 27, 1906, p. 11.

66. Newspaper clipping, June 1905, scrapbook no. 73, p. 198, OHS.

67. *Portland Oregonian,* Jan. 19, 1905, p. 8; (Portland) *Oregon Daily Journal,* Feb. 17, 1905, p. 4; *Portland Evening Telegram,* Jan. 24, 1905, p. 6.

68. *Portland Oregonian,* Jan. 5, 1911, p. 10.

69. *Portland Evening Telegram,* Feb. 2, 1911, p. 6.

70. *Portland Evening Telegram,* Jan. 28, 1911, p. 6; *Portland Oregonian,* July 25, 1909, p. 1.

71. Newspaper clipping, scrapbook no. 88, p. 88, OHS; (Portland) *Woman's Tribune,* Feb. 4, 1905, p. 12.

72. *Minutes of the Twenty-Sixth Annual Convention of the Oregon's Woman's Christian Temperance Union,* 1909, pp. 42–43; *Minutes of the Twenty-Eighth Annual Convention of the Oregon's Woman's Christian Temperance Union,* 1911, pp. 41–42. Pleck, "Whipping Post," indicates that suffrage workers tended to divide on the whipping post.

73. (Portland) *Oregon Daily Journal,* June 7, 1905, p. 1; City of Portland Arrest Books, 1905 to 1911, City of Portland Archives and Records Center, Portland, Ore.; Multnomah County Circuit Court records; Marion County Circuit Court records, Oregon State Archives, Salem.

74. Newspaper clipping, June 1905, scrapbook no. 73, p. 198, OHS.

75. *Portland Oregonian,* Aug. 2, 1907, p. 9.

76. (Portland) *Oregon Daily Journal,* July 22, 1905, p. 4.

77. Mult. Co. nos. 34798, 36277.

78. (Portland) *Women's Tribune,* July 8, 1905, p. 45.

79. Oregon State Association Opposed to the Extension of Suffrage to Women, *An Appeal to Voters and Arguments against Equal Suffrage Constitutional Amendment* (n.p., [1906]), p. 22.

80. Newspaper clipping, June 1905, scrapbook no. 73, p. 198, OHS.

81. *Portland Oregonian,* Feb. 26, 1908, p. 8.

82. *Congressional Record,* 59th Cong., 1st sess., 1906, vol. 40, pt. 3:2448, cited in Pleck, "Whipping Post," p. 141.

83. *Portland Oregonian,* Feb. 13, 1911, p. 6.

84. *Portland Evening Telegram,* Oct. 18, 1916, p. 6.

85. Newspaper clipping, June 1905, scrapbook no. 73, p. 198, OHS.

86. *Portland Evening Telegram,* July 20, 1905, p. 3.

87. Bertram Wyatt-Brown, in *Southern Honor: Ethics and Behavior in the Old South* (New York: Oxford University Press, 1982), pp. 462–93, offers an intriguing Durkheimian analysis of the scapegoating of an antebellum southern wife killer. Oregon wife beaters did not receive public whippings, but reporters from newspapers, the modern equivalent of the town square, made their abasement a public event.

88. The frequency of violence, however, tended to decline as occupational status rose: 3.18 for laborers, 2.84 for semiskilled and skilled workers, 2.96 for blue-collar proprietors and managers and white-collar workers, and 2.68 for professionals and white-collar proprietors and managers. To determine frequency of violence, I used a five-point scale, essentially a three-point scale (1, 3, and 5) with borderline cases assigned a 2 or a 4. A score of 1 indicates only one example or instance of violence. A score of 3 means that the violence occurred more than once but apparently did not occur frequently. Frequent acts of violence were coded as 5, with "frequent" defined as three acts of violence within a three-month period. Descriptions of violence such as "continually" were coded as 5. A score of 2 was given to cases in which the violence could have occurred more than once or only once. A score of 4 was given to cases in which the violence could have occurred frequently, but may have been only sporadic. The occupations for the four categories are as follows (the first two are considered working class):

Laborers: fishermen, helpers in blue-collar occupations, housekeepers, janitors, laborers, loggers, miners, ranch hands, sawmill workers (no skills indicated), scavengers, watchmen.

Semi-skilled and skilled: bakers, barbers, bartenders, bill posters, blacksmiths, boatswains, boiler makers, brewers, bricklayers, butchers, carmen, carpenters, cement makers, chippers with steel companies, cigar makers, conductors, coopers, dispatchers, drivers, electricians, engineers, farmers, finishers, firemen, foremen, grocers, harness makers, horseshoers, hypnotist's assistants, linemen, longshoremen, machinists, mates, millers, millwrights, oilers, painters, peddlers, plumbers, porters, printers, shinglers, sign painters, steam fitters, stewards, stove mounters, switchmen, taxidermists, teamsters, tinners, waiters.

Blue-collar proprietors and managers, white-collar workers: actors, advertisers, artists, bookkeepers, clerks, contractors, draftsmen, grocers, blue-collar managers, musicians, small-business owners, photographers, police, postal workers, blue-collar proprietors, realtors, salesmen, saloonkeepers, secretaries, solicitors, (small) speculators, stenographers, surveyors, teachers, telephone operators.

Professionals and white-collar proprietors and managers: attorneys, dentists, manufacturers, merchandise brokers, ministers, money brokers, physicians, white-collar proprietors.

The men's occupations were determined from city directories and from the divorce suits.

89. Mult. Co. nos. 44918, 45483, 45696.

90. Interpretations emphasizing violence in nineteenth- or early-twentieth-century working-class families include: Ellen Ross, "'Fierce Questions and Taunts': Married Life in Working-Class London, 1870–1914," *Feminist Studies* 8 (Fall 1982): 572–602; Peter N. Stearns, *Be a Man! Males in Modern Society,* 2d ed. (New York: Holmes & Meier, 1990), pp. 93–94. Immigrant status was determined from the 1900 manuscript census and occasionally from the divorce suits.

91. City of Portland arrest books, 1905 to 1911. The figures for the nonwife assaults are from two one-year periods, one from 1905 to 1906 and the other from 1910 to 1911. Just over 40 percent of assault and battery cases in both categories were dismissed by the court or by the person assaulted.

92. Working-class men constituted about 79 percent of those arrested, foreign-born men 33 percent, and African American men 5 percent, all higher figures than their proportion of Portland's husbands. City of Portland arrest books, 1905 to 1911. I found occupations listed in the arrest books or, more commonly, traced them through city directories. It is difficult to know if the high number of arrests of men in certain social groups was due largely to police bias or to the wives of such groups being more apt to call on the police. *Portland Oregonian,* Nov. 11, 1907, pp. 1, 4. Karen Taylor, "Patriarchy and Male Oppression: Suffering the Responsibilities of Manhood," in Pamela R. Frese and John M. Coggeshall, eds., *Transcending Boundaries: Multi-Disciplinary Approaches to the Study of Gender* (New York: Bergin & Garvey, 1991), pp. 62–63, reports that very few battering husbands in Melbourne, Australia, or Boston received more than a fine from 1850 to 1900, and that even wife killers faced relatively light punishments.

93. Mult. Co. no. 31220.

94. Mult. Co. no. 31827.

95. Mult. Co. no. 31026.

96. Mult. Co. no. 37650.

97. Mult. Co. no. 30711. Pamela Haag, "'The Ill-Use of a Wife': Patterns of Working-Class Violence in Domestic and Public New York City, 1860–1880," *Journal of Social History* 25 (Spring 1992): 468–70, and Christine Stansell, *City of Women: Sex and Class in New York, 1789–1860* (New York: Alfred A. Knopf, 1986), pp. 80–83, argue that working-class women in mid-nineteenth-century New York relied heavily on each other for protection from their husbands and for more general mutual aid. I have found, however, that men intervened more often against violent husbands than women did. See also Ross, "'Fierce Questions and Taunts.'"

98. Mult. Co. no. 36147.

99. Mult. Co. no. 37847.

100. Mult. Co. no. 37224.

101. Mult. Co. no. 36710.

102. Mult. Co. no. 36104.

103. Mult. Co. no. 36356.

104. *Portland Oregonian,* Sept. 7, 1907, p. 16.

105. *Portland Oregonian,* July 13, 1902, sec. 3, p. 1.

106. *Portland Oregonian,* Jan. 7, 1907, pp. 1, 3.

107. Mult. Co. no. 37500.

108. Mult. Co. no. 36951.

109. Mult. Co. no. 31329.

110. *Portland Oregonian,* Feb. 19, 1910, p. 18; Mult. Co. no. 45340.

111. *Portland Oregonian,* Feb. 9, 1910, p. 10.

112. Multnomah County Circuit Court cases.

113. *Reports of Cases Decided in the Supreme Court of the State of Oregon* (San Francisco: Bancroft-Whitney, 1914), 47: 47.

114. *Report of the Social Survey Committee of the Consumer's League of Oregon on the Wages, Hours and Conditions of Work and Cost and Standard of Living of Women Wage Earners in Oregon with Special Reference to Portland* (Portland, Ore.: Keystone Press, 1913), p. 24, passim.

115. Mult. Co. no. 31422.

116. Mult. Co. no. 30730.

117. B.G.A.S., file for case no. 2420; James Allen, "Illusions of Serenity: The Impact of the Judicial System on the Development of Social Policy against Domestic Violence, 1870–1930," B.A. thesis (Reed College, 1992).

118. Leslie Woodcock Tentler, *Wage-Earning Women: Industrial Work and Family Life in the United States, 1900–1930* (New York: Oxford University Press, 1979), p. 175.

119. Mult. Co. nos. 31333, 45283.

120. Mult. Co. no. 31827.

121. Multnomah County Coroner's Investigation Books, 1900–1910, Multnomah County Medical Examiner's Office, Portland, Oregon.

122. x2=6.133, df=1, P<.025, N=38 for foreign-born versus those with native-born parents.

123. The likelihood of intervention fell as class status rose in the four occupational categories: 39 percent; 38 percent; 31 percent; and 16 percent.

124. Mult. Co. no. 31220. George eventually succeeded in grasping her throat.

125. Mult. Co. no. 36068.

126. Mult. Co. no. 37642.

127. Mult. Co. nos. 36935, 36224. Ross, "'Fierce Questions and Taunts,'" argues that London working-class women of the late nineteenth and early twentieth centuries frequently stood their ground against violent husbands or even precipitated violence.

128. *Portland Oregonian,* May 5, 1908, p. 13.

129. *Portland Oregonian,* March 3, 1909, p. 14.

PART 3
WORK

Women have always worked in their own homes, cleaning and raising children, sewing and entertaining, nursing, supervising, and organizing. These responsibilities did not disappear when, in addition, by need or by choice, women took on occupations outside the domestic realm. In this collection, we look at some examples of Northwest women engaged in paid work. Among these cases are in-depth examinations of their work as political office-holders and defense industry employees during World War II. Like farming and journalism—other occupations we encounter in this book—factory work and political leadership have been dominated by males. Such woman-dominated fields as nursing, teaching, clerical work, social work, prostitution, hairdressing, cannery work, and domestic work would reveal different patterns. To study these patterns in the Northwest, we must await further scholarship.

The historian Maurine Weiner Greenwald explores a debate that took place in Seattle immediately after World War I, an era when the city was widely known for its radicalism. "Should married women work for wages?" the *Seattle Union Record* newspaper asked its readers. Greenwald explores the replies of men and women respondents in this essay. She finds that working-class feminists, concerned with gender rights as well as class solidarity, did not voice the same arguments as middle-class feminists. Rather, some proponents advocated work on the grounds of sexual equality, the importance of economic and personal independence from husbands, and the clear capability of women. Others argued for the comfort of the working-class family. Opponents recognized the domestic and child-rearing demands on women, in an era before anyone suggested that husbands might share in those tasks. They also underlined the scarcity of post-war job opportunities and insisted that the survival of working-class community depended on married women's absence from the competition for wage work. Greenwald's portrait of Seattle's Union Card and Label League broadens our sense of working-class women's commitment to labor issues. She traces members who used the organization to engage in an impressive spectrum of activities supportive of union members and their families, including social activities, benevolent work, and consumer boycotts.

The region has not been wanting in examples of successful woman lawyers, judges, and physicians. Mayor Bertha Knight Landes's career, however, was the culmination of generations of women's dreams. Seattle led the nation, in 1926, as the first large American city to elect a woman as mayor. Doris H. Pieroth's portrait of Mayor Landes reveals that the first generation of women office-holders relied on skills, experiences, and beliefs acquired in the woman's sphere. While Landes benefited from a college education and a spouse supportive of her public roles, her life pattern resembled that of most middle-class women. That is, of primary importance were husband, children, and church. An interest in and a talent for volunteer work led her gradually to climb within women's organizations, taking higher and higher offices in larger and grander organizations, until she presided over the entire Seattle Federation of Women's Clubs. There, like most clubwomen of her day, she defended woman's involvement in civic reform as "municipal housekeeping," or the proper and logical extension of her role in the domestic sphere. For almost a century, multitudes of feminists had asserted that the differences between men and women should serve as a basis for woman's involvement in public life, not her banishment from it. Domestically cultivated talent, perceptions, and knowledge could lend special, valuable insights to public issues and problems. That her peers catapulted Landes to the Seattle City Council and mayoralty was unusual for its time, but her belief in a woman's special viewpoint was not.

Mayor Landes promised to represent women's values in government and to transform government by women's presence. This made it inevitable that she stand for decency, enforcement of prohibition, regulation of cabarets and dance halls, civil service, improved recreation, municipal ownership of utilities, city council government, and opposition to corruption. Pieroth suggests that Landes's very firmness on these issues, and her refusal to compromise for political gains, ensured her failure to win reelection. Women's vision of an honest operation of a real democracy ultimately could not undermine the entrenched system. Landes's failure to implement and protect her platform brought grave disappointment to newly enfranchised women.

The Great Depression of the 1930s inhibited many of women's hopes for full participation and wide influence in American society, but World War II opened doors to new opportunities in the marketplace. Now all hands were needed to produce for the defense industry, and Northwest women were suddenly encouraged to relegate family responsibilities to second place and take up war-related tasks. Where they had previously been concentrated in low-paying, low-status occupations, now they were invited to work in more lucrative fields, heretofore almost exclusively the province of men. Karen Beck Skold addresses this phenomenon in the Portland area, where three Kaiser Corporation shipyards hired women in great numbers. Skold raises questions about their training, duties, motivations, obstacles, satisfactions, and disappointments, and explores their wages, hours, and working conditions . How did their workplace experiences compare with men's? Did they enjoy cooperation, or did they suffer harassment by male colleagues? How did they balance wage-earning with responsibilities at home?

Skold describes the widespread participation by women who came to represent, during the years 1942–45, a significant portion of the shipyard labor force. Attracted by high wages, better jobs than had been available before, a chance to provide patriotic service to their country and try new opportunities, they equaled men in productivity and hoped to continue their work after the war emergency was over. Skold praises the high quality day-care centers available in Portland and Vanport, Oregon, and Vancouver, Washington, which suggested a new social willingness to provide facilities for women who had responsibility for children.

For all the positive experiences of this wartime period, however, sexism by no means disappeared at the workplace. Women were over-represented in unskilled positions, as laborers, helpers, and welders, and women over age thirty-five had to resign themselves to sweeping and other menial jobs. Women were under-represented as journeymen in most crafts, and Oregon saw only one loftlady, three woman riggers, and one woman wiring on the 50-foot masts of Liberty ships. Ultimately, the aberrant nature of women's swift career and wage advancement became apparent, at the war's end. Women were rapidly dismissed and sent back to the home or to traditionally female wage-earning occupations, as men returned from the military to reclaim "male" jobs.

Working-Class Feminism and the Family Wage Ideal: The Seattle Debate on Married Women's Right to Work, 1914–1920

MAURINE WEINER GREENWALD

American feminists in the early twentieth century included a segment of working-class women, participating alongside the better-known middle-class and elite adherents of feminist ideas. Class boundaries did not stop the flow of ideas. Working-class feminists cited the writings of Charlotte Perkins Gilman on housewifery, Olive Schreiner on married women's employment, and Doris Stevens on woman suffrage. Women wage earners marched in suffrage parades between 1910 and 1920 and convinced brothers, fathers, and male coworkers to vote in favor of extending the franchise to women. During and after World War I, such women began to express a new concern for personal satisfaction and a new ambition at work. In this period working-class women sometimes behaved in extremely disorderly ways, rejecting traditional ladylike behavior to fight "like men" for their dignity and economic rights. They promoted their beliefs in workplaces and homes, social clubs, union halls, neighborhood stores, and local newspapers.[1] Working-class women participated in the early-twentieth-century revolt against traditional gender roles, but their activism is only part of a larger story still unfolding. Many questions still remain about the origins and outlines of working-class feminism. How did working-class women reconcile feminist ideas with the gender and class traditions in their communities? Did working-class women fashion a distinctive variant of feminism out of their own experiences and observations? How did working-class opponents of feminism conceive of women's place in a laboring community?

A controversy on married women's employment that erupted in Seattle between 1918 and 1920 reveals both the distinctive features of working-class feminism and the range of working-class opinion on the issue. Seattle is a good choice for such a study because in the early twentieth century it was an extremely class-conscious town with a vibrant labor movement that included women as union and auxiliary members, organizers, and officials. As compared with trade-union movements elsewhere in the United States at that time, Seattle's was distinctly left of center with a strong, although controversial, commitment to industrial unionism, labor-owned businesses, and workers' control of industry. The workers who supported the labor movement were predominantly white and were native-born Americans, or Scandinavian, British, or Canadian immigrants, or the children of such immigrants. Stereotypically thought of as a city of metal workers and lumberjacks—a man's town—Seattle was also a "city of women." By the second decade of the twentieth century, working-class men and women were accustomed to cooperating in union business, boycotts of employers, political campaigns, and social celebrations. Working-class women also regularly collaborated with middle-class clubwomen to lobby for the federal suffrage amendment and for state laws protecting women workers and indigent mothers.[2]

The issue of married women's employment provides an excellent opportunity to explore how female and male members of the same class responded to feminist ideas and concerns. The right of married women to work for wages outside the home, regardless of economic necessity, has been a key tenet of modern feminism. In the early twentieth century, feminists believed that wage work would emancipate married women from economic dependence on their husbands and social isolation in the home. The legitimacy of married women's employment was debated vociferously in the era of the First World War, when the United States underwent a turbulent mobilization for war and a painful readjustment to peace. The debate found an audience in popular magazines, newspapers, novels, academic journals, monographs, and feminist and labor publications. From 1918 to 1920 the *Seattle Union Record*, the official organ of the Washington State Federation of Labor, published letters, questionnaires, and news reports on the topic. Even in Seattle, where working-class women and men formed a close partnership, the debate over married women's wage work raged with ferocity, eliciting an array of responses.[3]

The Seattle controversy reveals a variety of working-class views on women's place in American society and reactions to changing economic and social circumstances. Men and women took both sides of the debate—variously defending, questioning, and opposing married women's right to paid employment. The rationales of individual respondents usually turned on one of three positions, two that favored married women's employment, one that opposed it. Proponents expressed either an explicit commitment to feminism or an avid desire for a higher standard of living. Opponents of married women's employment resolutely underscored their allegiance to the ideals of a family wage and a moral economy.

The Seattle debate over married women's employment clearly demonstrates, on the one hand, that feminist ideas were an integral part of Seattle's working-class culture and public discourse. Economic autonomy and personal independence became increasingly important to married working-class women in the early twentieth century, just as those goals became important to married middle-class women.[4] But working-class feminist ideas were not identical images of middle-class ones. Seattle's working-class feminists adopted and adapted feminist ideas to fit the particular circumstances of their lives and community. Working-class feminists defended equal rights for women and tailored a dual commitment to equal rights for women *and* workers. Such dualism distinguished working-class feminism in Seattle from its middle-class counterpart. This study places special emphasis on the particular sources, outlines, and concerns of working-class feminism.

On the other hand, some members of the Seattle working class supported married women's labor force participation as a way of improving families' standards of living, not primarily as a way of enhancing wives' social and economic status. These advocates saw married women's employment as part of a family strategy of acquiring a large share of the goods and services available in modern America.

Working-class feminists in Seattle clashed head on with opponents of married women's employment who subscribed to the ideals of the family wage and the moral economy, two of the most revered precepts of the Seattle labor movement. Wage work by married women violated both ideals; both condemned it as improper and unfair. The family wage ideal, in which the male breadwinner earned enough to support his wife and children, constituted a class aspiration shared by men and women. The ideal of the moral economy postulated that financial need alone should determine who had a legitimate claim to wage work. From both perspectives, married women had no right to work except in cases of absolute economic necessity. Proponents of the family wage and the moral economy believed that their ideas represented the fairest arrangement possible in a highly competitive labor market with chronic unemployment.[5]

This triptych of views of married women's employment in Seattle in the World War I era demonstrates how complex the intersection of class and gender has been. By looking at the way that women and men in an unusually

This cartoon from the *Seattle Union Record* (6 February 1915) featured housewives' power to improve unionists' employment and wages.

class-conscious city thought about a particular gendered issue, this case study underscores the importance of class and community traditions in shaping people's responses to feminist ideas in the early twentieth century and reveals the difficulties that feminists faced in balancing their individual and collective aspirations as women with loyalties felt as members of the working class.

BACKGROUND TO THE DEBATE

Seattle was a distinctly union town with a history of militancy and labor radicalism. The *Seattle Union Record* was owned and controlled by the Central Labor Council (CLC) of Seattle, an unusually loyal coalition of 110 unions that at its peak in early 1919 had 65,000 members, some 4,000 of whom were women. Approximately 42 percent of the 153,000 wage earners in Seattle belonged to the CLC unions, an unusually strong showing for the time. In 1919 council members proudly proclaimed that their organization was among the strongest city labor federations in the United States.[6] Seattle residents could outfit their families and homes with union-made clothes and appliances, serve union-processed food, eat at unionized restaurants, and purchase homes built by union craftsmen.[7] The Seattle CLC also distinguished itself by being more radical than the American Federation of Labor, with which it was affiliated, and most other citywide labor organizations in the country. The Seattle organization endorsed the concept of industrial unionism (having workers in various trades and crafts in one industry belong to the same association), promoted the election of pro-union candidates for public office, and favored the nationalization of key industries. The Seattle labor movement saw itself as very class-conscious, intent on bringing about workers' control of industry and supporting labor's claims to just treatment throughout the United States. Labor organization and socialist politics were closely linked in Seattle, as elsewhere in the Pacific Northwest.[8]

In 1919 male industrial workers in the metal trades and shipyards and craftsmen in the building trades dominated the Seattle labor movement, but women participated in CLC affairs as members of unions, auxiliaries, and clubs. The principal female unionists were waitresses, laundry workers, garment makers, boot and shoe workers, bookbinders, musicians, and candy workers.[9] During World War I, Seattle's women barbers, domestic servants, elevator operators, hotel maids, and telephone operators joined the labor movement. The wives of unionized workers organized auxiliaries to their husbands' unions. Such auxiliaries, associated with the unionized carpenters, electrical workers, building craftsmen, boilermakers and ship builders, typographical workers, and postal clerks, hosted social affairs, attended to the personal needs

"Lady" barbers, active members of the Seattle labor movement, supported married women's employment *(courtesy Special Collections, University of Washington Libraries, UW Neg. 8964)*

of trade union families, and occasionally supported legislative campaigns.[10] Other than the women trade union leaders, the most active women in the working-class community were the wives of skilled workers and union officials, who established clubs to promote the purchase of union-made goods, raise money for union causes, boycott businesses deemed unfair to labor, and lobby state legislators. As the number of working-class clubwomen grew, so did their importance to the Seattle labor movement. During the controversy over married women's employment the clubwomen were at the very center of the debate.

The public debate over married women's employment in the early twentieth century was a response to long- and short-term changes in women's job options and participation in the labor force. The federal censuses indicate that during the first twenty years of the twentieth century women's occupational opportunities expanded in the fields of trade, communications, education, and office work, marking a shift away from women's long-standing concentration in agriculture, manufacturing, and domestic and personal service.[11]

The new jobs attracted married as well as single women into the American labor market. Between 1900 and 1920 the proportion of married women in the female labor force increased by 53 percent, jumping from a little over 15 to nearly 23 percent. In the decade from 1910 to 1920, married women, like their single counterparts, sought jobs as factory operatives, telephone operators, salesclerks, government employees, teachers, and office workers in preference to traditional female employment in agriculture and household maintenance.[12]

Changes in women's employment patterns in Seattle followed the national trends. Both the number of employed women and married women's labor force participation increased between 1900 and 1920. In those twenty years, the number of Seattle women who worked rose 594 percent (4,774 to 33,114), while the number of married women who worked jumped 831 percent (881 to 8,203). The city's general population in the same twenty-year period rose 291 percent (80,671 to 315,312). Married women, excluding divorced and widowed women, were 18 percent of Seattle women wage earners in 1900 and 25 percent in 1920; the figures were slightly higher than the national averages for those census years.[13]

The percentage of married women workers in Seattle rose in every occupational category in the early twentieth century, but by 1920 it was most pronounced in manufacturing, transportation, trade, and domestic and personal service. One-fifth to nearly one-third of female factory operatives, telephone operators, salesclerks, waitresses, barbers, and servants were married and living with their husbands. The effects of married women's wage work on the labor market, the labor movement, and family life in Seattle became an issue of heated public debate during and immediately following World War I.

The shift in women's employment patterns that resulted from wartime mobilization and postwar demobilization engendered a debate over married women's employment in Seattle. During the war, women's wage work acquired unprecedented public prominence and contributed significantly to the American economy as new employment opportunities opened for women. Particularly after the second draft of 1918 had markedly reduced the number of men available for civilian employment, women workers became a precious resource. They seized the opportunity by switching workplaces in search of better wages and working conditions. The mobilization conferred new dignity on women's wage work, as businessmen and politicians congratulated women for outstanding contributions to the nation's wartime economic welfare.[14]

As counterpoint to such accolades, intraclass tensions between men and women erupted as women changed from traditional to nontraditional employment throughout the United States. General economic and social tendencies and particular local circumstances—both local political culture and specific features in a community's industrial life—determined relations among coworkers. Male unionists reacted with hostility when employers hired women to dilute skilled labor, break strikes, lower wages, or introduce new technology. Acrimony between men and women workers flared especially in metalworking plants, foundries, offices, coal mines, and on streetcar lines. Men rejected women workers' introduction into new fields most vehemently when they perceived a threat from women's economic competition.[15]

Although the Seattle labor force was dominated by the shipbuilding and lumber industries, which traditionally employed only men, women gained entry for the first time in 1917 and 1918 into a few male-dominated occupations. Women drove taxicabs, operated drill presses in machine shops, delivered mail, worked as common laborers in lumberyards, substituted for men in can production, and assisted male electricians in factories. As was true elsewhere, in Seattle women obtained wartime jobs that required little training or skill.[16] Such workers were relatively vulnerable compared to women employed in traditionally female jobs—as telephone operators, candy and cracker workers, laundry operatives, teachers, hotel maids, and domestic servants—who could look to organized labor for financial and moral support when they struck for union recognition and higher wages.

Male trade unionists in Seattle responded to women's employment during the war with a host of strategies designed to defend their job benefits and extend them to women. Fearful that women would undermine their wages and working conditions, machinists, electricians, and timber workers reluctantly recruited women into their ranks and vigorously enforced equal-pay clauses. The Seattle barbers' local admitted "lady" barbers in defiance of their national constitution's provision barring women members. Trade unions taxed their members to support women strikers and new organizing efforts. At the urging of women unionists and unionists' wives, the Seattle Central Labor Council hired a full-time female labor organizer expressly to work among women. The Seattle unions sent representatives to the state capital to lobby for an increase in the minimum wage for women. Such union policies benefited both women in nontraditional jobs and women in so-called female occupations.[17]

The increasing presence of married women workers in the labor force presented a special problem for the Seattle labor movement. The city's trade unionists unanimously agreed on the importance of organizing women into unions, paying them equal wages, increasing their minimum wage, and supporting female strikers, but the legitimacy of married women's right to work outside the home raised key social, economic, and moral issues that split the Seattle trade union community. The new trend brought into question both the long-standing ideal of a family wage for the male breadwinner that would enable him to support his entire family and the customary division of labor between husbands and wives. The debate also prominently featured questions about the relationship between individual rights and class obligations, particularly the notion of a moral economy in which need alone (not individual rights) determined a person's legitimate claim to wage work in a competitive economy. Labor solidarity in Seattle eroded as members of the trade union community took their stands on the issue of married women's employment rights.

The debate over married women workers erupted in Seattle after trade unions and Washington State agencies adopted policies to exclude married women from wage work during and just after the war. The *Seattle Union Record* printed 82 letters by 78 individuals (52 women and 26 men) on this subject in 1918, 1919, and 1920. The first round of letters to the *Record* commented on the April 1918 International Association of Machinists' resolution that members should prevent their wives from working in industry on the grounds that they would rob more needy persons of employment. A second round of letters responded to the October 1918 Seattle CLC policy of discouraging "supported" married women from entering industry. A third round of debate occurred in 1919, sparked by events in Seattle and Tacoma, Washington. The Civil Service Bureau in Tacoma had recommended that the Tacoma City Council prohibit the promotion of currently employed married women and the hiring of additional married women. The Seattle CLC intensified the discord by disqualifying two married women from running for the elected position of CLC organizer for women workers. Judging by the many respondents who identified themselves by name, the debate engaged the most privileged sector of the working class—male and female union officials, skilled male workers, and the wives of labor aristocrats.[18]

WORKING-CLASS WOMEN'S WARTIME ATTITUDES TOWARD MARRIED WOMEN'S EMPLOYMENT

In expressing views on the propriety of married women working for wages the letter writers to the *Seattle Union Record* also revealed much about their attitudes toward women's place inside and outside the home. Many women whose letters were published in the *Record* expressed unqualified approval for married women's wage work, challenging male privilege in the marketplace. They attacked the traditional division of labor that assigned men the exclusive role of breadwinning and restricted women to domestic and child-rearing tasks. These champions of married women's employment deserve the label feminist as it was used between 1910 and 1920, the period when it first gained currency and legitimacy in the United States. Feminists believed in sex equality, opposed man-made barriers to women's full participation in American society, and embraced group consciousness and collective action by women to promote their views. Seattle women developed their own variant of feminism that grew directly out of their allegiance to a working-class community. The unwavering defense of married women's employment as individually and socially desirable was indeed a central principle for all feminists.[19]

The Seattle feminist respondents emphasized the importance of women's right, regardless of marital status, to enjoy economic independence, individual development, and personal autonomy. These writers invoked the terms *justice, democracy, individuality, freedom, equal opportunity, and equal development* to define and justify their position. Repeatedly affirming women's right to determine what they would do after marriage, they criticized male trade unionists for discriminating against married women. A characteristic response to the International Association of Machinists' resolution barring members' wives from industry asked sarcastically, "Did any organization ever pass a rule that men who have fathers to support them, or rich wives, who for any reason don't have to work, should stay out of industry to give other folks a chance? Not a bit of it." Mrs. K. L. asserted, "I don't think it's very democratic to put strings on one class of people and say they shan't work." Mrs. A. S. agreed, "[Working for wages] is a question for the individual woman to settle and not for machinists' unions to tell their members how to boss their wives." One woman compared the machinists to the mythical cavemen who ruled their women with brute force and tyrannical behavior. The women were protesting, in effect, the right of one group of wage earners to delimit or deny another group's freedom to work.[20]

The work-and-marriage advocates stressed the importance of selecting workers for jobs on the basis of individual preference, talent, experience, and training. Lillian Stevenson, a labor activist and member of the Waitresses' Union, asked, "What has marriage got to do with [women's employment] except that it makes a woman more able?" Mrs. Lorene Wiswell Wilson, president of the recently established Seattle Women's Trade Union League, argued that "those who work for a better order of society believe that every individual should have, regardless of sex, the opportunity to do for the service of all the kind he or she likes best."[21]

The feminist respondents fortunately left a trail of clues about the experiences that had shaped their attitudes on women's rights. They had followed no single route. Like middle-class women attracted to feminist ideas from 1910 to 1930, the Seattle working-class women came to feminism by way of their wage work, marital experiences, or civic activities. Whatever the nature of their journey, all feminists believed that women were productive members of society both within and outside the home. Many of the anonymous women who corresponded with the *Seattle Union Record* accentuated their wage work and personal difficulties in supporting themselves and their families. Wage earning had taught them that they were not paid as well as men or regarded with the same respect. For some female respondents the commitment to equal rights derived from their wartime experiences in wage and voluntary work. One married woman, newly retired from the labor force, credited the war with enlarging women's perspective.

> Since we had this great war, the women have got their eyes opened and gained a great advantage over men.
>
> Now these so-called weak women can step out and do work of all kinds and live independently and don't need to bow their heads and wait for a man to get ready to give them a small part of his wages, and maybe not any. I say let these women work, if they want to.[22]

The wife of a union business agent argued that her traditionally male job as a common laborer gave her not only "courage" but confidence and physical strength as well. Mrs. Anne Stewart linked the national recognition of women's voluntary wartime activities to married women's postwar aspirations for paid employment. "Now if the married woman has found that she has a commercial value . . . [and] if her services are rendered free, is she to be blamed that she still try for a 'place in the sun'?"[23]

For others the advocacy of women's rights derived from a perceived sense of the inequalities inherent in a patriarchal marital relationship. Gertrude Kallberg, wife of an electrician, urged women to work for wages to reinforce their personal independence and prepare for economic independence in case they faced marital discord, divorce, or desertion.

> [A woman] should not only be allowed to work, but be encouraged to become financially independent.
>
> It is a fact today that the average man sticks to a woman and supports her, and the children if there be any, just so long as the economic road is smooth, and she lives her life to suit him and his whims—in other words, as long as he pleases so to do.
>
> When the way grows rough, or the inner urge or law of her being forces a woman to live her own life in her own way, then trouble comes, and the man in the case often walks off and leaves her or the babes if there be any, without support.[24]

Many of the Seattle feminist respondents had learned about feminism through participation in the Women's Union Card and Label League, the key organizational link between working-class women and middle-class women and middle-class clubwomen in the city. The club played a major role in Seattle's labor movement. League members were the wives, daughters, and other female relatives of male trade unionists; some were wage earners as well as housewives. League women urged employers to adopt the union label and consumers to purchase only union-label goods. Many league efforts aimed to influence the behavior of women as consumers, but the organization also supported the eight-hour day, equal pay and trade union organization for women, and abolition of child labor. The league nurtured a commitment to feminism and strengthened members' resolve to combat gender discrimination within and outside the labor movement. A distinctly feminist consciousness emerged within the Seattle working class as league members promoted or challenged particular labor movement policies, discussed feminist writings, attended lectures by well-known women activists, worked with middle-class clubwomen, and responded to changing economic conditions. The league activists came to identify themselves as "houseworkers" and "women workers in the home" who wanted to liberate women from confinement to the household.[25]

In a special publication for the 1913 American Federation of Labor convention held in Seattle, the Card and Label League officers were portrayed as an integral part of the local labor movement *(courtesy Special Collections, University of Washington Libraries, UW Neg. 8965)*

As the organization grew in size and importance from 1914 through the war years, the women became accustomed to speaking for their interests as members of the working class and as women. Organized in 1911, the league began to flourish when it affiliated with the women's movement in 1914. At its peak the league had a membership of five hundred women, including most of the working-class female activists in the city. The league's many activities attest to the members' resourcefulness, vigor, and influence. The league's Fair Committee visited the owners of tailor shops, dairies, factories, and department stores to pressure them to hire union labor and use union labels. The committee also developed and published a "Fair Shopping List," naming businesses that made or sold union-made goods or employed union labor. On occasion the league helped organize citywide boycotts of businesses that refused to recognize union demands. The women faithfully raised money for striking workers, promoted labor-owned enterprises, collected signatures on petitions to repeal or retain state laws, and campaigned for political candidates endorsed by the labor movement. In hard times they fed unemployed women and tried to find jobs for them. The league also consistently supported campaigns to organize women wage earners into trade unions. The clubwomen attended to the social needs of the labor movement by hosting card parties, picnic luncheons, and masquerade balls. For their members' birthdays and wedding anniversaries, they sometimes orchestrated surprise parties with elaborate meals and personal gifts. Ill, bereaved, and needy members of the trade union community could expect clubwomen to minister to them. On Labor Day the league women, dressed in their finest attire, proudly marched with children from their junior affiliates at the head of Seattle's holiday parade and organized meals and recreation for the holiday participants. The Women's Union Card and Label League was, in short, an integral part of the Seattle trade union community.[26]

As their diverse activities suggest, the Seattle working-class clubwomen set their organizational agendas as members of the working class *and* as women. They attended to the most pressing needs—economic, political, social, or medical—of the laboring community as a whole and to the particular concerns of housewives and female wage earners. Viewing housewives as workers in their own right, they tried to gain visibility and respect for housewives' economic and social contributions to the Seattle working-class community. Indeed, the Seattle women used the term *houseworkers* interchangeably with *housewives,* emphasizing the centrality of work in housewifery. They thus supported the union label and labor-owned companies both as the wives of trade unionists and as houseworkers responsible for consuming only goods made under safe and sanitary conditions at fair wages. In the same vein, they looked out for the welfare of women workers, whose disadvantaged position in the labor market made them especially vulnerable to exploitation. They publicly proclaimed the direct link between their actions as women on behalf of other women in the home and work force and their actions as unionists' wives on behalf of the larger laboring community. In 1914 league activists boldly announced in the *Seattle Union Record* their intention of spreading a feminist "social consciousness" among working-class women. The club members regarded themselves as "wide awake, alert" women "whose minds and souls have outgrown the limitations of the arena of the cook stove and the 'four walls'" of the home. They disdained "bourgeois 'pink teas' and other antediluvian forms of . . . 'entertainment'" and bravely proclaimed a program to "embody the spirit of the best in the labor movement and the woman movement of today." To reach their ambitious goals, they scheduled discussions of writings by feminist theorists and labor activists. Discussions focused on works such as Olive Schreiner's *Woman and Labor* and Alice Henry's *Trade Union Woman,* which in distinctive ways promoted wage earning by married women. League members participated in the 1916 Leap Year Feminist

Ball, the motto of which was "Woman Is Man's Equal in All Things." Six hundred party-goers attended, dressed in costumes symbolizing "woman's emancipation from present customs." Dedicated to keeping current, they attended or read about lectures on birth control and sexual freedom by Margaret Sanger and Emma Goldman. The league enthusiastically sponsored public meetings for the feminist writer Charlotte Perkins Gilman and the suffrage leaders Doris Stevens, Anne Martin, and Carrie Chapman Catt. A kindergarten teacher looked after small children so that women with child-care responsibilities could attend league meetings regularly and become "social mothers."[27]

As a feminist, class-conscious organization modeled on the CLC, the league not only educated its members but also strove to influence public policy toward women, workers, and women workers. A delegation of four league members even tried to persuade the county commissioners to reserve a room in the new city and county building especially for women's groups to hold their meetings. League members joined representatives of forty-two other women's organizations to develop a legislative bureau in the state capital to lobby for day nurseries for working mothers, the abolition of child labor, an increase in the minimum wage for women, and the passage of an equal-pay law. When the controversy erupted over married women's employment, the Women's Union Card and Label League members were well versed in feminist ideas and accustomed to challenging customs and policies that discriminated against women.[28]

In openly defending married women's right to work for wages, league members directly rejected the notion that marriage limited women to the role of housewife. Echoing Olive Schreiner's insights, they informed their analysis of housewifery with a historical understanding of the changing nature of household labor since industrialization. They argued that housework no longer involved the arduous, time-consuming manufacture of daily necessities. Factories manufactured clothes. Gas and electrical equipment were replacing iceboxes and wood and coal-burning stoves. Houses with central heating required far less labor than ones with fireplaces and potbellied stoves. Commercial foods provided an attractive alternative to homegrown varieties and laborious food preservation. League members bemoaned women's loss of status as a consequence of industrialization and stressed the emotional rewards that would follow married women's employment. They argued that satisfying paid labor would improve relations between husbands and wives by giving otherwise isolated, bored, neurotic women an opportunity to exercise their intellects and become more loving partners to their husbands.[29]

Edith Levi, wife of a business agent for the Waiters' Union and herself a leader of the Card and Label League, emphasized the importance of women doing work to fit their individual talents and interests. "We should be allowed to do that which we are adapted for, otherwise we are living an unnatural life." Mrs. Mary Saunders, secretary of the Education Department of the Cooperative Food Products Association and a member of the league, insisted, "If I haven't a domestic kink in my nature I have a right to delegate the work in my home to some one [*sic*] who has."[30]

Other members of this working-class league underscored women's right to individual and creative expression through useful work. "Why should getting married banish women to the kitchen forever after, when she is supposed to be free and equal with men? Women are not all born cooks and housekeepers any more than men are born bricklayers," wrote Mrs. A. S. One woman likened her home, no matter how comfortable, to a "mausoleum" if she had to be confined to it every day. In an unusually long letter, Mary Archibald, an office or store clerk, explained how she had arrived at her views on the limits of domesticity. She married young and settled into a full-time domestic role without much satisfaction.

> I found, before too many years, that I was a square peg in a round hole. I was not domestic by nature. I loved my home, but I hated the everlasting monotony of putting the sugar-bowl on the table and taking it off again three times a day; of wanting something of beauty as well as utility in my surroundings, and never being able to afford it. . . . And this is my quarrel with marriage. There are too many square pegs in round holes, and if women enter industry in large numbers, I believe, it will force a reorganization, not only of industries, but of the home—to the advantage of both.[31]

In responding to the problem of "square pegs in round holes," a few of the letter writers proposed a radical reorganization of private housekeeping as a solution to the drudgery and lack of respect for domestic labor. The advocates of household reorganization echoed Gilman's writings on domesticity and social change and mentioned her by name several times. In her widely read book *Women and Economics*, published in 1898, Gilman painted a portrait of women as mental and emotional midgets, stunted in their growth by confinement to the home and by their economic dependence on men. Gilman reasoned that women's lack of emotional, mental, and economic independence would have dire consequences, in the language of her day, for the evolution of the race. Only with women's emergence from the household cocoon into the demanding world of paid employment could they experience a metamorphosis, attaining full personhood and insuring the health of

These women (Mrs. Minnie Ault is at left) represented the *Seattle Union Record* at a masquerade ball held by the Card and Label League to raise money for the labor movement

future generations. Gilman proposed a change in domestic life modeled on the division of labor and use of experts for particular tasks in industry. Women's emancipation from domestic chores was possible, Gilman argued, if collective living arrangements featuring kitchenless apartment buildings with child-care facilities, central dining rooms, and professional household cleaning services replaced the traditional household.[32]

The *Record* respondents who favored the reorganization of housework agreed that the traditional organization of domestic labor produced drudgery, isolation, inefficiency, and degradation. Some advocated the employment of specially trained cooks, housecleaners, and nurserymaids to replace the jack-of-all-trades housewife. Minnie Ault, president of the Card and Label League, business agent for the Bookbinders' Union, and wife of the *Record*'s editor, suggested that trained nurses care for the children of working mothers in day-care centers. Others looked to the collective laundries, kitchens, and dining rooms that Gilman advocated but expressed reluctance to transfer child care from the home. Mrs. A. Camp briefly described a way women might share their tasks and be recompensed too:

> I have thought that a group of from five to ten houses should have co-operative buildings behind, consisting of a kitchen, laundry, nursery, dining room, and visiting hall. The women living in these houses would meet in the visiting hall and arrange their work for the week, each taking turns at it. . . . The women of the 10 houses could arrange to pay wages for their work, and would feel more respect for themselves than taking money from their husbands for no just reason.[33]

Mrs. Anne Stewart also favored wages for housework so that a housewife's work would command equal "commercial" value to her "husband's earning power." Although the proposals for domestic organization varied considerably, from industrializing housework to paying wages for housewifery, they had a single aim. In the future, as a trained nurse remarked, "woman, once the slave of the home, would be free to develop herself."[34]

Like Gilman and her middle-class followers, the *Record* respondents did not suggest redistributing domestic labor or child rearing equally between wives and husbands so that both could work for wages full time and share household maintenance and parenting. The Seattle proponents of plans to reorganize housework did not perceive the gender bias in their schemes for social change. Although their proposals were radical in some respects, many of their ideas reflected the traditional sexual division of labor in the home. The advocates of changes in housework assumed that domestic labor and child rearing were "women's work." Only two women mentioned the importance of a father's role in child rearing. One of them recommended "an ideal of complete comradeship" in which both wives and husbands would work for wages until they had children, at which time both would stay home and raise them. More typically men's responsibilities to contribute anything besides their earnings to domestic life were simply ignored by the letter writers. No one suggested that men be hired as cooks, housecleaners, or child caretakers. The proposals challenged the conditions under which housework was performed, but they left intact the centuries-old tradition of assigning domestic chores and child rearing to women. A special reverence for motherhood probably contributed to the writers' inviolable association of household labor and parenting solely with women. League members emphasized the importance of women's role as mothers both in the family and in the civic arena.[35]

Although the Seattle feminist respondents referred to Gilman's ideas on domestic reorganization, their proposals probably derived as much from their experience as consumers in Seattle as from their reading of feminist literature. Their notions about housework may have developed from a familiarity with Seattle's numerous, but short-lived, working-class cooperative enterprises. From late 1918 until early 1920, Seattle unionists and their relatives boasted about their thriving consumer and producer cooperatives. Two citywide chains of cooperatives provided milk, groceries, meat, and fuel as well as shoe repair, coal and wood supplies, and cleaning and tailoring services. The predominantly consumer co-ops brought housewives together in neighborhood clubs to socialize and discuss their role as shoppers intent on promoting fair prices and labor conditions. The consumer cooperatives underscored the social importance of housewives' buying habits. The domestic reorganization envisioned by Seattle feminist respondents was in keeping with cooperative ventures in other fields in their city.[36]

The *Record*'s working-class feminists approached the problem of labor market competition in terms of gender rights and class obligations. They were conscious of themselves not only as women who wanted the right to work for wages, regardless of their marital status, but also as members of a community of workers who had trouble getting and keeping jobs as the economy converted from a war to a peacetime basis. Their commitment to paid employment was an expression of their belief in personal autonomy. They viewed the right to earn wages as inalienable, as inextricably tied to the American belief in individual liberty. But these women did not subscribe to the view that individual rights mattered above all else. They wanted the Seattle labor movement to combine individual rights with group responsibility. The feminist respondents valued individual liberty as well as family, class, and community obligations.[37]

Since these women were aware of both gender and class identities, they felt obliged to deal with the fear that married women's employment would increase unemployment among single women and single and married men. They had to answer the argument that it was immoral and unjust for supported married women to work when some families could not make enough to survive. The Seattle working-class feminists had to consider how to solve the problem of labor competition without sacrificing married women's right to work. They looked to workers' control of industry, a long-standing goal of Seattle labor, to make it possible for everyone who wanted work to find a job. They also strongly endorsed the labor movement's guiding principle of "all for one and one for all."[38]

Lillian Stevenson captured the radical sentiment of the working-class feminists when she asserted, "Barring industry to married women may relieve competition a little, but are we trying to uphold the competitive system? Pick on the system, and not on married women!" The Seattle feminist respondents would certainly also have applauded the letter from the woman who signed herself "From one who believes in FUNDAMENTALS." "The workers will never get anywhere," she asserted, "until they stop wasting time on trying to keep people out of jobs and set out to control industry from top to bottom." To improve labor market conditions for women without threatening male workers or single women with job competition, Seattle delegates to the 1919 Washington State Federation of Labor convention advocated a shorter workday and the organization of women into trade unions. They proposed that the workday "be so shortened that there would be a place in industrial, business, or professional life for everyone who desired to enter it." A two-hour workday was their "ultimate ideal" so that "women . . . could combine care of their home with work outside." Edith Levi of the Card and Label League requested that the federation organize unorganized women in order to "uphold the standards of living to which our husbands, brothers, fathers and sweethearts are justly entitled." In short, these women tried to persuade Seattle trade unionists that women and men could unite for the benefit of the entire working class.[39]

The *Record* feminists' dual commitment to individual rights and group obligations meant that they weighed and evaluated each issue separately. They were not ideological purists or feminist theorists. They accepted or rejected feminist ideas to fit the circumstances of their lives as women and as members of a community of workers. The working-class feminists in Seattle, like middle-class reformers, recognized that social and economic conditions at times made women the weaker and more vulnerable sex. As working-class women, they knew that most women wage earners worked long hours for very low pay. Their sensitivity to differences within the working class contributed to a certain pragmatism in applying equal-rights principles. They favored equal rights for women as well as labor legislation that offered women special protection. At conventions of the Washington State Federation of Labor, they introduced resolutions in favor of minimum-wage laws for women and pensions for indigent mothers. With support from the Women's Union Card and Label League, the Washington Federation of Women's Clubs, and the Seattle Women's Trade Union League, the Seattle feminists called for repeal of union policies against married women's employment. Despite the women's impressive record of labor solidarity, the Seattle unions rejected all such proposals.[40]

This portrait of Seattle suggests that working-class feminism in the early twentieth century was a broader, richer, fuller, more radical phenomenon than previously thought. Working-class feminism has most often been discussed in two contexts—the cross-class relations of working-class and elite women in the New York and Chicago branches of the Women's Trade Union League, and the participation and influence of working-class women in the suffrage movement.[41] Female trade union leaders in the early twentieth century have a reputation as staunch advocates of economic independence, equal pay for equal work, and suffrage, but the portrait of working-class feminists in Seattle offers insight into other facets of working-class feminism. From a philosophical standpoint, working-class feminism in Seattle underscores the importance of women as houseworkers, consumers, labor activists, and wage earners, no matter their marital status. The foundation for those multiple roles was a conviction that family and community should acknowledge the dignity of women's work—whether paid or unpaid. The Seattle working-class feminists understood that the simultaneous reorganization of industry, of housework, and of commercial enterprises was an essential precondition for women's full participation in American life. They implied that only a full-scale restructuring of the marketplace and home would bring about women's emancipation. In their view, women's emancipation depended on a strong working-class movement for workers' control of industry and labor-owned enterprises; women's solidarity and workers' solidarity were inextricably entwined.

The double aims of working-class feminism—gender rights and class solidarity—were precisely what set it apart from the middle-class variant of feminism. Modern feminism, according to Nancy Cott, was "full of double aims, joining the concept of women's equality with men to the concept of women's sexual difference, joining the aim of antinomian individual release with concerted social action, endorsing the 'human sex' while deploying political solidarity among women."[42] The double aims of middle-class feminism were directly related to feminists' simultaneous recognition of women as a group and women as individual human beings. At the heart of modern feminism is a dual belief: Women are first and foremost human beings, the same as men, to be respected for their individual potential, abilities, talents, intelligence, interests, and achievements, *and* women ought to act as a group to break down the socially constructed barriers to their full participation in society, thus enabling each woman to realize her individuality. Working-class feminists in Seattle triangulated from their experience. They defended individual rights and opportunities for women and urged women to join together to promote those rights, but they understood that individual opportunity was determined by social and economic status as well as by gender. Individual choices were inherently unequal as long as the social order reproduced gender and class hierarchies. Ultimately nothing short of a new social order involving workers' control of industry, government-sponsored child care, protective laws for working women, consumer cooperatives, domestic reorganization, and women's rights could adequately address the Seattle working-class feminists' multiple concerns.

The feminist respondents in Seattle did not speak for all the *Record* letter writers. Other women qualified their approval of married women's labor force participation, and a few disapproved of the practice. These qualifications and objections reveal further gender and class complexities shaping the discussion of married women's employment and highlight the diversity of opinion within the Seattle working class.

In contrast to the feminist respondents, other women who favored married women's employment regarded wage labor as a way of improving families' standards of living rather than as a desirable goal for its own sake. Such women did not mention the burdens of housework. For them homemaking was a venerable and highly respected occupation. Work for personal satisfaction and economic independence played no part in their statements. Employment meant money to these commentators, and money conveyed buying power.

These women discussed the inadequacy of most men's earnings and interpreted marriage as a partnership involving a dual role for women. Each family, they argued, had to define its own acceptable standard of living. Having adequate income for home ownership, retirement funds, household furnishings, commercial entertainment, medical care, and education most concerned these women. A woman who signed herself "Still on the Job" explained, "I am going to work to help my husband have something [for his] years of hard work." To those who sanctioned married women's employment only for economic necessity, a female trade unionist asked, "Who is to decide [what real need is]? Suppose my husband's wages are enough to keep the family from starving, but if we want to get the children's teeth fixed, and have the right kind of doctor, and give them a good education, we need more money than he is making. . . . No one can settle by regulations 'what real need' is." These women affirmed the right of workers to obtain a full measure of American prosperity. Mrs. Myrtle Howarth, business agent for the Hotel Maids' Union and wife of a hoisting engineer, argued that "scraping" by was simply unacceptable when married women's employment could provide "the beauties of life." Such women championed employment as a means to a higher standard of living for individual families, not as a means to personal independence and self-esteem for individual women.[43]

Women with that outlook regarded wage work itself as strenuous, exacting, and tiring. Unfortunately few of the women letter writers to the *Record* indicated what work they performed. A former stenographer complained that much of women's work in mass production involved dead-end, repetitive, highly routinized tasks. She mourned the passing of women's preindustrial craft work as weavers and basket makers. "There's a lot more to satisfy your soul in such work than in going down to Ames' [shipyard] boiler shop." Women expressed the hope that their husbands would receive higher wages or that their joint employment would soon allow the women to retire to domestic responsibilities full time. "And God knows," one woman wrote, "I'll be glad . . . to quit." Wage work was for such women important primarily for its material rewards.[44]

The women respondents who supported married women's employment as a strategy for bettering their families' incomes nonetheless disagreed about the appropriateness of wage earning by mothers. These respondents invoked motherhood as a rationale either for staying home or for seeking paid employment. A few women strongly objected to married women working if they had young children. They argued that preschool children needed the special attention and care that only a mother could provide. An anonymous respondent asserted that "if there are children, the mother should stay home and do the very best she can for them. . . . When there are no children a married woman should have just as much right to do any work she can best do as a single woman." The same woman suggested that the federal government pay mothers for "raising good healthy and well trained children."[45]

Other letter writers adopted the contrary position, bolstering the case for married women having jobs by appealing to a general concern for children. Rosa Adams expressed this perspective very well.

> Not one woman in a thousand gets up early and stands the hardship of a working woman's life for mere nothings. [A] true mother would rather work than take her children out of school or deny them the advantages the present day demands. The things that one time were a luxury are nowadays necessities: art, music and education are necessities to the home now.[46]

The message was clear: mothers owed their children the best opportunities for nurturing, schooling, and personal development. How to realize that goal was a matter of considerable contention. Women interpreted motherhood either as a strong deterrent to their employment or as an incentive to supplement their husbands' wages by working outside the home. Not surprisingly, married women wage earners argued in favor of working to better standards of living, while full-time mothers objected to married women's employment.[47]

Some women, principally trade unionists and single wage earners, disapproved of married women's employment because of the limited number of jobs and the uncertain future of the labor movement after the war. The objections of those commentators to married women's wage work were quite distinct from the nonfeminist view that married women simply belonged in the home. Among all the female respondents only one woman, Mrs. C. G. R., dogmatically asserted that any married woman who did "justice" to her housework and who had a husband who was "any good" and could "hustle a job" would have no time for other work. Despite her categorical view, she admitted to having worked after her own marriage until she was laid off, when she then had to make the best of housewifery.[48]

In contrast to Mrs. C. G. R., the other female opponents of married women's wage work expected married women to engage in activities outside the home. They rejected only the wage-earning option for supported married women. Their opinions were influenced by a concern for the economic welfare of working-class families as a whole. They believed that housewives whose husbands could meet their basic needs should refrain from taking jobs in order to leave those economic opportunities for the very needy. Their arguments suggest a belief in a moral economy in which available work would be shared, so that every family would have at least a minimum subsistence. If a husband could pay his family's essential expenses, his wife had no right to a job outside the home. These women subscribed to the traditional sexual division of labor insofar as they assumed that husbands should work and wives should not. According to their perspective, marriage invalidated a woman's

In November 1917 Seattle "hello girls" (telephone operators) joined a five-state strike to get the Pacific Telephone Company to recognize their new union. In street demonstrations they associated militancy with patriotism *(courtesy Museum of History and Industry, Seattle)*

claim to equal treatment in a highly competitive job market except in cases of economic necessity. The advocates of a moral economy associated married women's employment with an individual acquisitiveness diametrically opposed to their faith in a mutualistic ethic. To them, mutualism meant spreading available work among as many families as possible, with priority given to male breadwinners or single mothers and widows. Faced with a topsy-turvy economy with alternating patterns of labor surpluses and labor shortages, such women viewed the family wage ideal as the only realistic and ethical choice.

Ironically, another argument against allowing supported married women to work outside the home rested on the premise that workers ought to show their solidarity. Three women union activists—Miss May Duffy, business agent for the Seattle telephone operators' union; Miss Sophie Pugsley, women's organizer elect for the Central Labor Council; and Mrs. Hilda O'Connor, a widow and the secretary of the Laundry Workers—pointed out that many women married to trade unionists had scabbed during the wartime and postwar strikes of candy workers, laundry operatives, and telephone operators. To prevent a repetition of such behavior the women union leaders should support the Seattle Central Labor Council's effort to prohibit supported married women from entering industry. Scabbing from within labor's ranks was considered traitorous in Seattle, and it prompted union officials representing metalworkers, auto mechanics, musicians, shipyard employees, and painters to inform their members that they would be physically barred from working if their wives or close relatives acted as strikebreakers.[49]

The handful of young single female wage earners whose letters appeared in the *Record* felt personally threatened by married women workers. A teenaged girl who had diligently searched for work for three weeks in January and February 1920 declared in a tone of desperation, "If these married women were not . . . taking the work away from single girls there would not be half as many suicides and girls that go wrong." A Miss M. B. referred to the popular pin money theory of women's work. She pointed an accusing finger at married women for lowering female wage rates by working for "anything or nothing" to buy luxury items rather than the necessities of food, clothing, and shelter.[50]

The competitive labor market obviously undermined any sense of sisterly solidarity among the proponents and opponents of married women's employment.[51] Feminists were equally concerned about the employment opportunities of married and single women and recommended a shorter workday and aggressive union organizing campaigns to make more jobs available and to strengthen the labor movement. To those who objected to married women's wage work, the feminists' strategies seemed an insufficient remedy for recurrent episodes of unemployment and strikebreaking. Such commentators emphasized instead reasons for giving priority to the needs of certain members of the working-class community, the justice of the family wage, and the sanctity of class solidarity.

SEATTLE MEN'S VIEWS: FROM APPROVAL TO DISAPPROVAL

Men's responses to the question of married women's labor force participation varied as much as women's. Some men unconditionally supported married women's employment, some offered qualified support, others categorically condemned the idea.

TABLE

Seattle Women's Occupations and Marital Status, 1900 and 1920*

Fields of Employment	1900 Women Workers	1900 % Married	1920 Women Workers	1920 % Married
Manufactures	1,006	23.4	4,298	32.5
Transportation	75	1.3	1,388	20.3
Trade	228	16.6	4,664	31.6
Public Service	n.a.	n.a.	38	29
Professional Service	717	15.2	5,020	16.7
Domestic and Personal Service	2,090	20.6	8,675	32.8
Clerical Occupations	603	8.3	8,967	14.7

*The 1900 census list of women's occupations was adjusted to conform to the 1920 categories. The census statistics on married women exclude divorced and widowed women. The 1900 census lists the divorced and widowed separately, but the 1910 census combines them with single women. Married women's labor force participation rate cannot be calculated for Seattle because neither the state nor the federal government recorded the total number of married women in Seattle for these census years.
SOURCES: U.S. Bureau of the Census, *Special Reports: Occupations at the Twelfth Census* (Washington, D.C.: U.S. Government Printing Office, 1904), p. 732; U.S. Bureau of the Census, *Fourteenth Census of the United States*, vol. 4: *Population, 1920, Occupations.*

Several men argued in the same terms as the women who supported married women's unconditional right to work. They linked the oppression of women to the oppression of the whole working class and called for a new social order as a solution. Frank Turco of the Blacksmiths' Union declared:

> I believe in freedom. Woman should do what she sees fit. As long as the workers believe in a woman staying at home because she is tied up to a certain man, just so long . . . we'll have slavery. Man cannot be free as long as woman is not free.

An anonymous respondent echoed Turco's sentiment. "It seems to me that the 'freedom of womankind' is ultimately bound up with the freedom of the proletariat. For we see that in those countries where the workers as a class have overthrown the rule of their exploiters, there do women enjoy equality of opportunity with their brothers." "Rubberneck" sarcastically examined the assumptions underpinning the CLC's 1918 decision to discourage supported married women from entering industry.

> If an active man should marry a talented, high-salaried woman, and if after the wedding, all the women of the community should call a mass meeting to denounce the man for continuing to go about his daily occupation on the ground that one member of the household was supporting two or more, wouldn't Mr. Average Man say that this was petticoat government of the worst type? The policy of the Central Labor Council in opposing "supported" married women . . . is trouser government of the worst type.

Phil Pearl, business agent for the Barbers' Union, also used the language of equal rights to support women's right to choose. "I hold that a married woman has as much right to work as anybody." He appreciated the fact that some women disliked housework and wanted to do something else. Wage work enhanced women's lives by helping them develop "independence and originality."[52]

Turco and "Rubberneck" were unusual in offering an unequivocally feminist point of view. Other men who unconditionally approved of married women's employment nonetheless insisted that women must abstain from undercutting men's wages. These male respondents endorsed married women's goal of holding jobs, but at the same time they accused married women workers of a willingness to work for low wages and hence to undermine union solidarity. Such men used the forum provided by the *Seattle Union Record* both to support the rights of all workers and to chastise married women for allegedly hurting the labor movement. A respondent who signed himself "A Student of Equality and Fair Play" speculated that no union would object to married women's wage work if the women would insist on equal pay for equal work, but antagonism between men and women was inevitable as long as women violated trade union principles. L. W. Buck, secretary of the Washington State Federation of Labor, also criticized women for undermining the labor movement's commitment to equal pay for equal work. He offered the pin money explanation, claiming that women work "just for 'extra money.'" At the same time Buck supported the right of a married woman to work "since we let her do all the voluntary work she is willing to do." Limiting married women to volunteer work seemed unfair to Buck. After accusing married women of unjust job competition and strikebreaking, "Wormholes," a timber worker, concluded, "I have been a union man for years and have all the respect in the world for a worker of the opposite sex, be she a mother or a miss. But for the love of Mike, girls, when you take a job, be sure it's fair and demand a man's wages for a man's work, and I am sure no one will have a kick coming."[53]

Male opponents of married women's employment also raised the issue of fairness, but in a different context. They branded the employment of married women whose husbands earned a decent living as immoral and unjust to the needy. Individual rights, they argued, were of secondary importance to the welfare of the group in an economic order that pitted individual against individual. James Duncan, secretary of the CLC and one of the most influential labor leaders in Seattle, offered the fullest statement of this position.

> The question is not one of rights. Rights are yielded for the common good by every individual who enters organized labor. Married women who are supported . . . have a legal right to enter industry if they desire, but when labor through organized effort reduces hours of work to the limit of its ability to absorb the army of unemployed, no supported married woman has a moral right to answer the call of the unscrupulous employer to enter the competitive field for pin money to the disadvantage of the single girl who must work to live.

Duncan's opinion was expressed in dichotomies: individual rights versus group rights, immorality versus morality, married women versus single women, pin money versus subsistence wages. Herman Rose, assistant business agent for the Waiters' Union, also subscribed to the notion of a moral economy in which the good of the group was more consequential than an individual's rights. "I am absolutely opposed to married women working. There are too many single men and single women walking the streets hungry." Like the female opponents of married women's employment, Duncan and Rose stressed the primacy of a moral economy and associated it with the family wage ideal of adequately paid husbands supporting their wives. The only time married women had a right to work for wages was when their husbands could not adequately provide for them and their children.[54]

Other opponents of married women's employment defined their position in terms of traditional gender roles. Only a few who opposed such employment in letters to the *Record* explicitly stated that married women should devote themselves solely to the home. Walt Chapman, a machinist, was representative of these contributors. In one of his several letters to the *Record*, Chapman argued that women who disliked housework should be legally forbidden to marry workingmen. Like Frank Rust, manager of the Labor Temple, the CLC headquarters, who believed that "woman was put on earth to raise children and a man to protect her in that function," Chapman was clearly a strong advocate of "separate spheres" for men and women. He would have agreed with Rust's assertion that "raising a family should occupy a woman until she is 45 years old."[55]

CONCLUSION

The Seattle debate on married women's employment revealed three distinct outlooks—commitments to feminism, to a higher standard of living, or to a family wage ideal. It is impossible to tell precisely from the existing sources which viewpoint attracted the most adherents in the Seattle working-class elite. The family wage/moral economy argument seems to have been especially compelling for male and female trade union leaders, while the female club leaders, many of them housewives, adopted a feminist perspective. The standard of living argument had adherents in both groups. Each attitude was rooted in real circumstances of the time and informed by particular experiences of family, workplace, trade union, and civic life, and each reflected relatively distinct sets of ideas and priorities. This rich diversity of views suggests that no single voice can represent an entire gender, class, or community.

The Seattle controversy demonstrates that feminist ideas were an important part of working-class culture and public discourse that women tailored to suit their dual commitment to equal rights for women *and* for workers. Even though financial obligations motivated married women to take jobs outside the home, working-class feminists in Seattle argued that work fulfilled other needs as well. Despite the low market value of women's labor and the poor working conditions awaiting women workers, wage labor gave women a sense of self-respect and self-worth comparable to what it gave men. The feminist women in Seattle's working class tried to reconcile their commitment to equal rights with their concern for the needs of their class as a whole. They believed that the welfare of their class mattered as much as their individual aspirations. They subscribed to the ideal of collective control over working conditions through trade unions and other working-class institutions and accepted the legitimacy of demanding social and economic sacrifices from members of a class-conscious community. But they were unwilling to preserve customary gender traditions—especially the male breadwinner/female homemaker dichotomy—should doing so diminish their rights as human beings.

The feminist respondents in the *Seattle Union Record* attempted to reconcile their ideology with class loyalty by insisting on a modification in the practice of mutual obligation. They directly challenged the fairness and appropriateness of the family wage ideal, which held that an adequate wage was one that allowed a husband to provide for his wife and children. Irate at the implication that women's wage work would then be considered superfluous at best, feminists sought to prove that married women's employment would actually enhance working-class life. In their eyes a cooperative relationship between husbands and wives as wage-earning partners could improve labor conditions for everyone. Although they saw themselves as part of a group committed to social and economic change, in practice their ideals of class loyalty and women's rights at times conflicted, resulting in bitter intraclass tensions.

The case of Seattle's working-class feminism suggests that this ideology had an existence independent of the feminism of middle-class and elite women. Working-class feminists in Seattle were influenced by the writings, speeches, and public actions of middle-class feminists, but they were equally influenced by and devoted to the working-class ethic of mutualism. Because of their dual devotion to gender and class rights, they tended to think about women's emancipation in more radical terms than did most middle-class feminists. From their vantage point the need to reorganize industry, commerce, and housework was an essential prerequisite for the emancipation of women. The acrimonious war of words that took place in Seattle over married women's employment suggests that feminist ideas posed a special philosophical challenge to working-class women. Individual rights and mutual obligation based on class identity were not easily reconcilable. The belief in the right of married women to earn wages without regard to economic need collided head on with the working-class commitment to a moral economy.

The *Seattle Union Record* respondents who conditionally approved or disapproved of married women's employment argued that some members of the working-class community had greater needs than others. If the American economic system could not provide work for everyone, then those with greater economic needs, as determined by their ability to meet essential expenses, deserved the opportunity to work more than others did. Those who believed in a moral economy considered the family wage to be the only equitable arrangement possible in a highly competitive and volatile labor market. They rejected the right of supported married women to work for wages and subscribed to the traditional sexual division of wage-earning labor as an alternative to unrestricted competition between unemployed or poorly paid wage earners and those who were better off. At the same time the advocates of a moral economy were sympathetic to married women's need for public recognition of their roles as housewives and mothers. They also respected the voluntary activities of married women, which provided valuable services to the working-class community. The view that married women belonged only in the home, caring for children and domestic chores, did not appeal to the privileged sector of the working class. The fact that gender traditionalism was of little concern to the *Seattle Union Record* respondents suggests that Seattle wage earners were keenly aware of the large-scale social changes that were reshaping home life and nurturing women's aspirations for expanded roles in American society.

Although the controversy over married women's employment was debated in the Seattle labor movement and the *Seattle Union Record* from April 1918 until the winter of 1920, it was always overshadowed by other homefront developments, especially after the war. The several-day Seattle General Strike in February 1919 weakened the labor movement. From within, bitter factional struggles and jurisdictional disputes crippled the movement. From outside, police raids, arrests, and court battles put organized labor on the defensive, while employers launched a powerful and determined open-shop movement that ultimately undermined organized labor's economic power in the city. By the summer of 1919, the Women's Union Card and Label League, the champion of women's rights, regretfully reported that its membership and influence had dramatically declined. Integrally tied to the trade union movement, the league was an accurate barometer of the weakened state of organized labor in Seattle. Under the circumstances, the Seattle Central Labor Council could do little to discourage the continued increase in married women's entry into the labor market during the 1920s.[56]

The Seattle debate suggests that married women's employment was motivated by economic pressures *and* by a change in married women's attitudes toward housewifery and wage work. Public opinion polls have only recently documented widespread approval for married women's employment, but the *Record* correspondence suggests earlier roots for such a societal value change.[57] The *Record*'s letters collectively imply that for two issues—whether married women should hold jobs outside the home and what place women workers should have in American society—new social values were emerging in the era of the First World War.

NOTES

This essay originally appeared in the *Journal of American History* 76, no. 1 (June 1989): 118–49.

1. Nancy Schrom Dye, *As Equals and as Sisters: Feminism, the Labor Movement, and the Women's Trade Union League of New York* (Columbia: University of Missouri Press, 1980), pp. 122–39; Elinor Lerner, "Immigrant and Working Class Involvement in the New York City Woman Suffrage Movement, 1905–1917: A Study in Progressive

Era Politics," Ph.D. diss. (University of California, Berkeley, 1981); Elinor Lerner, "Family Structure, Occupational Patterns, and Support for Women's Suffrage," in Judith Friedlander et al., eds., *Women in Culture and Politics: A Century of Change* (Bloomington: Indiana University Press, 1986), pp. 223–36; Ellen Carol DuBois, "Working Women, Class Relations, and Suffrage Militance: Harriot Stanton Blatch and the New York Woman Suffrage Movement, 1894–1909," *Journal of American History* 74 (June 1987): 34–58, esp. 46–52; Nancy F. Cott, *The Grounding of Modern Feminism* (New Haven: Yale University Press, 1987), pp. 20–34; Maurine Weiner Greenwald, *Women, War, and Work: The Impact of World War I on Women Workers in the United States* (Westport, Conn.: Greenwood Press, 1980), pp. 13–45, 87–184; Alice Kessler-Harris, *Out to Work: A History of Wage-Earning Women in the United States* (New York: Oxford University Press, 1982), pp. 217–49; Alice Kessler-Harris, "Independence and Virtue in the Lives of Wage-Earning Women: The United States, 1870–1930," in Friedlander et al., eds., *Women in Culture and Politics,* pp. 3–17, esp. 12–13; Jacquelyn Dowd Hall, "Disorderly Women: Gender and Labor Militancy in the Appalachian South," *Journal of American History* 73 (September 1986): 354–82.

2. Robert L. Friedheim, *The Seattle General Strike* (Seattle: University of Washington Press, 1964), pp. 23–54. Left-wing developments in the Northwest are detailed in Carlos A. Schwantes, *Radical Heritage: Labor, Socialism, and Reform in Washington and British Columbia, 1885–1917* (Seattle: University of Washington Press, 1979); and Carlos A. Schwantes, "Leftward Tilt on the Pacific Slope: Indigenous Unionism and the Struggle against AFL Hegemony in the State of Washington," *Pacific Northwest Quarterly* 70 (January 1979): 24–34. U.S. Bureau of the Census, *Fourteenth Census of the United States,* vol. 3: *Population Characteristics of States, 1920* (Washington, D.C.: U.S. Government Printing Office, 1923), p. 1093. The title of Christine Stansell's study of New York applies as well to Seattle. See Christine Stansell, *City of Women: Sex and Class in New York, 1789–1860* (New York: Knopf, 1986).

3. Articles discussing married women's employment can be found in such magazines as *Woman's Home Companion, Atlantic Monthly, Collier's, Ladies' Home Journal, Literary Digest, Scribner's Magazine, Nation, Harper's Magazine,* and the *Saturday Evening Post.* The *Journal of the American Association of University Women, Annals of the American Academy of Political and Social Sciences, Survey Magazine,* and *Woman's Press* (a Young Women's Christian Association publication) published articles on the controversy over married women's employment. The Women's Bureau of the Department of Labor issued many bulletins about the economic contributions of working wives to their families. Contemporary surveys include Virginia MacMakin Collier, *Marriage and Careers: A Study of One Hundred Women Who Are Wives, Mothers, Homemakers, and Professional Workers for the Bureau of Vocational Information* (New York: Channel Bookshop, 1926); Grace L. Coyle, *Jobs and Marriage? Outlines for Discussion of the Married Woman in Business* (New York: Woman's Press, 1928); and Cecile

Tipton LaFollette, *A Study of the Problems of 652 Gainfully Employed Married Woman Homemakers* (New York: Teachers College, Columbia University, 1934). Feminist theorists offered book-length arguments for married women's employment. See Alice Beal Parsons, *Woman's Dilemma* (New York: Thomas Y. Crowell, 1926); Lorine Pruette, *Women and Leisure: A Study of Social Waste* (New York: E. P. Dutton and Co., 1924); Suzanne LaFollette, *Concerning Women* (New York: A. and C. Bone, 1926). For a detailed history of the Seattle labor newpaper, see Mary Joan O'Connell, "The *Seattle Union Record,* 1918–1928: A Pioneer Daily," M.A. thesis (University of Washington, 1964).

4. Scholars agree that seventy or more years ago, married working-class women earned wages to ensure basic family support or to improve the family standard of living. From such a perspective, women's desire for economic independence or personal autonomy and self-respect played no part in the decision of working-class married women to work for wages. See, for example, Leslie Woodcock Tentler, *Wage-Earning Women: Industrial Work and Family Life in the United States, 1900–1930* (New York: Oxford University Press, 1979), pp. 139, 141, 144, 153, 160, 177–78; Lois Scharf, *To Work and to Wed: Female Employment, Feminism, and the Great Depression* (Westport: Greenwood Press, 1980), pp. 37–38; Winifred Wandersee, *Women's Work and Family Values, 1920–1940* (Cambridge, Mass.: Harvard University Press, 1981), pp. 7–26; Sarah Eisenstein, *Give Us Bread but Give Us Roses: Working Women's Consciousness in the United States, 1890 to the First World War* (Boston: Routledge and Kegan Paul, 1983), pp. 124–25, 132, 145; and Lynn Weiner, *From Working Girl to Working Mother: The Female Labor Force in the United States, 1820–1980* (Chapel Hill: University of North Carolina Press, 1985), pp. 84–88.

5. The term *moral* economy was first used by E. P. Thompson in his analysis of eighteenth-century food riots in England. He argued that the crowd actions against soaring prices and hunger were based upon "a consistent traditional view of social norms and obligations, of the proper economic functions of several parties within the community, which taken together, can be said to constitute the moral economy of the poor." See E. P. Thompson, "The Moral Economy of the English Crowd in the Eighteenth Century," *Past and Present* no. 50 (1971): 76–136, esp. p. 79. In a similar fashion, it can be argued that some members of the Seattle working class subscribed to a kind of moral economy in determining who had a legitimate claim to wage work during periods of labor scarcity. Heidi Hartmann, "The Unhappy Marriage of Marxism and Feminism: Towards a More Progressive Union," *Capital and Class* no. 8 (1979): 1–43; Jane Humphries, "The Working Class Family, Women's Liberation, and Class Struggle: The Case of Nineteenth Century British History," *Review of Radical Political Economics* 9 (Fall 1977): 25–41; Gita Sen, "The Sexual Division of Labor and the Working-Class Family: Towards a Conceptual Synthesis of Class Relations and the Subordination of Women," *Review of Radical Political Economics* 12 (Summer 1980):

76–86; Jane Humphries, "Class Struggle and the Persistence of the Working-Class Family," *Cambridge Journal of Economics* 1 (September 1977): 241–58; Hilary Land, "The Family Wage," *Feminist Review* 6 (1980): 55–77; Martha May, "The Historical Problem of the Family Wage: The Ford Motor Company and the Five Dollar Day," *Feminist Studies* 8 (Summer 1982): 399–424; Martha May, "Bread before Roses: American Workingmen, Labor Unions and the Family Wage," in Ruth Milkman, ed., *Women, Work & Protest: A Century of U.S. Women's Labor History* (Boston: Routledge and Kegan Paul, 1985), pp. 1–21.

6. Scholars differ about the number of trade unionists in Seattle in 1919. For an estimate of 65,000, see O'Connell, "*Seattle Union Record,*" p. 86; and Harvey O'Connor, *Revolution in Seattle: A Memoir* (New York: Monthly Review Press, 1964), p. 126. The percentage of union members in Seattle's work force has been calculated from the number of Seattle wage earners listed in the 1920 federal census (153,776) and the number of trade unionists listed by O'Connell and O'Connor. See U.S. Bureau of the Census, *Fourteenth Census of the United States,* vol. 4: *Population, 1920 Occupations* (Washington, D.C.: U.S. Government Printing Office, 1923), p. 128. The number of trade unionists in late 1918 is given as 60,000 in Friedheim, *Seattle General Strike,* pp. 24–25. Seattle's 48,000 trade union members included 4,000 women according to State of Washington, Bureau of Labor, *Twelfth Biennial Report, 1919–1920* (Olympia, 1920), pp. 32–34. Perhaps the Seattle labor movement had 65,000 members at the beginning of 1919 and only 48,000 by the end of that tumultuous year.

7. *Seattle Union Record,* weekly edition, June 15, 1918, p. 1. On April 24, 1918, the *Record* began publishing a daily edition in addition to its established weekly format.

8. For an excellent analysis of the different political perspectives of unions affiliated with the Seattle Central Labor Council (CLC), see Friedheim, *Seattle General Strike,* pp. 23–54. Chroniclers of Seattle history mention that CLC delegates to the American Federation of Labor conventions regularly cast what was often the only dissenting vote against the reelection of Samuel Gompers. See O'Connor, *Revolution in Seattle,* pp. 110–11; and Anna Louise Strong, *I Change Worlds* (New York: Henry Holt and Co., 1935), p. 73.

9. The number of women trade unionists in Seattle grew from 568 to 4,000 (604 percent) between 1916 and 1919. For a detailed list of union membership by sex, see State of Washington, *Tenth Biennial Report of the Bureau of Labor Statistics and Factory Inspection, Years 1915–1916* (Olympia, 1916), pp. 153–54; State of Washington, Bureau of Labor, *Eleventh Biennial Report, 1917–1918* (Olympia, 1918), pp. 85–87; State of Washington, Bureau of Labor, *Twelfth Biennial Report, 1919–1920* (Olympia, 1920), pp. 32–34. There were 6,000 women members in 20 Seattle unions in 1917, according to the *Seattle Union Record,* Dec. 8, 1917, p. 7.

10. *Seattle Union Record,* March 6, 1915, p. 5; April 17, 1915, p. 7; May 1, 1915, p. 7; April 22, 1916, p. 7; May 13, 1916, p. 5; June 10, 1916, p. 5; Feb. 17, 1917, p. 5; March 30,

1917, p. 7; July 7, 1917, p. 6; July 14, 1917, p. 7; Sept. 8, 1917, p. 4; Sept. 29, 1917, p. 7; Feb. 16, 1918, p. 7.

11. On pre–World War I changes in women's employment, see Greenwald, *Women, War, and Work,* pp. 5–12.

12. U.S. Bureau of the Census, *Historical Statistics of the United States, Colonial Times to 1970,* 2 vols. (Washington, D.C.: U.S. Government Printing Office, 1975), 1:133. Although according to the federal census a mere 9 percent of all married women in the United States worked for wages outside the home in 1920 and only 12 percent in 1930, the extent of married women's employment was greater. As contemporary observers pointed out, the 1920 census underreported the number of married women wage earners because the census takers combined women workers who were widowed, divorced, or separated from their husbands with single (never married) women. Community studies of women wage earners conducted by the Women's Bureau in the early twentieth century demonstrated that married women constituted a larger percentage of the total number of women workers reported in the federal census when widowed, divorced, and separated working women were added to the working wives whose husbands lived with them. The 1920 census recorded married women's percentage of the female labor force as 24, while the Women's Bureau discovered that married women comprised between 32 and 47 percent of wage-earning women in particular communities when married women with and without husbands were counted together. Most women took jobs because their husbands' earnings could not cover daily necessities or because they were the principal breadwinners. But an increasing minority of married working-class women earned wages for other reasons. See, for example, Agnes L. Peterson, "What the Wage-Earning Woman Contributes to Family Support," in Viva B. Boothe, ed., *Women in the Modern World, Annals of the American Academy of Political and Social Science* 143 (1929): 74–93, esp. 78–79.

13. For data on Seattle, see U.S. Bureau of the Census, *Special Reports: Occupations at the Twelfth Census* (Washington, D.C.: U.S. Government Printing Office, 1904), p. 732; *Fourteenth Census of the United States,* vol. 4: *Population, 1920: Occupations* (Washington, D.C.: U.S. Government Printing Office, 1923), p. 863; and *The Fourteenth Census of the United States (1920),* vol. 1: *Population* (Washington, D.C.: U.S. Government Printing Office, 1921), p. 311. For the national figures on married women's labor force participation, see U.S. Bureau of the Census, *Historical Statistics of the United States,* 1:133.

14. Greenwald, *Women, War, and Work,* pp. 3–45.

15. Ibid., pp. 87–184.

16. *Seattle Union Record,* Jan. 5, 1918, p. 7; Nov. 10, 1917, p. 3; Nov. 17, 1917, p. 7; weekly edition, Aug. 17, 1918, p. 4; weekly edition, June 8, 1918, p. 4; June 23, 1917, p. 8; Jan. 19, 1918, p. 3; Feb. 9, 1918, p. 7; Feb. 23, 1918, p. 7; March 2, 1918, p. 4. See also U.S. Department of Labor, Women's Bureau, *The New Position of Women in American*

Industry, Bulletin no. 12 (Washington, D.C.: U.S. Government Printing Office, 1920), pp. 41–92.

17. On recruitment into unions, see *Seattle Union Record*, Oct. 13, 1917, p. 7; Jan. 19, 1918, p. 7; weekly edition, June 8, 1918, p. 4; weekly edition, June 22, 1918, p. 1; weekly edition, Sept. 28, 1918, p. 3; weekly edition, May 10, 1919, p. 1; King County Central Labor Council, Minutes, March 27, April 3, Sept. 11, Oct. 2, 1918, June 4, Oct. 1, 1919, box 8, King County Central Labor Council Records, Manuscript Collection, University of Washington Libraries. On strike support, see *Seattle Union Record*, Sept. 8, 1917, p. 7; Oct. 6, 1917, p. 1; Oct. 13, 1917, p. 1; Nov. 10, 1917, p. 7; Nov. 17, 1917, pp. 1, 3; Minutes, Sept. 24, 1919, King County Central Labor Council Records. On the issue of hiring a woman organizer, see *Seattle Union Record*, Feb. 17, 1917, p. 7; Aug. 11, 1917, p. 7; Aug. 18, 1917, p. 7; Aug. 25, 1917, pp. 1, 7; Oct. 6, 1917, pp. 1, 4; Nov. 3, 1917, p. 7; Jan. 12, 1918, p. 5; weekly edition, April 25, 1918, p. 6; weekly edition, Nov. 4, 1919, p. 7; Minutes, Oct. 8, Oct. 22, 1919, King County Central Labor Council Records. On the minimum wage, see *Seattle Union Record*, Aug. 18, 1917, p. 1; Minutes, Jan. 2 and July 24, 1918, King County Central Labor Council Records. Official statements on these matters can be found in the *Proceedings of the Eighteenth Annual Convention, Washington State Federation of Labor Held at Bellingham, Washington, June 16–21, 1919* (Tacoma, n.d.), pp. 122, 126, 128, 136–37, 150.

18. Most of the letters were published with initials or aliases like "Disgusted Housewife" and appeared either on the *Seattle Union Record's* "Woman's Page" or in the column of Ruth Ridgway, a pseudonym used by various staff members. During the period covered in this article, Ruth Ridgway was either Mary L. Chamberlain, a former *Survey* magazine staff writer, or Mary Ahlgren, "a former federal wartime social worker." Chamberlain is mentioned in Harry E. A. Ault to Mary L. Chamberlain, July 9, 1921, folder 15, box 4, part 1, Harry E. A. Ault Papers, University of Washington Libraries; and Ault to Sylvia, April 12, 1922, folder 16, Ibid. Ahlgren is mentioned in Earl Shimmons, "The Seattle Union Record," typescript, 1923, p. 87, folder 9, box 7, Ibid. The original letters from the *Seattle Union Record* readers have not been preserved, so it is impossible to determine whether the writers represented a cross section of the Seattle working class in occupation, ethnicity, or race. The letters almost always reveal the sex of the letter writer and sometimes the respondent's marital and occupational status. The correspondence on the "Woman's Page" has the advantage of identifying the authors by name and sometimes by organizational affiliation and marital status. Among the women correspondents, 21 of the 52 (40 percent) signed their names; 12 of the 26 men (46 percent) signed. Thus 33 of the 78 letter writers (42 percent) can be identified by name. The Seattle city directories, 1918–20, helped identify the occupations of the letter writers. The women's and men's occupations are mentioned in the text of the essay.

19. Cott, *Grounding of Modern Feminism,* pp. 3–6; Parsons, *Woman's Dilemma,* pp. 270–90; Pruette, *Women and Leisure,* pp. 88–96; LaFollette, *Concerning Women,* pp. 189–206.

20. *Seattle Union Record,* daily edition, April 24, 1918, p. 4; April 29, 1918, p. 8; ibid., daily edition, May 8, 1918, p. 8.

21. Ibid., daily edition, Oct. 25, 1919, p. 9.

22. Cott, *Grounding of Modern Feminism,* pp. 22–24; *Seattle Union Record,* daily edition, Sept. 8, 1919, p. 3.

23. *Seattle Union Record,* daily edition, Nov. 12, 1919, p. 9; June 17, 1919, p. 5.

24. Ibid., daily edition, July 1, 1919, p. 5.

25. Kathryn Oberdeck drew my attention to the association between working-class and middle-class feminists in Seattle 1910–20. See Kathryn Oberdeck, "'Not Pink Teas': The Working-Class Women's Movement in Seattle, 1905–1918," *Labor History* 32 (Spring 1991): 193–230. On housewives as houseworkers see *Seattle Union Record,* Jan. 24, 1914, p. 8; April 20, 1918, p. 7. The Women's Union Card and Label League professed its class consciousness; Ibid., Feb. 28, 1914, p. 4.

26. For a brief history of the Seattle Women's Union Card and Label League, see *Seattle Union Record,* daily edition, June 10, 1919, p. 7. For the league's chronology, the best source is Oberdeck, "'Not Pink Teas.'" Other label leagues existed in Tacoma, Spokane, Aberdeen, Olympia, Walla Walla, and Yakima, Washington. See *Seattle Union Record,* weekly edition, Aug. 10, 1918, p. 3. On the union-label campaigns, see ibid., Aug. 22, 1914, p. 5; Sept. 5, 1914, p. 5. On the league women's political activities and support for strikers and the unemployed, see July 11, 1914, p. 8; Feb. 28, 1914, p. 8; Dec. 5, 1914, pp. 1, 5; Dec. 12, 1914, p. 4; Dec. 19, 1914, p. 4; Nov. 13, 1915, p. 1; Dec. 4, 1915, p. 7; March 24, 1917, p. 7; weekly edition, May 8, 1918, p. 4; weekly edition, July 12, 1919, p. 4. On their social concerns, see Sept. 12, 1914, p. 5; May 29, 1915, p. 7; June 12, 1915, p. 7; June 26, 1915, p. 7; Jan. 29, 1916, p. 8; June 24, 1916, p. 7; July 8, 1916, p. 7; Jan. 13, 1917, p. 7; and March 3, 1917, p. 7. On Labor Day preparation and performance, see July 21, 1917, p. 7; Sept. 8, 1917, pp. 1, 7.

27. *Seattle Union Record,* Feb. 21, 1914, p. 4; Jan. 10, 1914, p. 8. See also Feb. 28, 1914, p. 4. On the Seattle Women's Union Card and Label League educational meetings, see Jan. 10, 1914, p. 5; Feb. 28, 1914, p. 4; March 7, 1914, p. 5; May 23, 1914, p. 5; March 3, 1917, p. 7; and March 24, 1917, p. 7. Married women's employment was discussed in Olive Schreiner, *Woman and Labor* (New York: F. A. Stokes Co., 1911), pp. 117–29; Alice Henry, *The Trade Union Woman* (New York: D. Appleton and Co., 1915), pp. 217–43. The feminist ball was described in the *Seattle Union Record,* Jan. 29, 1916, p. 8, and Feb. 19, 1916, p. 1. On visiting lecturers see April 8, 1916, p. 7; June 17, 1916, p. 2; Aug. 26, 1916, p. 1; Oct. 28, 1916, p. 7; Nov. 3, 1917, p. 7; and Nov. 4, 1919, p. 7. On child care and "social mothers," see Feb. 21, 1914, p. 4; Feb. 28, 1914, p. 4; and March 7, 1914, p. 5.

28. On meeting space for women, see *Seattle Union Record,* Oct. 24, 1914, p. 4; and May 20, 1916, p. 7. On the Federation of Trades Union Women & Auxiliaries, see Feb. 11, 1916, p. 7; June 10, 1916, pp. 1, 7; June 17, 1916, p. 7; July 15, 1916, p. 7; Aug. 26, 1916, p. 7; Sept. 16, 1916, p. 7; Jan. 20, 1917, p. 7; Feb. 24, 1917, p. 7; March 24, 1917, p. 7; April 21, 1917, p. 7; July 21, 1917, p. 7; Sept. 15, 1917, p. 7; Sept. 22, 1917, p. 7; Oct. 13, 1917, p. 7; Nov. 24, 1917, p. 7; March 23, 1918, p. 7. Reports of the Woman's Legislative Council of Washington can be found May 30, 1914, p. 5; Dec. 9, 1916, p. 7; Dec. 11, 1916, p. 7; Nov. 17, 1917, p. 7; *Washington State Federation of Women's Clubs Bulletin,* 1 (August 1917): 26; 2 (February 1918): 29–30 (copies in Pacific Northwest Collection, University of Washington Libraries).

29. Schreiner, *Woman and Labor,* pp. 45–49; *Seattle Union Record,* Feb. 7, 1914, p. 7; daily edition, May 27, 1919, p. 3. League members probably also gained an historical perspective on housewifery from Theresa Schmid McMahon, an instructor of labor history and labor law at the University of Washington who worked very closely with the labor and women's club movements. McMahon's published dissertation chronicled the distinctive impact of industrialization on working-class and middle-class housewives. See Theresa Schmid McMahon, *Women and Economic Evolution Or The Effects of Industrial Changes upon the Status of Women,* Bulletin of the University of Wisconsin 496 (Madison, 1912), pp. 28–80. For McMahon's ties to organized labor, see Theresa McMahon, "My Story," typescript, p. 33, folder 1, box 1, Theresa Schmid McMahon Papers, University Archives, University of Washington Libraries. For her involvement in the club movement, see *Seventeenth Annual Report of the Washington State Federation of Women's Clubs, 1913–14,* pp. 62–63 (copy in Pacific Northwest Collection, University of Washington Library).

30. *Seattle Union Record,* daily edition, May 27, 1919, p. 3; Oct. 25, 1919, p. 9.

31. *Seattle Union Record,* daily edition, April 29, 1918, p. 8; daily edition, Dec. 31, 1919, p. 9.

32. Charlotte Perkins Gilman, *Women and Economics: A Study of the Economic Relation between Men and Women as a Factor in Social Evolution,* ed. Carl Degler (New York: Harper and Row, 1966), pp. 95, 153, 240–69.

33. *Seattle Union Record,* daily edition, May 27, 1919, p. 3. For Minnie Ault's union affiliation, see ibid., daily edition, Jan. 19, 1918, p. 7. For her comments on child care, see Oct. 25, 1919, p. 9, and daily edition, Sept. 3, 1919, p. 4.

34. Ibid., daily edition, June 17, 1919, p. 5; May 27, 1919, p. 3.

35. Ibid., daily edition, July 29, 1919, p. 5; Scharf, *To Work and to Wed,* pp. 28–29.

36. Dana Frank informed me about the importance of Seattle's consumer cooperatives. Frank, *Purchasing Power: Consumer Organizing, Gender, and the Seattle Labor Movement, 1919–1929* (New York: Cambridge University Press, 1994). The region's communitarian socialist tradition is briefly discussed in Schwantes, *Radical Heritage,* pp. 87–90. In 1897, during his adolescence, Harry Ault, later editor of the

Seattle Union Record, lived in the Equality Colony, a cooperative community. See O'Connell, "*Seattle Union Record,*" p. 15.

37. Sophia Kramer, a dedicated trade unionist and editor of the *Record*'s "Woman's Page," was probably responsible for an article chastising businesswomen who violated the eight-hour principle and worked many more hours each day just so that they could be "successful." See *Seattle Union Record,* March 24, 1917, p. 7.

38. The Seattle CLC endorsed a resolution from a Boston cigar makers' local outlining a plan for reorganizing the U.S. government and the nation's industries under the control of the AFL, "a conception of a trades union state in control of the workers." The CLC members "laughed" to think of Gompers, a former cigar maker, being compelled "to stand for an extremely revolutionary program." See *Seattle Union Record,* weekly edition, May 17, 1919, p. 1.

39. Ibid., daily edition, Oct. 25, 1919, p. 9; May 23, 1918, p. 8; July 1, 1919, p. 5. The Seattle resolution favoring a short workday is mentioned in the *Seattle Union Record,* July 1, 1919, p. 5, but it does not appear in the published convention proceedings. The resolution to organize unorganized women can be found in *Proceedings of the Eighteenth Annual Convention, Washington State Federation of Labor,* p. 150.

40. Joseph Frederick Tripp, "Progressive Labor Laws in Washington State, 1900–1925," Ph.D. diss. (University of Washington, 1973), pp. 86, 91; Joseph F. Tripp, "Toward an Efficient and Moral Society: Washington State Minimum Wage Law, 1913–1925," *Pacific Northwest Quarterly* 67 (July 1976): 97–112, esp. 99–100; *Seattle Union Record,* Aug. 1, 1914, p. 5; Oct. 24, 1914, p. 4; Jan. 23, 1915, p. 5; May 1, 1915, p.7; Sept. 16, 1916, p. 7; March 3, 1917, p. 4; weekly edition, Jan. 19, 1918, p. 5; weekly edition, May 24, 1919, p. 1; weekly edition, Oct. 25, 1919, p. 9. For a catalog of married women's legal and social handicaps, see Sophie L. Wepf Clark, "The Status of the Wife in America," *Washington State Federation of Women's Clubs Bulletin* 2 (February 1918): 27–29 (copy in Pacific Northwest Collection, University of Washington Libraries).

41. Dye, *As Equals and as Sisters,* pp. 110–39; DuBois, "Working Women, Class Relations, and Suffrage Militance," pp. 46–47.

42. Cott, *Grounding of Modern Feminism,* p. 50.

43. *Seattle Union Record,* daily edition, July 29, 1919, p. 5; May 23, 1918, p. 8; Oct. 25, 1919, p. 9.

44. Ibid., daily edition, June 10, 1919, p. 7; July 29, 1919, p. 5.

45. Ibid., daily edition, Nov. 26, 1919, p. 9.

46. Ibid., daily edition, Oct. 16, 1919, p. 11.

47. Middle-class women were also divided over the issue of wage earning for mothers of young children. See Scharf, *To Work and to Wed,* pp. 30–36; and Cott, *Grounding of Modern Feminism,* pp. 193–202.

48. *Seattle Union Record,* daily edition, July 1, 1919, p. 5.

49. Ibid., daily edition, Oct. 25, 1919, p. 9; Oct. 13, 1919, p. 9; Feb. 11, 1920, p. 7;

Aug. 18, 1917, p. 1; Nov. 10, 1917, p. 4; weekly edition, July 5, 1919, p. 2; weekly edition, May 10, 1919, p. 1; King County Central Labor Council, Minutes, July 2, 1919, King County Central Labor Council Records.

50. *Seattle Union Record,* daily edition, Feb. 11, 1920, p. 7; daily edition, April 24, 1918, p. 4.

51. Nancy A. Hewitt, "Beyond the Search for Sisterhood: American Women's History in the 1980s," *Social History* 10 (October 1985): 299–321, esp. p. 315.

52. *Seattle Union Record,* daily edition, Nov. 6, 1919, p. 11.

53. Ibid., daily edition, June 10, 1918, p. 6; May 31, 1918, p. 8. "Wormholes" often wrote letters to the editor of the *Timberworker,* a one-page newspaper published as part of the *Seattle Union Record.* I assume that "Wormholes" was a lumber worker.

54. *Seattle Union Record,* daily edition, Nov. 6, 1919, p. 11.

55. Ibid., daily edition, May 4, 1918, p. 6; daily edition, Nov. 6, 1919, p. 11.

56. Strong, *I Change Worlds,* pp. 72–85; Friedheim, *Seattle General Strike,* pp. 146–76; Schwantes, *Radical Heritage,* pp. 214–16; *Seattle Union Record,* daily edition, June 10, 1919, p. 7. In the early 1920s, the Card and Label League inducted only a handful of new members. See King County Central Labor Council, Minutes, Jan. 28, 1920, Nov. 1, 1922, May 2, 1923, King County Central Labor Council Records.

57. Hazel Erskine, "The Polls: Women's Role," *Public Opinion Quarterly* 35 (Summer 1971): 275–90, esp. 283–89; Hazel Erskine, "Opinion Roundup," *Public Opinion* 2 (December 1979/January 1980): 19–43, esp. 33.

Bertha Knight Landes: The Woman Who Was Mayor

DORIS H. PIEROTH

With her election as mayor of Seattle in 1926, during a decade that promised more for women in politics than it delivered, Bertha Knight Landes became the first woman mayor of a major city in the United States. She has been largely ignored by historians or depicted as a prohibitionist killjoy, a figure of ridicule whose term in office can be dismissed simply as "two turbulent years of 'petticoat rule.'" This essay is a look past the caricature to the woman whom the Seattle voters trusted enough, and with whom they were sufficiently comfortable, to elect to public office.[1]

She belongs to the progressive tradition, that seeming paradox of altruism and pragmatism that, for all the diversity of its reform efforts, was intent on the moral regeneration of a society becoming increasingly urban, industrial, and multicultural. She was thirty-two years old in 1900—a nineteenth-century woman who, in her twentieth-century career, espoused moral uplift, public decency, and effective civic management in such areas of urban life as health, safety, and wholesome recreation. She championed the city manager form of government and municipal ownership of utilities. Her public career came during the life of the Eighteenth Amendment, and for good or ill, her reputation became inextricably tied to enforcement of the prohibition laws. She was dedicated to duty and service, guided by science and reason—a practical, law-abiding, and moralistic woman who operated under an internal restraint that was reinforced by contemporary culture.

Her political career began in 1922. She and Mrs. Kathryn Miracle broke the all-male barrier to city government that spring with their election to the

Seattle City Council, Mrs. Landes by the unprecedented plurality of 22,000 votes. She came to office as a "nonpolitician," backed primarily by women's organizations and an informal network of establishment groups and individuals. Although she grew as a politician and became more politically astute, she failed to strengthen or broaden her power base and to fashion a strong political organization of her own. She appears to have lacked one thing necessary to have made a truly productive and lasting contribution to municipal reform—personal political ambition. Or, if she possessed it, she suppressed it. By the time she glimpsed some vision of her political possibilities, the door had closed on them and she was denied reelection as mayor.

She brought to the role of public servant fifty-three years of previous experience as daughter, sister, student, wife, pioneer, mother, community leader, and clubwoman. She was born Bertha Ethel Knight on October 19, 1868, in Ware, Massachusetts, the daughter of Charles Sanford Knight and Cordelia Cutter Knight. She was the youngest of nine children, the sister of two boys and six girls. On her father's side there was said to be a "dash of French Huguenot," which showed itself "in the olive complexion, dark hair and big black eyes of his children." In 1926 the *New York Times* described Bertha as "below medium height with olive skin and drab brown hair," noting that "the keen brightness of her eyes is her most arresting feature."[2]

Although both the Knights and the Cutters could trace forebears to early Massachusetts Bay, there is little to suggest great family wealth. Her father worked as a painter in the village of Ware after his discharge from the Union Army; he moved the family 20 miles east to Worcester and entered the real estate business when Bertha was five years old.[3]

Worcester, an industrial center with a population of 41,000 in 1870, had been, before the war, a center of militant resistance to the Fugitive Slave Law. It was also an important nineteenth-century educational center, the home of Worcester Polytechnic Institute, Holy Cross College, a state normal school, and Clark University.[4]

Bertha Knight grew up in that city, in a family later described as providing "the best of home influences, a father and mother of old American stock, of that sterling uprightness, and devotion to duty, that 'plain living and high thinking' that has produced so many of our best in literature, arts and statesmanship." While the Knight children "were rigidly taught to abide by the law," the family was evidently close, secure, and loving. Bertha thought her mother the most wonderful woman she had ever known; she especially admired her devotion to the nine children and to the care of her husband, whose Civil War wounds had left him an invalid by the time Bertha turned eight.[5]

Indications of a close family with a strong sense of family obligation are apparent in Bertha's years as a young adult. She had graduated from Classical High School in Worcester and was living at home in August 1887, when her sister Jessie married David Starr Jordan, who was then the president of Indiana University. In the fall of 1888, just shy of her twentieth birthday, Bertha went to Bloomington to live with the Jordans and to enroll as a student at the university. She was there that October, undoubtedly providing help and support when Jessie's first child was born into a household that also included Jordan's two children by his first wife.[6]

Following her graduation from Indiana in 1891, Bertha returned to Worcester to live with her mother and to teach until her own marriage three years later. In Bloomington she had met and become engaged to Henry Landes, a geology student from Carroll, Indiana, who had gone on to Harvard for a master's degree.

Bertha seems to have chafed somewhat in the role of single daughter under her mother's roof and she perhaps anticipated difficulty breaking away. In a long and eloquent letter written in the last summer of their long engagement, her fiancé reacted to the latest word from her:

> I am so glad that you find your life happier than you had expected. It takes a load off me when I find you cheerful. . . . You must not be blue dearie, it don't pay. Your letter was not blue by any means—but very cheerful. I am very sorry that mother is ill, and that you have to work so hard. Please do not do too much, but keep as strong as you can. . . . I am very much surprise[d] at the turn Charlie [her brother?] and May have taken. I should think that if they came over they would . . . stay there permanently. It certainly would be a nice thing all around. And how easily it will be for you to leave home when you can. It will very [e]ffectively settle your dilemma. Now if other things would only shape themselves in such good fashion we might get married before many months after all. . . . I know but little more than I did a week ago. You must expect developments very slowly.

The "other things" included his finding a job at the end of that summer, which he had spent with a United States Geological Survey team. Despite the precarious state of the nation's economy in 1893, he did secure employment that fall, classifying and arranging the geological collection for the New Jersey State Museum. They were married on January 2, 1894, and made their first home in Trenton.[7]

At Indiana, Bertha Knight and Henry Landes had attended a university that was experiencing an intellectual renaissance and enduring political and economic stress. Its student body of fewer than 300 included between 30 and

40 women. Bloomington, with a population of 3,500, "was still a backwoods court house town," with flickering electric lights and muddy streets; it had no registered saloon, but it boasted twelve churches. Founded in 1820, Indiana University had known only clergymen as presidents prior to the appointment in 1885 of the biologist David Starr Jordan, who helped the school redefine its mission within the context of the humanities and the social and physical sciences. There was extensive curriculum revision, and emphasis on physical science led Henry to a career in geology, while Bertha studied for her degree in the new Department of History and Political Science, whose young chairman, influenced by the Johns Hopkins Seminar, stressed American history and politics.[8]

David Starr Jordan touched the lives of thousands of students, and his influence on Bertha and Henry Landes is readily apparent. Although a "Darwinian extrovert among Hoosier fundamentalists" at Indiana, the liberal scientist was still somewhat old-fashioned and strongly opposed to drinking. His sister-in-law was seventeen years his junior, and in her years as a student, living for a time in his home, she had ample opportunity to be exposed to his ideas and style, his commitment to science and reason, and his politics. They corresponded after the Jordans had moved to California, where he served as the first president of Stanford, and she traveled occasionally to the Bay Area during her years in public office. He consoled her following her defeat in 1928, telling her he was not surprised at the election's outcome and asking, with Thoreau, "When were the good and true ever in the majority?"[9]

It is quite likely that conversation at the Jordan dinner table in Bloomington included politics, both civic and academic. The university was always faced with appropriations struggles and battles with legislators who at one time wanted "not only to cut the University's . . . funds but even to close the institution." Bertha Landes's experience on a campus pressed politically and financially, and whose administration she had observed from a unique vantage point, came with her to the role of faculty wife the year after her marriage. Henry Landes, on Jordan's recommendation, was appointed professor of geology at the University of Washington, and the Landeses arrived in Seattle in the fall of 1895. Newly occupying its present campus, the school was on the threshold of growth and improvement. Its immediate future was stormy, however; a Populist legislature, elected in the sweep of 1896, cut the university's requested appropriation from $90,000 to $78,000, and faculty salaries were among the nation's lowest. During the Landeses' first seven years, the university saw a succession of four presidents. A fifth, Thomas Kane, served until January 1914, when he was replaced by an acting president—Henry Landes.[10]

The Landeses rightly qualify as Seattle pioneers; the university's new location was on a heavily wooded site well beyond the city, and they were among those university people who chose to live near the new campus and become active participants in the life of the community. They built their home at the pivotal intersection of Brooklyn Avenue and Northeast 45th Street; it was a large, two-story frame house with a hospitable and inviting front porch.[11]

The Congregational Church, long the only church in the district, was a center of community activity; geared intellectually to serve university families, it became a focal point for the Landeses, who had joined the fledgling congregation early on their arrival. By 1899, Henry had become its treasurer and a trustee, and Bertha was to serve two terms as president of its Women's League—in 1903 and again in 1918. Dean Frederick Padelford later described their community at the time of his own arrival:

> In 1901 the University District was distinctly a town in the making—a few unpaved streets, wooden sidewalks, cottage homes, bits of lawn on which the cows from the Green Lake farms were daily trespassers, a cluster of stores at the corners, and a little community church, bare and graceless as frontier churches are wont to be. But it was a warm-hearted and strictly democratic community, almost entirely made up of people in their twenties and thirties, all of them from somewhere else, and all ambitious and confident of achievement. The atmosphere was electric, charged with youth and energy. The environment, both physical and social, was flexible, and with singular unanimity the members of the community went about the task of molding it into something fine and worthy.[12]

In such an environment and among such people, the Landeses reared their family. Bertha bore three children; the first, a daughter, Katherine, was born when her mother was twenty-eight. She was a beautiful and talented child, and her death in 1905 at the age of nine from complications following a tonsillectomy can only have been a crushing blow. There were two sons—Roger, who did not survive infancy, and Kenneth, who followed his father's career choice to become professor of geology at the University of Michigan. Two years after Katherine's death, nine-year-old Viola was adopted into the family, whose circle for many years included a blind and aged uncle of Bertha's. She devoted the years prior to World War I to home and family. Her outside activities were related to the church, to schools and PTA, to social services such as the Red Cross, and to women's clubs.[13] During the year of the acting presidency, the Landeses entertained students and faculty on frequent occasions, giving the first alumni homecoming reception, which was attended by more than four hundred people. Bertha Landes's home was once again that of a university president awash in politics, and in the spring of 1914 there was speculation that Landes would be named to the presidency permanently. The speculation ended with the appointment of Henry Suzzallo.[14]

For any woman carving a career, Henry Landes would have been an exceptional husband; he gave his wife unwavering support. She fully appreciated this and said at one time that he "is as interested in having me live a full, rich life as he is in having one for himself." He understood and acknowledged the contributions of women, and as dean of the College of Science at the university, he provided a source of counsel and support for women on the faculty. Both the nursing and home economics departments considered him one of their best friends. He was described by a longtime friend as "always happy, gallant and gay," and a student who ran afoul of the faculty and was dealt with by Landes said that he was "a man of inflexible honor and exalted ideals. . . . Moreover, he possesses infinite tact, a rare sense of justice, and a rarer sense of humor."[15]

It was widely speculated during Bertha's campaign in 1922 that *he* would be the councilman in truth, and letters to the editor asked such things as "Will she do as Henry tells her—if elected?" There is no evidence that he controlled that council seat, although he obviously was her staunch ally and a chief adviser. She said that he was "a tower of strength in times of stress and made many sacrifices without complaint that I might give my time and strength to my civic service." One such sacrifice by the former Indiana farm boy could have been the postelection move from their home (then at 4511 18th Avenue N.E.) to an apartment in the Wilsonian Hotel, a move that lightened her domestic duties, some of which she continued to carry even while mayor.[16]

Both Landeses saw her career as duty and service rather than an opportunity for fulfillment of her own ambition, and they both justified her political activities within the context of woman's proper place. In 1926, Henry Landes found nothing "revolutionary" about his wife's election as mayor, saying, "It's simply the natural enlargement of her sphere. Keeping house and raising a family are woman's logical tasks, and, in principle, there's no difference between running one home and a hundred thousand." The city as simply a larger home was a theme of many of her speeches and public comments; one of the nationwide lecture tours that she made was called "Adventures in Municipal Housekeeping." Throughout her public career she held to the old values, and she sought to reconcile woman's "proper place" with her newly emergent opportunities in a wider sphere.[17]

In 1921 Mrs. Landes was president of the Seattle Federation of Women's

Clubs; she was involved in university community affairs, active in campus circles as a faculty wife, and a leader in the University Congregational Church. The quintessential clubwoman, she had honed her skills in public speaking and parliamentary procedure during years of active leadership in such clubs as the Woman's Century Club and the Women's University Club. As federation president, she was a driving force in planning and directing the highly successful week-long Women's Educational Exhibit for Washington Manufacturers. This exhibit of Washington State products was staffed by more than one thousand clubwomen who had become enthusiastic supporters of local industries at a time when the city and the region were in the throes of economic depression and severe unemployment. The business community was impressed with the women's efforts in behalf of the state's economy and the Seattle Chamber of Commerce president praised Mrs. Landes for her role, telling her that he was "particularly impressed with the character of the interviews you have given out, showing as they do that you have caught the great vision of civic usefulness and responsibility."[18]

That year, Mayor Hugh Caldwell created a five-member commission on unemployment to deal with the city's problem, and he appointed one woman—Bertha Landes. Another member of that commission urged her to run for the city council. She had successfully bridged the gap between woman's traditional world of home, church, and club and the world of business and civic service; she was now a strong, serious, and worthy candidate for public office.[19]

She couched her 1922 council campaign in perfectly acceptable terms for a woman. While asserting that the time had come for women to be represented in governing bodies, she stated clearly that woman's first duty was to home and family. Many of her campaign statements seemed aimed at reconciling those two points, and they frequently smacked of apology for a candidacy justified as duty and service and for a candidate who disavowed any political ambition. As she filed for office she said, "It is not only the right, but the privilege and duty, of women to take part in the administration of public affairs." She stressed time and again the right of 40 percent of the voters to representation on the council, and said that if elected she would "support the moral and welfare projects in which women are primarily interested."[20]

During the campaign, noting the large number of women candidates in the country, she said, "This woman's movement is the logical outcome of two things: 1. Suffrage [and] 2. Commercialization of many of the activities which formerly centered in the home, such as the laundry work, baking, sewing and so forth." She also thought, though, that women might not be so anxious to demand the right to representation, which suffrage gave them, if men had "been able to interpret and express women's viewpoint on matters relating to the home, the welfare of women and children and the moral issues." The viewpoints of both men and women, she believed, were "as necessary for a well-balanced theory of city government as for a well-managed house. Home standards should be city standards, and this man has not realized." Since technology had ended much household drudgery, women had more time for outside activities, and "if [a woman] is not to be a parasite, something abhorrent to her nature, she must turn her energies to public service of some kind." While Mrs. Landes emphasized that woman's task is "to make the home and rear the future citizens," she urged civic involvement for the woman "who has reared her family and has . . . a trained intelligence to offer in service to her country . . . and who can render it without detriment to home or family interest."[21]

That first campaign and its organization were considered "absolutely unique in the political annals of the city." It was run by a group of five women—Mrs. Landes and four staunch backers from among the city's clubwomen, who were described as "typical Seattle housewives." One of them, Mrs. R. F. Weeks, said, "We wanted political experience; we were all amateurs." She stressed that they had run a low-budget operation in order to avoid "slush funds [which] mean either paid campaign workers or promised jobs"; they wanted Bertha Landes to enter office with clean hands, beholden to no faction.[22]

On May 2, 1922, the day of the general election, the candidate issued one final statement: "Our campaign is over. It has been strictly a women's campaign to elect a woman to the city council without entangling alliances, to represent woman's thought and viewpoint. . . . Our idea was to serve the best interests of the city; not to further the political ambitions of any one woman."[23]

From her seat on the council license committee, Mrs. Landes spearheaded the move for an ordinance that provided for the tighter regulation of cabarets and dance halls. In June 1924, she was elected council president and became acting mayor when Mayor Edwin J. "Doc" Brown was in New York attending the Democratic National Convention. She caused a furor and received attention in the national press when she fired Brown's police chief, William Severyns, for failing to rid his department of corruption, which he himself had widely publicized, and for his insubordination in an exchange of letters with her. She won reelection to the council in 1925 by a margin well below her phenomenal showing of 1922, but as municipal election time approached the following year, her name cropped up as a potential mayoral candidate.

We urge you to
Work and Vote For

BERTHA K. LANDES

We ask your support

All Seattle needs LANDES for Mayor

Our Public Utilities
Our Industrial Future
Our Growing Children
Our City's Good Name

Each and every one a reason why you should

WORK AND VOTE

We indorse LANDES FOR MAYOR:

W. E. FORKNER	MRS. HAM BONNAR
DR. DAVID C. HALL	MRS. J. W. MARLATT
JOHN H. REID	MRS. E. F. PUGSLEY
BYRON PHELPS	MRS. NORMAN COMPTON
W. WALTER WILLIAMS	MRS. WYLIE HEMPHILL

Poster for mayoral campaign *(courtesy Museum of History and Industry, Seattle)*

She was extremely reluctant to run for mayor and saw herself as a candidate only if none other emerged with a chance of defeating Doc Brown. It was not until the last day of filing, during which she changed her mind several times, that she made her final decision. She was heavily influenced by leaders in women's organizations that had been the backbone of her council campaigns and by pressure from backers of an initiative—also on the ballot—to establish city manager government in Seattle. In favor of the city manager plan and optimistic about its passage, she perhaps felt less diffident about entering the race because of the likelihood of the mayor's office being superseded.[24]

Her mayoral campaign occurred against the backdrop of the celebrated "Rum Trial" of the Seattle policeman-turned-bootlegger Roy Olmstead, a coincidence that kept the spotlight on Mrs. Landes's concern for morality and law enforcement. The trial tended to substantiate links between Brown and bootleg interests and to corroborate assertions she had made during the Severyns firing in 1924. She was elected on March 9, by a margin of just under 6,000 votes in what was then a record voter turnout.[25]

As mayor she sought strict law enforcement, sound management for the municipal electric utility (City Light), a firmer financial base for the troubled street railway department, improved traffic safety, and quality appointments based on merit. She could and did take pride in such accomplishments as enhanced and expanded recreational programs in the park department and the return to profitable operations for the streetcar system. Although she had assured the Municipal League that as mayor she would "attend to other duties than 'greeting actresses at incoming trains,'" Mrs. Landes was gracious in her ceremonial tasks; notable among them was welcoming to Seattle both Charles A. Lindbergh, recently returned from his Atlantic flight, and Queen Marie of Rumania, on her widely heralded tour of the United States.[26]

In 1928, the once reluctant candidate was being touted in some quarters as a candidate for governor, but she wanted to be reelected mayor. A two-year term was, according to the incumbent, "not long enough to work out and put in effect a constructive program." She told reporters, "Frankly, I like being mayor. I haven't seen any reason, since taking office, why a woman can't fill it as well as a man." Another thing that appealed to her as a woman was a "hope to show that a woman could not only get an office, but could 'make good' and win indorsement of voters for a second term."[27]

She began her reelection campaign armed with a good record in office and the same type of support she had commanded since 1922. But, "within the space of a short election campaign, the incumbent mayor went from a betting odds' favorite . . . to resounding defeat." She lost to Frank Edwards, a man completely unknown politically and without any record of public service or community involvement. The conventional explanation for her ouster has been that by pressuring the police department into making liquor raids she lost valuable support and that by 1928 "Seattle was tiring of reform and of Mrs. Landes."[28]

Although enforcement of prohibition was without doubt a factor in the election, it was not the whole story. She herself attributed her defeat to a combination of "a nine months' campaign on the part of my opponent, excessive expenditure of funds, and sex prejudice."[29]

Indeed, the Edwards campaign was of unprecedented length and cost; it had started the preceding summer and utilized hundreds of paid precinct workers, citywide billboards, and film footage of the candidate at City Light projects on the Skagit River. Edwards's reported expenditures failed to include much of that, prompting the prosecuting attorney to consider an investigation of his funds. However, such a probe could be initiated only by the defeated candidate, and she never did request an investigation.[30]

Lacking the facts, which might thus have been uncovered, speculation as to the source of Edwards's money centers on those favoring a more open city and less stringent law enforcement and on private power interests. Both groups had long-standing cause to oppose Mayor Landes.

A backer of municipal ownership of utilities throughout her career in public office, the mayor sided with J. D. Ross, the popular and increasingly powerful head of City Light, in his plans for developing the power potential of the upper Skagit River. Although overshadowed by her sensational dismissal of the police chief, two other actions Mrs. Landes took as acting mayor in 1924 may have earned her the opposition of private power. One was the signing of a new contract for Ross, which had been held in abeyance by Mayor Brown for six months, and the other was proclaiming June 18 as Power Day, in support of the drive to gain ballot qualification for the Bone bill, an initiative that would authorize expanded opportunities for public utilities.[31]

The financial woes of Seattle's street railway system, the city's $15 million white elephant inherited from Mayor Ole Hanson's glory year of 1919, brought Mrs. Landes face to face with the firm that had sold the city the system—Stone and Webster, parent company of Puget Sound Power and Light. The refusal of banks in the Seattle Clearing House Association to honor railway warrants in December 1927 forced the mayor to go beyond measures that cut operating expenses and to negotiate refinancing of the system. The success of this depended on state enabling legislation, and while making the city's case before the lawmakers in Olympia, "she clashed with private power company officials over the bill's contents."[32]

Activities of the Civil Service League also contributed to her ouster from office. That organization of municipal employees actually sought out Edwards and encouraged him to run, and "firemen and policemen openly compaigned for him while on duty." The mayor had alienated many streetcar men by making deep cutbacks in personnel in order to ensure the system's solvency.[33]

Sex prejudice, as Mrs. Landes put it, looms as no small factor in her defeat. In her study of the 1928 election, Florence Deacon stresses the pervasiveness of the issue and sees it as both an overt and a subtle factor. She characterized the successful Landes campaign of 1926 as a "nonthreatening" one in which the candidate "did not step out of the traditional woman's role: she was simply to be a municipal housekeeper." In contrast, for the reelection race, the mayor "was too busy running the city to present an adequate campaign. She didn't take time to play up the role of 'little woman' and housewifely mother." Deacon concludes that the voters would not accept Mrs. Landes in other than the traditional role. Her opponent stressed his experience as a business*man* and much of his literature promoted "Frank Edwards, the *man* you would be proud to call mayor." The issue of a woman mayor was a constant theme in the press, pro-Landes papers decrying the fact that the only criticism of the incumbent was that she was a woman. It was implied at every turn that a city of Seattle's stature really needed a man for mayor. The Portland *Oregonian* chided the city for defeating a mayor considered the superior of most of her predecessors:

> We suspect . . . that Mrs. Landes was defeated solely because Seattle wishes to be known as a he-man's town. . . . [I]t wants a mayor's office where one can put one's feet on the desk. . . . [The Commercial Club] wants a mayor whose presence does not call also for letting everyone's wife in to the festivities. . . . [I]t is the fashion for cities to personify their dignity and importance through the male sex. . . . Yet out here in the far west where men are reputed to be men a proud and hustling city was mayored by a woman. Many a bearded cheek in Seattle has blushed in the last two years over this imagined shame upon a he-man's town.[34]

If the public woman was beset by the he-man factor, the private woman seemed beset by an inner restraint that kept her from using her political power effectively and to her own advantage. Nonetheless, Bertha Landes held strong convictions about the role of government and the place of women in relation to government, and she was firm in her commitment to progressive measures.

The mayor's progressivism suggests the influence of David Starr Jordan, whose abiding interest in politics comprised a strong opposition to the spoils systems and an ongoing concern for civil service reform. Jordan and Theodore Roosevelt, who met when Roosevelt spoke on the Indiana campus in 1888, shared political convictions, and the views of the two men informed those of Bertha Landes. Her appointment policy as mayor was one Jordan could approve—one intended, in Roosevelt's words, "to take politics out of politics." A forgotten element in her clash with Doc Brown in 1924 was his alleged abuse of civil service regulations; after her brief tenure as acting mayor she continued to serve on the council's efficiency committee, which conducted a wide-ranging investigation of the Civil Service Commission.[35]

Mrs. Landes preserved the reprint of the text of a speech Roosevelt gave in 1893, and she quoted from it to advise the 1927 graduating class of Yakima High School to become involved in civic affairs. In choosing to avoid politics, she warned, "You are simply saying that you are unfit to live in a free community." That particular Roosevelt speech could almost have served as her political credo:

> The first duty of an American citizen is that he shall work in politics. . . . [He should remain in political life] only as long as he can stay in it on his own terms, without sacrifice of his own principles. . . . [W]hen a public servant has definitely made up his mind that he will pay no heed to his own future, but will do what he honestly deems best for the community; without regard to how his actions may affect his prospects, not only does he become infinitely more useful as a public servant, but he has a far better time. He is freed from the harassing care which is inevitably the portion of him who is trying to shape his sails to catch every gust of the wind of political favor.[36]

She presented her views on municipal government, home, and womanhood in a speech prepared for delivery shortly after her election as mayor. Echoing Frederic C. Howe, she noted that the city "is said to be the hope of Democracy," and deplored people's reluctance to become involved politically: "The majority of our people desire civic decency and public morality but they don't desire them sufficiently to be willing to sacrifice very much of their time, strength or money to procure them." She reminded her listeners that the family is the smallest unit of government, that "government centers around the home," and that "the underlying principle [of government] is the satisfaction of all the needs of the people." For her, the most important function of government "is creating the proper atmosphere, mental, moral and physical, for the rearing of children and the activities of adult life. The city is really only a larger household or family with its problems increased manyfold through its diversified interests and the cosmopolitan nature of its members." The city must "supervise and regulate commercial amusements within her borders—keep down vice and immorality with a firm hand and . . . control the moral conditions under which her people live." In a personal message for the women in the audience she said:

> Let me tell you . . . that though I am a public official and a so-called politician, that I am first and always a woman . . . that I am a wife and mother but a mother whose children are grown . . . that I yield to no one in my respect for wifehood and motherhood and regard those professions as the very highest ones which any woman can fill. . . . I now want to urge you to assume your personal respon-

sibility for civic betterment. If woman is indifferent and fails to realize her responsibility... then is the outlook gloomy and the future uncertain.... [Even the mother of small children] must pay some attention to what is going on outside the walls of her home.... The woman of mature years who has raised her family certainly has an added responsibility for civic conditions, for which she has not only leisure but a maturity of judgment which should be used for the public good."[37]

Mrs. Landes remained firm in her belief that a woman should have raised her family before seeking office; she preferred also that a woman not be dependent on the job for a living because financial freedom encouraged objectivity and independence. This sounds naïvely idealistic, but though she did not change her basic belief, she did become more practical. She came to see politics as the art of the possible. While she was mayor, she spoke of the "necessity for compromise in small things in the hope of providing for greater ones," and she acknowledged the difficulty of reconciling one's ideals with reality.[38]

She had assumed that her greatest contribution on the city council would be supporting women's traditional health and welfare measures, representing others rather than initiating and leading. Two things thrust her into a leadership role—the need for a dance hall ordinance and conditions within the police department, including the insubordination of the police chief. In the former instance, she had the active and open backing of leading men in the community; in the latter, she took matters into her own hands, while a few men offered advice in the background. The episode of the police chief weighed heavily on her. She later said that she had been given power; she believed in God; she felt like a martyr; and "Oh, I didn't want to do it!" With something akin to a sense of calling, she did what she had to do, feeling somewhat victimized in the process.[39]

When the call came, or pressure was applied, to be a mayoral candidate, she felt no special urge to be mayor, but asked herself, "[Am] I the person to help my city realize its possibilities?" Again, potential power was thrust on her; she had not sought it. Once again she answered the call and did her duty. Toward the end of her term as mayor, as she came to relish the opportunities and the power of her office, she said:

Municipal housekeeping means adventure and romance and accomplishment to me. To be in some degree a guiding force in the destiny of a city, to help lay the foundation stones for making it good and great, to aid in advancing the political position of women, to be the person to whom men and women and children look for protection against lawlessness, to spread the political philosophy that the city is only a larger home—I find it richly worthwhile![40]

She had come to public life from among Seattle's middle-class clubwomen, but during her time in office she encountered a much broader spectrum of Seattle's women. She came to appreciate women wage earners and their concerns as well as the business and professional women who made up the Seattle Soroptimist Club, of which she was a charter member. Her expanded contacts seem to have made her more understanding of the economic problems of women and perhaps less prone to sit in judgment. In the dance hall ordinance battle of 1922, she softened her stand to some extent after receiving in her home three women who worked in one of the establishments targeted for closure and who came to plead economic necessity. She was reportedly determined to wipe out vice in the city, having been informed "that the same type of women are here today that were here some years ago, when we had a wide open town, and that gambling and all other vices of those days are again in vogue." Yet her visitors "did not make a bad impression. We had a pleasant talk. I got their viewpoint. It was enlightening, but I have nothing to say about it." Two of the women were working to support their children; they could earn $4.00 or $5.00 a night in the dance halls, in contrast to $13.45 a week in a factory or $2.40 for an eight-hour shift in a restaurant. Whatever her reasons, Mrs. Landes did settle for dance hall regulation and supervision rather than closure in the final version of the ordinance.[41]

She remained sympathetic to women's causes after she left office; the Depression underscored the economic plight of women. In 1931 she was the principal speaker for a successful lobbying of the city council that was organized by the Women's Protective Association in opposition to a proposed charter amendment barring married women from city employment. She headed the women's division of the city's Commission for Improved Employment early in the Depression; its main project was the operation of three sewing rooms that provided employment for women and clothing for needy children. Mrs. Landes showed concern for the self-esteem of the women in the sewing rooms: she declared that the city, in helping such women "avoid the dole," must make "every effort to provide work and see that work is paid for so that there is no feeling of accepting charity." During her term as president of the American Federation of Soroptimist Clubs, from June 1930 to June 1932, one of that organization's major concerns was relief for older women, who as a group suffered disproportionately from unemployment.[42]

That she was a prohibitionist is a fact. But it is open to question that she merits the reputation as a "blue-nose" moralist intent on spoiling all the fun of the roaring twenties. During the mayoral race in 1926, in an effort to divert the issue from being solely "whether you want an open town or a blue law one," the *Seattle Star* said, "Bunk! Mrs. Landes isn't a blue law person. She wants only what a vast majority of our citizens want—a fair degree of decency and some dignity in public office."[43]

She never did promise to "entirely eradicate bootlegging and illegal sale of liquor." She did say, however, "that there would be no longer open and flagrant violation of any law—be it the prohibition law or any other law." She fought repeal and thought that many seeking it were "men and women who can afford financially the 'high cost of drinking' . . . [and who wish to] break down the protective law which the 18th Amendment has built around society . . . apparently in order that they may go their way unhampered and with a less guilty conscience." She herself personified restraint and self-control, and at the heart of her prohibitionism was her contention that "all prohibitive laws have arisen as a result of a lack of personal restraint on the part of individuals and the placing of an over-emphasis on the right of personal liberty."[44]

While she cannot be classified as a civil libertarian, neither should she be thought a bigot; in the context of her times, on occasion she appears comparatively enlightened, and her activities and statements indicate an objective and rational approach to race relations. She was a member of the board of directors of the city's Soroptimist Club, which took the lead in eliminating the "white only" restriction for membership in that organization; she was president of the national organization when all reference to race as a membership qualification was deleted from its constitution. Her reported opposition in 1921 to interracial marriage was based on the ground that "where the two races are so different, the result could mean nothing more than incompatibility." That is a rational note for an era marked by agitation for immigrant exclusion and by virulent racism—a time in which fifty hooded and robed members of the Ku Klux Klan could be seated in a body for Sunday services at Seattle's First Presbyterian Church and be described by the Reverend Mark Matthews as worshipping "reverentially."[45]

Bertha Landes was blessed with a sense of humor, even in regard to liquor. She saved the printed lyrics of a song parody that had been sung to her while she was mayor. Set to the tune of "Maryland, My Maryland," it went:

> You took our booze and took our gin,
> Mayor Landes, mayor dear!
> And made it hard for us to sin,
> Mayor Landes, Mayor dear!

When we had Doc and Roy and Bill
We felt quite safe to drink our fill;
Now hooch there ain't, though we be ill—
Mayor Landes, mayor dear!

Now, kindly woman that thou art
Mayor Landes, mayor dear!
Please, prithee, show a woman's heart,
Mayor Landes, mayor dear!

Let down the bars, we'll stand in line;
Fill once again ou[r] empty stein;
We'll vote for you; we like you fine—
Mayor Landes, mayor dear!

In her ill-fated campaign for reelection, unable to get her opponent to meet her in debate, she staged mock debates with an empty chair. The *New York Times* reported that "she laughs as she conducts these one-sided debates and appears to get as much 'kick' out of them as her hearers, and the audience is usually in an uproar."[46]

She met defeat in 1928 in much the same manner that she had encountered other developments in her life—realistically and without false modesty; stoically but with some humor. The day after the election she told the Rotarians, gathered for their Citizenship Day luncheon, that they were "imposing a severe test upon her to laud voters for 'intelligent citizenship' in view of their decision of the previous day." She took pleasure in the knowledge that she could leave office with the conviction she had given Seattle a "constructive administration" and that the city was cleaner than it had been for years.[47]

Later, however, she indicated that she had been abandoned by her supporters. Although she avowed no regrets, there is disappointment in her words:

> The people who had put a woman into office to house clean for them "rested upon the comfortable assurance that all was going well and they could rest upon their oars." . . . So . . . they left their woman mayor to the wolves . . . an unguarded sheep. . . . Then the wolves came down *en masse* and, to all practical purposes, devoured her. They sent her back, providentially, to private life. She had worked day and night with very few play days for two years. . . . She was not exactly weary in well doing, for she fought long and hard to win, but at the same time she took her defeat with a certain sense of relief and without bitterness or deep regret.[48]

Mayor Landes greets Arctic explorer at train station
(courtesy Museum of History and Industry, Seattle)

Reflecting on her performance in office, she once said, "I tried to uphold the ideals of womanhood." For her, that meant exhibiting strength, intelligence, and courage, and taking the slings and arrows stoically. Her formula for political success for women included "courage without tears . . . personal charm . . . poise . . . endless physical energy . . . a sense of humor . . . but most of all—no tears." An overly sensitive woman would "be hurt by the many unpleasant things people do and say. And before she knows it she [would] be in tears, which would bring disgrace on womankind!"[49]

She had wanted full equality in name and in truth, once saying she was a councilman, "not a council woman, please note. And I threaten to shoot on sight, without benefit of clergy, anyone calling me the mayoress instead of the mayor. Joking aside, I am fighting for a principle in taking that stand. Let women who go into politics be the real thing or nothing! Let us, while never forgetting our womanhood, drop all emphasis on sex and put it on being public servants."[50]

In the summer of 1933, she and Dean Landes conducted the first of a series of University of Washington-sponsored study tours to the Far East, and they led a group during each of the next three summers. On the return trip in 1936, Henry Landes became ill, developed bronchitis, and died shortly after arriving back in Seattle. The former mayor agreed to lead the tour alone the following year, but this was among the last of her public activities. Even though by 1939 her own health had become a problem, she continued to live at the Wilsonian, and she maintained her independence. During those later years, she encountered the thinking of the Unity School of Christianity, the Kansas City-based organization that stressed faith healing and a sort of self-help, matter-of-fact approach to the spiritual. That Mrs. Landes would turn to it seems quite in keeping with her character, and it is not surprising that among the Unity School literature that she kept was the motto: "I meet every situation in my life with perfect poise, for I am secure in the realization that God guides, protects and prospers me." In 1941, in part because of poor health, Bertha Landes moved from Seattle to Pacific Palisades, California. She died November 29, 1943, at the age of seventy-five, at her son's home in Ann Arbor.[51]

Bertha Landes graduated from college at the dawn of the progressive era of political and social reform, but she was not enfranchised until the age of forty-three. Although a leader in church, club, and community, she remained on the sidelines politically until, as a woman whose personal identity was first and foremost wife, mother, and homemaker, she was called upon at fifty-three to begin a new career in elective office.

Her political career had strong overtones of the progressive tenets of efficiency and regulation in public affairs, but her term as mayor did not mirror institutional reorganization that had taken place under Progressives elsewhere, nor did it produce any lasting social change. It seems rather that she fought a rearguard action in which she tried to reestablish in the city a rational and efficient approach to civic affairs, to strengthen municipal utilities, to improve services and programs for the betterment of the people, and to enforce the laws that she considered essential for the health and welfare of all.

Unlike other and earlier Progressives, Mayor Landes built no political machine of her own. The short, two-year mayoral term worked against her enlistment of able, and younger, strategists with long-range goals and ambitions of their own, and her reliance on a core group of women supporters, amateurs all, who lacked political staying power, added neither strength nor breadth to her campaigns.

She failed to effect reforms and she failed at reelection. It can be argued that the causes of the failures were the two things that made her tenure unique—her espousal of progressive measures and her sex. By the mid-1920s, a progressive was already something of a political anachronism, and her 1928 defeat may be seen as further evidence that the progressive movement had died or gone underground to await rebirth in the New Deal. As a woman she confronted the same forces, both subtle and not so subtle, that still account for gender inequality in politics; even within herself she was restrained by having been born and bred to a nineteenth-century woman's "proper place."

She reconciled the role of woman-in-the-family and that of woman-in-public office by combining them. She simply proclaimed the city a larger home, a concept acceptable to her and to contemporary culture. But the attempt to achieve political success took her beyond the stereotype of municipal housekeeping to meet politics on its own terms, and she found herself, a woman beyond the home, at odds with her culture if not with herself.

NOTES

This essay appeared in *Pacific Northwest Quarterly* 75 (July 1984): 117–27.

1. George W. Scott, "The New Order of Cincinnatus," *Pacific Northwest Quarterly* 64 (1973): 137 (quotation). Two exceptions to this treatment are Florence J. Deacon, "Why Wasn't Bertha Knight Landes Re-elected?" M.A. thesis (University of Washington, 1978), and *Notable American Women, 1607–1950,* s.v. "Landes, Bertha Ethel Knight."

2. David Starr Jordan, *The Days of a Man,* 2 vols. (New York: World Book Co., 1922), 1:326 (quotations); *New York Times,* March 28, 1926.

3. *Notable American Women,* s.v. "Landes"; *Biographical Cyclopaedia of American Women,* vol. 2, s.v. "Landes, Bertha E. Knight."

4. *Encyclopaedia Britannica,* 9th and 11th eds., s.v. "Worcester, Massachusetts."

5. *Biographical Cyclopaedia,* s.v. "Landes" (first quotation); Blanche Brace, "Well . . . Why Not?" *Woman Citizen* 11 (September 1926): 9 (second quotation); Julia N. Budlong, "What Happened in Seattle," *Nation* 127 (Aug. 29, 1928): 197.

6. Jordan, *Days of a Man,* 1:326–27.

7. Henry Landes to Bertha Knight, July 9, 1893, box 1, Bertha K. Landes Papers, University of Washington Libraries; G. E. Goodspeed, "Memorial of Henry Landes," *Proceedings of the Geological Society of America for 1936* (June 1937), pp. 207–13.

8. Thomas D. Clark, *Indiana University: Midwestern Pioneer,* 4 vols. (Bloomington: Indiana University Press, 1970–77), 1: 214, 219–20, 236 (quotation), 237.

9. Ibid., pp. 211 (extrovert) and 239; Jordan to Bertha Knight Landes, March 14, 1928, box 1, Landes Papers.

10. Clark, *Indiana University,* 1:212 (quotation); Charles M. Gates, *The First Century at the University of Washington, 1861–1961* (Seattle: University of Washington Press, 1961), pp. 60, 62, and 123.

11. Photographs, box 1, Landes Papers.

12. Frederick M. Padelford, "The Community," *University Congregational Church Fiftieth Anniversary Program* (1941). In 1928, Bertha Landes became the first woman to serve as moderator of the Washington Conference of the Congregational Church.

13. *Pacific Wave* (Seattle), April 7, 1905; "Memorial of Henry Landes"; Matthew O'Connor, "Biography of Bertha Knight Landes" (typescript), box 1, Landes Papers; Budlong, "What Happened in Seattle," p. 197.

14. *University of Washington Daily,* Nov. 30 and Feb. 20, 1914 (hereafter *Daily);* Gates, *First Century,* p. 142.

15. Clipping, Feb. 9, 1927 (Landes quotation), box 2, Landes Papers; Cora Jane Lawrence, "University Education for Nursing in Seattle, 1912–1950," Ph.D. diss. (University of Washington, 1972), p. 75. Grace Denny to Landes, Sept. 1, 1936, Effie Raitt to Landes, 1936, and Eva Ronald Benson to Landes, Aug. 28, 1936 (friend's quotation), box 1, Landes Papers; *Daily,* Feb. 25, 1914 (student quotation).

16. *Seattle Star,* April 15, 1922 (campaign quotation); typed fragment (n.d.) (Landes quotation), box 1, Landes Papers; "Interesting Westerners," *Sunset* 58 (February 1927): 46.

17. *New York Times,* March 28, 1926.

18. *Seattle Spirit,* April 28, 1921, p. 1; Robert S. Boyns to Bertha K. Landes, April 19, 1921 (quotation), box 1, Landes Papers.

19. Bertha K. Landes, "Does Politics Make Women Crooked?" *Collier's* 83 (March 16, 1929): 36.

20. *Seattle Star,* March 2, 1922 (first quotation); *Seattle Post-Intelligencer,* March 10, 1922 (second quotation).

21. Bertha Landes, "Women in Government," *Seattle Star,* April 4, 1922.

22. Ibid., April 21 (first two quotations) and 5 (Weeks quotations), 1922.

23. Ibid., May 2, 1922.

24. *Seattle Times,* Jan. 23 and 24, 1926; *Seattle Post-Intelligencer,* Feb. 3, 1926. Brown was a Democrat, and it is likely that Mrs. Landes was a Republican; however, the mayoral election was nonpartisan.

25. *Seattle Post-Intelligencer,* Jan. 29 and 30, Feb. 3, 4, and 21, 1926; *Seattle Star,* March 10, 1926.

26. *Seattle Post-Intelligencer,* Feb. 3, 1926.

27. Ibid., Oct. 30, 1927.

28. Norman H. Clark, *The Dry Years: Prohibition and Social Change in Washington* (Seattle: University of Washington Press, 1965), p. 199 (last quotation); Deacon, "Why Wasn't Landes Re-elected?" pp. 62 (first quotation) and 114.

29. Undated clipping fragment, box 2, Landes Papers.

30. *Seattle Times,* March 5, 10–13, 1928; Deacon, "Why Wasn't Landes Re-elected?" pp. 72–73, 93.

31. *Seattle Star,* June 13, 1924 (text of proclamation); *Oregonian,* June 29, 1924; Landes to Oliver Erickson, Aug. 11, 1927, box 87, Seattle Lighting Department Records, University of Washington Libraries; *Seattle Times,* June 27, 1927.

32. Deacon, "Why Wasn't Landes Re-elected?" pp. 47–59 (57, quotation).

33. Ibid., pp. 114 and 93 (quotation).

34. Ibid., pp. 115 (first three quotations) and 79 (fourth quotation); *Argus,* Jan. 7, Feb. 4, and June 2, 1928; "Revolt of the He-Men," *Oregonian,* March 15, 1928.

35. Jordan, *Days of a Man,* 1:306 (quotation). As mayor, Bertha Landes appointed civil service commissioners of her own choosing, one of whom was Dave Beck, then a young, rising force on the Seattle labor scene.

36. "Yakima School Speech" (n.d., typescript), and Theodore Roosevelt, "Good Citizenship and Public Office," reprint (Jan. 26, 1893), box 1, Landes Papers.

37. Text of speech, "The Problem of the Large City," pp. 1, 5, 6, 7, 12–14, box 1, Landes Papers.

38. *Kansas City Times,* Dec. 2, 1937, clipping, box 2, Landes Papers; *Soroptigram,* March 1927 (mimeographed) (quotation).

39. Budlong, "What Happened in Seattle," p. 197.

40. Bertha Landes, "Steering a Big City Straight," *Woman Citizen* 12 (December 1927): 7 and 37.

41. *Seattle Post-Intelligencer,* Oct. 14 (first quotation) and Oct. 16 (second quotation), 1922.

42. Ibid., Dec. 2, 1931; Lois Jermin to Bertha Landes, Dec. 3, 1931, box 1; box 1 (re:

Commission for Improved Employment) and box 2, undated clipping (quotation) and clipping, May 31, 1933, Landes Papers; *American Soroptimist,* September 1962, p. 10.

43. *Seattle Star,* March 2, 1926.

44. Statement by Bertha K. Landes at a hearing before the House Judiciary Committee, March 12, 1930, box 1, Landes Papers.

45. *Soroptimist Yearbook,* December 1925, p. 8; 1926, p. 2; 1932, p. 40. Ruth Bachtel, "President's Report," read at Soroptimist Founder's Day Meeting, Seattle, Oct. 8, 1980; *Seattle Star,* Dec. 29, 1921 (quotation) and April 3, 1922. The allegation was made in "Recollections," *Puget Soundings,* June 1976, p. 15, that Mrs. Landes was "very prejudiced" and that she "instigated a program of cataloguing people" by color for the purpose of restricting the movements throughout the city of people of darker color. I have been unable to find any evidence to corroborate such a claim.

46. "Mayorland, Dry Mayorland," box 1, Landes Papers; *New York Times,* March 11, 1928.

47. *Seattle Post-Intelligencer,* March 14 (constructive) and March 15 (severe test), 1928.

48. Bertha Landes, "An Alumna in Politics," *Indiana Alumni Magazine* (April 1939), box 1, Landes Papers.

49. Undated clipping (first quotation), and clipping from *Honolulu Advertiser,* ca. 1938 (quotations), box 2, Landes Papers.

50. Landes, "Steering a Big City Straight," p. 7.

51. *University District Herald* (Seattle), June 6, 1941; *Seattle Times,* Nov. 29, 1943; "Society of Silent Unity," p. 5 (motto), box 1, Landes Papers.

The Job He Left Behind: Women in the Shipyards During World War II

KAREN BECK SKOLD

During the Second World War, Portland, Oregon, was one of the major centers of the American shipbuilding industry. Hundreds of Liberty ships, tankers, aircraft carriers, and other ships were built between 1941 and 1945 by a labor force numbering 125,000 at its peak. What was remarkable about this army of workers was that one-fourth were women. They were welders, burners, electricians, and shipfitters, working in jobs once the exclusive domain of men. Climbing scaffolding on the hulls or descending into the ships' holds, they earned the same pay as the men, wages that were the highest of any industry at the time. The importance of women's labor was recognized in the media campaigns recruiting more women, and by the creation of child-care centers at the workplace.

The boom in shipbuilding was short-lived. Yet women gained access during the war years to skilled trades and high wages from which they had traditionally been excluded. What was the meaning of this experience? Was a model of equality between women and men in the labor force briefly created? How much change really occurred in the definition of "women's work" and "men's work" under the pressure of the war emergency?

This essay shows, first of all, how and why women entered the shipyards, and what the process meant in terms of increased opportunities. Second, it compares the actual work done by women and men. And, finally, it examines women's postwar plans and what happened to them when the shipyards closed.

WOMEN ENTER THE SHIPYARDS

The sudden, rapid growth of the shipbuilding industry changed Portland from a quiet, provincial city into wartime boomtown. Three huge shipyards built and operated by the Kaiser Corporation dominated the industrial life of the area. Here ships for the U.S. Maritime Commission were built at record-breaking speed. In addition, several local companies built small craft for the Navy. The first of the Kaiser yards, the Oregon Shipbuilding Corporation, was built in 1941, and absorbed most of the area's supply of unemployed men. Shortly after Pearl Harbor, Kaiser was granted a contract to build a second yard across the Columbia River from Portland in the small town of Vancouver, Washington. Then, in March 1942, a third Kaiser yard began at Portland's Swan Island.[1] The demand for labor thus increased sharply at the same time that the supply of healthy young men was being decreased by the draft.

Beginning in the summer of 1942, Kaiser recruiters sought unemployed men in cities such as Minneapolis and New York, promising to pay their transportation costs as an advance on wages. Before long a housing crisis developed in Portland, as migrants arrived faster than the war housing projects were built. The bottleneck in housing was broken with the construction of Vanport, the "world's largest housing project," built in 110 days by Kaiser and other construction firms on swampland midway between the three Kaiser yards. A year after ground was broken, Vanport was the second largest "city" in Oregon, with 40,000 residents. Between 1940 and 1944, nearly a quarter of a million migrants came into the Portland-Vancouver area.[2]

The consequent strain on schools, housing, transportation, and other services was typical of defense industry centers. War industries were not built with the location of adequate labor supply in mind. Workers had to move to the jobs, given the inducement of high wages.

Meanwhile, another source of labor had begun to be tapped. Plans were made quite early to hire women in the Kaiser yards. In January 1942, the Vancouver school board learned that women would be used to help "man" the shipyard, barely under construction, and it decided to admit ten women to the school district's defense training classes. In April, when Oregon Ship hired two women as welders on the outfitting dock, it became the first of the nation's Maritime Commission yards to employ women in production work. As word spread, first private, then public welding schools began sending more women to the yards.[3]

The women who began to enter the yards in 1942 were not the only workers new to the industry. The Kaiser company estimated that only 2 percent of its workers had ever built ships before.[4] The incorporation of masses of inexperienced workers, necessary because of the vast expansion of the industry, was made possible by changes in the organization of work. Before the war, shipbuilding had been a small industry; ships were individually built by skilled workers who served long apprenticeships to learn all aspects of their trades. The war brought standardization of products to the industry, and made preassembly of ships practical. Welding replaced riveting as the means of joining steel plates, because it was faster and easier to learn. These changes, combined with the specialization of tasks, made possible the use of unskilled labor. Detailed planning by management split apart the forty to seventy skills that made a craft, so that each could be learned with a brief period of training. Specialization in the preassembly phase meant that a crew of workers built the same section of a ship over and over. But there were limits on skill breakdown in shipbuilding. The basic skills of cutting, shaping, and joining steel could not be learned as quickly as assembly-line jobs. As F. C. Lane notes: "There was still a considerable range of skills in the shipyards even after scientific management had broken down the jobs."[5]

The unions did not oppose the dilution of skills, because neither wages nor union status was threatened by the change. Craft rules were relaxed to permit workers with limited training to do jobs traditionally reserved for the "first-class mechanic," provided they got the same wages and joined the union. The dues of the new members enriched union treasuries, and closed-shop agreements prevented management from using the job breakdown to undermine the unions. In addition, the old-time craftsmen moved rapidly into foreman and supervisory positions.

Government-funded War Production Training, administered by state and local school boards, enabled new workers to learn specific skills in a short period. Free defense training classes were offered by Portland and Vancouver vocational schools. Soon welding schools were opened in all the major shipyards, and paid trainee programs began in March 1943 to help meet the critical need for more welders. At the peak of the training program, a government agent, Augusta Clawson, enrolled in the Swan Island welding school to discover ways of improving training and reducing turnover, especially among women. At her suggestion, an orientation program for the newly hired was started, which included a special session for women workers conducted by the women's counseling department. A few months later, the turnover rate for women production workers dropped to just slightly above that of men.[6] The training program, coupled with the breakdown of crafts into component parts, made it easy for women and other inexperienced workers to enter shipbuilding.

Another barrier to the employment of women fell when unions admitted women to membership. Workers in the Portland yards, as in most West Coast shipyards, were represented by the American Federation of Labor (AFL) craft unions. Even those conservative unions soon recognized that if women had to be hired in the shipyards, it was preferable that they work under union jurisdiction. In September 1942, the Boilermakers Union, which controlled two-thirds of all shipyard jobs, voted to admit women. This decision came a few months after the first women welders were hired in Portland.[7]

Increasing rapidly from dozens to hundreds to thousands, women became a significant part of the overall labor force in the shipyards. From only 3 percent of the total payroll in January 1942 (all office workers at that point), women grew to 15 percent by January 1943 and to 28 percent a year later. Both total employment and women's employment rose steeply through the end of 1943. During 1944, employment fluctuated because of uncertainty about the future of shipbuilding contracts. The Kaiser yards lost 10,000 workers in the first half of the year, but the percentage of women remained high. A production drive at Oregon Ship and Vancouver in the latter half of the year brought employment up again, and women made up as much as 30 percent of the work force. At this point 28,000 women were working in the Kaiser shipyards and several thousand more in smaller Portland yards.[8]

Women were hired earlier and in greater numbers in Portland than in most of the nation's shipyards. When the U.S. Women's Bureau made visits to forty-one shipyards in the fall of 1943, few had employed women as long as one year, and six had yet to hire women. But in the three Portland-Vancouver Kaiser yards, 27 percent of the employees were women by April 1944; on Swan Island the figure was 32 percent, compared with 18 percent in Kaiser's Richmond, California, yards, and 8 to 10 percent at most eastern shipyards.[9] The main reason was that the sudden growth of shipbuilding in a low-population area created a greater labor shortage than in other areas of the country. Male workers were always the preferred labor force, and women were hired only when it was clear that sufficient men were not available. This point was simply reached sooner in Portland, a small city in a rural state. The eastern shipyards were located near highly populated areas, and they also had most of the nation's trained shipbuilding workers since many of the yards dated from prewar times.

Women entering shipbuilding gained access to high wages, to equal pay, and to jobs from which they had formerly been excluded. Wages in shipbuilding were the highest of any defense industry, averaging $63 a week in September 1943. This reflected the importance of the industry to the war effort. Shipbuilding was also noted for its high proportion of skilled to unskilled workers. Sixty percent of the workers were journeymen, who earned $1.20

an hour as a basic rate. The rest were mostly helpers, earning 95 cents an hour. Wages were set by the job, so women and men in the same job category earned the same pay.[10] Despite the skill breakdown, the crafts that women workers entered involved more interesting and varied work than most jobs available to them in the past. Even the simplest welding job, that of tacking, required two weeks to learn and longer to master; it could provide a sense of accomplishment greater than cleaning houses, waiting on tables, or filing letters. Workers were not tied to one spot, as on an assembly line, but moved about as the work demanded. In addition, women did not enter the industry at the bottom, as is often the case when they move into a formerly male job. The first women hired were welders; only later did women branch out into unskilled helper and laborer jobs, as well as into other crafts.

Recruitment campaigns stressed high wages and the capabilities of women workers. A major mobilization campaign was held in Portland in June 1943, under the auspices of the U.S. Employment Service, the War Manpower Commission, and the Office of Civil Defense. The mayor declared Working Women Win Wars Week, and a door-to-door canvass to find women able to take war jobs was publicized by the local media. Women war workers demonstrated their skills on lathes and other machines in the display windows of downtown department stores.[11] The Kaiser employee publication urged shipyard men to "help your yard lick the manpower problem" by recruiting their wives: "If your wife, or any woman of your acquaintance, is between 18 and 35, not employed in essential industry, active, in good physical condition, and not overweight, tell her about these well-paid welding jobs." Starting at 95 cents an hour during training, welders could earn from $62 a week on day shift to $72 on graveyard.[12]

The importance of women's labor to the war effort was recognized by the creation of government-funded child-care centers. Community-based centers, funded through the Lanham Act, were opened in Portland, Vanport, and Vancouver. Of greater importance to shipyard mothers were the two Kaiser child-service centers, nationally known for their quality and innovations in workplace child care. Located at the shipyard entrance, so parents could drop off their children on their way to work, the centers operated on all three shifts, and could accommodate up to 350 children each. The best child development experts were recruited to run the centers, which became showcases proving that young children could thrive in group care for long hours. Meals and snacks were planned by a well-known nutritionist, and an infirmary cared for mildly ill children. Another notable feature was "home service food," precooked meals that workers could purchase at the child-care centers, take home, and reheat for dinner. High quality child care was made possible by the unusual method of funding: the cost of child care was absorbed by the Maritime Commission when it purchased the ships.[13]

The shipyard child-care centers were a result, not a cause, of the high percentage of women workers. The child-care centers did not open until November 1943, after the period of greatest increase in the female labor force. Although the centers were reputed to be the largest in the world, the number of children cared for was small compared with the total number of women workers. At their peak in the summer of 1944, the Swan Island and Oregon Ship centers cared for a total of more than 700 children. But there were roughly 16,000 women workers in these two yards. The centers provided much-needed services to many shipyard mothers, but they could not have affected the total number of women workers very much.

Women were attracted to shipyard work for a combination of reasons, but high wages was the most important. Many women learned of opportunities for shipyard jobs from their husbands or other friends and relatives already working in the yards. One woman said that she worked in the shipyard "to make money. My husband was working there. We hadn't been married too long, and we decided that if I was going to work I might as well work where the pay was a little more."[14] Women who were the sole support of their families were especially interested in the high wages. A divorced mother of two was working on a Work Projects Administration (WPA) job when the program was phased out because of the war. She was given a choice of training for a shipyard job or of working in a child-care center. She inquired about the pay, found that child care paid $35 a week compared with $62 a week in the yards, and said "I'll take the shipyards."[15]

For some women, the chance to do different or more interesting work was as important as the high wages. One young mother of three followed her husband to Portland from Nebraska when he found a railroad job there. Explaining her interest in welding, she said: "Dad had a blacksmith shop. We lived in the country. I was always around metal and fire burning, drills and the whole bit. I really liked it. Even as a child I'd rather be outside than inside."[16] Another woman was working as an egg candler in Portland when she heard from her husband, a welder, that women were being hired for shipyard work. "I just thought I'd like to weld," she said. "That was the reason I went. I just wanted to."[17]

Concern about the war was also a factor, especially for those women who had relatives in the service. A woman from Oklahoma said, "I came out here because I had three sons and a son-in-law in service and I felt like I should be doing something to help." But she also noted that the wages were much higher than in her factory job, and that it was a chance for her to make a change in her life: "I wanted to get away. I was a widow, my family was raised. I thought this would be a good opportunity for me to do something different."[18]

WOMEN'S WORK IN A MAN'S WORLD

Women's entry into shipbuilding challenged the sexual division of labor and traditional notions of femininity. The first woman office worker at Oregon Ship recalled in a 1944 interview that "for more than a year, no woman was allowed to walk along the ways or in any construction area for fear she would be injured." A cartoon in the shipyard newspaper in the spring of 1942 ridiculed the notion that women might be hired in production work, picturing housewives in aprons and high heels ineptly handling machinery.[19] Although some men had declared they would walk out if women were hired, no one actually did. The first women welders were stared at, whistled at, and then grudgingly accepted as a war necessity.

But uneasiness about women's new work roles remained. Rumors that welding caused sterility in women were persistent, reflecting a concern that women were losing their femininity. Strict dress regulations for women were based as much on "principles of concealment and sexless propriety as on concern for safety," according to Katherine Archibald, a sociologist who worked in a California shipyard for two years. "Like soldiers infiltrating enemy lines, women in the shipyards had to be camouflaged lest the difference in sex be unduly noted and emphasized," she wrote.[20]

Regardless of how men felt about it, women were doing men's work, and doing it quite well. Only six months after the first women welders were hired, a study comparing male and female welders in all seven Kaiser shipyards showed that women nearly equaled men in productivity. In the fall of 1942 the shipyard newspaper described a woman who had outwelded all the men on her crew doing difficult overhead welding on the hull of the ship. Women soon entered other jobs in the yard. By the end of 1942, women at Oregon Ship were working as burners, crane operators, duplicators, electricians, expediters, machinists, reamers, riggers, shipfitters, laborers, and helpers in eleven different crafts. In June 1943, they were rapidly replacing men as truck and delivery car drivers. Soon there were few job categories without women.[21]

Although barriers were clearly broken, it is necessary to ask a further question: To what extent were women doing the same work as men? Studies have shown the prevalence of segregation by sex in the labor force, and its remarkable persistence over time, despite changes in the occupational structure and in the sex composition of particular jobs.[22] As the shortage of male labor pulled

Iona Murphy, a welder in assembly building, Oregon Shipbuilding Corporation, November 1942 *(courtesy Oregon Historical Society, OrHi 56117)*

Alberta Delano and Orrel Weidman at the drill press at the Commercial Iron Works electric shop, March 1943 *(courtesy Oregon Historical Society)*

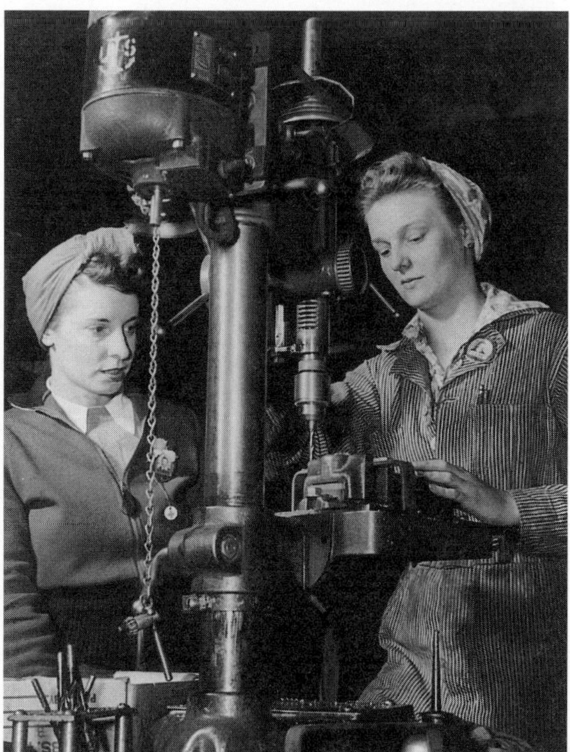

women into the shipyards, were they hired in the same jobs as men? Or were they channeled into some types of work and not others?

The extent of difference between women's and men's jobs can be measured by an index of segregation. This index compares the occupational distribution of the two groups, and tells the percentage of the labor force that would have to change jobs in order to create an equal distribution of jobs by sex. For example, in a situation of equality, if 20 percent of the men were welders, then 20 percent of the women would be welders also. An index of segregation was calculated for each of the three Kaiser shipyards, based on data collected by the War Manpower Commission in 1942 and 1943. The amount of segregation was substantial. Approximately half of all women or all men working in the shipyards would have had to change jobs in order to equalize the occupational distribution of women and men.[23]

In order to understand why this occurred, it is necessary to look at the kinds of jobs women held. A careful examination of the data for all three yards revealed that in general women were overrepresented as welders and underrepresented as journeymen in the other major crafts. Women were overrepresented as helpers and laborers; in some of the unskilled jobs, nearly all the workers were women.

The reasons so many women were welders are fairly clear. As the War Manpower Commission report put it, "Welding is the craft that has absorbed most women—mainly because of the urgent need for thousands of welders in modern shipbuilding, but also because women can be trained for welding more easily than most other shipbuilding jobs" (WMC 1:51). The demand for welders was always high, because virtually all joining of steel was done by welders. Speed of production thus depended more on the availability of sufficient welders than on any other group of workers. The skill breakdown and the paid, in-plant trainee program made it easy to recruit and train women in this craft. After two weeks of training, novice welders could be put to work in the yard as tackers, making temporary welds to hold pieces in place until the seams were fully joined by production welders. It was the demand for more welders that first opened shipbuilding work to women, and at first women were hired only for this job. Thus it is not surprising that women were highly concentrated in this craft. Although women were a significant percentage of all welders (over 40 percent at Swan Island in the summer of 1943), welding was never a predominately female job. A comparison of data for the three yards, collected at different times, shows that the overrepresentation of women as welders decreased as the number of jobs in which women were employed increased.[24]

When women entered crafts other than welding, they remained a small percentage of their craft and of all women workers. The reasons for this are less clear-cut, but some examples of women working in crafts that remained overwhelmingly male suggest possible explanations. It was very easy for women to become welders, but to enter other crafts sometimes required a great deal of persistence and initiative on the part of the woman, and in some cases the cooperation of male co-workers.

The first full-fledged "loftlady," promoted to her job in December 1943, was an example of persistence as well as special ability. A former housewife, she went to shipfitting school and did so well that she was encouraged to take courses in loft training. After one day in the mold loft (where templates, or patterns for pieces of the ship were made), she decided she needed more training. After 200 additional hours of training at Vancouver High, she went back to work in the loft. The superintendent assigned her to the office for some time, where she checked detail prints with structural changes. She showed such ability that she was promoted. It was almost unheard of for a woman to become a loftsman, according to the shipyard newspaper, because "not one woman in a thousand has become interested enough in mechanical craftsmanship to equal her ability."[25]

The only woman who did wiring atop the 50-foot masts of the Liberty ships came to the yard as an electrician's helper. She asked for the job climbing the masts, agreeing that if she failed to do the job as well as a man, they could replace her. She was still on her job, and liked it, over a year later. This confident young woman lived on a ranch with her parents, and hoped for a career in aviation after the war. An article entitled "Slender Blonde Does Good Job as Rigger" told the story of another atypical woman, one of only three who had successfully tackled that job. Riggers were usually "husky ex-lumberjacks," and their job was to attach loads to cranes and then guide the crane operator with hand signals. She attributed her success to the cooperation of a fellow worker. "I never could have made the grade if it hadn't been for Joe Harris, the other crew member. He taught me a lot of tricks in rigging to take the place of the brawn a woman rigger doesn't have."[26] Presumably, women not fortunate enough to work with a "good Joe" had a more difficult time.

Hierarchies of pay and of responsibility may also have played a part in limiting women's access to certain jobs. While most journeymen earned a basic rate of $1.20 an hour, in some crafts, presumably those requiring greater skill, the pay was $1.33. Loftsman was one such job, and as the example cited above shows, only a woman of exceptional ability and persistence was able to break the barrier to this craft. A similar job was layer-out in the mold loft, which also paid $1.33 an hour. The account of one woman who was finally able to transfer from welding to layout suggests that it was not a lack of ability that kept women out, but a desire to maintain a male monopoly on a good job. She described the work as follows: "They have patterns and you lay them out on steel, then trace around them to cut out parts for the ship. It's just like making a dress." She needed no extra training to do this job well, because she found her high school home economics background in pattern making sufficient. As she put it, "Patterns are patterns." The mold loft would have been a logical place for the shipyards to make use of women's traditional skills. But few women worked there. The reason, according to this woman, was that "the men who were qualified layout people felt that they should get the jobs because they were men."[27]

Even when there was no wage differential, the work relationships between crafts may have influenced the placement of women. In her book based on her experience working at Swan Island, Augusta Clawson noted that welders had a "strange status" in the shipyard: "Shipfitters and shipwrights often cannot go on with their jobs until a spot has been fixed by a chipper, burner, or welder. The consequence is that they are always yelling for us. 'Come and tack this!'—or 'Burn that'—or 'Chip this.' It gives the impression that we are working for them although we are really on the same pay and job."[28] Frequently the welders and burners were women. Chipping was not done by women, but it was often done by black men. In contrast, only 10 percent of the shipfitters at Swan Island were women, and there were no women shipwrights. Jobs that involved directing the work of others may have been considered more appropriate for men. And women may have shared this attitude. Clawson recorded her experience working with a woman shipfitter whom she described as a "slave-driver."

Basically, however, in all crafts where the supply of men was sufficient, barriers to the employment of women journeymen remained. Because welders were needed, the shipyards made it easy for women to enter that craft; paid trainee programs were located right in the shipyard. But training in many other crafts was less conveniently located, lasted longer, and was not paid. Women with an immediate need for income preferred entering the yards as helpers or trainees. Many women learned of job possibilities in other crafts only after they had become welders, and it was often difficult to transfer. To enter other crafts often took special efforts, skills, or good luck.

Aside from welding, there was a concentration of women in helpers' jobs. Forty-two percent of all women at Swan Island and 50 percent at Vancouver were helpers. In both these yards, the occupational data were collected at a time when the number of women employed was approaching its peak. The data from Oregon Ship, in contrast, represented an earlier phase. At the end of 1942, only 8 percent of Oregon Ship's production workers were women, and the majority of them were welders. At the other yards in 1943, more women were helpers than were in any other category. Thus the expansion of job opportunities for women took place in large part in the unskilled categories. While a greater variety of skilled jobs were held by women in 1943 than in 1942, most women entered unskilled jobs.

Why were so many women helpers? The reason is suggested by a quotation from the War Manpower Commission report, which noted that "women have been filling gaps in increasing numbers where men are not available or not willing to accept this kind of employment" (WMC 2:29). Apparently, as the labor shortage grew more severe, it was difficult to find male workers for the low-wage, unskilled jobs. One woman who worked as a tank cleaner commented that "the men didn't want to do menial jobs anyway. They wanted money. They'd go for electrician or welding."[29]

Some of the unskilled job categories were filled almost entirely by women. In an industry in which all work had previously been done by men, and in which women were a minority of the labor force, the existence of any job category that was predominately female is significant. It suggests that such jobs were now identified as "women's work." For example, laborers were 80 percent female at Vancouver and 90 percent female at Swan Island. A detailed job breakdown for Vancouver, in which helpers were identified by crafts, revealed eleven jobs that were over 60 percent female, and three in which women constituted over 90 percent of the workers. Fully one-quarter of all women workers were found in these three "women's jobs": painter helper, tool checker, and shipwright helper (WMC 3:22).

Why were women channeled into some unskilled jobs rather than others? Sometimes the nature of the work, not always reflected in the job title, lent itself to sex stereotyping. The job of sweeper, for example, did not appear in any occupational classification. Sweepers were hired as laborers, shipwright helpers, and boilermaker helpers. The reason nearly all laborers at two of the yards were women, and most shipwright helpers were women in another, may have been that their actual job was sweeping. Sometimes women ended up sweeping regardless of their job title or training: "In the plate shop all new women employees start with the crew of 150 women who sweep up and clean up in that area. Regardless of experience or ultimate job desired, if the new employee is a woman, her first job is sweeping."[30]

Older women were often found in these unskilled jobs. The division of labor by age may have intensified the division based on sex, since older men were more likely to have had access to some skills or training that could be useful in the shipyards. The preferred age for women welder trainees was eighteen to thirty-five, so women over thirty-five often found themselves in helper or laborer jobs. While less skilled than welding, these jobs were not necessarily light and easy. Augusta Clawson noted that a number of women in her welding class had started as laborers. "Apparently they were terribly overworked," she wrote. "They were paid 88 cents an hour and had to pick up and carry heavy metal all day. Lots of women have quit such jobs."[31] Other women, accustomed to hard work and chores considered menial by others, were proud of their endurance. A sixty-five-year-old woman who "picked up used rod and emptied skiffs on the ways" didn't miss a day's work during the hard winter of 1943–44. "I came here from my own farm in Idaho that I worked myself," she said, "and I guess I'm used to hard work and cold weather."[32] Another woman, who worked as a scaler, scraping welded seams smooth, said: "When you bring up ten children, you work hard and you do a lot of things that aren't pleasant. This job is helping to win the war, and I feel I'm doing my bit."[33]

The separation between men's work and women's work in the shipyards may have been greater than is indicated by the data on occupational distribution. Evidence suggests that within the same job categories, women and men were doing different types of work, with the women concentrated in the less-skilled, more routine aspects of the job. This is most clear in the case of welding, where the distinction between tackers and welders lent itself to a sex-based division of labor. Frequent references to tackers as women in a variety of sources suggest that women were more likely to be tack-welders, never moving on to more skilled types of welding. Most women electricians were probably wiring lights in the electrical shops, rather than installing them on the ships.[34]

There are other indications that women and men in the same jobs were doing different work. A report on labor requirements listed workers needed both by craft and by sex. Why did Swan Island need 215 *male* welders and 166 *female* welders that week, unless they were to be assigned to different types of work? (WMC 2:28). Women were typically pictured in all-women crews in the shipyard newspapers, and most women interviewed said they had worked in all-female crews. While this practice sometimes contributed to women's solidarity as they entered a male-dominated workplace, it may also have reflected a difference in the type of work done by women.

Traditional distinctions between the sexes were maintained in the matter of promotion to supervisory positions. Although there was an acute shortage of supervisory personnel, women were rarely considered suitable for promotion. The War Manpower Commission report noted that "the increase in the proportion of marginal and women workers due to the draft and other causes had materially reduced the supply of leader material" (WMC 1:63).

Helper and laborer leadwomen were the main exception. All forty-five leadwomen and the only forewoman at Swan Island were supervising helpers or laborers. At Vancouver, 68 percent of helper leadmen were women. The probable reason there were leadwomen over helpers and laborers crews is that they earned less than the average journeyman's wage; laborer leadmen, for example, earned $1.15 at the most.[35] In addition, they were supervising mostly women in those jobs.

Sometimes women were promoted in the crafts. Welding was the obvious job where leadwomen might be expected, since women had begun welding earlier than any other craft. A woman pictured in the shipyard newspaper in the fall of 1942 was identified as a welder leadwoman. But by the time the occupational data for the War Manpower Commission reports were collected, there were no welder leadwomen. A former welding leadman said that men objected when several women were promoted, even though they were on all-women crews. "There was quite a little friction over that," he said. "The men resented it very much. Some of them were oldtime welders and had to take a back seat to these women."[36] Other women who were interviewed recalled no leadwomen on welding crews. "There was absolutely no hope of a woman going in as a leadman," said one former welder. "That was strictly male."[37] One exception was a crew of women welders at one of the smaller shipyards that had a leadwoman and a female welding instructor. But that was not until mid-1944, and it was the first such crew in that yard.[38]

Even more exceptional was a machinist leadwoman, since few women were even journeymen in that craft. She and her crew of eight men and five women were responsible for installing locks on steel doors, and similar tasks. The shipyard newspaper pointed out that she was probably the only woman on the West Coast to hold down a job of that kind. Not surprising, she liked her job, and said, "If there is any place for me after this war is over, I'd like to continue in this type of work."[39]

In general, the pattern of job segregation may be summarized as follows: Women were overrepresented as unskilled workers, and in some of these jobs nearly all the workers were women. Women were underrepresented as journeymen, except in welding. Women were promoted to leadman only over helpers and laborers, with a few exceptions. In addition, women and men in the same job categories may have been doing different types of work. The barriers that channeled women into some jobs rather than others were not rigid, however, and women with exceptional talent or persistence could gain access to most shipyard jobs.

The labor shortage broke the barrier to employment of women, and women entered welding because of the critical demand for workers in this craft. In general, women were hired to fill gaps where the supply of men was insufficient. The gaps increasingly were in the unskilled, lower-wage jobs, some of which became "women's jobs." The skill breakdown and the training programs, which made it easy to utilize women's labor, also facilitated the development of sex-based segregation in shipyard jobs.

Despite the opportunities that shipbuilding offered to women, in the form of high wages (even as helpers), and access to new jobs and skills (even diluted skills), the pattern of men's work and women's work reasserted itself. While women welders challenged traditional conceptions of appropriate work for women, the principle that men and women are fundamentally different kinds of workers was maintained in the organization of shipyard work.

POSTWAR PLANS AND REALITIES

How did women feel about their shipyard jobs? Surveys showed that half of them wanted to keep their war jobs. In September 1943, one shipyard newspaper asked women to fill out "coupons" stating whether or not they wanted to keep their present jobs after the war. The results, reported in a Portland newspaper, revealed that "women welders were 60 percent for staying in overalls. Other women workers, ranging from electricians to tarp sewers, were 50% for staying on the job." A sheet-metal worker interviewed by a reporter said, "I hate to think of leaving $65 a week to come back to dishes and diapers." This expressed the feelings of many women. However, neither the number nor percentage of women workers who responded to the voluntary survey was recorded.[40]

A comprehensive survey of workers at the Kaiser shipyards, conducted in January 1944, produced a similar finding. Nine-tenths of the yards' 91,000 workers were interviewed concerning their postwar plans. Of the women, 53 percent said they wanted to continue in industrial work, 8 percent were undecided, and the rest planned to seek other jobs or to return home. That fall, the women's counseling department at Oregon Ship found that 45 percent of the women wanted to continue in the same type of work after the war. They had interviewed 872 women, probably one-tenth of the total. Did the 8 percent drop represent a real change of opinion? It is difficult to know. The shipyard newspaper pointed out that the figure was quite high, considering that the yard had been on a seven-day week for the past three months. In any case, it is more important that three different types of surveys at three different times produced roughly similar results.[41]

Despite their desire to continue in industrial work, it soon became clear that there would be no place for women in "men's jobs" after the war. Shortly after V-E Day, an article in the shipyard newspaper proclaimed "The Kitchen—Women's Big Post-War Goal." What women really wanted, the article stated, was to "put aside the welder's torch" and give it back to the men. They wanted to get out of their "unfeminine" work clothes and look for a "vine-covered cottage," where they could put up frilly curtains and grow geraniums. The message was emphasized by a drawing of a woman in work clothes and tin hat racing home, reappearing dressed in ruffled apron and high heels, washing dishes and singing gaily while two angry children fought at her feet. The article was supposedly based on interviews with one hundred women in the yards. Of the sixty-five women who were working in nonclerical jobs, there were only seven who "stated flatly that the home life had no appeal for them and that they would stay in industry if given half a chance." This drastic change of opinion is understandable, however, given the conditions of the interviews. The article noted that men kept interrupting the questions to insist, "They ought to go home. Women haven't any business trying to do men's work," and that many women agreed with these remarks because it was "a time-honored way of satisfying the male ego." In general, the women were reported to be "philosophical about the fact that there will probably be no place for them in industry doing the tasks ordinarily performed by men after the war."[42]

When the war with Japan ended in August 1945, shipyard production declined rapidly. Cancellations of Navy and Maritime Commission contracts for ships led to heavy layoffs. From 65,000 workers on August 1, the shipyards were down to 25,000 by October. A year later, only 4,500 remained. Ship repair, conversion, "mothballing," and scrapping operations kept some shipyard workers employed for a while. But these jobs were reserved for men. The last three women welders at Oregon Ship got their "quit-slips" at the end of October 1945. A few women remained in unskilled jobs. A tank cleaner worked at Oregon Ship until it closed, then worked at a small shipyard through December 1946. "I was the last housekeeper there," she said.[43]

Women's work in the shipyards had come to an end. The child-care centers at Oregon Ship and Swan Island closed abruptly on September 1, 1945. The enrollment had been declining for several months, reflecting layoffs of women before the war ended. One of the centers became an elementary school, but a proposal to keep a small preschool program was vetoed by the school board. As a result of a national campaign, government-funded centers got their support extended to March 1946. But the purpose of child-care funding was to aid production for the war effort, and the emergency was over.[44]

In the job market, old lines were redrawn. Job opportunities were clearly differentiated by sex, age, and race, and skills acquired in the shipyards were discounted. Employers were becoming "choosy." Once willing to hire anyone because of the labor shortage, many now specified "not over 45 years, male, and white." There was a demand for skilled mechanics, but employers were interested in prewar skills: "The quickly acquired skills of the lush shipyard days are a drug on the market. Inside electricians who pushed a yellow or red wire through a hole, or [those] who sprayed paint on a ship or were emergency welders are not considered skilled according to the yardstick of employers."[45] This automatically excluded women, whose only access to the skilled trades had been in the shipyards.

The jobs available to women were in traditionally female areas, at wages considerably lower than those in the shipyards. The governor's postwar planning commission noted that the war had ended at a good time, when Oregon's seasonal industries could absorb many of the unemployed: "Fruit and vegetable canneries especially favor female help." A year later, women on the night shift in the canneries earned 85 cents an hour, while men earned $1 for "harder duties." In December 1945, there were few job openings in the higher-paid brackets, but there were plenty of jobs for 65 cents an hour. At the end of 1946, women trained as stenographers, nurses, and office workers were needed. "An equal demand is for domestics and laundry workers, with few accepting those jobs."[46]

Women's unemployment after the war was dismissed as unimportant because of the convenient belief that all women were "housewives" who didn't really need to work. In September 1945, 60 percent of Oregon's unemployment claims were filed by women. As late as March 1946, it was noted that "more women than men from the shipyards are filing claims each week. This was anticipated, for housewives who worked in the shipyards or aircraft industries have returned to their domestic affairs, but they are not over-looking any checks that may be coming to them."[47] In fact, no more than 40 percent of shipyard women listed their previous occupation as housewife, and many of them needed to continue working after the war.[48] Statistics showed that "84% of American working women in 1944 and 1945 were employed because of economic necessity and were self-supporting and/or financially responsible for other members of their family."[49]

What actually happened to women shipyard workers after the war? No systematic records were kept. Unions, which lost thousands of members in a few months, did not make any checks on what had happened to their former members. It was assumed that these people had left the state or, in the case of women, had "returned to their household duties." But the pattern is clear: women were pushed back into "women's work," whether in the home or in traditionally female-employing industries.[50] Examples from interviews illustrate the process. One black woman, who had been a scaler in the shipyard, was unemployed for several months after the war. She finally found seasonal work picking chickens and turkeys in a poultry factory, then worked in a laundry for the next nine years. A young mother of three had to quit welding when the night shift at her yard shut down. She and her husband had managed child care by working on different shifts. For the next five years, she was mostly at home, and had several more children, but managed to work off and on as a waitress, in a knitting mill, and in a department store. Then she found full-time work as a meat wrapper, a job she held for the next twenty-two years. A middle-aged widow, who had earned $1.20 an hour as a shipyard electrician, returned to her prewar job as an elevator operator at 25 cents an hour. She had to sell her house in order to survive.[51] The line between women's work and men's work had been reestablished; not until the early 1970s would women have access to those jobs again.[52]

The wartime demand for labor briefly opened new opportunities to women. Barriers to the skilled trades fell, and women entered shipbuilding, the highest-paying defense industry. Access to skills and high wages was especially great in the Portland shipyards, which hired women earlier and in greater numbers than most of the nation's shipyards. The importance of women's labor was recognized by the creation of model child-care centers at two Kaiser shipyards, demonstrating that high-quality workplace child care was possible, given sufficient resources.

Although women's entry into shipbuilding challenged the sexual division of labor, the basic distinction between men's work and women's work was not altered. To a great extent, women and men in the shipyards were doing different types of jobs. Women filled in where men were unavailable or unwilling to work. Thus women were concentrated in welding and in the unskilled helper jobs. Within the crafts, they were often assigned to the more routine operations. The same skill breakdown and in-plant training programs that eased the employment of women also helped channel them into certain types of jobs. That job segregation by sex persisted in the midst of dramatic changes in the type of work done by women suggests its importance as a structural feature of the labor force.

Although shipyard jobs were sometimes arduous and routine, many women preferred them to their prewar work. Half of all women shipyard workers hoped to continue in industrial jobs after the war. But employers' preferences for young white men with prewar skills confined women to the low-paying jobs where they had always been found. Women's unemployment was disguised and discounted by the myth that all women war workers were "housewives" whose husbands could support them. In reality, however, the segregated job market ensured a plentiful supply of cheap female labor for seasonal industries like the food-processing plants in Oregon and for the post-war expansion of clerical and service jobs.

While the war did create some preconditions for greater equality between women and men at work, such as equal pay, child care, and access to new skills, the changes were temporary. In an economy in which full employment was possible only during a war, and in the absence of a self-conscious women's movement, or of an effective labor movement willing to defend the rights of working women, there was little chance of consolidating these gains.[53] Women were temporary substitutes for men in a labor shortage. Like farm women helping out at harvest time, women in industry could do "men's work" when necessary, but it remained "men's work."

NOTES

Reprinted from Carol R. Berkin and Clara M. Lovett, eds., *Women, War and Revolution,* by permission of the publisher, Holmes & Meier Publishers, Inc., 30 Irving Place, New York, NY 10003. Copyright 1980 by Holmes & Meier.

1. U.S. War Manpower Commission, *A Survey of Shipyard Operations in the Portland, Oregon, Metropolitan Area* (Portland, 1943), 3 vols. (hereafter cited as WMC 1, 2, or 3).

2. Kaiser Industries Corp., *The Kaiser Story* (Oakland, Calif., 1968); Vanport City, Oregon Schools, *6000 Kids from 46 States* (Portland, 1946); U.S. Bureau of the Census, *Population,* Aug. 12, 1944, series CA-2, no. 6.

3. "Yards to Give Women Jobs," *Oregonian,* Jan. 30, 1942; *Bo's'n's Whistle,* May 7, 1942, p. 6. *Bo's'n's Whistle* (hereafter cited as *BW* with appropriate date) was the employee publication for the Kaiser shipyards in Portland. "Kaiser Shipyards Lead U.S. in Employment of Women," *Oregonian,* April 27, 1944.

4. Kaiser Industries Corp., *The Kaiser Story,* p. 31.

5. Frederick C. Lane, *Ships for Victory* (Baltimore: Johns Hopkins Press, 1951), p. 239.

6. WMC 2:45–46. See also Oregon State Board of Education, Division of Vocational Education, "Descriptive Report of Vocational Training for War Production Workers," 1945; WMC 1, 2, and 3; Augusta Clawson, *Shipyard Diary of a Woman Welder* (New York: Penguin Books, 1944).

7. Paul R. Porter, "Labor in the Shipbuilding Industry," in Colston E. Warne et al., eds., *Yearbook of American Labor* (New York: Philosophical Library, 1945), pp. 345–60; "Boilermakers to Admit Women in Ranks of Union," *Oregon Labor Press,* Sept. 25, 1942.

8. “Employment in the Three Kaiser Yards,” *BW,* Jan. 14, 1944, pp. 4–5; “Employment Rolls Stable in 1944: Personnel Nears ’43 Peak as Workers Heed War Demands,” *BW,* Dec. 29, 1944, p. 3.

9. Dorothy K. Newman, “Employing Women in Shipyards,” Women’s Bureau *Bulletin,* 1944, 192-6; *Oregonian,* Jan. 30, 1942.

10. Porter, “Labor in Shipbuilding”; Oregon Shipbuilding Corp., “Occupational Codes and Classifications,” 1945; “Ladies in Overalls,” *BW,* Sept. 27, 1942, p. 18.

11. “Civilian Defense Leaders Open Women-in-War Drive,” *Oregonian,* June 22, 1943.

12. “How You Can Help Your Yard Lick the Manpower Problem,” *BW,* June 3, 1943, p. 3.

13. Carol Slobodin, “When the U.S. Paid for Daycare,” *Day Care and Early Education* (Sept.-Oct. 1975): 23–25; Kaiser Corp. Inc., Portland Yards and Oregon Shipbuilding Corp. Child Service Centers, “Final Report, 1943–45.”

14. Interview 14, Beaverton, Oregon, May 16, 1976. The author interviewed a number of former shipyard workers in 1976. The original tapes and transcriptions of these interviews are now available at the Oregon Historical Society, Portland.

15. Interview 7, Portland, Oregon, Feb. 14, 1976.

16. Interview 8, Portland, Oregon, Feb. 15, 1976.

17. Interview 22, Lake Oswego, Oregon, June 20, 1976.

18. Interview 6, Beaverton, Oregon, Feb. 14, 1976.

19. “OSC Yard Opening Recalled by Woman,” *BW,* Sept. 29, 1944, p. 4; *BW,* March 26, 1942, p. 8.

20. Katherine Archibald, *Wartime Shipyard: A Study in Social Disunity* (Berkeley: University of California Press, 1947), p. 22. Rumors of sterility are mentioned by Clawson, and in *BW,* June 3, 1943.

21. Kaiser Corp. Inc., Richmond Shipyard No. 3, “Women in Shipbuilding,” Jan. 1, 1943; “Mabel Can’t Do That to Us,” *BW,* Nov. 5, 1942, p. 9; WMC 1:26; “Woman Power in the Three Kaiser Shipyards,” *BW,* June 17, 1943.

22. For example, see Edward Gross, “‘Plus Ça Change . . . ?’ The Sexual Structure of Occupations Over Time,” *Social Problems 16* (Fall 1968): 198–208.

23. Data from WMC 1, 2, and 3. Index based on eighteen major job categories, excluding office workers. Results were: Oregon Ship, 55 percent; Swan Island, 48 percent; Vancouver, 57 percent. For explanation of index of segregation, see Gross, “‘Plus Ça Change . . . ?’”

24. Comparing the percentage of all women with the percentage of all workers who were welders, women were overrepresented as welders by 28 percent at Oregon Ship in December 1942, by 11 percent at Swan Island in August 1943, and by only 2 percent at Vancouver in October 1943.

25. "Loftlady," *BW*, Dec. 23, 1943, p. 12.

26. "High Climber," *BW*, Jan. 28, 1944, p. 13; "Slender Blonde Does Good Job as Rigger," *BW*, Sept. 29, 1944, p. 4.

27. Interview 10, Portland, Oregon, May 14, 1976.

28. "'Gus' Comes Back: Welder-Author Visitor," *BW*, May 12, 1944, p. 2; Clawson, *Shipyard Diary*, p. 123.

29. Interview 23, Portland, Oregon, July 11, 1976 (wife in a joint interview).

30. "The Story of 130 Dozen Brooms," *BW*, May 20, 1943, pp. 10–11.

31. Clawson, *Shipyard Diary*, p. 48.

32. "Hard Job 'Natural' for Idaho Woman," *BW*, Sept. 29, 1944, p. 4.

33. "These and All Shipbuilding Mothers Honored May 14," *BW*, May 12, 1944, p. 1.

34. References to women as tackers from interviews, Clawson, *BW;* to women as inside electricians from interview 5, Portland, Oregon, Feb. 13, 1976, and Postwar Readjustment and Development Commission (PRDC), "Progress Report," November 1945.

35. Oregon Shipbuilding Corp., "Occupational Codes and Classifications," 1945.

36. Interview 23 (husband in a joint interview).

37. Interview 7.

38. "All-Women Welding Crew," *Stem to Stern*, June 2, 1944, p. 7.

39. "Machinist Leadwoman Position Unusual Job for Woman," *BW* (Vancouver), Dec. 15, 1944.

40. "Women at WISCO," *Stem to Stern*, Sept. 9, 1943; Ellen Mills Ewing, "Postwar Poser: Pants or Aprons?" *Oregonian*, Nov. 21, 1943 (magazine section).

41. Two-thirds of all shipyard workers hoped to continue in industrial work. "Workers Shy Postwar Plans," *BW*, March 10, 1944, p. 7; "Many Women Plan to Stay in Industry," *BW*, Nov. 24, 1944, p. 3.

42. BW, May 11, 1945, p. 7.

43. PRDC, August 1945, October 1945; Oregon State Employment Service, "Analysis of Oregon Labor Market," October 1947; "Women Welders Out," *BW*, Nov. 2, 1945, p. 8; interview 23.

44. Child Service Centers, "Final Report"; Minutes and Reports of the Day Care Committee, Portland Council of Social Agencies, 1945; Howard Dratch, "The Politics of Child Care in the 1940s," *Science and Society* 38 (Summer 1974): 167–204.

45. PRDC, October 1945; PRDC, December 1945, p. 5.

46. PRDC, August 1945, p. 3; PRDC, September 1946; PRDC, November 1946, p. 3.

47. PRDC, September 1945; PRDC, March 1946, p. 6.

48. The figure of 40 percent former housewives is derived from the report that 11

percent of all shipyard workers listed "housewife" as previous occupation. Other listed occupations were not broken down by sex. From *BW,* March 10, 1944, p. 7.

49 Lyn Goldfarb, *Separated and Unequal: Discrimination Against Women Workers After World War II* (Washington, D.C.: Union for Radical Political Economics, n.d. [prob. 1976]), unpaginated, quotation from 11th page.

50. PRDC, November 1945.

51. Interview 12, Portland, Oregon, May 15, 1976; interview 8; interview 5.

52. Several women interviewed had returned to welding in Portland shipyards in the early 1970s.

53. Even a progressive union like the UAW did not defend the jobs of its women members. See Goldfarb, *Separated and Unequal.*

PART 4
RACE AND ETHNICITY

Job and other opportunities have been far more limited for women of color than for white women. Severe discrepancies have existed, and continue to exist, in housing, education, income, and health care. For all but a handful of women of color, leisure time to agitate for political rights or municipal reform has been almost impossible to come by. At the same time that the inequities are being documented, however, new research is revealing additional, affirmative dimensions to the history of people of color. This approach celebrates the distinguishing aspects of black, Native American, Hispanic, and Asian cultures. Furthermore, this endeavor can uncover alternate role models, particularly among the women who have shouldered the double burdens of racism and sexism.

Sylvia Van Kirk examines Native American women and fur traders on the North American coast, when our current Pacific Northwest fell under the dominion of the English Hudson's Bay Company. She reminds us that, until the mid-nineteenth century, both the United States and England claimed the region. She also documents a staggering number of ways that Native American women assisted visiting fur traders to succeed at their work and enjoy comfortable lives in the late eighteenth and early nineteenth centuries. She catalogs women's economic services, including trapping marten for pelts, making moccasins and snowshoes, preserving meat, preparing fish or pemmican, and hunting rabbits and partridge for food. Native American women collected berries, wild rice, roots, and gum, made maple sugar, paddled and steered canoes, planted, and harvested. In addition, they washed and cleaned, spoke several languages, and served as interpreters, diplomats, and peace makers. They were also wives of trappers, mothers of children, and consumers of kettles, cloth, knives, needles, and axes. If they have been invisible in the textbooks, they were not invisible to their communities.

The anthropologist Lillian A. Ackerman observes women's roles within Native American culture in "Sexual Equality on the Colville Indian Reservation in Traditional and Contemporary Contexts." She conducted numerous interviews, including forty-five with elders aged sixty to ninety, from eleven tribes (Sanpoil, Nespelem, Colville, Lakes, Southern Okanogan, Methow, Chelan, Entiat, Columbia, Wenatchi, and one band of Nez Perce). She finds great differences between Indian and Euro-American women's sexual equality. Contrasting the reminiscences of the 1920–30 era with descriptions of modern life and tribal arrangements, she notes real changes in politics, economy, religion, and domestic life. Nevertheless, the women of both eras experienced equal access, or a different but balanced access to power, authority, and autonomy. The author perceives that women on the Colville Reservation have not had in the past, and do not have now, the secondary status in key realms of life experience that has been accorded women in mainstream society.

Jerry García provides us with an overview of a Chicana's experiences in the Northwest since the 1940s. He conducted an oral history interview with Texas-born Dora Sánchez Treviño (b. 1947), a Chicana who has lived in the agricultural community of Quincy, Washington, since 1963. Reading her own words and the analysis García provides, we meet a woman who has occupied many roles in the last half-century—daughter, wife, mother, widow, student, housekeeper, Roman Catholic, Democrat, union activist, dental assistant, agricultural worker, teacher's aide, social worker, restaurant operator, child-care worker, and, in 1978–79, councilwoman. She has also worked through voluntary organizations, including LAA (Latin American Association) and PLUMA (Progressive League of United Mexican Americans), to improve living and working conditions for Chicanos in Quincy. The many roles she plays in her complex life sometimes intersect and sometimes work at cross purposes.

There are great hazards in relying on sweeping generalizations about immigrants. A multiplicity of forces shaped the experiences of various newcomers to this land. The individual's sex, age, nationality, religion and marital status, experiences abroad, migration patterns in America, societal tolerance for their upward mobility through schools, jobs, and neighborhoods, the level of prosperity in the adopted community, its rural or urban character, the time period of arrival—all exerted some influence. Our tired assumptions—that most immigrant women were housebound and dependent, that they functioned as preservers of Old World traditions and resisted change, and that rural transplants to urban centers continued to bear many children, more than they could support—clearly have a limited usefulness. Here, actually, they distract us from the facts. The broad lesson, then, is one of caution. Let us avoid a disregard for the ethnic diversity that was and remains broad.

The two essays drawing on oral histories prove that interviews can be a valuable source for researchers, documenting activities unrecorded elsewhere. The route to personal reminiscence is accessible; anyone with curiosity can collect material from willing subjects. Yet interviews are troublesome too, for they leave the reader uncertain of the ways in which the subject is unique or representative of her time. For that reason, we are grateful to García and Ackerman for substantiating original transcripts and analysis with additional source material from newspapers, yearbooks, the census, and the scholarly literature.

The Role of Native Women in the Creation of Fur Trade Society in Western Canada, 1670–1830

SYLVIA VAN KIRK

In essence the history of the early Canadian West is the history of the fur trade. For nearly two hundred years, from the founding of the Hudson's Bay Company in 1670 until the transfer of Rupert's Land to the newly created dominion of Canada in 1870, the fur trade was the dominant force in shaping the history of what are today Canada's four western provinces.

This long and unified experience gave rise in western Canada to a frontier society that seems to have been unique in the realm of interracial contact. Canada's western history has been characterized by relatively little violent conflict between Indian and white. I would like to suggest two major reasons why this was so. First, by its very nature, the Canadian fur trade was predicated on mutual exchange and dependency between Indian and white. The Indian not only trapped the fur pelts but also provided the market for European goods. Until very recently, the fur trade has been viewed as an all-male affair, but new research has revealed that Indian women played an active role in promoting this trade. Although the men were the hunters of beaver and large game animals, the women were responsible for trapping smaller fur-bearing animals, especially the marten, with its highly prized pelt.[1] The notable emergence of Indian women as diplomats and peacemakers also indicates that they were anxious to maintain the flow of European goods such as kettles, cloth, knives, needles, and axes that helped to alleviate their onerous work.[2]

The second factor in promoting harmonious relations was the remarkably wide extent of intermarriage between incoming traders and Indian

Sally, daughter of an Okanogan chief, who married Alexander Ross, fur trader *(courtesy Manitoba Provincial Archives)*

women, especially among the Cree, the Ojibwa, and the Chipewyan. Indian wives proved indispensable helpmates to the officers and men of both the British-based Hudson's Bay Company and its Canadian rival, the North West Company. Such interracial unions were, in fact, the basis for a fur trade society and were sanctioned by an indigenous rite known as marriage *à la façon du pays*—according to the custom of the country.

The development of marriage *à la façon du pays* underscores the complex and changing interaction between the traders and the host Indian societies. In the initial phase of contact, many Indian bands actively encouraged the formation of marital alliances between their women and the traders. The Indians viewed marriage in an integrated social and economic context; marital alliances created reciprocal social ties, which served to consolidate their economic relationships with the incoming strangers. Thus, through marriage, many a trader was drawn into the Indian kinship circle. In return for giving the traders sexual and domestic rights to their women, the Indians expected reciprocal privileges such as free access to the posts and provisions.[3]

As a result of this Indian attitude, it was soon impressed upon the traders that marriage alliances were an important means of ensuring good will and cementing trade relations with new bands or tribes. The North West Company, a conglomerate of partnerships that began extensive trading in the West in the 1770s, had learned from its French predecessors of the benefits to be gained from intermarriage and officially sanctioned such unions for all ranks (from bourgeois down to *engagé*).[4] The Hudson's Bay Company, on the other hand, was much slower to appreciate the realities of life in Rupert's Land. Official policy formulated in faraway London forbade any intimacy with the Indians, but officers in the field early began to break the rules. They took the lead in forming unions with the women of prominent Indian leaders, although there was great variation in the extent to which the servants were allowed to form connections with native women.[5]

Apart from the public social benefits, the traders' desire to form unions with Indian women was increased by the absence of white women. Although they did not come as settlers, many of the fur traders spent the better part of their lives in Rupert's Land, and it is a singular fact in the social development of the Canadian West that for well over a century there were no white women.[6] The stability of many of the interracial unions formed in the Indian country stemmed partly from the fact that an Indian woman provided the only opportunity for a trader to replicate a domestic life with wife and children. Furthermore, although Indian mores differed from those of the whites, the traders learned that they trifled with Indian women at their peril. As one old voyageur explained, one could not just dally with any native woman who struck one's fancy. There was a great danger of getting one's head broken if a man attempted to take an Indian girl without her parents' consent.[7]

It is significant that, just as in the trade ceremony, the rituals of marriage *à la façon du pays* conformed more to Indian custom than to European. There were two basic steps to forming such a union. The first was to secure the consent of the woman's relatives; it also appears that the wishes of the woman herself were respected, as there is ample evidence that Indian women actively sought fur trade husbands. Once consent was secured, a bride price had then to be decided; this varied considerably among the tribes but could amount to several hundred dollars' worth of trade goods. After these transactions, the man and woman were usually conducted ceremoniously to the post where they were now recognized as man and wife.[8] In the Canadian West, marriage *à la façon du pays* became the norm for Indian-white unions, being reinforced by mutual interest, tradition, and peer group pressure.[9] Although ultimately "the custom of the country" was to be strongly denounced by the missionaries, it is significant that in 1867, when the legitimacy of the union between Chief Factor William Connolly and his Cree wife was tried before a Canadian court, it was found to have constituted a lawful marriage. The judge declared a valid marriage existed because the wife had been married according to the customs and usages of her own people and because the consent of both parties, the essential element of civilized marriage, had been proved by twenty-eight years of repute, public acknowledgment, and cohabitation as man and wife.[10]

If intermarriage brought the trader commercial and personal benefit, it also provided him with a unique economic partner. The Indian wife possessed a range of skills and wilderness know-how that would have been quite foreign to a white wife. Although the burdensome work role of nomadic Indian women was somewhat alleviated by the move to the fur trade post, the extent to which the traders relied upon native technology kept the women busy.

Perhaps the most important domestic task performed by the women at the fur trade posts was providing the men with a steady supply of "Indian shoes" or moccasins. The men of both companies generally did not dress in Indian style (the buckskinned mountain man was not part of the Canadian scene), but they universally adopted the moccasin as the most practical footwear for the wilderness. One wonders, for example, how the famed 1789 expedition of Alexander Mackenzie would have fared without the work of the wives of his two French-Canadian voyageurs. The women scarcely ever left the canoes, being "continually employ'd making shoes of moose skin as a pair does not last us above one Day."[11] Closely related to the manufacture of moccasins was the Indian woman's role in making snowshoes, without which winter travel was impossible. Although the men usually made the frames, the women prepared the sinews and netted the intricate webbing that provided support.[12]

Indian women also made a vital contribution in the preservation of food, especially in the manufacture of the all-important pemmican, the nutritious staple of the North West Company's canoe brigades. At the posts on the Plains, buffalo hunting and pemmican making formed an essential part of the yearly routine, each post being required to furnish an annual quota. In accordance with Indian custom, once the hunt was over the women's work began. The women skinned the animals and cut the meat into thin strips to be dried in the sun or over a slow fire. When the meat was dry, the women pounded it into a thick, flaky mass, which was then mixed with melted buffalo fat. This pemmican kept very well when packed into ninety-pound buffalo-hide sacks, which had been made by the women during the winter.[13]

But pemmican was too precious a commodity to be the basic food at the posts themselves. At the northern posts, the people subsisted mainly on fish, vast quantities of which were split and dried by the women to provide food for the winter. Maintaining adequate food supplies for a post for the winter was a precarious business, and numerous instances can be cited of Indian wives keeping the fur traders alive with their ability to snare small game such as rabbits and partridges. In 1815, for example, the young Nor'Wester George Nelson would probably have starved to death when provisions ran out at his small outpost north of Lake Superior had it not been for the resourcefulness of his Ojibwa wife who, during the month of February, brought in fifty-eight rabbits and thirty-four partridges.[14] Indian women also added to the diet by collecting berries and wild rice and making maple sugar. The spring trip to the sugar bush provided a welcome release from the monotony of the winter routine, and the men, with their families and Indian relatives, all enjoyed this annual event.[15]

As in other pre-industrial societies, the Indian women's role extended well beyond domestic maintenance as they assisted in specific fur trade operations. With the adoption of the birch-bark canoe, especially by the North West Company, Indian women continued in their traditional role of helping in its manufacture. It was the women's job to collect annual quotas of spruce roots, which were split fine to sew the seams of the canoes, and also to collect spruce gum, which was used for caulking the seams.[16] The inexperienced and undermanned Hudson's Bay Company also found itself calling upon the labor power of Indian women, who were adept at paddling and steering canoes. Indeed, although the inland explorations of various Hudson's Bay Company men such as Anthony Henday and Samuel Hearne have been glorified as individual exploits, the men were, in fact, entirely dependent upon the Indians with whom they traveled, especially the women. "Women," marveled one inlander, "were as useful as men upon Journeys."[17] Henday's journey to the Plains in 1754, for example, owed much of its success to his Cree female companion, who provided him with much timely advice about the plans of the Indians, in addition to a warm winter suit of furs.[18] The Hudson's Bay Company men emphasized to their London superiors the value of the Indian women's skill at working with fur pelts. In short, they argued that the economic services performed by Indian women at the fur trade posts were of such importance that they should be considered as "Your Honours Servants."[19] Indian women were indeed an integral part of the fur trade labor force, although, because their labor was largely unpaid, their contribution has been ignored.

The reliance on native women's skill remained an important aspect of fur trade life, even though by the early nineteenth century there was a notable shift in the social dynamic of fur trade society. By this time, partly because of the destructive competition between rival companies that had flooded the Indian country with alcohol, relations between many Indian bands and the traders deteriorated. In some well-established areas, traders sometimes resorted to coercive measures, and in some cases their abuse of Indian women became a source of conflict.[20] In this context, except in new areas such as the Pacific Slope, marriage alliances ceased to play the important function they once had. The decline of Indian-white marriages was also hastened by the fact that fur trade society itself was producing a new pool of marriageable young women—the mixed-blood "daughters of the country." With her dual heritage, the mixed-blood woman possessed the ideal qualifications for a fur trader's wife: acclimatized to life in the West and familiar with Indian ways, she could also adapt successfully to white culture.

From their Indian mothers, mixed-blood girls learned the native skills so necessary to the functioning of the trade. As Sir George Simpson, governor of the Hudson's Bay Company emphasized in the 1820s: "It is the duty of the Women at the different Posts to do all that is necessary in regard to Needle Work,"[21] and the mixed-blood women's beautiful beadwork was highly prized. In addition to performing traditional Indian tasks, the women's range of domestic work increased in more European ways. They were responsible for the fort's washing and cleaning; "the Dames" at York Factory, for example, were kept "in Suds, Scrubbing and Scouring," according to one account.[22] As subsistence agriculture developed around many of the posts, the native women took an active role in planting and harvesting. Chief Factor John Rowand of Fort Edmonton succinctly summarized the economic role of native women in the fur trade when he wrote in the mid-nineteenth century: "The women here work very hard, if it was not so, I do not know how we would get on with the Company work."[23] With her ties to the Indians and familiarity with native customs and language, the mixed-blood wife was also in a position to take over the role of intermediary or liaison previously played by the Indian wife. The daughters of the French-Canadian voyageurs were often excellent interpreters: some could speak several Indian languages. More than once, the timely intervention of a mixed-blood wife saved the life of a husband who had aroused Indian hostility.[24] Indeed, in his account of fur trade life during the Hudson's Bay Company's monopoly after 1821, Isaac Cowie declared that many of the company's officers owed much of their success in overcoming difficulties and in maintaining the company's influence over the natives to "the wisdom and good counsel of their wives."[25]

In spite of the importance of native connections, many fur trade fathers wanted to introduce their mixed-blood daughters to the rudiments of European culture. Since the place of work and home coincided, especially in the long winter months, the traders were able to take an active role in their children's upbringing, and they were encouraged by company officials to do so.[26] When the beginnings of formal schooling were introduced at the posts on the Bay in the early 1800s, it was partly because it was felt to be essential that girls, who were very seldom sent overseas, should be given a basic education that would inculcate them with Christian virtue.[27] Increasingly, fathers promoted the marriage of their daughters to incoming traders as the means of securing their place in fur trade society. In a significant change of policy in 1806, the North West Company acknowledged some responsibility for the fate of its "daughters" when it sanctioned marriage *à la façon du pays* with daughters of white men, but now prohibited it with full-blooded Indian women.[28]

As mixed-blood wives became "the vogue" (to quote a contemporary), it is notable that "the custom of the country" began to evolve more toward European concepts of marriage. Most important, such unions were coming to be regarded as unions for life. When the Hudson's Bay Company officer J. E. Harriott espoused Elizabeth Pruden, for example, he promised her father, a senior officer, that he would "live with her and treat her as my wife as long as we both lived."[29] It became customary for a couple to exchange brief vows before the officer in charge of the post, and the match was further celebrated by a dram of liquor to all hands and a wedding dance. The bride price was replaced by the opposite payment of a dowry, and many fur trade officers were able to dower their daughters quite handsomely.[30] Marriage *à la façon du pays* was further regulated by the Hudson's Bay Company after 1821 with the introduction of marriage contracts, which emphasized the husband's financial obligations and the status of the woman as a legitimate wife.

The social role of the mixed-blood wife, unlike that of the Indian wife, served to cement ties within fur trade society itself. Significantly, in the North West Company, many marriages cut across class lines, as numerous Scottish bourgeois chose their wives from among the daughters of the French-Canadian *engagés* who had married extensively among the native people. Among the Hudson's Bay Company men, it was appreciated that a useful way to enhance one's career prospects was to marry the daughter of a senior officer.[31] Whatever a man's initial motivation, the substantial private fur trade correspondence that has survived from the nineteenth century reveals that many fur traders became devoted family men. Family could be a source of interest and consolation in a life that was often hard and monotonous. As Chief Factor James Douglas pointedly summed it up: "There is indeed no living with comfort in this country until a person has forgot the great world and has his tastes and character formed on the current standard of the stage[;] . . . habit makes it familiar to us, softened as it is by the *many tender ties* which find a way to the heart."[32]

However, the founding in 1811 of the Selkirk Colony, the first agrarian settlement in western Canada, was to introduce new elements of white civilization that would hasten the decline of the indigenous fur trade society. The chief agents of these changes were the missionaries and white women.

The missionaries, especially the Anglicans who arrived under the auspices of the Hudson's Bay Company in 1820, roundly denounced marriage *à la façon du pays* as being immoral and debased.[33] But while they exerted considerable pressure on long-cohabiting couples to accept a church marriage, they were in no way champions of miscegenation. In fact, this attack upon fur trade custom had a detrimental effect upon the position of native women. Incoming traders, now feeling free to ignore the marital obligations implicit in "the custom of the country," increasingly looked upon native women as objects for temporary sexual gratification. The women, on the other hand, found themselves being judged according to strict British standards of female propriety. It was they, not the white men, who were to be held responsible for the perpetuation of immorality because of their supposedly promiscuous Indian heritage. The double standard, tinged with racism, had arrived with a vengeance!

Racial prejudice and class distinctions were augmented by the arrival of British women in Rupert's Land. The old fabric of fur trade society was severely rent in 1830 when Simpson and another prominent Hudson's Bay Company officer returned from furlough, having wed genteel British ladies.[34] The appearance of such "flowers of civilization" provoked unflattering comparisons with native women; as one officer observed, "This influx of white faces has cast a still deeper shade over the faces of our Brunettes in the eyes of many."[35] In Red River especially, a white wife became a status symbol: witness the speed with which several retired Hudson's Bay Company factors married English schoolmistresses after the demise of their native wives. To their credit, many company officers remained loyal to their native families, but they became painfully anxious to turn their daughters into young Victorian ladies, hoping that with accomplishments and connections, the stigma of their mixed blood would not prevent them from remaining among the social elite. Thus in the 1830s, a boarding school was established in Red River for the children of company officers: the girls' education was supervised by the missionary's wife, and more than one graduate was praised for being "quite English in her Manner."[36] In numerous cases, these highly acculturated young women were able to secure advantageous matches with incoming white men, but to some extent this was only because white ladies did not in fact make a successful adaptation to fur trade life. It had been predicted that "the lovely tender exotics" (as white women were dubbed) would languish in the harsh fur trade environment,[37] and indeed they did, partly because they had no useful social or economic role to play. As a result, mixed marriages continued to be a feature of western Canadian society until well into the mid-nineteenth century, but it was not an enduring legacy. Indian and mixed-blood women, like their male counterparts, were quickly shunted aside with the development of the agrarian frontier after 1870. The vital role native women had played in the opening of the Canadian West was either demeaned or forgotten.

NOTES

This essay originally appeared in *Frontiers* 3, no. 9, and is reprinted by permission.

1. Sylvia Van Kirk, *Many Tender Ties: Women in Fur Trade Society, 1670–1870* (Norman: University of Oklahoma Press, 1980; Winnipeg, Man.: Watson and Dwyer, 1980), pp. 72–73.

2. The most outstanding example of Indian women who, although not married to whites, were active peacemakers and diplomats are Thanadelthur, a Chipewyan, and Lady Calpo, a Chinook. See ibid., pp. 66–71, 76–77.

3. The few cases of violent conflict, such as the Henley House Massacre of 1752, were caused by the traders' failure to respect this bargain. See ibid., pp. 41–44.

4. Ibid., p. 28.

5. Ibid., pp. 28–29, 41–42.

6. After an ill-fated venture in 1686, British wives were officially prohibited from traveling to Hudson Bay. It was not until 1812 with the Selkirk settlers that women were again officially transported to Hudson Bay. A French-Canadian woman in 1806 was the first and one of the few white women to come west in the North West Company canoes. See Van Kirk, *Many Tender Ties,* pp. 173–80.

7. *Johnstone et al. v. Connolly,* Appeal Court, Sept. 7, 1869, *La Revue Legale,* 1:280 (hereafter cited as Connolly Appeal Case, 1869).

8. Van Kirk, *Many Tender Ties,* pp. 36–37. For a discussion of the motivation of the Indian women, see chap. 4.

9. This does not mean that sexual exploitation of Indian women was unknown in the Canadian West. Prostitution certainly existed, and the marriage relationship could be abused as in white society.

10. *Connolly vs. Woolrich,* Superior Court, Montreal, July 9, 1867, *Lower Canada Jurist,* 11:230, 248.

11. W. Kaye Lamb, ed., *The Journals and Letters of Sir Alexander Mackenzie* (Cambridge, Eng.: Cambridge University Press, 1970), p. 220.

12. Van Kirk, *Many Tender Ties,* pp. 54–55.

13. Ibid., p. 56.

14. Journal, Jan. 29–June 23, 1815, George Nelson Papers,Toronto Public Library. See also Van Kirk, *Many Tender Ties,* pp. 58–59.

15. Van Kirk, *Many Tender Ties,* p. 57.

16. Ibid., p. 61.

17. J. B. Tyrell, ed., *Journals of Samuel Hearne and Philip Turnor, 1774–1792,* Champlain Society, vol. 21 (Toronto, 1934), pp. 252–53.

18. Van Kirk, *Many Tender Ties,* p. 64.

19. Hudson's Bay Company Archives, B.239/b/79, fols. 40d–41 (hereafter HBCA).

20. Van Kirk, *Many Tender Ties,* pp. 90–91.

21. R. H. Fleming, ed., *Minutes of Council of the Northern Department of Rupert's Land, 1821–31,* Hudson's Bay Record Society, vol. 3 (London, 1940), p. 378.

22. Hargrave to Christie, June 13, 1832, James Hargrave Correspondence, vol. 21, Public Archives of Canada.

23. HBCA, D.5/18, fols. 535d–536.

24. One of the most famous cases was that of James Douglas, a clerk in northern British Columbia, whose high-handed treatment so outraged the Carrier Indians that he might have been killed but for intervention of his mixed-blood wife, Amelia, and the wife of the interpreter. See Van Kirk, *Many Tender Ties,* pp. 111–13.

25. Isaac Cowie, *The Company of Adventurers* (Toronto: W. Briggs, 1913), p. 204.

26. Van Kirk, *Many Tender Ties,* pp. 97, 99, 106, 131.

27. Ibid., pp. 103–104.

28. W. S. Wallace, ed., *Documents Relating to the North West Company,* Champlain Society, vol. 22. (Toronto, 1934), p. 211.

29. Connolly Appeal Case, 1869, p. 286.

30. Van Kirk, *Many Tender Ties,* pp. 108, 115.

31. Ibid., pp. 108–109.

32. G. P. de T. Glazebrook, ed., *The Hargrave Correspondence, 1821–1843,* Champlain Society, vol. 24 (Toronto, 1928), p. 381.

33. Van Kirk, *Many Tender Ties,* pp. 153–56.

34. They also violated "the custom of the country" by callously casting aside their former mixed-blood partners. For a full discussion of this episode, see Sylvia Van Kirk,

"The Impact of White Women on Fur Trade Society," in *The Neglected Majority: Essays in Canadian Women's History,* ed. Susan Mann Trofimenkoff and Alison Prentice (Toronto: McClelland and Stewart, 1977), pp. 27–48.

35. Hargrave to Charles Ross, Dec. 1, 1830, Hargrave Correspondence, vol. 21, PAC.

36. Glazebrook, ed., *Hargrave Correspondence,* p. 229.

37. Ibid., pp. 310–11.

A Chicana in Northern Aztlán: An Oral History of Dora Sánchez Treviño[1]

JERRY GARCÍA

Accounts of the Chicano experience in the United States have steadily increased for the past thirty years, particularly for the Southwest and Midwest.[2] By and large, efforts have focused on these locations due to the historical concentration of Chicano communities there. However, Chicano communities outside of the Southwest and Midwest continue to grow. The Pacific Northwest is an area that has seen a rapid increase in Chicano population. In the decade between 1980 and 1990, Washington, Idaho, and Oregon recorded significant increases in Hispanic population.[3] For example, Washington State now has the eighth largest Chicano community in the United States and ranks tenth in growth.[4] Despite this growth and a Chicano presence in Washington that dates back at least to the 1800s, there are only a sparse number of studies that explore the Chicano experience in the Evergreen State.[5] Furthermore, studies specifically examining the Chicana experience in the Pacific Northwest are nearly nonexistent.

Because traditional sources have left out Chicanas in the Pacific Northwest, this paper attempts to capture that experience by utilizing oral history as a basic form of research. Chicano culture has long-established ancestral forms of oral histories, which are passed on from one generation to the next. The use of the *corrido* or songs is part of that rich tradition.[6] Nevertheless, Chicanos have rarely used oral history as a tool for research until the very recent past. Since the 1970s Chicanos from a variety of fields have used oral interviews to glean information on the origins of their communities. For Chicanos in the Pacific Northwest, oral histories are a valuable tool that can

Dora Sanchez Treviño,
Quincy High School yearbook picture in 1963

provide a panoramic view of ethnic communities that would otherwise not be seen. The researcher Devra Anne Weber suggests that oral histories enable us to challenge the common confusion between the dismal conditions of the agricultural labor system and the internal life of workers. They reveal the relationship between the economic system of agriculture and community, politics, and familial and cultural life. Oral histories help answer fundamental questions about class, gender, life and work, cultural change, values, and perceptions that are ignored in traditional sources.[7] This is true for Chicanas in Quincy, Washington. The following interview with Dora Sánchez Treviño elaborates on issues of gender in the workplace and being Chicana in an Anglo-dominated community. Written documents in Quincy say very little about the contributions or existence of Chicanas in the community. The use of oral history will illustrate its importance as a tool and reveal that Chicanas in Quincy have been active in all modern periods of development within the community.

Chicanos who came to Quincy in the 1940s arrived via the Yakima Valley of Washington State, which had been the hub for agricultural workers since the 1920s. Prior to the completion of the Columbia Basin Irrigation Project in 1952, individuals and families who were able to find work in the area sporadically contributed Chicano labor.[8] In the late 1940s companies such as Cedargreen Farms and the Elmer Gerkin Ranch established small food-processing plants in Quincy, offering year-round employment.[9] While Mexican communities in the Yakima Valley were thriving in the early 1950s, very few Mexicans ventured north into the Columbia Basin region. When the area became the beneficiary of a major federal irrigation project, the new program expanded the agricultural capabilities of the previously dry land, and as a result, Mexican agricultural workers found expanded opportunities in Quincy, Moses Lake, Warden, and Othello, Washington.

Since the late 1940s Quincy has experienced two periods of major Chicano migration and one stage of direct immigration from Mexico. The initial phase occurred in the late 1940s and early 1950s. The second phase of migration, in the early 1960s, coincided with the expansion of Columbia Basin agriculture and the need for additional labor in the Quincy Valley. This growth and development was instrumental in drawing Chicanos to Quincy. During the last stage, from approximately the mid-1980s to the present, immigrants began arriving directly from Mexico.

Shortly after World War II a small number of Chicanos initiated the first phase of migration into the Columbia Basin, including Quincy. Officially, no Chicanos resided in Quincy during the first four decades of the twentieth century.[10] However, high school yearbooks for the 1940s and 1950s contain pictures and names of individuals of Mexican ancestry. Historically, census statistics have not provided an accurate representation of the Chicano population.[11] In 1950 Quincy's population consisted of 804 people, with an insignificant number categorized as "other."[12] Oral interviews conducted by the author in Quincy have revealed that the Chicano pioneers of the community were not recent immigrants from Mexico, but U.S. citizens of Mexican descent who followed long-established migratory routes north out of the Southwest.[13] Specifically, the majority of the Chicanos arriving in Quincy during the late 1940s and early 1950s came from Texas, in particular the Río Grandé Valley in south Texas.[14]

The arrival of Jesse Gonzales and his family, in 1948, marks the earliest known immigration of Chicanos to Quincy for permanent residence. This family was typical of the Chicanos arriving in Quincy in the late 1940s and early 1950s. The Gonzales family left Texas in the 1930s to follow the sugar beet crop up into Montana. From there the family moved to the crops in Wyoming. After almost a decade of following this route out of Texas, they arrived in Toppenish, Washington, in the early 1940s. By 1948 the Gonzales family had moved to the Quincy Valley to work for Cedargreen Farms and, along with a few other families, set the foundation for the Mexican community. During the following decade the number of permanent Chicano residents increased, but many continued to migrate from Texas to Washington. As the Columbia Basin Irrigation Project expanded crop production, recruitment of a stable, cheap, and permanent work force began.

As the second phase of migration developed in the early 1960s, the Quincy Valley farms expanded to over 100,000 acres and sustained a variety of labor-intensive crops.[15] The family of Rita Puente demonstrated the continuing growth of the Chicano population in the Quincy area. During the late 1940s her family followed traditional migratory routes through Illinois, Michigan, and Indiana. In 1951 the Puente family migrated to Sunnyside, Washington, to pick asparagus. After working in the fields for five or six months, they returned to Texas by following the crops through California. This became the migration process for Rita and her family until the early 1960s, when they eventually made Quincy their permanent home. Rita Puente, in her capacity as the only female labor contractor in the area, facilitated the recruitment of many Chicano families to the region.[16]

During this second phase, the first signs of a Chicano social and cultural community appeared, beginning with the annual Mexican fiesta, which originated in the late 1950s. Additional activities followed the establishment of the Latin American Association (LAA) in 1964.[17] By 1965 the members of the LAA were raising funds for charitable donations and community activities. The association sponsored the annual Mexican fiesta, donating the proceeds to the Catholic church. Dora Treviño, by being involved with the LAA, established her political roots and became an active member within the Chicano community. A second organization, the Progressive League of United Mexican Americans (PLUMA), established in 1967, played a major role in organizing the agricultural workers of Quincy.[18]

The small Chicano trickle of the 1950s and 1960s grew to approximately 1,000 by 1970 and then stabilized. This increase and permanency of the Mexican community began to challenge the white population in the Quincy Valley. Socioeconomic, religious, and political problems exposed the size of the population and the need to develop solutions to community issues. For example, a group of Chicanos in 1970 attempted to develop Quincy United Enterprises to produce school and institutional furniture. Their plan called for a public offering of stock to be sold to Mexican Americans who would own and operate the enterprise as a self-help industry. The objectives of the company were never met due to its inability to raise the required seed money.[19] In January 1973, Chicano high school students protested what they called unfair treatment by teachers and school administrators by walking out of their classes. This demonstration resulted in the formation of an advisory committee consisting of Chicano parents and school officials.[20] Friction between the Anglo and Chicano communities persisted throughout the 1970s.

By the mid-1980s Quincy witnessed another increase in its population. This period marked the beginning of the third stage of Mexican migration. However, it was distinct from the first two because the increase was the result of recent arrivals from Mexico.[21] Additionally, the growth in the Mexican population was linked to the expansion in year-round employment in industries related to agriculture.[22] The 1990 census indicated that the city's population was 3,758, which included 1,401 people of Hispanic origin, and 93 percent of those were of Mexican origin.[23] Not included in the census was a large Hispanic migrant population that spent part of the year in Quincy.[24]

As of 1996 Chicanos made up approximately 40 percent of the total population of the city of Quincy[25] and, according to the Quincy School District Office, represented 55 percent of the student body.[26] But numbers do not necessarily provide equality, political power, or socioeconomic parity. The Chicano community of Quincy has suffered from the exhausting hours in the sun, package sheds, and other areas of the local agrarian economy. Currently, Chicanos are still occupying the lowest-paying jobs, representing the smallest percentage of homeowners, and having the highest "push-out" rate in the school district.[27]

When examining the history of Chicanos in Quincy, one can document the experience via interviews. An oral interview with Dora Treviño extracted a tremendous amount of information concerning not just Treviño's experiences, but those of Chicanas in general. In the following interview, Treviño provides a glimpse of her childhood and of the dynamics of a traditional patriarchal Mexican family. Her relationships with her brother and eventually with her husband display some of the cultural norms within this patriarchal system. Starting at a very young age, Treviño engaged in a wide range of occupations that included weeding sugar beet fields, being a teacher's aide, and professional employment with a state agency. This background has allowed her to witness from many levels the position of Chicanas in the Quincy workplace. Her description of her high school experiences in Quincy illustrates the type of race and class relations that existed between Anglos and Chicanos in the early 1960s. Her involvement with Chicano organizations, union activism, and local politics illustrates all of those issues from a Chicana perspective. Dora Treviño's life in Quincy may not be representative of all Chicanas in the community, but through her eyes we can see a portion of the overall experiences of Chicanas in Quincy.

I chose to feature the history and experience of Dora Sánchez Treviño because she has lived in Quincy since the early 1960s and has firsthand knowledge of the growth and development of the community. Additionally, she has been the only woman of color to hold political office in Quincy (councilwoman).[28] Specifically, I wanted to glean information from Treviño on her experiences as a Chicana in Quincy, and I wished to compare her experiences with those of other Chicanas in Quincy and of Chicano men.[29] Although it is only one history, Treviño family history provides insight into the type of Chicano families arriving in Quincy during the early 1960s. Finally, her personal journey, as a Chicana, mother, wife, and as a professional worker, provided her with a variety of views and experiences.

I have known Dora Treviño and her family practically all of my life. Our families arrived in the region several years apart but traveled many of the same migration routes out of the Río Grandé Valley before finally settling in Quincy. I graduated from high school with one of her brothers and a year after one of her sisters. Still, I was oblivious to her family and personal history until the day I interviewed her.[30] I hope that her story provides an understanding of the Chicana experience in the Pacific Northwest.[31]

García: Can you please provide some background information about yourself and your family?

Treviño: My maiden name is Sánchez and my married name is Treviño. I was born in Uvalde, Texas, March 29, 1947. My mother, Ignacia, was born in either Seguin or Brownsville, Texas. My father, Abel Sánchez, was born in Piedras Negras, Mexico, right across from Eagle Pass, Texas. However, since the age of two he was raised in a German town called Lockhart, Texas, about 40 miles from Austin. I do not know too much about my grandparents except that one was born in Texas and the other in Mexico. I moved to Quincy in February 1963 and I had just turned 15 years old. My parents came later, in July 1963. I arrived in Quincy from Austin, Texas, and was shocked to see this little town, tumbleweeds everywhere, and a school district that had very little to offer Mexicans.[32]

García: How many brothers and sisters do you have?

Treviño: There are ten of us. There are five boys and five girls. From the oldest to youngest, it is Chencho, Jesse, Renaldo, Guadalupe, Jesus, Eva, Oralia, Carolina, Maggie, and I.

García: Why did you arrive before your parents?

Treviño: Because two of my brothers were running a swathing and combine business in Quincy. My oldest brother, Chencho, wanted someone to come and help him with the household, and he initially wanted my older sister. My oldest sister was a senior in high school in Austin, and she refused to go before she graduated. Back then the Mexican men in the family were used to getting what they wanted, so I was sent to Quincy.

García: What year did your family begin to migrate from Texas?

Treviño: I used to hear my father talk about the family migrating back in the 1930s. Half of my family was born in Montana and the other in Texas. It was not until the late 1950s that our family actually stayed put for any duration. It was around the early 1930s that my father began to farm in Montana. During this time period our family would just go from Texas to Montana and back. When my father returned to Texas he usually worked in construction.

García: Do you remember where in Montana your family migrated?

Treviño: Oh yes, it was right on the northeast region of Montana. The place was called Fairview, Montana, right on the state line of Montana and North Dakota. It was very cold.

García: What time of the year would your family leave for Montana?

Treviño: Our family would leave from April until October, when the sugar beet harvest ended. In between those months we would thin and weed the sugar beets. We would do this several times until the beets were ready to be harvested. My father used to tell us about how they cut the beets back in those days. They used a short cutter and blocked the beets and they were hand loaded into sacks or trucks.

García: What type of work would the women do in Montana?

Treviño: They did the same work. They would work side by side with the men.

García: Which women are you talking about?

Treviño: My mother, aunts—it seemed like the whole family was out there. All the brothers and wives would travel together. They lived in a little house, which the grower provided for them. But I was too young to work in the fields at this time. The last time I was in Montana I was only 12 years old. At this age I do remember doing a lot of the cooking for the crews.

García: What were your first impressions or experiences when you arrived in Quincy?

Treviño: My father sent me all by myself to Quincy on a bus. I was 15 years old, and I cried all the way to Waco, Texas. I was coming to a region that was very unfamiliar. I arrived in the middle of winter and it was extremely cold.

García: What kind of expectations did you have when you left Texas on your way to Washington?

Treviño: When I left Texas in 1963 I was in tears because I had never been away from my parents other than just an overnighter. I cried most of the way and can't remember when I stopped. Seeing Washington was very nice. It was a very beautiful place as I came through the Yakima Valley. You could see a big difference between the Yakima Valley and the Quincy Basin. In Quincy it was so dry and barren.

García: How did your parents let you know that you were going to Washington?

Treviño: Well, I actually was foolish enough to volunteer. So they did not confront me with it. As I mentioned before, the oldest male in our family, Chencho, had a lot of power and pull and whatever he wanted he received. He told my parents that he needed one of my sisters, Lala, who was my oldest sister so that she could cook, clean, and take care of the house in Washington. However, right away fear came to her because she was going to graduate that year from high school. Back then many people did not think education was important for women. And I knew how my mother felt about education, and she tried real hard to get us one. The boys in our family did not care so much for an education, but she knew us girls wanted one. My mother really had to fight whatever my brother said. I finally told my mother she could not send Lala because she was so active in school, and I volunteered to go. She asked me if I was sure? I said yes because I adored my brother no matter how demanding he was. We all idolized him because he was the oldest. So my mother said okay and took me to church to be blessed. Being blessed by the church was very common whenever someone left on a trip. The whole family would go so the priest could bless us. So, it was not like I was forced to go.

García: What did your mother talk to you about before you left?

Treviño: She told me that things were going to be harder for me because my brother was very strict. My mother was strict, but she would take us to dances, but we could never go by ourselves. She told me that I could not expect the same thing with my brother. And she was right; I was not allowed to do anything.

García: During this time period were you allowed to date?

Treviño: When I was back home in Texas I was allowed. I started dating at a very young age, about thirteen, but I was not allowed to go anywhere by myself. I had to take my other brother Ray, my sister Lala, and one of my cousins. So, it was like taking *la familia.* When I arrived in Quincy my brother decided that no one was good enough for me. It was the big brother protection thing. I was not allowed to date.

García: How did you feel about the way your brother treated you?

Treviño: I would get so mad, but I did not hate him. I realized that we had to live with rules. Out of all the girls I was considered the "rebel." Again, I remember my mother telling when I got to Quincy to make sure that I got up early to do my chores and to go to school.

García: What was it like going to high school in Quincy in 1963? What was the background of the students?

Treviño: I can give you the names of the other Mexicans who were in school with me. Alicia Gonzales was a junior, and there was Joe Gonzales who was also a junior, but they did not mix with the other Mexicans in the school. They were not related. They were more into. . . they were more involved at school. I feel that they believed they had to shun their own identity as Mexicans so they could be more accepted by the white students. I guess if they expressed they were Mexicans they would not have a chance in high school and would be treated differently by the white students.

García: How were you and the other Mexican students different from Alicia and Joe Gonzales?

Treviño: When I arrived in Quincy all the Mexican students hung out with each other. Me being new and not knowing anyone, Alicia Gonzales came and introduced herself and told me, "This is what you do to be accepted by the white students." I could feel the other Mexican students waiting to see what I was going to do. When I came to Quincy I did not have any friends. And then Roger Mata and Cecelia Saenz looked after me. I was treated differently by the white students. Unlike some of the other Mexicans, I attempted to get along with everyone. I told myself that I was there to get one thing done and that was to finish high school. Some of the other Mexican students did try to put me down, especially when I was a junior because I was trying to get involved in school activities and I had white friends. I believe many of them thought that I felt I was better than them.

García: What were some of the labels used to describe people of Mexican descent?

Treviño: You never heard the term *Chicano.* Most of the time you were either a *Mexicana* or someone trying to act like a *gabacha* [white]. If it were the Mexicans trying to put you down, they would say, "Se creer gabacha." The term *Chicano* was considered low class by my parents, so they would not allow us to use that term.

García: Was *Mexican American* ever used that you were aware of?

Treviño: Once in awhile you would hear that term. More often it was *Spanish American.* We were taught not to say *Mexican American* because if you claimed your heritage you were branded right away.

García: You also mentioned that when you first arrived to Quincy High School some of the Mexican students warned you about racism. Did you ever experience some type of racism while in school?

Treviño: I started school in the middle of the school year, and there was a clear stereotype of Mexicans who came in later than usual. No matter what the circumstances were, you were labeled a "migrant." And, many of the white students looked down on migrant school children. I am not putting migrants down because my parents were migrants until they finally settled down, but I've always been against stereotypes. The assumption was made that new Mexican students were here for the harvest. I remember one of my Anglo teachers telling me, "Oh, you are here for the harvest and the weeding." At that time I had no idea what she was talking about, and I looked at her, puzzled. I thought that maybe I should answer yes. From that time on I began to get the feeling that maybe I should answer yes to the things they wanted to hear.

García: What was it like growing up in your family? What did the women do in your family? Or what were the responsibilities of the women?

Treviño: During the growing season in Quincy we had to get up at 4:00 A.M. and help with the household. While we were in school we were not expected to go work. Our primary responsibilities were to be sure that the house was clean and have dinner ready when our mother and father came home. Many of the kids I went to school with had to put in a few hours of work before they went to school. After the school year ended, we went to work in the fields. We usually weeded onions, sugar beets, and radishes. In other ways I felt our family was unique because our mother allowed us to stay home on the condition that we maintained the household and cook. If we went to work it was a choice. Nineteen sixty-three was the first year that I worked. I worked for the Yoshino brothers and they were paying $1.25 per hour. We thought, "Wow, that is a lot of money." My sister Lala and I would take turns working each week. One week I would stay and take care of the house, and we would switch every other week. We would split the earnings we made.

García: Describe some of your experiences while working in the fields.

Treviño: The first year my sister and I started we had never worked in the sugar beets before. We would show up in shorts, sandals, and no hat, shortsleeve shirt, sunglasses, and no gloves. We also used the short hoe that no one was using anymore. Many of the other workers would get mad at us because they thought we were mocking them. Everyone else of course were protecting themselves from the elements by wearing the appropriate clothing. By the end of the day we had blisters on our hands because we did not have gloves. Everybody had a big sombrero, long-sleeve shirt, gloves, and a rag to cover their faces. We didn't care, we thought we were going to be tanning. We thought it would be great to be dark. By our second year we had learned our lessons and were completely covered.

García: What is the formal educational background of your parents?

Treviño: My father had a second-grade education and my mother a sixth-grade education.

García: What kind of influence did your parents have on your staying in school?

Treviño: My mother had the greatest influence. She made every accommodation for us so that we would not miss school. One of the main reasons we stopped migrating was because my mother wanted us to finish high school, and when my parents eventually moved to Quincy in late 1963 it was a great help. My mother's father also died when she was school age and that prevented her from finishing. Six out of ten of my siblings completed high school. I graduated from Quincy High School in 1965. My mother always had a direct influence. She was always telling me to think of the future. I believe that is why she always had me going with her to all those meetings. She wanted me exposed to different ideas.

García: Dora, can you discuss what kind of experience your mother had living in the Pacific Northwest and in Quincy?

Treviño: My mother was a wonderful lady and a proud woman. As I mentioned before, in our household my mother made many of the decisions, especially when it came to finances. I remember my mother making my father believe he was making all the decisions, but in reality she had [a] great deal of influence within the household. My mother had a very quiet demeanor, but she knew how to get things done. After I finished high school, my mother went to work in the sheds, and I felt so sorry for her because then she would come home and work. I mean, she would work like a man out in the packing sheds, and then [be] expected to come and do the housework.

García: When a "traditional" Mexican wife is described, do you feel your mother fit this role?

Treviño: In a way she did. By that I mean she was a very strong woman and she would not be very vocal in the house, but she was more a person who would wait and later come forth with a very firm decision. I also feel that she does not fit the traditional role. However, because she worked both outside and inside the home and never complained, I feel that [she] fit the traditional role. When it came to our education and our future, she was very firm and told my father what was going to happen.

García: When your mother arrived in Quincy did she get involved with the community?

Treviño: I remember going with her to city hall because she knew we were going to be here for awhile. She wanted to register to become a voter in Quincy, and I'll never forget the clerk asking my mother in a very rude voice, "What do you want?" My mother just looked at her and said she wanted to register. She asked my mother if she was a U.S. citizen. My mother stated yes, and this woman asked where she was born. My mother had a problem hearing out of one of her ears, and she responded with "What?" Then my mother looked at me and said, "¿Qué dice? ¿Qué dijo?" (What is she saying? What did she say?) I said, "¿Dijo qué dondé nacio?" (She said, "Where were you born?") My mother then tells me in Spanish, "In Texas." I told the clerk she was born in Texas. The clerk then asked if my mother could read and write in English. I turned to my mother and continued translating for her, and she told me to tell the clerk she [could] read and write English a little. The clerk responded by saying that she could not register because she was not fluent in English. So my mother never did register. This was very difficult for her because she used to stress how important it was for us [to] vote. That was in 1963, and my mother never did register in Quincy. I'll never forget the look on my mother's face when she was told she could not vote. She was used to voting in Texas on almost everything. She belonged to an organization in Texas, but I can't remember the name, where it was all women. It was a political organization where they would meet once a month. An attorney would come and talk about legislative issues coming up. My mother had [a] strong influence on me when it came to getting involved with community organizations. When she arrived in Quincy she would take me to all the meetings she was attending. In 1964 my father got involved with [the] Latin American Club.

García: Were there any women involved with the Latin American Club?

Treviño: Yes, there were, but not very many. I was involved because I was asked to be the secretary of the organization at a very young age. In 1966 Jovita Valdez was very much involved with the organization, also May Gonzales. Those two women were very involved with the Chicano community during that period. It was through them that I learned so much.

García: What kinds of issues were addressed in the Latin American Club?

Treviño: At that time it was human rights issues, labor laws, and discrimination. The Latin American Club would do fund raising for the community as well as holding an annual banquet to recognize graduating Mexican students.

García: What were your plans after finishing high school?

Treviño: Well, one of the things my mother always did was take me to meetings. She was very much involved with the Altar Society of the Catholic church. We went to the Altar Society meetings because they always had a variety of speakers. At one particular meeting I attended there were these two female speakers who were very much involved with politics. One of them was Emily Weber, who was from a very well known family in the area. At these meetings she was discussing new grassroots programs that were being started by President Johnson.

I started looking into these programs, particularly one called Community Action. After high school I had no intention of working in the fields. I never wanted to end up working in the potato sheds; it just was not my thing. As I spoke with Emily Weber, she told me about this program that would cater to migrant children to keep them out of the fields while their parents worked. I wanted to work in that program, but the Quincy School District would never tell me when the applications would become available. Eventually, with my persistence, they did give me one and I filled it out.

García: What positions were you applying for?

Treviño: I was applying for a teacher's aide position. When I was hired in 1965 they only had three Mexicans who were working in the program. Most of the teacher's aides that were hired were the daughters of the white teachers. They did not advertise the positions at all, which made it difficult for other Mexicans to know about these jobs. I knew because I asked after speaking with Emily Weber.

García: Had you made plans to go to college?

Treviño: Yes, I applied to the Institute of Medical Technology in Minneapolis. My older sister Oralia was already attending. This institute had an 18–month program in the medical field, and it was the only place I applied to.

García: What happened after the summer that you were a teacher's aide?

Treviño: Well, I realized I would not be going to college until January 1966 so I applied for work at the local warehouses. I was hired but treated very bad by the foreman. They insisted on yelling at all the new workers, and safety procedures within the warehouse were never followed. After I had a minor accident at the warehouse, my brother made me quit. He told me I was not going to work there anymore and got a loan for me [to] start school earlier.

García: How did Minneapolis work out for you?

Treviño: I was there until May of 1966. I returned to Quincy with the intention of just staying for the summer and returning to

Minneapolis, but my sister Oralia changed everything by getting engaged to some guy from Larson Air Base near Moses Lake. Without her I was unable to return by myself.

García: Why didn't you return to Minneapolis and complete school without your sister?

Treviño: I actually did finish in May 1966 and returned back to Quincy. However, my sister and I planned on living together in Minneapolis because we both had technical degrees, but those plans were stopped when she got married when we returned to Quincy for the summer in 1966.

García: Do you remember the size of the Mexican population in Quincy when you were a teacher's aide?

Treviño: During the regular school year in the 1960s you may have had a total of ten Mexican families in Quincy. However, during the growing season, that would increase to about a hundred families. Most of the families came from the Río Grandé region of south Texas. Now most are coming from California.

García: How many Mexicans were eventually hired for the Migrant Summer Program?

Treviño: In 1965 when I first started there were only three. I did not work there the summer of 1966. In 1968 about a fourth of the employees were Mexicans, but they never hired a Mexican teacher. Anglos filled all of the teaching positions. My sister Carrie later became the nurse for the summer program.

García: Between 1965 and 1974, what direction did your life take?

Treviño: When I came back in 1966 from college I was not sure what I wanted to do. I had received my certificate as a dental assistant. I was unsure, so I did child care. This was in 1966. In 1967, the first Title I programs came out. These were programs that were used for helping students who were falling behind in their academics. In Quincy, the majority of these students would be Mexican. Again, not much advertisement was done. I called the school to find out some information. I filled out an application with Jerry King. While I was waiting to find out about the position, I went back to work in the warehouse. It was at this time [that] the union movement began in Quincy. I could see why. At the warehouses the workers were treated horribly. Safety was not a concern, they did not get their breaks, and they were pushed around. The Teamsters came in, and I started going to their meetings. I would come back and start talking to people. Then I went door to door talking to people about the union. The big warehouse in Quincy was the Yoshino's plant. I started telling people about our worker's rights and important health issues and concerning the union. We started having our meetings at the Women's Youth Hall, which used to be the Quincy Library on B Street.

García: Who was organizing these meetings?

Treviño: The Teamsters was the union, but Ray Deeks was the organizer. Here I was, 19 years old and trying to tell people about their rights. Again, they were treated badly. They would not get breaks, if they got one it was only to go to the bathroom. These people would be standing all day long. I started getting concerned about this. The foreman tried to block my contact with people. When they found out that I was helping to organize, they had me laid off. When I confronted them, they just said they did not need me anymore. After this I began to get more involved with the union. When the union finally offered me a job as an organizer, I turned it down because being a union organizer was not what I wanted to do. At that time I had other plans for my life, and being part of the union effort full time was not in my plans. Ray Deeks in 1966 offered me the job, but I turned it down. It just was not what I wanted to be. I felt that being part of the agriculture community was not going to be my life, so I moved to Portland, Oregon. In 1967 I was called back to Quincy for an interview for the teacher's aide job in Quincy.

García: When you worked in Quincy as a teen-ager and young adult, how were you or women in general treated in comparison to men?

Treviño: In the fields I do not remember very much about being treated any different from the men because we all started at the same hours and we left at the same time. However, in the warehouses and packing sheds was a totally different situation. I used to get so mad and I was always very vocal and as a result I was always the very first one to get laid off.

García: What were you upset about?

Treviño: In the potato sheds the women were always put on the conveyer belts to sort the potatoes, and it was constant and rapid work. And the men never worked on the belts but would be paid between ten and twenty-five cents more an hour. The excuse was that men did heavier work, but their work was a lot slower and they had periods of rest in between loading the potatoes onto trains or whatever. Women rarely received any breaks during the day, and the less pay was what really bothered me. Also, women stood on their feet all day, and if any women needed a bathroom break they had to wait for someone to take their place on the belt line. I knew that there must have been laws about allowing people bathroom breaks in the workplace. I was not sure, but I voiced my concern all the time.

García: What was the result of your voicing your concern?

Treviño: Many times I would just take my break in [the] morning, but none of the other women would follow me, so I ended up by myself. And because of this, the foreman would always lay me off first. I really felt this was a type of harassment. The men and women should have been treated fairly and equally. Men were always going on breaks because they had down time in between their loading. There was a clear distinction between what kind of work men did and women did in those warehouses. Men always got paid more, and the idea of applying to a "man's" job was unheard of in those days.

García: Did you get the job as a teacher's aide?

Treviño: Yes, I got the job. So I moved back to Quincy. In December of 1967, I got married. I ended up staying here in Quincy the rest of my life.

García: What was it about your husband that made you decide he was the one to marry?

Treviño: It is difficult to explain, but we just fell in love. However, things did change once we got married. He was a very domineering person and did not believe women should do something without the husband saying so.

García: Before you married your husband, did you date or have any other serious relationships?

Treviño: I really did not get serious with anyone because my plans were not to get married at a young age.

García: What was your notion of an ideal husband?

Treviño: Someone who could take care of himself, be very involved with the community, but ethnicity was not an issue. When Robert and I decided to get married I was nineteen and two months pregnant. I did not have to get married because I was pregnant, but I was afraid of what my father was going to say. I felt he was going to disown me. In the end my father took the position that there was very little he could do and gave us his blessing.

García: What happened to the unionization effort in Quincy?

Treviño: In the Yoshino plant the workers voted to go union. So the owner, Yoshino, instead of allowing it, decided to close it down, and he sold it. Then Lamb-Weston came in and bought the plant. I was still involved to [a] certain extent in helping the union. I would assist in sending people to Portland to see how unions worked there, and they would return to Quincy. Finally, Lamb-Weston was unionized.

García: How did marriage work into your career path?

Treviño: Well my husband, Roberto Treviño, started working for Community Action, one of the grass-roots programs of the War on Poverty. He had just left the service and became a federal project director. He was a director in Moses Lake. He covered all of Grant County. He was also involved with [the] Small Business Administration in an effort to target minority business owners. As it turned out, very few Mexicans were ever approached about starting up a business.

García: What were you doing after you got married?

Treviño: When I got married my husband did not want me working with the union. Again, it is that old Mexican tradition where the man rules the household.

García: How did you feel about that situation?

Treviño: I did not like it. I was always—well, my youngest son used to call me the Norma Rae of back then. My husband did not want me involved. He felt that a wife and woman should not be getting involved with big issues. He told me he was not sure if he could tolerate it if anyone came up to him and said anything about me. So, me being a woman and obeying and obedient back then, I withdrew from a lot of my activities during my marriage.

García: What were you involved with then during your marriage?

Treviño: My family and working at the school. It was now a nine-month position, and I worked during the summer in the migrant program. My husband from 1966 to 1970 worked for Community Action. After 1970 my husband got so sick that he quit that position, and we opened our own business.

García: What kind of business did you operate?

Treviño: We ran a restaurant. It was located on E Street near the Coast to Coast Store. The name of the business was called the "Q" or the Quincy Recreation Center. We ran it from 1970 to 1975. However, for some reason, we always had some problems. Part of the Mexican community did not want us catering to the whites, and if we did, we got boycotted.

García: What was your role in the restaurant?

Treviño: I worked at the school and then I would come to the restaurant afterwards and help with cashiering, waiting on tables, and fixing some of the food.

García: What kind of problems did you have?

Treviño: When I say the Mexicans were against us, what I meant was the younger Mexican generation. The older generation or working class were always nice, courteous. It was the younger kids who were becoming very militant. In 1973 they had a walkout from the high school. It was that bunch of kids. They were the ones who discouraged the whites from coming in. The whites were not avoiding our place because we were Mexican owned, but were being harassed by the young Chicanos.

García: What did you mean that some of the Chicano people did not want you and your husband catering to white people in your restaurant?

Treviño: It was a group of Chicano kids who hung out at our restaurant, or what I call loitering there, that felt my husband was discriminating against them because if they were not eating he wanted them out. And because of that they started saying that he only wanted white customers.

García: Were you involved in the Chicano movement in any way?

Treviño: Not really, I just remember [that] when the Chicanos had the walkout, the Quincy community was trying to keep it real quiet, but my husband had a friend in the *Wenatchee World* and he called him.

García: Do you remember why they had a walkout?

Treviño: No, not really. It had a lot to do with the Chicano movement. My sister Carrie was asked to walk out and she said she did not believe in it. When she refused, many of the Chicano students ignored her.

García: What happened to you and your family after 1975?

Treviño: Well, my husband got very ill with a sickness called lupus. Very little was known about the disease then. He became a manic-depressive and was taken to American Lake Veterans Hospital. We had to close the business. And when he came home, I had to quit my school job to take care of him. I had no choice. At that time I had very little knowledge about Social Security benefits, and when he came home he started receiving Social Security. It was also at this time that I had to ask for assistance from the government, and it broke my heart. No matter how low income we were, we always budgeted for the hard months. So when the winter of 1976 came around, I had no choice but to ask for assistance.

García: By this time you are running the household. How many children did you have?

Treviño: I had three altogether, but at this time only two. Between October 1975 and December 1975 I ran the business by myself, worked at the school, and took care of my kids. My employer, Jerry King, was very understanding. I would go to work and leave at ten to go run the business. I was working about three hours at the school to keep my medical benefits. On Sundays, I left at five in the morning to go see my husband. It was like that for three to four months. When he was released, I had no choice but to quit my jobs and ask for assistance.

García: After your first child was born, what were your options concerning having more?

Treviño: I decided to wait to have any more children because shortly after the first birth my husband began to get very ill. The future was uncertain so my option was to wait. After about three years I decided to go off contraceptives, and my husband stated that if I get pregnant, I get pregnant. I did get pregnant and had my second child, Ricardo, in 1971. After that we decided no more children because his illness was getting worse and worse. My husband died in 1978, and I had another child from a different individual. My third child was from another relationship in which this person came into my life when I was very vulnerable and I always wanted a third child. It was very difficult at [the] time because I was a woman, single parent, not married, and then I was pregnant. My third child's name is Agosto Renaldo Treviño, and he was born in 1981.

García: What happened after your husband came home?

Treviño: Well after three months Jerry King asked me if I was ready to come back to work, and I looked at my husband to see his reaction, but at this time my husband needed my care full time. I tried to convince him that if I went to work I could come back during my breaks and be with him. He finally realized it was not right to hold me back, so I went back to work. In the meantime he was in and out of the hospital. Finally in June of 1978 he went to the hospital and died that same month.

García: After the death of your husband, were you treated any differently by family members because you were now a single mother, widow, and single woman?

Treviño: After my husband died, I became very depressed and was taking the antidepressant Valium because I was very stressed out. I finally realized that my kids suffered so much with their father's sickness and now they had to see me go through depression. One day I just threw all of my pills away and decided that was it. I then went and told my boss I was ready to go back to work. When my husband was alive we really did not have much of a life because he was sick so much. He was seriously ill for over ten years. So my kids grew up seeing their father in pain. I forced myself [to] get off the pills and try to live a normal life. However, for over ten years a normal life for me was taking care of my husband because of his illness. That was all gone now. My sons and I actually mourned before his death and now we needed to start living. My in-laws could not understand why I did not mourn for [a] year and wear the traditional black clothing. I never believed in that, and mother felt the same way. We had so many relatives dying that if we followed that tradition we would always be wearing black. So, very soon after his death I started doing things with [the] children instead of staying home and mourning. I also started to go out more with my friends. My in-laws were the most difficult. They practically disowned me and started saying that I probably did not love my husband. There were other people also who did not accept what I was doing because of our Mexican culture. But I remember I put up with so much with my husband when he was ill, especially his mood swings, and he would become very abusive. The abuse would be physical and mental. He would hit me physically until finally I could not take any more. We were taught never to talk back to avoid confrontations.

García: Do you believe that his physical abuse towards you was related to his disease?

Treviño: Some of it might have been, but I believe he could not handle seeing me becoming more independent. As I became more independent I became more vocal when I did not see something that was right and he was not used to that. He was used to the notion that whatever he said was right.

García: Were you involved in other organizations?

Treviño: Yes, I was. My job at the elementary school did not remain static as a home visitor. I got more involved by working with students who were potential school drop-outs. The Quincy School District had the largest referral rate to the HEP program, which was a high school equivalency program. Basically, the students would get their general education degree and move on to either employment or to college. This was around 1979–80. I was really targeting the Chicanas. Many of the Mexican parents did not believe in their daughters going away for college.

García: Did you ever go into the high school to find out what the problem was?

Treviño: Yes. When I was doing registration and records I would notice that many of the students were missing certain credits to graduate. I brought this to the attention of the counselor. I knew about the new PASS program coming in. I took it upon myself to sign Quincy up for the program. The PASS program was basically a correspondence program that targeted low-income and agriculture families. I would take busloads of Chicano kids to workshops in Moses Lake because many of the universities were recruiting there. Otherwise they would never hear about it. They did not get it at home like the Anglo kids. It is my belief that in the white community, they probably talk about college a lot in the homes. In Mexican families they do not because there is no experience with the university life. Many Mexican kids are at a disadvantage because of this, and the schools do a poor job of pushing Mexican kids into the university. Many of the Mexican families leave that up to the schools, but it really does not happen.

García: Did you get involved in community politics?

Treviño: Yes, I was appointed to the Quincy City Council. This came about because one of our other Mexican community members, who had also been appointed by the mayor, realized they needed someone from the Mexican community on the council. So Charles Sulpuveda was appointed before I was. The mayor at that time [was] Ken McGrew. He was mayor for fourteen years. At that time not many people wanted to run for mayor.

García: As far as you know, was Charles the first Mexican to be on the council?

Treviño: Yes. But he moved out of town so he asked around to find someone else as a possible candidate to speak for the Mexican community. He is still around and still very much involved and well respected. He is on the police committee. He told Ken about me, and I was called in and I was appointed to the council. My first year on the council was 1978, and I was on for a year and a half. When the position came up for re-election, I did not run because I wanted to spend time with my children.

García: During the time you were with the council, did anything significant happen in regards to the Mexican community?

Treviño: Well, one of the hardest things was getting the affordable housing going near the junior high. Quincy has always had a problem with affordable housing. The community has made some small steps to correct this.

García: When you were appointed to the city council position, how did your family react?

Treviño: My family was very happy and honored I was appointed. The only person that I felt was not supportive, again, was my mother-in-law. She called me and sounded resentful about what I was accomplishing now that her son was dead.

García: When did you make a career change and why?

Treviño: That happened in 1986. However, before that occurred I really felt that I had not achieved anything with my life. I was about to turn forty and my life was passing by. I was really getting stressed out. I felt I needed a change. My oldest son was going to graduate in 1986. I was not really looking for a new job but my sister who worked at the Department of Social and Health Services (DSHS) called me and told me about a position there that was opening up and it was bilingual. I was sent an application and I filled out part of it. I received a call from a supervisor who wanted to know if I was still interested in the position. She agreed to stop by my home and help me finish filling out the application. She interviewed me and then two days later tells me I have been hired. I still had my job at the school and I was in the middle of this big project. It was difficult for me to leave at that time. I told DSHS that I could not start for a couple of months. Meanwhile, the project director at the school could not find anyone. But eventually they did find someone and I started at DSHS in March of 1986.

García: I want to back up just a little bit to the time when you were on the council. Were you the only woman on the council?

Treviño: No, there was another woman by the name of Mrs. Neville. She was a teacher.

García: As a woman on a predominately male council, especially as a Mexican woman, did you notice any kind of problems with being a woman? How were your ideas being accepted or were they being seriously considered?

Treviño: I felt no problems, but I was assigned to the street, water, and sewer committee. Being from the background that I had, I felt that I was assigned to the wrong committee. They should have assigned me to the police committee or somewhere else where I could use my expertise as Mexican community member, but on the street, sewer, and water committee? I brought it up, but all the committees were all set up and I stayed there. It was very boring.

García: Explain your career path since 1986 to the present.

Treviño: I started off in DSHS as a financial specialist. It was also the time when the new immigration laws were coming into effect, and I got involved with that. The INS official who was stationed in Wenatchee asked me to come and talk to the INS employees and give them some background on the people they would be legalizing. Basically, I explained how we helped Mexican immigrants and a background of the area. What kind [of] work they did, why they were coming into the DSHS office. The Immigration Reform and Control Act had a big impact on our department.[33] So I was put in charge of the limited-English customers, and my caseload went up to 700. I was a financial specialist for six or seven years. Then in 1992 I took a position as a financial specialist for Children Services. I was there for three years and returned to the welfare office in 1995 as [a] Financial Specialist III.

García: Please explain your duties at the present time.

Treviño: My duties now are implementing the new welfare reform laws and work first programs. There are many changes now because of the new immigration laws.

García: How did you get involved in the campaign of Patricia Martin, who is currently the mayor of Quincy?

Treviño: I got involved in her campaign because she shows a sincere interest in the Mexican community. She has been involved in the schools and with the Mexican community. She has always kept an eye out for the needy population of the community. I've seen her helping Mexican families winterize their homes by putting plastic sheeting over the windows. She has always been there for the community. She first ran in 1993 and was successful in her campaign. She was the only mayor that I can remember that has never had a conflict of interest because she does not work for anyone or own a business. She was strictly for the people.

García: Did you campaign for her?

Treviño: Yes, I did. I sent out literature, door knocking, phone calls, painting signs, etc. Then I got involved with her on another issue that she [is] fighting very hard on. This involves the issue of fertilizer. When she explained the dangers of the use of fertilizer, I could not believe it. Especially when I realized that the Mexicans are the ones exposed to these chemicals. There are so many heavy metals that they can't get rid of, and much of it has been turned into fertilizer. There is an old pond where they used to dump the chemical waste located by the high school. Many community meetings have taken place where Patty has been booed. You have to remember that this is an agriculture community. Some of the biggest companies are fertilizer companies like Quincy Farm Chemical and Cenex. Pete Romano, who owns Quincy Farm Chemical, was very much against Martin's campaign. They employ a lot of people and farmers buy their product. Cenex finances many of these farmers. Basically, Patty was trying to convince these companies to clean up their act. When the wind blows by this old pond, the wind carries the remnants of it throughout the whole town.

García: As a Mexican woman, what have been your positive and negative experiences in Quincy?

Treviño: Well, first of all, Quincy has been a growing community in regards to the Mexican population. When I first came here, it was so small. Now, when I go around town to all the businesses, I see many Mexican employees, especially women. There are times when I run into farmers around town and they recognize me, but they always try to place me as one of their laborers. Instead of recognizing me as a community activist, they stereotype me. They still look at Mexicans as laborers and nothing more. Other issues I face are at work. There is still the idea that many Mexican workers at DSHS are hired because of their skin color. They do not realize the experience that some people might have. I have been working with the Mexican community since the 1960s, and because of that I compete very well against individuals with college degrees. Some positions I received over supervisors because of my experience. There are always comments in reference to being a Mexican. It is a continuing battle that has not stopped. Here in Quincy, I believe we are ten or fifteen years behind the Yakima Valley in the sense that the valley has had people of Mexican descent involved in their communities to a greater extent. You see them in business, education, and administration, and all sectors of the community. In Quincy they are just starting. And Wenatchee is even further behind than Quincy is, so can you imagine? Wenatchee is like it was in the 1960s in Quincy.

García: Do you feel that there is resistance for change from the Quincy community?

Treviño: Yes, there is. Basically, the city council is made up of business owners who look out for their own interest. And most of them are Anglos except for Tony Gonzales, who works for Lamb-Weston and whose father-in-law is the manager of Cenex.

García: How long has Tony been on the council?

Treviño: Since 1992 or 1993.

García: Are you involved with the Democratic party?

Treviño: Yes, I am. I've been involved with the Grant County chapter of the state Democratic party.

García: Why are there very few Mexican women involved in politics?

Treviño: Well, that is a difficult question. Many believe it is boring and that it is for old women, but it is not, of course. Many do not want to be the only Mexican. I'm usually the only Mexican but I don't let it stop me. I was also involved in the Centennial Celebration in Washington in 1989. I won a silver medal for the two-person canoe race. I was told I was the only Mexican to receive a medal that year. So, you see, I don't let the color of my skin stop [me] from participating in activities.

García: Have you ever witnessed or experienced any type of sexism from the Chicanos in Quincy?

Treviño: No, I never really have. I am not sure why. Maybe because it is the way I carry myself and I somehow put a stop to it before it happens. Some might say that I intimidate some of the Chicanos. Maybe the only form that I experience is when I am running at noon and some Mexicanos will see me and whistle and say, "¡He mamasita!" (Hey baby!). That upsets me so much.

García: What kind of role has female companionship played in your life?

Treviño: I have a lot more male friends, however, my closest friends are females. I particularly have one female friend, Irma Sepulveda, that has played a big role in my life. When we were growing up we were not that close. It was not until she got married and she saw everything I went through in my marriage. We became close friends when later she also became a teacher's aide in Quincy. We just started confiding in each other about our marriages. When my husband passed away she was there for me. She has basically been there for me through all my crises. She also went through some hard times with her family, and I was there for her. Her kids I regard as my kids, and I would do anything for them. Since I never had a daughter, her daughter was the closest thing so when it came time for her *quinceañera* I helped arrange everything for the ceremony.[34] The easiest way to describe our friendship is I feel her pain and she feels mine. She does many things with me. She visits my relatives with me and we participate in church functions together. She is also my youngest son's *madrina* [godmother] and her husband is his *padrino* [godfather].

García: As you have aged in this community, have people treated you any differently?

Treviño: I am now fifty years old, and many people have seen me develop in the community. There are still many people who are a great deal older than I in the Chicano community. I feel that they have seen me as [a] role model for their children. I also believe that because they have seen me involved in so many activities Chicanos are starting to see that they can also get involved. I've actually seen it happening before me. There are many more people from the Chicano community that are now involved than there used to be. It has been a very positive experience, and many people comment about how strong I am.

García: What kind of future plans do you have?

Treviño: Well, I feel that I really need a change from my job. Not because I am tired of it, but I feel there is so much more I want to do while I am strong. I want to travel and possibly go into business with my sister. We are thinking of opening up some type of store or even a restaurant. I am very athletic so I want to devote more time to do that. I'm involved with many athletic events, and I do it mostly to stay in shape, but also it allows me to meet people.

García: Sometime in the future would you like to get married again?

Treviño: That is one of the questions that everyone brings up. I have become so independent now, and my father says I will not get married again because I do not want any male telling me what to do. He sometimes gets mad at me. I tell him that after growing up with him, my brothers, and being married, and all of them telling me what to do, maybe he is right, I do not want to get remarried. I am not saying I will never remarry, it just is not in my plans right now. It is not a high priority. My high priority is me.

García: From your perspective, have Chicanas changed over the years in Quincy?

Treviño: From what I have seen, Chicanas have become more outgoing and working in positions that was never seen before. No longer do you just have Chicanas working just in low-skill positions. But what is needed is more involvement by Chicanas in the community. I would love to see more Chicanas involved in politics, especially with the women's Democratic party in our region. Right now I am the only one. They need to realize that there is a lot of power by using the vote. I belong to the AFL-CIO and have been very active in the union, but I am one of only a few Chicanas involved in the whole state of Washington. I know there [are] hundreds of Chicanas working for the state, county, or municipal agencies that could get involved, but don't. Also, I wish more Chicanas would come back to the community. There are many more Chicanas leaving now and getting a college education, and we need more like that here in Quincy as role models and to encourage other young students.

In her thirty-four years of living in Quincy, Treviño witnessed the growth and development of the Chicana community, as well as being one of its participants. During that time period, many Chicanas progressed from the agricultural fields to semiskilled and professional positions. However, according to Treviño, this development was difficult and painful. From an early age she confronted the issues of ethnicity and identity, racism, gender, sex roles, family, and marriage. Her own words tell a story of struggle, pain, joy, and eventually a sense of independence and peace with what she has accomplished and who she is.

Treviño's transition to the Pacific Northwest and enrollment in Quincy High School provided her first notion of racial identity. She arrived in Quincy at the age of fifteen, a sophomore in high school. Her family represented one of the many families from the second stage of Chicano migration to Quincy, at a time when the population consisted mostly of whites. In fact, Treviño recalled every Chicano student by name because of the small number of Chicanos enrolled at the time. She came from a high school in Texas in which blacks and Mexicans made up the majority to the Quincy School District, in which no blacks existed and only a handful of Mexican students. Most of the Mexican students who came from south Texas experienced similar culture shock. Some of them struggled to gain acceptance within the predominately white student population.

The early 1960s marks the beginning of the Chicano movement,[35] which did not reach Quincy until the late 1960s or early 1970s. Although the Latin American Association (LAA) existed, Chicanos functioned within the parameters of the established mainstream political system and used the LAA as a social club rather than an instrument for social change. The emergence of the Progressive League of United Mexican Americans (PLUMA) in 1967 changed the orientation of political organizing in Quincy and significantly affected the Columbia Basin. As a grass-roots entity, the league's primary goals were addressing economic development and political and social concerns. Additionally, PLUMA played an important role in developing Chicano cultural awareness, which had been lacking in the Quincy community.

In the early 1960s, Mexican students in Quincy did not use the term *Chicano.* According to Treviño, the prevailing label used in Quincy to describe people of Mexican descent was *Mexican-American.*[36] The ideas and terms used during the period provide an understanding of the dynamics of identity during the early 1960s.

> You never heard the term *Chicano.* Most of the time you were either a *Mexicana* or someone trying to act like a *gabacha* [white]. If it were the Mexicans trying to put you down, they would say, "Se creer gabacha." The term *Chicano* was considered low class by my parents, so they would not allow us to use that term.
>
> Once in a while you would hear [*Mexican-American*]. More often it was

> *Spanish-American.* We were taught not to use the term *Mexican-American* because if you claimed your heritage, you were branded right away.

According to these passages, several different labels were used to describe a woman of Mexican descent. While in high school, Treviño did not identify with the term *Chicana,* which was common. From the interviews it is clear that the label *Mexicana* prevailed among Treviño and her peers. Treviño's identification as a *Mexicana* reflected the values and customs of the patriarchal family structure in which she was raised and in which *la familia* was celebrated. The unequal gender relations within her family and in her community can be attributed to the traditional male domination within Mexican families. When Treviño challenged this system, she was accused of acting non-Mexican or trying to be "white." The term *gabacha* or *agabachada* (white identified) denoted cultural betrayal and assimilation of non-Mexican values and life-styles. As Treviño adapted to her new environment in Quincy and refused to confine herself to strictly Mexican friends, the term *gabacha* followed her throughout high school. However, as she became active within the community, she experienced less oppression from within her own cultural group and family.

Despite trying to "fit in," many Mexican students experienced some form of overt racism or stereotypes by the Anglo community. As explained by Treviño:

> No matter what the circumstances were, Mexican students were labeled "migrants." And, many of the white students looked down on migrant school children. . . . The assumption was made that new Mexican students were here for the harvest. I remember one of my Anglo teachers telling me, "Oh, you are here for the harvest and the weeding." At that time I had no idea what she was talking about, and I looked at her, puzzled. I thought that maybe I should answer yes. From that time on I began to get the feeling that maybe I should answer yes to the things they wanted to hear.

At an early age Treviño gained confidence and awareness of her identity by becoming involved in a multitude of organizations and struggles. Starting at the age of sixteen, she became a member of the Latin American Association. Her involvement with unionization began at the age of nineteen. She held political office in the 1970s, and her continued involvement with the Democratic party and community issues illustrates her commitment to progressive politics. However, when discussing her activism and contributions to the Mexican community in Quincy, she discounted her role and said that she could not remember being involved with the Chicano movement. Treviño represents one of the many Chicanas in Quincy whose daily life consisted of activism and struggle but who do not view their efforts as noteworthy.

Except for Catholic groups, organizations in Quincy such as the Latin American Association (LAA), the Community Action Council, and the Progressive League of United Mexican Americans were disproportionately male. Despite the small number of Chicanas involved in organizations, they made a significant impact on the community. When Treviño joined the LAA in the 1960s, two other Chicanas, Jovita Valdez and May Gonzales, were instrumental in providing guidance and leadership, not only for the organization but for Treviño as well. Jovita later organized and ran the Quincy Community Service Center as part of the Grant County Community Action Program, which advised migrants on local resources. May Gonzales remained active within the community by becoming involved with the Grant Community Action Council. Chicanas were also visible in church groups. Mexican women joined the Catholic Altar Society and provided spiritual guidance to the community by arranging wakes and rosaries and by organizing the celebration of the *quinceañera*. Additionally, the Catholic Altar Society provided Treviño with the opportunity to meet community leaders and activists. Finally, many Chicanas in Quincy benefited from the Great Society programs implemented by the Johnson administration in the 1960s. Programs such as the Migrant Day Care Center, the Quincy Community Center, the Grant County Community Action Council, and Northwest Rural Opportunities were all funded by the War on Poverty programs. Treviño, Jovita Valdez, and May Gonzales, to name just a few, received valuable training and leadership during this time period.

Throughout Dora Treviño's life, the interrelationships of race, class, and gender have manifested themselves. This is particularly true when discussing labor issues, and Treviño provides ample evidence of oppression based on gender. For example, when she was growing up and migrating from state to state with her extended family, she observed men and women working side by side, doing the same type of work.

> Our family would leave from April until October, when the sugar beet harvest ended. In between those months we would thin and weed the sugar beets. We would do this several times until they were ready to harvest. The women did the same work as the men.

Later in life, Treviño observed and felt the inequities of the sexual division of labor, not in the fields but in the more structured environment of the warehouses. It appears that when women worked in the fields with men, men and women did the same work and were paid equally.

> In the fields I do not remember very much about being treated any different from the men because we all started at the same hours and left at the same time. However, in the warehouses and packing sheds was a totally different situation. I used to get so mad and I was always very vocal and as a result I was the first one to get laid off. In the potato sheds the women were always put on the conveyer belts to sort potatoes, and it was constant and rapid work. And the men never worked on the belts but would be paid between ten and twenty-five cents more an hour. Women rarely received any breaks during the day, and the less pay was what really bothered me.

According to Treviño, while working in the fields females and males did the same work and very little tension existed. However, in the warehouses, where positions were filled based on gender, foremen exhibited a number of unfair practices, and Chicanas were relegated to the lowest-paying work. After witnessing the poor treatment of women and workers in general, Treviño involved herself in the unionization efforts in Quincy.

> At the warehouses the workers were treated horribly. Safety was not a concern, they did not get their breaks, and they were pushed around. The Teamsters came in, and I started going to their meetings. I would come back and start talking to people. Then I went door to door talking to people about the union. . . . The foreman at the warehouse tried to block my contact with people. When they found out that I was helping to organize, they had me laid off.

Between the late 1940s and the present, the Chicano labor force contributed significantly to the development of the Columbia Basin, with Chicanas composing a large proportion of the work force. However, the most significant contribution to the growth of the Quincy Valley economy is credited to the early pioneers, who were white Americans. Such a myopic view fails to recognize the equally important contributions of the pioneer Chicano laborers. The economic growth of Quincy was based on two important and related factors. On the one hand, the establishment of the Columbia Basin Irrigation Project initiated the economic growth of the area; however, the growth and expansion of the economy required abundant and cheap labor. Chicano labor met the need.[37]

Treviño's oppression as a Chicana went beyond the workplace. Growing up in a traditional patriarchal structure, she first encountered the forces of that system when she was sent to the Pacific Northwest from Texas to serve her brother. Although she admits she went voluntarily, the fact remains that either she or her sister was going to be sent to Washington.

> My oldest brother, Chencho, had a lot of power, and whatever he wanted he received. He told my parents that he needed one of my sisters, Lala, who was my oldest sister so she could cook, clean, and take care of the house in Washington.

Treviño ended up convincing her parents to let her go to Washington so that her older sister could finish high school.

Although Treviño's family exhibited many of the norms and values of a patriarchal family, her mother, Ignacia, did not fit the "traditional" role of a Mexican mother. In many cases the family exhibited forms of a matriarchal structure. Ignacia made many, if not all, the financial decisions for the family. Treviño also received her first lessons in the political arena from her mother, who was active in Texas politics and later became involved with a number of organizations in Quincy. Additionally, it was Ignacia who placed the importance of educating her daughters above the need for the supplemental income they could bring into the family. Ignacia actively resisted the traditional role of a Mexican mother by pursuing activities outside of the home, including employment in the warehouses. However, as Treviño points out, her mother did continue a dual role.

> In our household my mother made many of the decisions, especially when it came to finances. I remember my mother making my father believe he was making all the decisions, but in reality she had [a] great deal of influence within the household. After I finished high school my mother went to work in the sheds, and I felt so sorry for her because then she would come home and work. I mean, she would work like a man out in the packing sheds, and then [be] expected to come and do the housework.
>
> In a way [my mother fit the role of a "traditional" Mexican mother]. By that I mean she was a strong woman and she would not be very vocal in the house, but would . . . wait and later come forth with a very firm decision.

The pattern of male dominance continued when Treviño left home and got married. She admits that her husband was controlling and abusive and that he limited her activities.

> When I got married my husband did not want me working with the union. Again, it is that old Mexican tradition where the man rules the household. . . .

> My husband did not want me involved. He felt that a wife and a woman should not be getting involved with big issues. He told me he was not sure if he could tolerate it if anyone came up to him and said anything about me. So, me being a woman and obeying and obedient back then, I withdrew from a lot of my activities during my marriage.

The characteristics displayed by the Sánchez Treviño family reveal several forms of the traditional patriarchal family. This can be observed with Treviño's relationship with her brother and later her husband, for both demanded obedience and control over her life. However, within the household male dominance was countered by the influence and authority of Treviño's mother, Ignacia. In many instances Ignacia dominated the decision-making process in the family, and the household became acutely egalitarian when she was employed. Dora's relationship with her husband contained similar patterns of traditional controlling mechanisms. Like Ignacia, Dora Treviño enjoyed independence and influence within her household that later helped her recover from years of abuse. Overall, the Treviños demonstrated strong emphasis on familism, or the traditional norms of the patriarchal family, but the Sánchez Treviño women did not allow themselves to be confined by the rigid boundaries of such a structure.

Following the death of her husband in 1978, Treviño's life changed dramatically. After a period of transition she realized that, as a single parent with two young children, she needed to focus on the future. During this stage of her life she focused on her children and the community. In 1978 she was appointed by Mayor Ken McGrew as the first woman of color to sit on the Quincy City Council. Additionally, she began to work actively with young Chicanas in the high school, preparing them for college. By 1986, Treviño felt a new sense of independence, and she worked with the largest state agency. She became more involved with the Mexican community than she had been since 1978. In late 1997, Treviño joined other community activists in an attempt to prohibit local farmers and several fertilizer companies from dumping toxic waste near school facilities.

During all of her activities, Treviño had a chance to observe how the Chicano experience changed.

> Quincy has been a growing community in regards to the Mexican population. When I first came here it was so small. Now, when I go around town to all the businesses I see many Mexican employees, especially women. There are times when I run into farmers around town, and they recognize me, but they always try to place me as one of their laborers. Instead of recognizing

> me as a community activist they stereotype me. They still look at Mexicans as laborers.

Treviño views the Chicano community in a larger context. Because of her job and involvement with the state Democratic party, she has been able to analyze the development of other regions. She reports that the Yakima Valley provides better business and community opportunities for the Mexican population. In Wenatchee, Washington, where she works, she observes a continual conflict of cultures between the Anglo and Mexican communities. She attributes this to the rise of the Mexican population and the unwillingness of the Anglo community to accept the fact that Mexicans are no longer moving back and forth from Mexico or state to state. She places Quincy between Yakima and Wenatchee, Yakima having the least resistance to change and Wenatchee the greatest.

Since the death of Treviño's husband in 1978 she has not remarried, and one of my last questions was about her plans for the future and whether or not they might include marriage. Her response to this question sums up her relationship with men since she was a child.

> That is one of the questions that everyone brings up. I have become so independent now, and my father says I will not get married again because I do not want any male telling me what to do. I tell him that after growing up with him, my brothers, and being married and all of them telling me what to do, maybe he is right, I do not want to get remarried. I am not saying I will never remarry, it just is not in my plans right now. It is not a high priority. My priority is me.

Treviño admits that she has had more male friends than female. However, she is quick to indicate that female companionship has provided the closest friendships. She has drawn tremendous support from Patty Naigle, former mayor of Quincy, and her longtime friend Irma Sepulveda. During Naigle's campaign for the mayor of Quincy, a strong friendship emerged between Treviño and Naigle. Additionally, the two were in the vanguard for legislative change in regards to the disposal of fertilizer waste and products. Treviño indicated that her friendship with Irma Sepulveda revolved around family, church, and strong support during times of crisis. She describes their friendship in these terms:

> Irma Sepulveda . . . has played a big part in my life. . . . When my husband passed away she was there for me. She has basically been there for me through all my crises. She also went through some hard times with her family, and I

> was there for her. . . . The easiest way to describe our friendship is I feel her pain and she feels mine.

Women have played an important role in Treviño's growth. Her mother had a significant impact during her early years, as did other women who were community activists. Since the death of Treviño's husband, she has relied on the support and companionship of females, particularly as confidantes.

The interview with Treviño does not provide a complete picture of Chicanas in the Pacific Northwest. However, it does begin to place Chicanas into the incomplete history of the region. By allowing us to view her life, even if from afar, Treviño allows us a glance at the daily life of a Chicana in the Pacific Northwest. This perspective shows the conditions in which many Chicanas live their daily lives. Treviño's story adds to the notion that Chicanas' life experiences are different from both Chicanos' and white women's.

NOTES

1. Aztlán is considered the homeland of the Mexica (Aztecs). After founding Tenochtitlán (present-day Mexico City) in 1325, the Mexica chronicled that they had originated from the north, most likely from the state of Nayarit, only four hundred miles from Mexico City. However, early Spanish chroniclers, influenced by the Spanish search for the seven cities of gold, placed Aztlán's location in the southwestern United States. Since the 1960s Chicanos have used the concept of Aztlán as a cultural icon/symbol and homeland. I use it in the title of this paper to denote that Chicanos have moved beyond what are considered the traditional boundaries of Aztlán (the southwest) and to emphasize that Aztlán is a concept of identity not exclusive to the Southwest.

2. Many generations of Mexicans had considered the term *Chicano* to be a pejorative in-group reference to lower-class persons of Mexican descent. In the 1960s the term was adopted by young Chicanos to reassert pride in their indigenous past and their right to self-determination and as a unifying symbol against racism by Anglos against people of Mexican descent.

3. Carlos Maldonado and Gilberto García, eds., *The Chicano Experience in the Northwest* (Dubuque, Iowa: Kendall/Hunt Publishing Company, 1995), p. 38. Washington went from 121,286 to 206,018, a 70 percent increase; Oregon from 66,164 to 110,606, a 67 percent increase; Idaho from 36,560 to 51,679, a 41 percent increase.

4. Roberto M. De Anda, *Chicanas and Chicanos in Contemporary Society* (Boston: Simon & Schuster Company, 1996), p. 15. According to the 1990 census, there are more than 155,000 individuals of Mexican descent in Washington State. If the umbrella rubric "Hispanic" is used, Washington then has more than 206,018. See Guadalupe Friaz,

"A Demographic Profile of Chicanos in the Pacific Northwest," in Maldonado and García, *The Chicano Experience*, pp. 35–65.

5. Erasmo Gamboa, "Mexican Migration into Washington State: A History, 1940–1950," *Pacific Northwest Quarterly* 72 (July 1981): 121.

6. A *corrido* is a narrative ballad composed in Spanish that recounts the historical circumstances surrounding a protagonist.

7. Devra Anne Weber, "*Raiz Fuerte:* Oral History and Mexicana Farmworkers," *Oral History Review* 17, no. 2 (1989): 48.

8. U.S. Department of the Interior, *Water and Resource Service Project Data* (Denver: U.S. Government Printing Office, 1981), p. 380. The Columbia Basin project was the largest reclamation project in United States history. The arrival of water had a tremendous impact on agricultural communities, which continue to attract farm laborers.

9. Washington State Extension Service, *Emergency Farm Labor Specialist Report,* April 21, 1947, p. 1.

10. U.S. Department of Commerce, Bureau of the Census, *A Report of the Seventeenth Decennial Census of the United States, Census Population: 1950, Number of Inhabitants,* vol. 1 (Washington, D.C.: U.S. Government Printing Office, 1952), Table 6.

11. U.S. Department of Commerce, Bureau of the Census, *Census of the Population: 1960, Characteristics of the Population,* vol. 1, pt. 49: *Washington,* p. xx. Since the beginning of this century, attempts to describe people of Mexican descent have resulted in confusion and inconsistencies in identifying the Chicano population. For the first two decades of this century, there was no rubric to describe people of Mexican descent. The 1930 census used the term *color* to differentiate between people who were white and nonwhite. This system of identification was used until 1980, when the Census Bureau began to use *Hispanic.*

12. Ibid., pp. 24–49.

13. By the 1920s, the migration routes north from Mexico and the southwestern United States had clear tributaries culminating in the Midwest, the Rocky Mountain region, and the Pacific Northwest.

14. Interviews conducted by the author in 1992, 1993, and 1997 document a distinct pattern of migration from a region known as the Río Grandé Valley in Texas, which would include communities such as Edinburg, Harlingen, McAllen, Pharr, Mission, Weslaco, and Mercedes. The majority of these people were following the growing and harvest season to the Pacific Northwest, and many already had friends or relatives in the region.

15. "So Huge It Escapes the Eye and Mind," *Quincy Post Register,* Dec. 5, 1952.

16. Interview with Rita and Manuel Puente, Quincy, Washington, April 11, 1992.

17. "Latin American Association Established," *Quincy Post Register,* March 21, 1964; "Latin American Association Donates Funds to Send Youths to Camp,"

Quincy Post Register, May 20, 1965, p. 1; "Roy Alvarez Presents Father Henaghan with a Check for $1400," *Quincy Post Register,* Aug. 12, 1965; "Latin American Association to Sponsor Movies," *Quincy Post Register,* Oct. 14, 1965; "Latin American Association Donates $100 to Quincy Community Float Committee," *Quincy Post Register,* May 2, 1968.

18. Interview with Andres Martinez, Feb. 27, 1993. PLUMA was one of the earliest and most successful grass-roots organizations to come out of Quincy. Martinez describes the organization as a political tool, not only for Quincy: chapters appeared in Moses Lake, Othello, and Warden—basically throughout the Columbia Basin.

19. "Newly Incorporated Firm to Issue Stock," *Quincy Post Register,* Jan. 15, 1970.

20. "Chicano Parents Form School Advisory Group," *Wenatchee World,* Jan. 18, 1973.

21. *Washington State Standard County/City Profile: Quincy* (Moses Lake, Wash.: Grant County Community Development, 1990, 1996), p. 1.

22. Ibid., p. 2. By 1990 there were twelve different industrial firms in Quincy employing more than 1,300 full-time employees. Except for Celite Chemical, all of them support the agricultural industry.

23. U.S. Census Bureau, *1990 Census of the Population and Housing By Place,* pt. 49: *Washington* (Washington, D.C.: U.S. Government Printing Office, 1992–93), p. 33.

24. *Washington State Standard County/City Profile: Quincy*, p. 1. No breakdown by race or ethnicity was available.

25. The City of Quincy Comprehensive Plan, 1996–2016, EX-6.

26. Quincy School District 144–01, P-105A School Enrollment Report (October 2, 1997), p. 6, Quincy, Wash.

27. The term "push-out" rate is used instead of "drop-out" because studies have shown that many Chicano students continue to receive an inferior education in comparison to white students, which tends to push students out of school. Chicano students continue to have one of the highest "push-out" rates in the nation.

28. Interview with Dora Sánchez Treviño, Quincy, Washington, Sept. 21, 1997.

29. I have attempted to be conscious of the fact that I am a male interviewing Chicanas. I have known these individuals since I was a child; they are all friends of my family. Additionally my coming from the same class background and not being a stranger to the community made the oral interviews more comfortable and easier.

30. Since 1993 I have interviewed fifteen individuals, four of them women. All of the interviews were conducted in Spanish and English. For this article I use primarily the interview with Dora Treviño.

31. Interview with Dora Sánchez Treviño.

32. The text of the interview was gathered from two sessions with Dora Treviño, September 21 and November 28, 1997.

33. In 1986 the Immigration Reform and Control Act (IRCA) was implemented.

It provided amnesty for undocumented individuals who could show proof of residence in the U.S. since 1982. Additionally, it imposed penalties on employers who hired undocumented workers.

34. A *quinceañera* is observed during the fifteenth year of a young woman's life. This ceremony has pre-Columbian roots that can be traced to the Mesoamerica region of Mexico and specifically to the Toltec and Maya cultures. It was customary to present a fifteen-year-old girl to the community and declare her an adult with all of the responsibilities that come with adulthood. With the Spanish conquest of Mesoamerica in the sixteenth century, this ceremony was combined with Catholicism and now reaffirms a young woman's commitment to the doctrine of the Catholic church. There is no similar rite of passage for males.

35. Generally, the Chicano movement is considered to have started in 1967–68, when Chicano students spontaneously walked out of classes in California, Texas, Colorado, and New Mexico, thus signaling the birth of the Chicano student movement. However, the 1960s Chicano movement can be traced back to earlier generations of Chicanos who fought valiantly since the beginning of the twentieth century for civil liberties and justice.

36. The hyphenated label *Mexican-American* has been associated with the concept of assimilation and has been rejected by Chicano activists.

37. Gilberto García and Jerry García, "Mexican Communities in the Columbia Basin Region in the State of Washington," unpublished work, p. 21.

Gender Equality on the Colville Indian Reservation in Traditional and Contemporary Contexts

LILLIAN A. ACKERMAN

Many anthropologists consider it doubtful that gender equality has occurred or might occur in any society, past or present.[1] Their opinion supports the idea that males are dominant over females in all societies.[2] The few studies demonstrating or suggesting the presence of gender equality in certain groups have so far had little influence in changing such views.[3] Further examples of gender egalitarian groups, then, are important to persuade social scientists and the lay public that such societies are not only possible but exist today. The culture of the Colville Indian Reservation in the recent past and in contemporary times presents just such an example of an egalitarian society.

The Colville Indian Reservation in the state of Washington is made up of eleven Plateau Indian groups. Gender equality was reported for the traditional Plateau Indian societies over forty years ago,[4] but was insufficiently described. A study focusing on the relative status of men and women in Plateau culture seemed in order, and the Colville Indian Reservation was chosen for the locus of this research.

The research described here was conducted in 1979–80 on two levels. First, elders, age sixty to ninety (in 1979), were interviewed regarding the status of the genders in their youth, a period dating from about 1910 to 1930 when the foraging economy was still predominant. This memory culture is called "traditional" here because, while many changes had been made from the "aboriginal" period, the foraging way of life was still a viable option, universally exercised. The memory culture recorded in 1979 may be compared with statements made to researchers around 1930 that gender equality existed in Plateau culture.[5] The 1930 period is used as a baseline and then compared with contemporary gender status, almost fifty years later.

Following interviews with elders, younger informants who work for wages or who have salaried employment were then asked to describe aspects of gender status in the contemporary culture. Their information was cross-checked through observation.

Forty-five people from eleven tribes (Sanpoil, Nespelem, Colville, Lakes, Southern Okanogan, Methow, Chelan, Entiat, Columbia, Wenatchi, and one band of Nez Perce) were interviewed in depth during the research. While some details regarding gender status varied within the political and religious spheres among these eleven groups, the variations were minor. In contrast, gender status was identical in the domestic and economic spheres for all groups, probably because of the customary intermarriage among Plateau peoples.

The method for evaluating gender status is based on Schlegel's definition of sexual equality. She defines sexual equality as the equal access, or the different but balanced access, of both genders to power, authority, and autonomy in the economic, domestic, religious, and political spheres. Power is the ability to act effectively on persons or things, to secure desired decisions which are not of right allocated to the individual or to his or her role.[6] Political influence, widely used in Plateau society, falls into this category. Authority is the institutionalized right to make a decision and expect obedience. Autonomy is the right to take independent action without control by others.[7]

Using these definitions, tables were made for each of the four social spheres in both periods, and data gathered during fieldwork were classified and assigned to each sphere under the cells for power, authority, and autonomy for each sex. This process resulted in a summary statement of the degree of participation by each gender in each of the four social spheres in two periods (see Table 1 as an example).

THE ECONOMIC SPHERE: TRADITIONAL CULTURE

In the past, the Plateau Indians were fishers, hunters, and gatherers, living in small villages under the authority of a chief.[8] By the 1920s, people lived on reservations and were scattered on small allotments that they farmed, but chiefs continued to be elected and acknowledged. Along with maintaining their small farms, people pursued traditional economic activities as well: men continued to fish and hunt, and women continued to gather vegetal foods. The power, authority, and autonomy of each gender in the economic sphere during this period are outlined in Table 1. The power cell is blank, since no examples of what I could call economic power were recalled by informants, although they may well have existed.

Table 1 shows that each gender provided approximately half the traditional diet, and both genders valued both flesh and vegetal foods equally. All informants agreed that flesh foods were not considered more important than vegetal foods. This is an important point, for Friedl writes that all hunting and gathering societies esteem meat as the most valued food in the diet. She argues that since men distribute meat to other men, only they can accrue the prestige necessary for political power. Women cannot participate in political power because they do not have the means (meat) to accrue prestige. This situation, according to Friedl's argument, results in males achieving universal dominance over women.[9]

Friedl's theory fails to fit the hunting and gathering phase of Colville Reservation history. To illustrate the point, meat distribution in the Plateau will be described.

The important fall hunting was always done by a group of men and women working together for several days or weeks. The men hunted while the women cooked, made camp, and helped the men drive the animals. After the hunt, the meat was butchered and evenly divided among the families in the camp. This was done as follows: in the evening, all the women in camp sat in a circle. Each woman was presented with a portion of the kill by a man who was not necessarily the hunt leader or the successful hunter. Often an older man was selected to divide and distribute the meat.[10] If a man lived alone, he sat in the circle with the women. This procedure of distribution in the Plateau refutes Friedl's theory that men acquire power through the presentation of meat to other men in all foraging societies.[11] The successful Plateau hunter did not distribute the meat, and so he could not earn political power in this manner. Further, when a man hunted or fished independently, he gave all the food he obtained to his wife, who did what she wished with it. Her first responsibility was to keep the family well fed, but surpluses of food were hers to trade or give away as she pleased.

To explore this question further, informants were asked specifically if good hunters were more influential politically than other persons—that is, if their opinions during political discussions were more highly valued than those of others. The answer was negative. Both genders said that men who were "good providers" of either meat or fish were influential with the chief and their peers, but women who were "good providers" of vegetal foods were equally influential, even though vegetal foods were rarely distributed outside the family. Nevertheless, the work of both genders was equally valued, and the foods they

TABLE 1

The Economic Sphere: Traditional Culture

Men	Women
POWER	
AUTHORITY	
Each gender provided about half of diet	
Flesh and vegetal foods equally valued and important in diet	
Economic skill (hunt, fish) leads to political influence	Economic skill (gathering) leads to political influence
Work of both genders considered equally important by both genders	
Only men made salmon weirs	Only women made lashings for weir tripods
Men fished	Women made nets
Men with Salmon Power built weirs	Women with Salmon Power ensured fish runs
Hunting leaders, Salmon Chiefs	Gathering leaders, salmon shamans
Men prohibited from proximity of root baking oven	Menstrual taboos
Men distributed meat	Women received meat
Boy's first kill ceremony	Girl's first gathering ceremony
Men own personal items and horses	Women own personal items and food
AUTONOMY	
Traders in horses, weapons, hides, fishing implements	Traders in foods, handicrafts
Male and female trade equally important	
Both genders were interpreters	
Both genders gambled	
Men made own weapons and tools	Women made own digging sticks for root gathering

Nancy Judge, Colville Reservation
(courtesy R. E. Ackerman)

obtained were equally valued. Thus political power was not gender specific in the Plateau, since the economic skill of either gender qualified a person to have political influence.

It should be noted on Table 1 that few economic aspects of life as described by informants were identical (indicated by crossing the midline of the table) for men and women in the past. I judged that most items were balanced or equivalent (noted by being placed in opposition on the table). Thus only men built salmon weirs, but informants reported that only women provided the lashings or thongs for the weir tripods without which they could not be built, and without which salmon could not be captured. Only men fished for salmon, but women provided nets.[12] Men with magical Salmon Power directed the building of the weirs. Women were ordinarily prohibited from approaching the weir, because menstrual blood could frighten the fish away.[13] If the fish run failed, however, a woman with magical Salmon Power was asked to clear debris from the fish traps, a task usually performed by males. Her magical power exerted during this task effected the return of the salmon run. Thus, while fishing was a male monopoly, women had important roles in the task.

Men with superior hunting ability (and with the proper magical power by definition) were chosen as hunt leaders during the communal hunts. Men with superior fishing ability (and the magical power) were chosen to build the weirs and supervise the taking of the fish. Women, too, had such leadership roles. Those with the appropriate magical power were gathering leaders who led others in finding edible plants. It was not necessary to have magical power to find roots, hunt, or fish, but such power was seen as making these tasks easier, especially when the resource was scarce during a bad season.

Large quantities of roots, an extremely important component of the diet, were dried in earth ovens for winter use. Baking roots well was an exacting task, made easier by magical power. It was believed that roots did not bake properly in the proximity of men, particularly unmarried men. Their presence was prohibited in the area.[14]

It is possible that the prohibitions placed on men balanced the similar menstrual taboos placed on women. Since these prohibitions are no longer in effect today, it is difficult to judge whether they were comparable in emphasis for both sexes. The pattern of prohibitions for both sexes, however, suggests that the prohibitions somehow reenforced the sexual division of labor. The menstrual taboo, at least in this culture, was not an indication of low social status, but was only one of several taboos that confirmed the complementarity of the genders.

The economic importance of both genders was symbolized by ceremonies celebrating a boy's first kill or first catch of fish and a girl's first gathering of vegetal foods. A boy might get his first deer about age twelve; a girl's first independent gathering might occur about age eight. These ceremonies continue today.

A married couple did not own material goods jointly. Women owned all food coming into the household, including the meat and fish caught by her husband. She also owned the house poles, the tipi covering, house mats, baskets, all prepared skins, plus a few horses to transport herself and her goods. Men owned only their weapons, clothes, and a number of horses. In case of divorce, men had only these kinds of goods to take away.

Both genders were involved in trade with Indians from other reservations. Women, as the sole proprietors of food, dealt mostly in that commodity, although they also traded handicrafts. Men traded horses, raw hides, and hunting and fishing implements, which they manufactured in earlier times. Informants of both genders judged that the trade of both genders was equally important.

In prereservation times, trading expeditions to the Pacific coast or to Montana required interpreters, and either gender filled this role, although women were said to learn languages more readily than men. Gambling was a prestigious economic activity in which large amounts of goods were redistributed. Both genders participated in this activity, but only with opponents of the same gender. It was believed that menstruating women would destroy the magic on which successful gambling was based.

Men and women each made their own economic implements, thus accentuating their economic autonomy. Men manufactured their hunting and fishing implements. Women fabricated their digging sticks, used for collecting roots, and baskets used in gathering roots, berries, and greens.

The factors listed in Table 1 suggest that the genders had not identical but equally balanced access to all aspects of the traditional economic sphere.

THE ECONOMIC SPHERE: CONTEMPORARY CULTURE

The foraging way of life became impossible for the Colville Reservation Indians around 1939. The building of Grand Coulee Dam destroyed many of the fish runs in the area. Hunting was curtailed by state law, and many of the gathering grounds were occupied by white farms. To survive, the Indians turned to the intensive working of their small farms and ranches, or to low-paid wage labor.

Half of the Colville Reservation lands were removed from Indian ownership in 1892 so that they could be opened to white settlement.[15] Commencing in the 1950s, moves were made by the federal government to force termination on the remaining reservation lands held communally. Only concerted action by many of the Indians defeated this move. In 1970, Congress decided against termination and awarded the tribal government more authority to run the reservation's affairs.

As a result of these and other changes, the economy of the reservation has altered from the past. In major respects, its economy is now similar to that of Euro-American society in that the tribal government staffs offices, manages forests, maintains roads, plans economic development, and administers health, education, and welfare programs. In other ways, the reservation economy remains a separate system. The tribal government does its own hiring by its own rules based on its indigenous cultural traditions. Since these rules differ from those of Euro-American society, the reservation cultural values become clear even in modern context. These values are evident in equal pay for equal work, the presence of female administrators, the ease with which female administrators work with either gender, and the equal importance given to work performed by both genders. These are all legacies of the past. Further, those who need work get it—reflecting, I believe, the foraging ethos of sharing.

The contemporary economic sphere, as it operates within the reservation, is outlined in Table 2. It is immediately apparent that access of both genders to the economic sphere is largely identical today instead of balanced as in the past. There are only two exceptions that may well be inequalities of access. One is that men outnumber women in the top three managerial positions on

TABLE 2
The Economic Sphere: The Contemporary Culture

Men	Women
POWER	
Influence exerted by both genders	
Access to management positions by both genders	
Top three managerial positions filled by men	
AUTHORITY	
First economic achievements of young people recognized	
Equally encouraged in training and employment	
Work considered equally important	
Jobs less gender typed than in Euro-American society	
Equal pay for equal work	
Authority equally effective in management jobs	
	Women's work seen generally as more efficient
AUTONOMY	
The decision to work autonomous for both genders	
	82% to 90% of women work
Trade proceeds owned individually	

the reservation. This may be a result of acculturation—that is, copying the authority structure of Euro-Americans, either because of a change in culture or the need of Euro-American governmental structure to do business only with men. On the other hand, this may be an indigenous element, since Plateau men have always served as spokesmen for the group with outsiders, and these three officials often deal with outsiders.

The other possible inequality of the genders in this sphere is that the quality of women's work is more highly valued than that of men's work today. Informants of both genders say that women are more efficient and conscientious in completing a task and in working eight-hour days. The contemporary opinion is reminiscent of the phrase "Men don't work," which elders of both genders use to describe the male economic role in the past. Of course men "worked," in the sense of providing fish and animal flesh for the diet; moreover, they risked their lives to defend the community. Their activities, however, occurred in strenuous spurts with leisurely periods in between, whereas women were more often occupied with tasks on a daily basis. Thus it is likely that the traditional economic role of reservation women may have better prepared them for the eight-hour days required from workers in an industrial society. The traditional pattern, on the other hand, did not prepare men for this. Furthermore, the incentive to earn money for its own sake, which equals power and prestige in white society, has no attraction for Indian men.

The traditional male intermittent work pattern may account for the observation that women in many North American tribes acculturate more readily to modern society than men do. It is argued, for instance, that differential acculturation among the Oglala Sioux occurs because women are able to continue their homemaker roles in contemporary times, thus experiencing less disruption than men. In contrast, men are completely deprived of their former roles as warriors and hunters.[16]

While this explanation seems obvious at first, it cannot apply to the Plateau tribes of the Colville Reservation, for there has been little continuity in women's roles either. Child bearing and rearing continue, of course, but all else is changed. Office employment is as different from gathering and preserving wild foods as lumbering is different from hunting. What remains from the past is the ethic that women do what they must to support the family, and even provide the major share of support if needed, as they did in the traditional culture. It is suggested here that the better adjustment of Plateau Indian women in contemporary times may be due to their being accustomed to sustained rather than intermittent work.

Other than the two exceptions discussed above, Table 2 shows an identical access of the genders to the economic sphere. Economic influence is exerted by both genders, and access to management positions appears to be attainable by women on an equal basis. Ceremonies celebrating a young person's economic "firsts" continue to be performed for both boys and girls. Young men and women are equally encouraged to get higher education, and both expect to be employed when adult. Women's work and men's work continue to be equally important. While jobs are somewhat gender typed in the Euro-American manner on the reservation, women are also found in male types of employment. They are lumberjacks, they run Caterpillar tractors, and they work as night "watchmen." They were being trained as miners in 1979 when a molybdenum mine was planned on the reservation (the project was terminated by the mining company when mineral prices fell). For all tribally paid positions, men and women receive equal pay for equal work. Problems of gender status in the workplace are not evident, and informants deny that there are any.

Today, both men and women make the decision to seek employment autonomously. Most women do not seek their husband's concurrence if they decide to work. Neither are they urged by their husbands to work. A woman's independence in making this decision is striking compared with a Euro-American woman's situation: she is expected to consult and negotiate with her husband before taking this step. Colville Reservation women expect to be employed unless they have preschool children and no child-care services are available. A recent survey shows that almost 82 percent of Colville women are employed.[17] The actual percentage may be higher, because some employment, such as providing child-care services to others, may not be reported in such a survey.

Today, trading among Plateau, Northwest Coast, and Plains tribes continues. Money from such trade is retained by the individual for personal use.

One may judge that, overall, the access of men and women to the economic sphere is equal in contemporary times. The fact that the access is identical rather than balanced as in the past is suggestive. It is possible that identical access of the genders to the economic sphere is the only way to achieve sexual equality in an industrial society.

THE POLITICAL SPHERE: TRADITIONAL CULTURE

The political sphere as it existed around 1910–30 will be addressed next (see Table 3). Reservation tribes were still foraging during this period, but were also farming small allotments. They continued to elect chiefs and form assemblies made up of both genders.

During this period, individual men and women with superior economic skills exerted equal influence on chiefs and their fellow band members, as described above. Although only men held the office of chief in most reservation tribes, it has been recorded that women could be chosen as chiefs or head political officers among the Southern Okanogan and Lakes tribes.[18] I discovered that a woman served as chief five generations ago among the Chelan as well. Another official, the "woman of great authority," shared power with a male chief in some groups and is recorded among the Southern Okanogan, Methow, and Chelan.[19] All the above tribes reside on the Colville Reservation today.

Contemporary informants of these four tribes deny that women ever served

TABLE 3
The Political Sphere: Traditional Culture

Men		Women
	POWER	
Those with superior economic skills had equal political influence		
		Wives advised chief
	AUTHORITY	
	Assemblies made up of both genders	
Male chief or head political officer		Female possible head political officer (chief) in past
		"Women of great authority" had judicial and advisory functions; called a "female chief"
Hunting and fishing leaders		Gathering leaders Chief's wife served as chief when husband away
		Chief's widow had right to nominate his successor; in some groups, she was temporary chief
	Could serve as peacemaker for tribe	
	AUTONOMY	
	Both genders spoke and voted in assembly	
	A married couple's votes did not need to coincide	
	Warriors of both genders	

as chiefs or head political officers. They confirmed, however, that a "woman of great authority" was elected to fill the office of judge and arbiter in criminal cases, notably feuds. Since the judicial function was reported by anthropologist Verne F. Ray to be the male chief's greatest prerogative, the "women of great authority" were then at least as important as the chief in those groups

TABLE 4
The Political Sphere: Contemporary Culture

Men	Women
POWER	
Access to political influence	
Age an advantage to either gender	
AUTHORITY	
Members of tribal council	
Men outnumber women on tribal council	
Both genders orate on ceremonial occasions	
Active on boards	
AUTONOMY	
Both genders speak publicly with equal frequency	
Married couples vote independently, do not know how spouse votes	
Equally active politically	

in which both existed.[20] Unfortunately, not much information regarding this role has survived today.

Chiefs were always advised in public affairs by their wives: this was an expected role. An indication of the importance of the wife's role is revealed by an incident occurring forty years ago when an otherwise suitable candidate for chief was rejected because his wife was considered unsuitable.

The chief's wife was influential in nominating the chief's successor after he died. In some groups, she served as chief until a successor was elected.

Lesser leadership roles were filled by women. One woman in contact times served as a peacemaker between her tribe and another. The gathering leaders mentioned above were influential politically as well as economically.

Both genders spoke and voted in assembly when a communal decision was being debated. Husband and wife voted completely independently of each other. If there was disagreement between them in the way they spoke or voted, it was not a matter for discussion later.

In prereservation times, a woman had the option to become a warrior even if she was married and had children. It was an autonomous decision that no one could veto. Such women were rare, but numerous enough to be remembered today.

In the traditional political sphere, a more uneven access of the genders appears. One may judge that there is a balanced access of the genders to political life on the chief level, although the opposite opinion also has some validity. However, below the chief level, equal political access of the genders is undeniable.

THE POLITICAL SPHERE: CONTEMPORARY CULTURE

In 1938 a tribal council took over the political functions formerly exercised by chiefs. Fourteen members sit on the tribal council today. Access to this political office is open to both men and women equally (see Table 4).

A number of women have occupied seats on the tribal council since 1938. Only two women were council members during the period of this study, but while they shared equal authority with the twelve male council members, their power or influence was greater. They earned this influence in the 1960s through their position as leaders in the fight against termination of the reservation. Even today, male council members seek their concurrence on solutions to problems, and they were seen to change their votes on important issues to coincide with those of the two women.

Women council members were more numerous in the past. In 1970, nine years before this study was made, six women and eight men sat on the council. Between 1963 and 1969, five women were council members. Informants said that women also served before those dates, and mentioned specific individuals.

Council women are usually assigned to the Health, Education, and Welfare Committee or the Enrollment Committee, subdivisions of the tribal council. These are seen as female concerns, although men sit on these committees as well. The work of these particular groups is perceived to be extremely important, for welfare concerns do not have the inferior status they have in Euro-American culture. The important Enrollment Committee determines the eligibility of a child for reservation membership, and consequently whether the child will participate in benefits such as per capita income. Women also serve on the council committees dealing with leases and timber sales—activities usually associated with males in Euro-American culture.

In the 1960s, the council met only once a month, for there was little business to be handled. Today, more work is needed to deal with problems coming before the council. Although the position of council member is full time and well paid, fewer women than before are willing to serve because extensive travel is now required for the job. Many women are reluctant to leave their children as frequently as the position requires.

The increased need for travel has come about since 1970, when greater autonomy was granted to the reservation. The extensive travel required today of council members seems to be a barrier to women—one that is perceived by both genders. Consequently, while the gender of a candidate does not seem to be relevant in winning office, and personality and talent are the important criteria, the social structure is changing enough to handicap women who wish to serve on the council. They cannot take young children with them on business travels, and they worry about adolescent children left alone at home. Only a few women can arrange for child care during long absences.

The polity loses more than the mere participation of women. Both male and female informants say that women are more suitable as council members because they generally do a better job and are more authoritative. They are seen as tougher, stronger, more outspoken, and more willing to challenge someone, whereas men as a group are more quiet and conservative. This is a generalization, of course, but one that was largely confirmed by observations made during tribal council meetings and conferences between Indians and whites.

Lesser political offices are filled by both genders in approximately equal numbers. Elders of both genders orate on ceremonial occasions, although in previous generations, men did so more frequently. All things being equal, reservation members tend to trust an older person over a younger one in a public role. Thus age in either gender is no handicap in running for office.

Autonomy in the political sphere today involves speaking publicly and voting autonomously. Husbands and wives never reveal how they cast their vote, either to each other or to anyone else before or after an election, whether the election is on the reservation or not. Someone married many years may guess how a spouse votes, but the matter is never discussed. This independence in voting is taken so seriously that one individual was incredulous when he learned that a Euro-American couple would discuss candidates with each other, and would probably influence each other's opinion and then vote identically.

In public meetings of a political nature, it was noted that both genders spoke publicly with about equal frequency. Men and women appear to be equally interested in the political issues concerning the reservation.

The access of the genders to the political sphere in the traditional period was a mixture of identical and complementary rights and privileges. The modern political arrangement displays an almost identical access of the sexes to this sphere (see Table 4).

THE DOMESTIC SPHERE: PAST AND PRESENT

Today, reservation women continue their roles as managers of the family's resources. The ultimate responsibility for the family's survival remains with her, as in the past. While foraging is still done on an occasional basis, employment provides the resources for the major economic needs of the family. If a man's wages are insufficient to meet family needs, his wife seeks employment, if she is not already employed. As noted above, her decision to do this is autonomous. She need not fear community disapproval, since employment is seen as the equivalent of gathering—that is, both activities sustain the family.

When divorce occurred in the past, the women who did not immediately remarry were able to support themselves completely through their gathering efforts. If they chose to live apart from parents or brothers, they traded surplus vegetal products for meat and fish. They received a certain amount of such foods in the communal distributions as well.

The same self-reliance is evident today. Most women do not expect long-term support for themselves and their children when divorce occurs; they are prepared to take complete responsibility. In fact, a female elder was heard to deride a young woman who was seeking support from her ex-husband. Because reservation women are self-reliant and confident, the loss of economic support is never an inhibiting factor when divorce is considered.

THE RELIGIOUS SPHERE: PAST AND PRESENT

The religious sphere in both periods is considered by informants to be the most important and valued aspect of the culture, and access to it by both genders is almost identical. Women as well as men became shamans in the past and were equally powerful. Women shamans were outnumbered by the men in some groups, but equal in number in other groups. Everyone of both genders sought and obtained guardian spirits.

Today, the native guardian spirit religion has persisted and is unchanged in terms of access by gender. However, several new religions have been added to the culture, with some consequent uneven access. For instance, in 1979, only men read the gospels and ushered in the Catholic church. The native Indian Shaker church, a combination of Christianity and the traditional guardian spirit religion, has a preponderance of female officials in the Colville Reservation branch of the church.

CONCLUSIONS

By examining the four sets of tables (only two sets have been presented here), it can be determined that, on the Colville Reservation, the access of both genders to the economic, political, domestic, and religious spheres is identical, or balanced, resulting in a condition of gender equality.

One of the implications of the study of gender status on the Colville Reservation in the past and present is that there is no automatic correlation between the level of socioeconomic integration and gender equality. Anthropologist Eleanor Leacock writes that sexual egalitarianism, like all equality, can exist only among hunting and gathering groups, but that it is destroyed in industrial societies.[21] Modern Colville Reservation culture indicates, however, that modern economic conditions are not incompatible with gender equality. On the contrary, gender equality has persisted as a legacy from the past despite erosion of the traditional culture in other areas. Where the Colville Reservation Indians have the power to control their society, they have not reduced women's status, but have adapted modern economic conditions to their ideology of gender equality.

NOTES

The research for this paper was made possible by fellowships from the Woodrow Wilson National Fellowship Foundation and the Educational Foundation of the American Association of University Women, and by grants from Sigma Xi and the Phillips Fund of the American Philosophical Society. Their support is gratefully acknowledged. I would also like to express gratitude to the many individuals on the Colville Reservation who helped me with their information, patience, and kindness, and also to the Colville Tribal Business Council, which gave me permission to do the research on the reservation. My thanks to Robert E. Ackerman and Linda S. Stone for helpful comments on various drafts of this paper. They do not necessarily agree with the ideas presented.

1. Sherry B. Ortner, "Is Female to Male as Nature Is to Culture?" in Michelle Zimbalist Rosaldo and Louise Lamphere, eds., *Woman, Culture and Society* (Stanford, Calif.: Stanford University Press, 1974), pp. 67–87; Michelle Zimbalist Rosaldo, "Woman, Culture and Society: A Theoretical Overview," in ibid., pp. 17–42.

2. William Tulio Divale and Marvin Harris, "Population, Warfare, and the Male Supremacist Complex," *American Anthropologist* 78, no. 3 (1976): 521–38.

3. Albert S. Bacdayan, "Mechanistic Cooperation and Sexual Equality among the Western Bontoc," in Alice Schlegel, ed., *Sexual Stratification: A Cross-Cultural View* (New York: Columbia University Press, 1977), pp. 270–91; Patricia Draper, "!Kung Women: Contrasts in Sexual Egalitarianism in Foraging and Sedentary Contexts," in Rayna R. Reiter, ed., *Toward an Anthropology of Women* (New York: Monthly Review Press, 1975), pp. 77–109; Eleanor Leacock, "Women's Status in Egalitarian Society: Implications for Social Evolution," *Current Anthropology* 19, no. 2 (1978): 247–75; and Alice Schlegel, "Male and Female in Hopi Thought and Action," in Schlegel, ed., *Sexual Stratification*, pp. 245–69.

4. Verne F. Ray, *Cultural Relations in the Plateau of Northwestern America* (Los Angeles: Publication of the Frederick Webb Hodge Anniversary Publication Fund, Southwest Museum, 1939), p. 24; L. V. W. Walters, "Social Structure," in Leslie Spier, ed., *The Sinkaietk or Southern Okanagon of Washington* (Menasha, Wisc.: George Banta Publishing Company, 1938), p. 96.

5. Ray, *Cultural Relations*, p. 24; Walters, "Social Structure," p. 96.

6. M. G. Smith, *Government in Zazzau, 1800–1950* (London: Oxford University Press, 1960), pp. 18–19.

7. Alice Schlegel, "Toward a Theory of Sexual Stratification," in Schlegel, ed., *Sexual Stratification*, pp. 8–9.

8. Ray, *Cultural Relations*, pp. 11–12.

9. Ernestine Friedl, *Women and Men: An Anthropologist's View* (New York: Holt, Rinehart and Winston, 1975), pp. 8–9, 13.

10. Richard H. Post, "The Subsistence Quest," in Spier, ed., *The Sinkaietk*, p. 22.

11. Friedl, *Women and Men*, p. 22.

12. Post, "The Subsistence Quest," p. 14.

13. Ibid., p. 17.

14. James A. Teit, *The Salishan Tribes of the Western Plateaus*, Bureau of American Ethnology, 45th Annual Report (Washington, D.C.: U.S. Government Printing Office, 1930), p. 185.

15. M. Gidley, *With One Sky Above Us* (1979; rpt. Seattle: University of Washington Press, 1985), p. 31.

16. Eileen Maynard, "Changing Sex-Roles and Family Structure among the Oglala Sioux," in Ann McElroy and Carolyn Matthiasson, eds., *Sex Roles in Changing Cul-*

tures, Occasional Papers in Anthropology (Buffalo: State University of New York, 1979), 1:12–13.

17. Colville Confederated Tribes Health Plan, Nespelem, Washington, 1979.
18. Ray, *Cultural Relations,* p. 24.
19. Walters, "Social Structure," pp. 95–96.
20. Ray, *Cultural Relations,* p. 22.
21. Leacock, "Women's Status," p. 255.

PART 5
THE ARTS

No matter how many responsibilities and hardships arise in family life, work experience, or political struggle, women have seldom failed to search for some touch of beauty in their lives. If it has oftentimes been difficult for them to obtain the training and patronage necessary to become acclaimed professional artists, they have sought to create and delight in accessible art forms that could fulfill their needs for self-expression. In this section, we explore women's interest in sound, color, texture, imagery, and design as expressed through poetry, music, and utilitarian objects like quilts.

Mary Cross, a quilt historian, reminds us that written documents and oral testimony are not the only sources scholars can use to interpret the past and women's contributions to it. Material artifacts, such as needlework, provide still another venue for examining women's work and creativity. Quilting enjoys a two-hundred-year tradition in America, demonstrating women's skill and frugality, pragmatism and aesthetic sense. It offers a window on the individual who completed the top of her bed covering and it sometimes also reveals her friendship circle, if she invited her peers to sew the three layers together with her. Mary Cross traces the enduring importance of quilts to Pacific Northwest women, from the pioneer settlers who made them on the Oregon Trail, en route to new lives on the frontier, all the way up to the present day.

In the late nineteenth century, when the Ladies Musical Club was founded in Seattle, women's clubs were flourishing all over America. In small towns and large cities alike, middle-class women of leisure, privileged to be exempted from wage-earning work, met weekly or monthly with like-minded friends for the purpose of self-improvement, charitable activity, or civic reform. Members of such clubs as the Walla Walla Woman's Club, Oregon Federation of Colored Women's Clubs, and Portland Women's Union discussed new books and great classics in literature, history, and philosophy oftentimes as part of their quest to solve social problems. The Woman's Christian Temperance Union, for example, focused on the problem of alcohol abuse. The National Congress of Mothers (which evolved into the PTA) stressed matters relating to child rearing. Church groups assisted impoverished neighbors or missions around the world. Northwest guilds raised money for the Washington Children's Home, an orphanage, and the Children's Orthopedic Hospital, both in Seattle.

On the face of it, Seattle's musical women met to strengthen their own knowledge and performance of classical repertoire. While they did so successfully, they simultaneously undertook to educate the general public on the frontier by bringing renowned musical artists from faraway Carnegie Hall in New York or the London stage to perform on the Pacific coast. One hundred years later, the organization still maintains a grand piano at the downtown branch of the Seattle Public Library, an instrument they purchased for public concerts. Not insignificantly, the members also demonstrated a strong civic responsibility, funding an ambulance for World War I, beds for the Children's Orthopedic Hospital, and settlement house classes for the foreign born.

Karen Blair's case study of the Ladies Musical Club offers a snapshot of Seattle women, far from America's centers of culture, yearning for beauty. It also illustrates the members' tenacious effort to make cultural contributions to their community as volunteers and to improve their city as citizen-activists. Their club goals invited them to leave the practice rooms and studios to learn about fund-raising, awarding scholarships, selling tickets, forming committees, budgeting money, and publicizing programs. The club provides us with an example of women determined to stretch the constraints of domestic roles and make a mark in the public arena, heretofore monopolized by their fathers, husbands, and sons. Like sister reformers in other clubs, who developed programs to address libraries, parks, street lights, vocational training, and preservation of forests, they left their mark on our cultural landscape.

"*Tsugiki*, a Grafting," by Gail Nomura, narrates the story of an individual artist, Teiko Tomita, a Japanese-born woman pioneer in Washington State. Much of the account would fit appropriately in this book's section on racial and ethnic diversity. Yet Tomita's extraordinary poetry compels us also to recognize the difficulties of producing art without the support of a group. No nourishment, criticism, or camaraderie from like-minded poets assisted Tomita during most of her artistic life. Instead, interruptions, injustices, and hard farm labor were the rule. Her creative drive and growth were self-generated, against all odds.

Tomita's parents arranged her marriage in Japan in 1920, to a countryman who farmed in Wapato, Washington, on land leased from the Yakama Indian Reservation. The Issei (first-generation) couple resembled a great many immigrants to America. They expected to earn enough from a few years of work in the New World to return to the homeland with sufficient profits for a comfortable life. They discovered, however, that their new lives were hard, profits scarce, and return impossible. Teiko Tomita's story, in other ways as well, represents that of other Issei women in the region. She left behind her family and country during the years when the United States government still permitted entry of Japanese brides for male Japanese settlers here (1908–24). She raised her children and farmed difficult land under spare conditions. Adversely affected by tightening American laws forbidding Japanese Americans to own, rent, lease, or sharecrop land, the Tomita family moved to the isolated town of Satus, where Teiko's husband supervised a white-owned nursery while she cooked for the laborers.

World War II tested the Tomitas' efforts to balance their ties to the United States and Japan. In an effort to demonstrate loyalty to the United States, they destroyed their mementos of the homeland. Relocation and incarceration—in Tule Lake, California, for the Tomitas—uprooted the family, forced the closure of their Sunnydale nursery business, and taxed their spirits. Unable to reassemble the pieces after the war, Teiko Tomita moved to an urban environment where, alongside women of every nationality, she became a worker in a garment factory.

Teiko Tomita's biography lends special insight into the Japanese American woman's experience, because of the poetry she wrote, in the manner of a journal, steadily recording her observations about life in America. Her *tanka* poems, translated by Nomura, offer the history of a woman whose strength and creativity did not falter despite numerous obstacles. For Tomita, the poetry provided private solace. For her many readers in Japan, it described both her family life in America and her broader societal concerns, including her postwar interest in the nuclear disarmament movement. Her poetry reveals to us her own "grafting"—in her life, as in her art—representing neither Old World nor New, but a unique blend of both.

Quilts in the Lives of Women Who Migrated to the Northwest, 1850–1990: A Visual Record

MARY BYWATER CROSS

In the last twenty years, the patchwork quilt has come to be recognized and accepted as a visual record of history that can be extremely valuable for accessing the public and private lives of the people who made them and owned them. This item of needlework—sometimes called a comfort, comforter, coverlet, coverlid, or blanket—is broadly defined as a "textile sandwich" of three layers held together with stitches. Most often associated with women, homes, and domestic responsibilities, quilts can provide a visual record of ordinary women's experiences. Their value is greatly increased when complemented by personal testimony, known as oral history, of the quiltmaker or owner.[1]

As current scholarship in women's history seeks to recover the daily lives, activities, and values of ordinary women as well as the role of women in community building, quilts have become part of that discovery. Many were made by women who came together in voluntary associations to produce and sell quilts in order to raise money for their churches, schools, and other community organizations. Traditional quilting bees became platforms for social crusades, political and fund-raising campaigns, and even military support efforts.[2] This tradition continues today in the efforts of both individual and group quiltmakers.[3]

By gathering information on quilts, along with their makers' biographies and stories, scholars can use the stitched works as a common denominator for the study of women's lives and family traditions. At the same time, the uniqueness of each quilt reflects the uniqueness of each quiltmaker's experiences.

The quilts included here show a diverse range of life experiences over time. They shift from examples of the most basic personal level of domestic security and sanctuary in an unfamiliar geographic location in the West to symbols of public or community interaction and even leadership roles of quilters within their networks. (See color plates following page 262.)

Pioneer women who made the journey west, for whatever reason, stayed to establish homes and families and adapted their patterns of living to overcome the challenges that faced them as individuals, wives, and mothers.

1. Quilt: Giesy Woolen Quilt
   Size: 81" x 77"
   Date: circa 1870
   Maker: Emma Wagner Giesy (1835–1882)
   Place: Aurora, Oregon
   Giesy came to the Pacific Northwest in 1853. She was the only woman in an overland trail party of ten Bethel, Missouri, scouts sent to select a site for the communal society led by William Kiel.

Emma Wagner Giesy was typical of the young women of the mid-nineteenth century who willingly accepted the challenge of striking out on the overland trail without really knowing what lay ahead of them. She was determined, hearty, and eager to take on responsibility for her own life and her role as a newlywed.

When William Kiel selected Emma's husband, Christian Giesy, as lead scout in search of a new site for a communal society, Emma refused to be left behind in Missouri, reportedly saying, "What trials of the wilderness trail you face, I will face, what privations and dangers you face, I will face."[4]

As was the case with many young wives, her pregnancy was an uncontrollable dimension of their lives. Emma's son was born a few short weeks after their arrival at Fort Steilacoom, where the party had gone to winter over because of the presence of other women for solace and a cow for milk.

The Giesys and others claimed and established farms on Willapa Bay in preparation for the entire communal society's move west. When Kiel arrived in 1855, he rejected the location as too isolated and chose instead Aurora, in the Willamette Valley. Yet the Giesys and other early settlers remained on their improved land. After her husband drowned in Willapa Bay in 1857, Emma continued to operate the family farm.

However, in 1861 she took her two young sons to the society's larger communal settlement of Aurora. By this time, society members had completed their migration. With her decision to join them, Emma Giesy demonstrated the pattern of families who went from the isolated self-sufficiency of individual farms to the cooperative support offered by growing communities. In Aurora, her family was able to share some of the regular routines and responsibilities with other communal society members.

Although this quilt is identified with a single family by the cross-stitched initials in one block, it does reflect the society's pattern of shared activity between 1855 and 1877. The woolen cloth, perhaps originally woven for dresses, as well as the batting were produced from the sheep raised in the community. The rich red and green colors are from natural dyestuffs, madder root and peach. The quilt belongs to the Old Aurora Colony Historical Society, Aurora, Oregon.

2. Quilt: Hexagon
   Size: 80 3/4" x 60"
   Date: Started 1869, finished 1900 (dated)
   Maker: Abigail Scott Duniway (1834–1915)
   Place: Willamette Valley, Oregon
   Duniway came to the Pacific Northwest in 1852, the daughter of an educated family from Illinois traveling overland to the Northwest. Family members established themselves in journalism and education.

Abigail Scott Duniway's quilt is a visual record of her years as a mother, wife, milliner, and woman suffrage activist. According to the typewritten documentation on the orange ribbon:

> This quilt was pieced in November 1869 by Abigail Scott Duniway of Oregon and was finished and quilted by her in November 1900, and donated to the First National Woman Suffrage Bazaar in honor of Theodore Roosevelt, the first champion of the equal Suffrage movement ever elected to a National office by popular vote.[5]

While pregnant in 1869, Abigail used the hat-lining fabrics from her successful Albany, Oregon, millinery shop to piece this single-template patterned quilt top. It was through operation of the shop that Abigail became familiar with the vast range of experiences shaping local women's lives. This awareness helped her to focus her work on women's rights, especially the right to vote.

It is ironic that this quilt is recognized today because it is well known that Abigail, a renowned suffragist, disliked sewing and especially patchwork. In one of her own editorials in her women's rights newspaper, she wrote:

> Any fool can make a quilt; and after we had made a couple of dozen over twenty years ago, we quit the business with a conviction that nobody but a fool would spend so much time in cutting bits of dry goods into yet smaller bits and sewing them together again, just for the sake of making believe that they are busy at practical work.[6]

Duniway preferred to devote her days to editing *The New Northwest* and stumping for women's political and social advancement. Her devotion to her cause earned her the honor of being the first Oregon woman to cast a ballot.

The quilt belongs to the Oregon Historical Society, Portland.

3. Quilt: Rose of Sharon variation

   Size: 62" x 77 3/4"

   Date: 1920–1935

   Maker: Eliza Jane Eynon Ricks (1856–1939)

   Place: Possibly eastern Oregon or Idaho

   Ricks came to the Pacific Northwest in 1917, in a move to LaGrande, Oregon, as a wife, mother, and member of the Church of Jesus Christ of Latter-day Saints. The Mormons homesteaded in the intermountain West to establish homes and create economic opportunities for their large families.

When Eliza was a young child, her parents were eager to gather in Zion in the American West after joining the Mormon church in England in the late 1850s. Finally, in 1863, her mother and three young children came West alone, leaving her father behind in England. Their ongoing struggle to survive the challenges of emigrating and pioneering in an unknown environment was daunting.

After Eliza married Jonathan Ricks in 1875, the new couple tried to establish farms in the high fertile valleys of Utah, Idaho, and Oregon. Each time they resettled, the cold weather took its toll either on the family's health or their farm crops.

Through it all Eliza Ricks demonstrated, in her writing and quiltmaking, a courageous ability to adapt to life's challenges. In her previously unpublicized reminiscence she wrote:

> We have had 12 children all of them good to their parents. 34 grand children and 2 great grand children. We have cared for 4 grand children and 5 not our own. It has been harder for me than for some better prepared for I was never in school in all my life. all I know I have taught myself. But you children know I can sew, spin, knit, weave and do every kind of work inside and out. With

> my husband I have helped to pay on all the Temples making quilts, carpets, rugs, knitting socks and mittens for me and my children and have paid our pennies to the Canadian and Hawaiian Temple. I have crossed the Atlantic Ocean and the American Continent to the Pacific ocean. I am 5 foot 4 inches tall, grey eyes, hair now grey but originally dark brown. weigh 180 and in good health.[7]

This bright quilt offers other clues about this woman's personality, her optimistic outlook, and her desire to be current in style and fashion. The quilt represents the new direction in quiltmaking in the first half of the twentieth century. The color choices and design style are those commonly seen at this time when women were either designing and marketing or purchasing kits, with a pattern and fabrics, to complete. It is difficult to tell if this is such a kit because there are none of the usual signs of prestamped cutting or quilting lines.

The quilt belongs to the Brigham City Museum, Brigham City, Utah.

4. Quilt: Grandmother's Garden
   Size: 89" x 102"
   Date: 1930
   Maker: Agnette Hendricksen Nilsen (1889–1952)
   Place: Astoria, Oregon

Nilsen came to the Pacific Northwest in 1913, emigrating alone from north of the Arctic Circle in Norway at the invitation of her husband-to-be, Elias Bernhard Nilsen.

In an effort to assure sales and encourage readers to make quilts for contests, the Sunday *Oregonian* newspaper published a series of patterns in 1930. The format of the quilt column was a weekly gathering of women called "Nancy Page's Quilt Club." Each column featured the next block pattern and gave advice for reproducing the design and making the quilt. Many newspapers of the day sponsored a regional contest in the early 1930s.

Agnette Nilsen involved her young daughter Annabell in this, her only quilt project. Annabell recalls the project vividly, "I remember at age seven, anxiously awaiting the *Sunday Oregonian* in order to find the next quilt floral pattern! I helped my mother to choose the fabrics and colors from the large box of scrap materials of dresses, shirts, etc." For Agnette Nilsen, the newspaper was an opportunity to teach herself the English language and keep abreast of the world beyond her Astoria, Oregon, neighborhood. She retained her inherited "Viking desire" for knowledge and travel throughout her life.

Emma Wagner Giesy's Woolen Quilt, "Running Squares"

Abigail Scott Duniway's Hexagon Quilt
(courtesy Oregon Historical Society, OrHi 98922)

Eliza Ricks's "Rose of Sharon" Quilt

Agnette Nilsen's "Grandmother's Garden Quilt," 1930

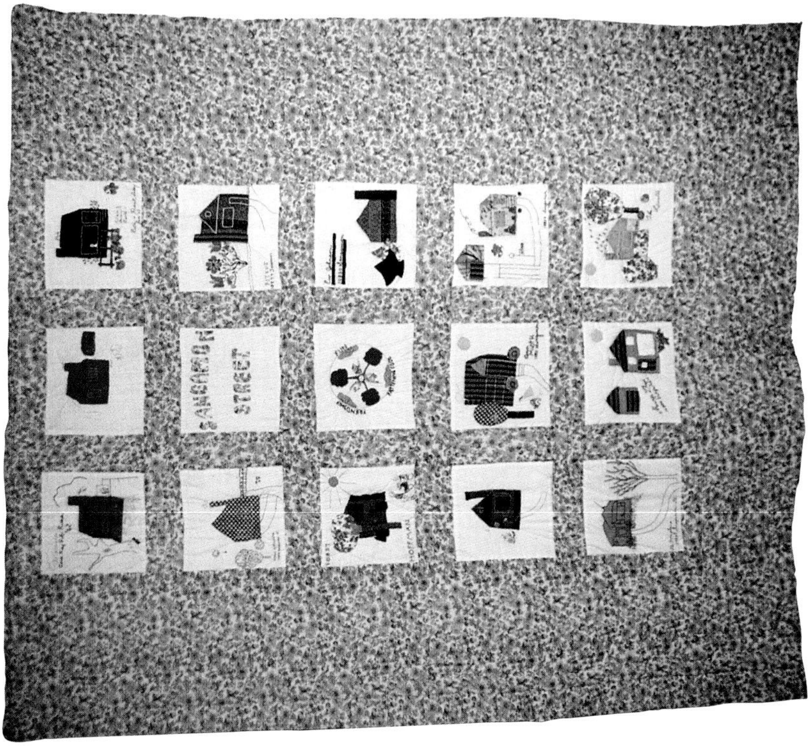

Sangamon Street Friendship Quilt, 1962

Mia's Quilt, 1986

In the late 1930s, she sold Avon products to finance a trip by Greyhound bus from Oregon to the Mexican border.[8]

The quilt is privately owned.

5. Quilt: Sangamon Street Friendship Quilt

Size: 78" x 89"

Date: 1962

Makers: Sangamon Street Ladies Cultural Society

Place: Chicago, Illinois

Phyllis Hoffman, the woman who organized the quilting activity, came to the Pacific Northwest in 1987. She and her husband retired to Spokane from Chicago to be near an adult daughter with special medical needs.

Hoffman's relocation is an increasing but familiar trend. From the mid-nineteenth century on, widowed quiltmakers and others have migrated west to be with families. Often, older adults have moved after retirement to be with adult children who can assist them in their lives.[9]

In the post-World War II era in Chicago, a subdivision of twenty-four houses was built in a two-block segment of Sangamon Street to provide housing for returning veterans and their families. The women, all home-based moms, founded the Sangamon Street Ladies Cultural Society to meet regularly in each other's homes. The name was chosen in order to qualify the group for the free informational programs that many of their husbands' employers had available to loan to qualified organizations. According to the quilt owner, one of their goals was to avoid gossip about the absentee members, a pastime that had proved the downfall for similar neighborhood groups. One quilt block shows other goals: "friendship, fun, and fattening food." For each meeting, the hostess chose a project for the women to do while they shared their lives over coffee.

Phyllis Hoffman made fabric templates of the five styles of houses along Sangamon Street. Each woman was to take her own home's pattern piece, appliqué it to a square of cloth, and personalize it by embellishing it with embroidery stitches and appliquéd fabrics. The group completed the quilt by the time of the local school PTA bazaar, but it was rejected as being the work of more than one woman. It became a treasure Phyllis Hoffman could carry away when she retired to Spokane.

The quilt, a compilation of twenty-three squares produced by midwest friends, reflects the migration theme. It shows change and separation yet reconnection with old neighbors and their families through the stitched record of a previously shared experience. The Hoffmans were some of the last to move from the Sangamon Street neighborhood.

The quilt has received recognition and achievement as a result of the new scholarship using quilts as visual records. Since arriving in the Pacific Northwest, the quilt was selected to be representative of the social passages of women's lives, and it was included in the 1994 Washington State quilt exhibition, "Quilt Heritage." To share the celebration of the quilt's newfound importance, the owner contacted the other twenty-three contributors, all of whom had moved away from Chicago by the late 1960s, and sent them exhibition catalogs.

The quilt is now privately owned.

6. Quilt: Mia's Quilt

Date: 1985–86

Size: Unavailable

Maker: "Coastal Quilters" for Mia, the daughter of Shelley Lobel and Bill Edbrook

The "Coastal Quilters" were a free-flowing, open-ended group of about sixty-five women, children, and men coming together from across North America, England, and Belgium over a period of roughly twenty-five years to settle on islands off Prince Rupert, British Columbia.

The quilts made by this group of people who migrated to an isolated corner of the Canadian Pacific Northwest vividly represent the alternative, independent, self-reliant, yet cooperative life-style of the 1960s. They had chosen to lead their lives communally in weather-enforced winter isolation. On the largest island of Digby, transportation is provided by boat and ferry and communication depends on electronics and postal services.

The group quiltmaking began in the late 1970s and early 1980s, when one friend agreed to pass her quilt block to another who wished to add a border. From this casual origin began the process of a "pass-the-medallion" method of quiltmaking, by which unplanned quilts would grow concentrically over a lengthy period of time as they moved from house to house. Each maker would add independently the fabric and design that she felt would enhance the evolving quilt top. Often, the only common denominators were consideration of previous color choice and knowledge of the person for whom the quilt was being made. This allowed each quilter to identify with the future recipient throughout the process of creating a design, choosing the fabrics, constructing their contribution, and assembling and quilting the quilt.

By 1986, the group of contributors grew in size to sixty-five people, and some relocated away from the islands to mainland places like Vancouver. The choice of style evolved to the "quilt by mail" block format set together with strips of fabric, with the only restriction being a standardized size. This process emulates their chosen life-style and values of independence and self-reliance, along with cooperation and connectedness.

The quilt is privately owned.

NOTES

1. Susan H. Armitage, "The Challenge of Women's History," in Karen J. Blair, ed., *Women in Pacific Northwest History: An Anthology,* 1st ed. (Seattle: University of Washington Press, 1988), pp. 233–41.

2. *Uncoverings,* a scholarly journal of the American Quilt Study Group, has published research documenting these themes since 1980.

3. See this volume's "Suggestions for Further Reading, Arts," for recent publications on Pacific Northwest quilts and quiltmaking.

4. Clark Moor Will, "Colony Mothers Help Write Colony History," typescript, Aurora Colony Historical Society Archives, Aurora, Oregon.

5. Quilt number 1721, Oregon Historical Society, Portland.

6. Abigail Scott Duniway, "Editorial Correspondence," *New Northwest,* July 15, 1880, cited in Ruth Barnes Moynihan, *Rebel for Rights* (New Haven: Yale University Press, 1983), p. 153.

7. Florence Smith Bowns, "History of Eliza Jane Eynon Ricks" (1937), Manuscript Collection, International Society of the Daughters of Utah Pioneers Museum, Salt Lake City, Utah, p. 5.

8. Interview with Annabell Miller, June 1990, cited in Mary Bywater Cross, "Reflections on an Oregon Quilt Contest," in Jeanette Lasansky, ed., *Bits and Pieces: Textile Traditions* (Lewisburg, Pa.: Oral Traditions Project, 1991), p. 106.

9. Mary Bywater Cross, *Treasures in the Trunk: Quilts of the Oregon Trail* (Nashville: Rutledge Hill Press, 1993), pp. 78–79, 108–109, 112–13.

REGIONAL ORGANIZATIONS FOR QUILT STUDY AND QUILT HISTORY

The American Quilt Study Group, P.O. Box 4737, Lincoln, NE 68504-0737. (402)472-5361. E-mail: aqsg@juno.com

The Association of Pacific Northwest Quilters, P.O. Box 22073, Seattle, WA 98122-0073. (206)622-2826. E-mail: apnq1998@cnw.com

The Canadian Quilt Study Group, 330 151 H Street, Blaine, WA 98230-5107. (604) 538-7551. FAX (604)533-7721. E-mail: narmstr@ibm.net; dhyndman@direct.ca

The Contemporary Quilt Art Association, P.O. Box 95685, Seattle, WA 98145-2685.

LaConner Quilt Museum, Gatches Mansion, P.O. Box 1270, 703 South 2nd, LaConner, WA 98257. (306)466-4288.

Latimer Quilt and Textile Center, 2105 Wilson River Loop Rd., Tillamook, OR 97141. (503)842-8622. E-mail: LatimerTextile@oregoncoast.com

The Seattle Ladies Musical Club, 1890–1930

KAREN J. BLAIR

"Everybody knows America wouldn't have any music if it weren't for women," observed the internationally renowned pianist Harold Bauer in 1924.[1] His remark saluted the phenomenon of women's music clubs, which blossomed in the United States from 1900 to 1930, and it held a large measure of truth. In thousands of communities during the early twentieth century, women founded and sustained amateur clubs that exhibited an impressive range of musical strengths and achievements.

On the verge of their long-awaited enfranchisement, women developed broad visions of their full participation in society. They dreamed of a world in which their equality would soar beyond the political arena. Many also determined that the richer offerings of civilization, like classical music, would be accessible not just to the wealthy, but to everyone. Women's music clubs became one vehicle for forwarding these aspirations.

Excluded from the male-dominated mainstream of musical performance and composition, women in the late nineteenth century began to form separate music associations of their own. Initially, these groups served to maintain and expand the musical knowledge and skills of women who, though trained in music in their youth, devoted the bulk of their days to running households and rearing families. The clubs soon came to embrace two additional important functions. The first of these was to assist the professional development of women performers and composers. To this end, the all-women's groups established music scholarships for girls, created opportunities for performances of new and old works, sponsored the MacDowell

Colony for creative artists, and supported women's orchestras. A second, civic-minded function, which became more prominent after World War I, was to build a nation in which every citizen could enjoy fine music. Working toward that goal, clubwomen brought artists of international reputation to perform in their towns and successfully fostered music education for immigrants in settlement houses and for youth in schools. Less obviously feminist in character, this second function strengthened the public role of women; more subtly, its progressive thrust challenged the elitist priorities of the male musical establishment.

The Ladies Musical Club of Seattle (LMC) is representative of the music clubs that grew and developed in America during the early twentieth century. The organization, which functions to this day, was formed in 1891, when twenty-four women, all musically trained in their youth, met at the home of Mrs. Ellen Bartlett Bacon. Their collaboration was "for the purpose of developing the musical talent of [the] members, and stimulating musical interest in Seattle."[2]

Like most of their counterparts elsewhere in the country, early members of the LMC were middle class and white. Most of the charter members and subsequent participants appear to have been leisured women, married to prominent professionals or businessmen in the community. Among them were the wives of Moses Gottstein, president of Gottstein Furniture Company; John C. Moore, physician; Gustov Schultz, druggist; Mitchell Gilliam, judge; W. D. Chandler, day editor of the *Seattle Times*; William Hickman Moore, city councilman; A. S. Hansen, accountant for the Hansen Baking Company; and Frank Van Tuyl, president of the Black Gold Channel Mining Company. They were women who had forsaken their early musical background, usually in piano or voice, for marriage, child rearing, and participation in Seattle's social, charity, and study clubs. Some, like the German-born pianist Martha Blanka Churchill, were experienced artists, anxious to maintain their facility. The daughter of a professor at the Hamburg Conservatory, Blanka had studied with Franz Liszt and performed internationally. It was while on concert tour in America that she met Frederick A. Churchill, a physician, and retired to make her home with him in Seattle. Rose Morganstern Gottstein had studied voice and sang at weddings in the city's churches. However, her husband, two sons, participation in the Temple de Hirsch, and volunteer work at the Children's Orthopedic Hospital demanded much of her attention, according to her grand-niece, Mary McCarthy, in *Memories of a Catholic Girlhood.*

Other members made determined efforts to advance their professional careers, insofar as they were able. Mary Carr Moore blossomed as a composer after arriving in Seattle with her physician husband in 1901. In 1912, she presented to the public her four-act grand opera, *Narcissa,* the story of the early Pacific Northwest missionary Narcissa Whitman. Other working composers in the club included Kate Gilmore Black, wife of an Alaska Fish Company vice-president and organist at Westminster Presbyterian Church. Amy Worth directed the Women's University Club Chorus for twenty-five years and published thirty songs, including one recorded by Lotte Lehmann. Daisy Wood Hildreth, whose husband was a salesman at Frederick and Nelson department store, also published her compositions.

Clara Hartle, who had studied voice in Chicago, came to the city when she married in 1904. For four decades, until her death, she instructed students, directed the University Methodist Church choir, and adapted fifteen operas to present in lecture-recital form to audiences all over the state. Cecilia Augsburg developed arts management skills through her LMC music circle. She had studied piano with Emil Liebling in Chicago and then headed the piano department of Kansas State Agricultural College. Having fallen in love with Seattle while performing on a concert tour, she settled in the city as a piano teacher. Her marriage to the druggist Gustov Schultz did not prevent her from becoming a concert manager of the Seattle Symphony Orchestra once she had proven herself as an impresario for the Seattle Musical Art Society.

In any given year, the LMC membership list also contained a handful of names of single women who made music their profession. Most, like Nellie Beach, Fidelia Birgess, Anna Grant Dall, and Leone E. Langdon, supported themselves as music teachers. Nellie Cornish founded a school for all the arts in 1914, known still as the Cornish Institute. She tapped the expertise of Martha Graham, Merce Cunningham, Mark Tobey, John Cage, and the wave of White Russians fleeing their country in 1917 to provide first-rate instruction for her pupils.

Others of the unmarried members were students, like Alice B. Toklas, who took her piano degree at the University of Washington's Conservatory in 1895, before her move to Paris and association with Gertrude Stein. Lillian Miller served as president of the LMC for a few months in 1900, but left for New York as soon as the opportunity arose to study composition with Edward MacDowell, the American composer.

The LMC never lacked for women eager to audition, by invitation only; membership conferred the privilege of paying dues and attending the monthly meetings from October to May. The club's serious attention to music in a community full of fervid women kept its lists full. By 1905, there were 98 active members; by 1916, 150; by 1921, 158; by 1932, 177. The group offered unique benefits to its own musicians, since the primary purpose of the association was performance by the members. If the constraints of the day prohibited a concert career for married women, at least members could maintain their skills by playing or singing for each other at meetings in each other's parlors. They were not only permitted but expected to perform regularly, alone, in duets, trios, string quartets (1922–27), other chamber groups, or in chorus (1913–22). Anticipating cases of stage fright, the early rules stated that "an active member who refuses to perform at the club concerts during six months, will forfeit her membership, unless her refusal has been caused by some reason considered adequate by the Executive Committee."[3]

Club members who were composers, as well as those who were performers, enjoyed regular hearings. Entire meetings devoted to Seattle compositions assured an airing of such works as "I Know Not Why," by Lillian Miller, "Oh Wind from the Golden Gate" for women's chorus by Mary Carr Moore, "Nocturne" and "Mazurka" for piano by Kate Gilmore Black, and songs by Amy Worth. This feature of club life was crucial for the growth of women composers, who in Seattle and elsewhere enjoyed few such opportunities outside the clubs. In this capacity women's clubs demonstrated their ability to provide a service to women that remained unmet by any other institution in society.

Western classics of the nineteenth century were popular choices for club performers, with Schubert, Beethoven, Wagner, and Tchaikovsky providing the staples. The women did not shy from contemporary music, however, and recent works by English (Elgar), American (Grainger), French (Debussy, Ravel, Saint-Saëns), and Russian composers (Rachmaninov, Borodin) were regularly performed. The newest atonal music, championed by Claire Reis and her League of Composers, was, however, generally ignored by clubwomen, as it was by the musical establishment of the day.

Perhaps surprisingly, LMC members defied general assumptions about European supremacy in music. They broke tradition in their support of American music, performing works by Edward MacDowell, Mrs. H. H. A. Beach, and Louis Gottschalk with regularity. In addition, they pioneered in collecting, analyzing, and listening to native folk music, especially Native American songs and Negro spirituals. This effort brought new respect to an unrecognized American musical heritage. In papers they prepared for their meetings and at conferences, they tapped the scholarship of women anthropologists like Alice Cunningham Fletcher, Frances Densmore, and Nelle Richmond McCurdy Eberhart who were collecting and publishing the music of North American Indians. Likewise, they turned to Natalie Curtis Burlin for lyrics and musical notation of plantation songs.

A notable exception to their commitment to native music was the ban by women's clubs on popular music, especially jazz, even when its elements were wedded to classical forms, as in *Rhapsody in Blue* by George Gershwin. Rejection of popular music served to symbolize opposition to a whole wave of new post-World War I freedoms that clubwomen perceived as shocking. The behavior of young single women—openly smoking, drinking, dancing, and traveling with men in automobiles—alarmed many adults. In Seattle, Cecilia Augsberger and other educators damned jazz as a "menace in the community." Clubwomen throughout the nation criticized the sensuous rhythms, dissonances, and incendiary lyrics of popular music for their corrupting influences. Some hoped that the permissiveness of the age might be checked by offering classical music as an antidote. Among Montana clubwomen, for instance, it was said that classics might replace that which was so "inexcusably worthless."[4]

But clubwomen did not espouse classical music solely as a means of subduing popular culture. Long before the advent of the jazz age, they were inspired by the positive idea of bringing the joy and knowledge of music to a wider public. They began by seeking to involve nonmembers in their programs. At first, they simply desired larger audiences for their own performances at club meetings. A member's satisfaction from effort spent on polishing pieces would be greater if she could reach beyond her immediate circle to play for a sizable crowd. Thus, the LMC, like its counterparts all over the country, began to permit "associate members" to attend a special monthly concert—October to May—for a fee, often slightly higher than official dues. Associates tended to be friends and relatives of club members, male as well as female; some associates were music lovers who lacked the talent, training, or courage to perform in public. Numbers of associates at the LMC grew from 217 in 1905, to 266 in 1916, to 360 in 1921, although only a small percentage of the associates actually attended each concert. For these eight occasions, the club required facilities more spacious than homes of participants. Therefore, the LMC rented halls and rooms—at the DAR, Plymouth Church, Unitarian Church, YMCA (1907–13), YWCA (1913–23), Women's University Club (1923–24), Olympic Hotel (the ballroom, 1925–44), Woman's Century Club (1944–60), and Seattle Public Library (1960–present).

Members did not long confine performance of their work to the closed club meetings and special concerts, but soon grew ambitious for wider exposure. They shared their work with other clubwomen in the region, performing, for example, at the Woman's Century Club Arts and Crafts Exposition held in 1906, and bringing their music to the meetings of other societies and conventions as well. An especially gala event for the LMC was the world premiere of *Narcissa,* by Mary Carr Moore, based on a libretto by her mother,

Sara Pratt Carr. Moore engaged a tenor and a soprano from the New York Metropolitan Opera and selected seventy local singers for her cast. Among them, naturally, were a great many women from the club, who performed in the chorus and as principals. The first grand opera ever composed and conducted by an American woman, *Narcissa* was produced at the Moore Theater in downtown Seattle in April 1912, winning critical acclaim that brought great satisfaction to members of the LMC.

Anxious to forward the musical growth of its members, the LMC also took seriously its additional goal of bringing good music to the Seattle community. To this end, the women imported the finest talents of the day to the far northwest corner of the nation. One of their major contributions to Seattle's cultural life was the establishment of a concert series that scheduled performances by four renowned recitalists each year. This plan originated in 1901, after the pianist Fannie Bloomfield Zeisler canceled her engagement in Seattle, discouraged by reports of the small turnouts at other classical concerts. A disappointed Rose Gottstein suggested that the club might assure some outstanding performances by guaranteeing the fee of the artist and then recouping the investment through a vigorous ticket sales campaign. Thus Gottstein, acting for the LMC, became Seattle's foremost impresario of classical music events. For nearly forty years, until her death in 1939, she made an annual visit to New York City's concert managers, armed with a purse of at least twenty thousand dollars, and secured four top artists of the concert stage for Seattle engagements. No wonder one local newspaper reporter cheered, "Folks, Meet Mrs. Gottstein: Puts Us on Music Map."[5] This work she did as a labor of love, receiving no payment but an autographed photograph from each performer she introduced. In thanks, the club presented her favorite charity, the Children's Orthopedic Hospital, with a two-hundred-dollar donation each year. Upon her death, the group also purchased a hospital bed in her honor, for five thousand dollars. It was a small price in view of the stellar talents she brought to the city.

Thanks to this series, the inhabitants of a remote city could count on regular exposure to the best-known virtuoso performers the world could offer. In the first decade, the club sponsored Fritz Kreisler, Josef Hofmann, and Harold Bauer. Twice, Walter Damrosch conducted the New York Symphony Orchestra with a sixty-member chorus that included vocalists from the Ladies Musical Club. Later, Jascha Heifetz, Sergei Rachmaninov, Pablo Casals, Lotte Lehmann, Yehudi Menuhin, Ignace Paderewski, Artur Rubinstein, Vladimir Horowitz, Rosa Ponselle, Efrem Zimbalist, Mischa Elman, and José Iturbi—a veritable *Who's Who* of international pianists, violinists, and singers—came to serenade the city.

Not surprisingly, the LMC felt a special responsibility to bring women to the stage. During the early years especially, a significant number of the professionals—eighteen of forty-seven—were female. Among the first were the Venezuelan pianist Teresa Carreño, the soprano Lillian Nordica, the contralto Ernestine Schumann-Heink, the singer Geraldine Farrar, and, to rectify past disappointments, Fannie Bloomfield Zeisler.

The prominence of such individual women performers did not mislead women into supposing that their sex had gained a firm footing in the male musical establishment. Male performers, orchestra conductors, critics, and teachers persisted in the view expressed by the writer Anthony M. Ludovici that "woman can at best make only an inferior display, even if she make any display at all."[6] In the orchestral world this attitude was rigid, causing the social critic and feminist Suzanne La Follette, in the 1920s, to rail against "the prejudice of male musicians . . . effective enough to exclude [women] from the personnel of our important orchestras."[7] Sir Thomas Beecham, conductor of the London and Seattle symphonies, summed up the inability of male musicians to take female colleagues seriously.

> I do not like, and never will, the association of men and women in orchestras and other instrumental combinations. . . . My spirit is torn all the time between a natural inclination to let myself go and the depressing thought that I must behave like a gentleman. I have been unable to avoid noticing that the presence of a half-dozen good looking women in the orchestra is a distinctly distracting factor. As a member of the orchestra once said to me, "If she is attractive, I can't play with her; if she is not, I won't."[8]

Of similar mind, José Iturbi refused to accept female graduates of the Eastman School of Music in the Rochester Symphony, which he conducted. Only a handful of women, usually harpists, managed to win places in symphony orchestras, until the Cleveland Orchestra admitted a few female musicians in 1923, and San Francisco four violinists and a cellist in 1925.[9] These steps, however, did not constitute a trend, and integration was slight until the 1970s.

Clubwomen sought to counter the exclusion of women from the musical mainstream in several ways. In 1913, the LMC began awarding music scholarships to girls, on the grounds that financial resources tended to be unavailable to them. In 1920, the club initiated an interest-free loan program for promising beginners, and it also aided students at the Cornish School. When women performers, barred from established symphonies, formed their own separate orchestras, women's music clubs everywhere sprang to their support, contributing money, selling tickets, filling concert halls, inviting them to play at their meetings and conventions, and publishing regular reports on their tours and critical triumphs.

The first of these all-women's orchestras, founded in Boston in 1888, was the Fadettes, named for a protagonist in George Sand's novel, *La Petite Fadette.* By 1920, they had performed six thousand enthusiastically received concerts all over North America. Dozens of other orchestras of women playing classical repertoire—in Salt Lake City, Chicago, Philadelphia, Los Angeles, New York, Minneapolis—were founded in the first third of the century and adopted by women's music clubs.[10]

The interest of clubwomen was not confined to women in the performing arts. They saw the importance of supporting women creators as well as performers. Not surprisingly, then, music clubs became financial backers of the MacDowell Colony in Peterborough, New Hampshire, a haven for composers, but also for writers, painters, and sculptors in need of solitude, work space, inexpensive room and board, and prepared meals. The colony was a project undertaken by Marian Nevins MacDowell, a German-trained pianist, upon the death of her husband in 1908. To fund the colony, she embarked upon a forty-nine-year career of regular concert tours to women's clubs and conventions, publicizing her dream of establishing a retreat "where working conditions most favorable to the production of enduring works of imagination shall be provided for creative artists."[11]

Marian MacDowell sought respect, enthusiasm, and money for her colony from the entire spectrum of American clubwomen. In return, she provided over 50 percent of the colony's facilities to creative American women, thereby forging a bond with clubwomen and winning their loyalty and firm support. MacDowell clubs sprang up all over the country. In Seattle, as elsewhere, women's music clubs named Marian MacDowell an honorary member, giving her not only their commendations but also their financial support. Funds from Seattle organizations like the Music Art Society, MacDowell Colony League, and Alpha Chi Omega helped sustain the colony, which still operates today. As long as Marian MacDowell maintained control, the bulk of colony awards went to women. Oddly enough, women working in arts other than music received the lion's share of awards and, later, of recognition. Nevertheless, a significant percentage of colony money continued to come from women's music clubs.

In their support of the MacDowell Colony, as in numerous other projects, music club women made common cause with other American clubwomen. Yet despite their history of encouraging women's abilities and influence, the music clubs had often been at odds with the general movement for women's rights. The turn of the century had seen steady efforts by women to win themselves the vote and find other avenues to political influence; to gain entry into trade unions, schools of higher education, and the professions; and to shape an American future that guaranteed democratic participation by all citizens. Many advocates of these goals discouraged attention to the arts, believing this arena incompatible with the rebuilding of society. Leaders of the politically moderate but powerful General Federation of Women's Clubs, for instance, disdained artistic endeavors, while revering civic reform. "Dante is dead," proclaimed President Sara Platt Decker at the turn of the century,[12] imploring her middle-class, leisured white constituency of half a million members to leave their poetry and pianos in order to lobby Congress for streetlights, public libraries, and child labor laws. Her agenda held no place for women's efforts to reform the cultural life of the nation.

It was the First World War that nurtured the already existing civic strain in the women of music clubs and led eventually to their increasing interest in the democratization of the arts. Patriotic community sings during the war stimulated pride in American songs. In every locale, Liberty Choruses formed in 1918 to lead citizens in public renditions of "Over There," "Swanee River," "A Long, Long Trail," and the national anthem. Huge, enthusiastic audiences filled theaters, halls, and churches; eventually, Chautauqua tents and outdoor sites were needed to accommodate these gatherings. The fervent response to American songs led clubwomen to appreciate the importance of cultivating the indigenous musical heritage and to seize the opportunity to extend the benefits of music to a far broader population than they had heretofore touched.

Although the strong anti-German feelings that swept the wartime nation caused some clubwomen to banish German compositions from their programs for the duration of the fighting, most desisted from such extreme measures. The war, nevertheless, caused them to reevaluate earlier assumptions that the German populace was inherently more receptive than the American listening public, and that German music conservatories must necessarily remain superior to American ones. A Washington State clubwoman wrote in 1917:

> Hundreds of thousands of this country's money have been spent yearly by students in music in European cities. . . . We have not the musical atmosphere of older civilizations. It is our privilege to see to it that this atmosphere is created and maintained, in order that American women may be trained under the protection of our own wholesome institutions.

> There are indications that we are about ready to replace our old-world culture with something radically our own. Let us make it unnecessary that any of our good American dollars shall be changed into marks in Leipsic [*sic*] or Berlin.[13]

Indeed, organizations of women provided hearty endorsement for the founding of the great American music conservatories, including the Juilliard, Curtis, and Eastman schools of music. In Seattle, the Cornish School found patronage that permitted expanded programs and the construction of an impressive school building in the wave of patriotic postwar enthusiasm for American musical education.

The drive for enhancing American prestige and power neatly allied itself with clubwomen's hopes for bringing better music to the nation. Members theorized that a common appreciation of classical music could fuse the American populace—people of every age, sex, background, and nationality—into a strong, united, and patriotic body of fine citizens who would create a superior democracy, disdainful of materialism, every bit as cultured and powerful as any nation on the globe. Clubwomen's devotion to this civic mission now overshadowed their emphasis on the musical training and advancement of women.

The clubwomen had an excellent opportunity to apply their civic theories when they found themselves with surplus cash—their profits from the community concerts they sponsored. With no interest in keeping substantial bank accounts, they initiated a spending campaign to elevate good citizenship while building musical taste in America. They chose to invest in groups that had not been reached by American musicians before. Thus, immigrants and children became the recipients of music club programming in the first third of the century.

Realizing that their public recitals were not attended by unassimilated immigrants, women's music societies frequently donated their profits to the burgeoning number of settlement music schools in the cities. If they were to bring good music to all citizens, the women had to encourage music lessons and other means of musical expression in the institutions located within immigrant neighborhoods. Thus, the settlements drew on women's clubs for assistance of endless variety, and the clubs provided money for instruction and supplies, teachers and coordinators, receptive audiences for settlement house performances, and invitations to immigrant musicians to play for club meetings.

The Ladies Musical Club was typical in its efforts to insure that the foreign population of Seattle would have access to music. It voted in 1914 to contribute to the new Settlement Music School in Seattle, an appendage of the settlement house in the Russian-Jewish neighborhood. Both settlement house and music school were sponsored by the Seattle branch of the National Council of Jewish Women, a group dominated by women of German-Jewish origins. The school borrowed programs that were effective elsewhere and emphasized the music that clubwomen respected. It provided piano and violin lessons and encouraged ensemble work as well. A boys glee club, several girls choruses, and an orchestra were established, and even the performance of operettas grew commonplace. Lessons with able music instructors, Jewish and Gentile, were inexpensive, pupils paying just "enough to make them appreciate the lessons and give them no slightest feeling of being objects of charity."[14] Full scholarships were made available to talented youth who had no financial resources for training.

Settlement house music programs were not limited to children, however. For the general foreign populace, harmonica bands, community sings, choruses for every age group, and celebratory pageants provided music; the programs featured classical and American music as well as native songs from every land. Thus, it was possible to hear mothers sing their folk tunes, kindergartners participate in rhythm bands, groups of boys harmonize sailor songs, young girls perform *Madame Butterfly*, and orchestras and choruses of all ages prepared a varied repertoire for neighborhood audiences on settlement anniversaries and national and religious holidays.

For these newcomers to American shores, clubwomen hoped that music would provide spiritual nourishment and solace in lives sapped by struggle. "If it means a great deal for the rich, who are surrounded by beautiful things[,] to have music in their homes, those who have only poverty have even greater need of it," remarked one settlement music supporter.[15] Clubwomen expected that music would act as a counterbalance to the immigrants' struggles, cultivating qualities contributing to good citizenship. As one of their leaders observed: "It is, of course, a truism that a healthy happy human being makes a better citizen than a morbid unhealthy one; and also that the more normal mental and emotional outlets the individual has, the more chance there is of his remaining healthy and happy and a good citizen."[16]

Some idealists among the clubwomen looked upon music shared by natives and immigrants as a true international language, a vehicle for communication among the diverse groups now settled in America or even, perhaps, around the world. Music, they thought, might contribute to international peace—"Art unifying mankind in the common cult of beauty."[17]

Practically, the women believed that music could instill democratic values in foreigners. Settlement music training could teach newcomers the tunes and lyrics of American patriotic songs. And by encouraging respect for the music

Ladies Musical Club String Quartet

In a series of

CHAMBER MUSIC CONCERTS

Concluding Concert of 1926 – 1927 – Series

WED. EVE. MAR. 2, at 8:15

1927

Margaret McCullough Lang – First Violin
Alice Williams Sherman, Second Violin

OLYMPIC HOTEL

Iris Canfield – Cello –
Louise Benton Viola

Junior Ball Room

Information at Marie Clippinger, Beacon 4016-J2
Tickets on sale at Sherman, Clay.

Members of the Seattle Ladies Musical Club formed a string quartet
(courtesy Museum of History and Industry, Seattle)

of the Old Country, clubwomen could demonstrate open-mindedness. Moreover, the settlement music schools provided access to classical musical knowledge, which in Europe was available only to the aristocracy. How the social workers must have glowed when one little girl declared, "Music is a luxury, but we get it here at Music School Settlement in New York for ten cents."[18]

Music club women believed that exposure to classical music could build good character and loyalty to American values not only in foreigners, but also in their own children. Soon after the war, state and national federations sent representatives into the public schools, promising that new music appreciation and participatory programs could insure everything from good posture to high grades. The women declared that the study of the classics could pull the U.S. through its "grave musical crisis" by checking "degeneracy in our modern public music into rag time" and by luring potential "delinquents" from "the suggestive words of popular songs" and the unacceptable behavior that they believed was sure to follow. So, too, music could enliven the small and sleepy communities from which youth, increasingly, was fleeing. "Make [your town] a lovely place to live in so that nobody cares to leave it," suggested one clubwoman to rural villages afraid of losing their population to the "wicked" cities.[19]

To make good their promises to modify youthful behavior through music education, women's groups quickly developed and then donated appropriate materials to public institutions. They purchased Victrolas and records for the schools and paid to bring symphony orchestras to schools or children to concert halls. In Arlington, Massachusetts, women's clubs deposited a great quantity of sheet music at the public library. The Ladies Musical Club in Seattle distributed bibliographies of music books at the libraries. It urged teachers to make their students aware of the music columns that the newspapers were printing in response to LMC pressure, and the growing number of classical radio programs. On Tuesday nights in 1925, for example, KJR broadcasted the Ladies Musical Club String Quartet on the "Puget Sound Savings and Loan Hour."

One easy way to build children's enthusiasm for the classics was to hold school competitions, which clubwomen sponsored. Musical Memory Contests induced children to memorize compositions by the great composers. Club members persuaded teachers to arrange spelling bee-style competitions, in which children would listen to a piece of music and identify the composition, composer, nationality, and dates, and the musical instruments featured. The LMC also sponsored essay contests on the values of music.

At local, state, and national levels contests were also held to reward young people already devoted to musical study. Beginning in 1915, the National Federation of Music Clubs awarded contest prizes in piano, violin, cello, organ, and voice. Later, the National Association of Colored Women, like multitudes of women's associations, invited students to their conventions, to perform solo, in duets, trios, quartets, and glee clubs, and gave medals and blue ribbons to the winners.[20]

Gradually, efforts to expand schoolchildren's familiarity with music led to after-school music clubs. These soon became institutionalized as regular music courses in the public schools. By the late 1920s, Seattle's music societies lobbied successfully for elective credit for high school students of music and for state accreditation for music teachers. Here was proof of the uniting of cultural and political action.

How acceptable to professional male musicians was women's involvement? Their efforts scarcely constituted a frontal assault on the male-dominated musical establishment of the early part of this century, yet many male critics expressed discomfort at the increased feminization of musical enthusiasts. Failing to appreciate that club members had subordinated their own musical development to champion established musical values among women, children, and immigrants, these men felt threatened by women's presence in the musical world. Walter Damrosch, conductor of the New York Philharmonic Orchestra, complained in his autobiography:

> Women's musical clubs began to form in many a village, town, and city, and these clubs became the active and efficient nucleus of the entire musical life of the community, but alas, again principally the feminine community. It is to these women's clubs that the managers turned for fat guarantees for appearances of their artists, it is before audiences of whom 75% are women that these artists desport themselves.[21]

Others, like George Reynolds, expressed their resignation to the phenomenon, and simply assigned cultural concerns to twentieth-century women as they assigned sports to men:

> Most of our Chambers of Commerce, men's organizations, you notice, are strong for good roads and golf links and Sunday baseball, to provide the amenities of life and opportunities for the enjoyment of the leisure with which our society seems almost to be threatened, but it is the women's clubs which mainly advocate those diversions of life which, from the days of primitive man, have enlivened his soul and ennobled his days, the great arts.[22]

Such acceptance of women's growing role in shaping musical taste was the exception. When the Curtis School of Music realized that two-thirds of its students were women when it opened in 1919, it limited acceptances until women represented only a third of the student body by the end of the decade. At Ginn and Company, publishers, the music department head Edbridge W. Newton attempted to bolster male participation in music by hawking its virtues to boys: "To be a good musician requires brains of the highest order. Boys, be not afraid to study music, there is nothing more worthy of the masculine mind."[23] Yet women persisted.

Indeed, the range of opportunities that music associations provided for members and their families was impressive. For the beginner, the loans and scholarships, the instruction and contests, the exposure and support, and even the safe dormitories for music students in strange cities aided the budding performer and composer. For the mature woman artist, who might have been a full-time, widely recognized professional in a world without sexism, the clubs reaffirmed her ability and nurtured its growth through acclaim. They constituted a crucial network for professional women. For example, the teachers shared educational techniques and news of job openings in schools; the ambitious concertizers and composers enjoyed hearings at regional meetings; contests yielded money, exposure, and acclaim.

To tap the enthusiasm of a growing associate membership with no musical skills, the clubs increasingly served to sustain the new auxiliaries and support associations that became the foundations of civic musical institutions. Their focus, away from the individual woman's training in favor of acquainting all segments of society with the classics and indigenous American songs, represented a massive effort unmatched anywhere else in society. Sheer tenacity pushed clubwomen beyond mere lobbying for access to music toward the instituting of contests, concerts, prizes, and classes in schools, settlements, and anywhere else the general citizenry might respond.

While members seldom attained praise from the male musical establishment, their efforts made an enormous impact on American musical life. This tireless cultivation of musical taste nurtured the respect Americans developed for and the enthusiasm they applied to the federal music program of the Depression years. So, too, the clubs' public program shaped the future supporters of the town symphony, the subscribers to the chamber music festivals, and the donors of the music schools throughout the nation.

Without a doubt, club members' motives were many. Their antipathy to popular music, their hopes of homogenizing the taste of youth and immigrants until it conformed to traditional standards, and blind patriotism—all these coexisted with the effort to develop an arena for women's influence in society, to revive the folk music of Indians, African Americans, and other neglected groups in the nation, and to share the musical beauty that had heretofore been monopolized by elites. On all counts, their organization was impressive, the variety and ingenuity of their projects were dazzling, and their success was broad. Women's societies, however detached from the musical mainstream, effectively shaped musical taste in the early twentieth century and served as a major force in American music.

NOTES

This essay originally appeared in G. Thomas Edwards and Carlos Schwantes, eds., *Experiences in a Promised Land: Essays in Pacific Northwest History* (Seattle: University of Washington Press, 1986), pp. 124–38.

1. Mildred Adams, "Foster-Mothers of Music," *Woman Citizen,* Jan. 26, 1924, p. 7.

2. The bulk of the paper's material was secured from the annual yearbooks of the LMC, in the Seattle Historical Society. The origins of the club are noted in C. T. Conover, "Ladies Musical Club's Epochal Cultural Services," *Seattle Times,* July 3, 1959; Mrs. A. E. Boardman, "Early History of the Ladies Musical Club," Golden Anniversary of Artists Concerts, 1900–1950, *Program*, p. 13; Hazel Gertrude Kinscella, "Seattle and the Pacific Northwest," in Quaintance Eaton, ed., *Musical USA* (New York: Allen, Towne, and Heath, 1945), pp. 195–206; and Clarence Bagley, *History of Seattle,* 3 vols. (Chicago: S. J. Clarke Publishing Co., 1916), 1: 615–16.

3. Ladies Musical Club, 1891–92 Constitution, p. 9.

4. "Jazz Is Under the Ban," *Music and Musicians* 1 (July 1921): 12; "A Music Club in Every Community, Is Slogan," *Miles City* (Mont.) *Daily Star,* Jan. 15, 1922.

5. *Seattle Star,* Sept. 19, 1924.

6. Anthony Ludovici, *Woman: A Vindication* (New York: A. A. Knopf, 1923), p. 320.

7. "Opening Doors," *Woman Citizen* 6 (Nov. 19, 1921): 187–88.

8. Sir Thomas Beecham, "The Position of Women," in *Vogue's First Reader* (Garden City, N.Y.: Halcyon House, 1942), p. 420.

9. Sophie Drinker, *Music and Women: The Story of Women in Their Relation to Music* (New York: Coward McCann, 1948), p. 239; "Wanted—The Open Door in Music," *Woman Citizen* 7 (Feb. 24, 1923): 15.

10. Christine Ammer, *Unsung: A History of Women in American Music* (Westport, Conn.: Greenwood Press, 1980), pp. 105–108.

11. "A Brief History of the MacDowell Colony," MacDowell Colony Archives, Peterborough, N.H.

12. Rheta Childe Dorr, *A Woman of Fifty* (New York: Funk & Wagnalls, 1924), p. 119.

13. Ida B. McLagan, "Music," in Washington State Federation of Women's Clubs *Bulletin* 2 (November 1917): 40.

14. Nicholas John Cords, "Music in Social Settlement and Community Music Schools, 1893–1939: A Democratic-Esthetic Approach to Music Culture," Ph.D. diss. (University of Minnesota, 1970), p. 37.

15. Ibid., 287.

16. Clarence A. Grimes, *They Who Speak in Music: The History of the Neighborhood Music School* (New Haven, Conn: Neighborhood Music School, 1957), p. 18.

17. Alice Duer Miller, *Barnard College: The First Fifty Years* (New York: Columbia University Press, 1939), p. 121; Washington State Federation of Women's Clubs, *Bulletin,* 1925.

18. Christine Rowell, "Where Children Love Music," *St. Nicholas Magazine* 47 (February 1920): 352.

19. General Federation of Women's Clubs, *Report of the Colorado Biennial Board for the Twentieth Biennial Convention,* Denver, 1930, p. 35; Massachusetts Federation of Women's Clubs, *Federation Manual,* 1922–23, p. 77; Washington State Federation of Women's Clubs, *Bulletin* 2 (November 1917): 42–44; Rhode Island Federation of Women's Clubs, 1915–16 Yearbook, p. 71; Alice Ames Winter, "The Technic of Being a Clubwoman," *Ladies Home Journal* 41 (August 1924): 6.

20. *National Notes* 28 (July 1926): 18.

21. Walter Damrosch, *My Musical Life* (New York: Scribner, 1926), p. 323.

22. General Federation of Women's Clubs, 1930 Biennial Report, p. 363.

23. Massachusetts State Federation of Women's Clubs, *Federation Manual,* 1921–22.

Tsugiki, a Grafting: A History of a Japanese Pioneer Woman in Washington State

GAIL M. NOMURA

In the imagination of most of us, the pioneer woman is represented by a sunbonneted Caucasian traveling westward on the American Plains. Few are aware of the pioneer women who crossed the Pacific Ocean east to America from Japan. Among these Japanese pioneer women were some whose destinies lay in the Pacific Northwest.

In Washington State, pioneer women from Japan, the *issei* or first (immigrant) generation, and their *nisei,* second-generation, U.S.-born daughters, made up the largest group of nonwhite ethnic women in the state for most of the first half of the twentieth century.[1] These issei women contributed their labor in agriculture and small businesses to help develop the state's economy. Moreover, they were essential to the establishment of a viable Japanese American community in Washington. Yet little is known of the history of these women.[2] This essay examines the life of one Japanese pioneer woman, Teiko Tomita, as a method of exploring the historical experience of Japanese pioneer women in Washington State.

Through interviewing Teiko Tomita, I have been able to gather certain facts about her life. But beyond this oral history, Tomita's experience is illumined by the rich written legacy of *tanka* poems she has written since she was a high school girl in Japan. The tanka written by Tomita served as a form of journal for her, a way of expressing her innermost thoughts as she became part of America. Tomita's poems give us insight into how she viewed her life in America and captured the essence of the Japanese pioneer woman's experience in Washington State. Indeed, *tsugiki,* the title Tomita gave to her section of a poetry anthology, meaning a grafting or a grafted tree, reflects her vision of a Japanese American grafted community rooting itself in Washington State through the pioneering experiences of women like herself.

The tanka provided a natural and common vehicle of expression for Japanese immigrants like Tomita. Coming from a country that had instituted compulsory education in the late nineteenth century, issei were often highly literate. But one did not have to be highly educated or uniquely gifted to compose tanka. Although the *haiku,* which is the Japanese short poem of seventeen syllables arranged in three lines of five, seven, and five syllables, is better known in the United States, the tanka is the more traditional poetic form. The tanka is a Japanese short poem consisting of thirty-one syllables arranged in five lines of five, seven, five, seven, and seven syllables successively. Japanese have from ancient times used the tanka to express their deepest emotions. Lyrical verse of the earliest collections of Japanese poetry used the brevity of the tanka form to speak of life, love, and grief of separation. Commoners as well as aristocrats wrote tanka, which for centuries remained the most popular means of poetic expression for men and women of all classes. Concentration and compression are the essence of the tanka, and in its brief thirty-one syllables Japanese were able to convey what might otherwise have required many pages, or even volumes.

Japanese immigrants like Tomita brought this poetic form with them to America and recorded their new lives through it. Issei-composed tanka in America reflected the imagery, feelings, and sensibilities of an immigrant generation taking root in a new land. Teiko Tomita used a traditional Japanese image, the cherry tree, in many of her *tsugiki* tanka to speak metaphorically of the grafting process of the Japanese immigrants to the root stock of America. Thus using the traditional poetic form and traditional metaphors, Tomita created new meanings expressing the issei immigrant experience. In writing of this immigrant experience so different from life in Japan, issei poets also created new metaphors and images and added new vocabulary. Tomita's early tanka in eastern Washington mention sagebrush and deserts unknown in Japan, and some of her tanka contain English words. The issei-written tanka was itself adapted to the new land, the poet adapting its content and language while maintaining its ancient form. Together with oral histories and other prose accounts, the tanka poems of Tomita give us a better understanding of the Japanese immigrant woman's experience in Washington State.

In an interview, Tomita recounted that she was born December 1, 1896, in Osaka Prefecture, Japan, the second of nine children born to the Matsui family.[3] She graduated from a girls high school, and while there learned to write tanka. Her teacher gave her the pen name "Yukari," which she used even in America. She went on to take a one-and-a-half-years' course at a normal school, which earned her a certificate to teach at the elementary school level. She taught until her marriage in 1920.

Most women in Japan at that time married before they were twenty-five, and as Tomita approached her mid-twenties she was urged to marry. Family-arranged marriages were the norm in Japan, rather than love marriages, since marriages were more of a contract between families than between individuals. Through a go-between, she was matched with her husband, Masakazu Tomita, who was farming near Wapato, Washington. She was shown his picture and told of his background and character. She met with his family in Japan, in the neighboring prefecture, and was impressed by them. Tomita and her husband-to-be exchanged letters for two years before their marriage, as a get-acquainted period. In late 1920, Masakazu Tomita returned to Japan for the marriage ceremony. The newlyweds then traveled in Japan for a couple of months before going to Wapato, in February 1921, to farm on the Yakama Indian Reservation.

Tomita's husband had promised her grandparents, who headed the extended family, that they would return in three years; and the grandparents consented, expecting her to work in America for three to five years at most. No one knew that the three-year stay would turn into more than six decades, though Tomita says that when she got to Washington and saw the poor conditions there, she knew they would not be able to return to Japan in so short a time. Indeed she would never again see her parents.

Tomita's poems indicate the feelings of issei women toward the families and life they left behind in Japan. Although starting a new life in America, the women still had solid roots in their homeland. Ties with their families were strong. In one poem Tomita recalls the parting words of her parents:

"Live happily,"
Said my parents
Holding my hands,
Their touch
Even now in my hands[4]

Tomita always remembered her parents' words of hope for her happiness in the new land. The warmth of her parents' love as expressed in their parting words and touch would sustain her through the years of separation. Tomita herself would pass this hope of happiness on to her own children in America.

Separation from her family gave Tomita new insights into the depths of family ties. This is apparent in a poem about her father that grew out of an incident that Tomita likes to recount over and over again. Marriage meant for her that her husband and children became the focus of her life and thoughts, and that work left little time to feel any longing to return home. She claims that she had no thoughts of returning to Japan, no sadness over her life in America. But her husband once saw her in the fields, shedding tears. He thought that she had become homesick after receiving a letter from her father. At dinner that night, he sympathized with her, saying he understood that she longed for her home, far away from the harsh land of Yakima. To his surprise, Tomita replied that she had no thoughts of returning to Japan. Rather, she had cried upon reading the letter, because it revealed a gentle, caring father she had not understood (*Hokubei hyakunen zakura*, p. 325):

The father I thought so strict
Where did he conceal
Such tender feelings
Revealed in those gentle letters
Many days I cried

"Those gentle letters" inquired after her well-being and happiness in the new land. Tomita came to have a fuller picture of her father than the severe figure of her childhood. She came to understand the love of father for child. The tears were tears of understanding.

The strength of ties with family and homeland over the thousands of miles separating them is apparent in another tanka by Tomita, encapsulating her emotions upon receiving a package from her family (p. 490):

When I think
It is from Japan
Even wrapping paper
Seems so close to me
It's hard to throw it away

Issei women had settled in the Yakima Valley since the 1890s, but even in 1921, when Tomita came to Wapato, the valley was still a raw frontier. Instead of moving from Japan to a richer life, Tomita embarked on a primitive pioneer life. In Kazuo Ito's book *Issei: A History of Japanese Immigrants in North America* (pp. 428–29), Tomita wrote that her Wapato house "was only a little better than a shack, being a two-room cabin hastily put together." Although everyone she knew in Japan had electricity, in Wapato "there was no electric light, so I had to polish oil lamps every morning. We had one small stove in there which took wood or coal, and from time to time I picked up roots of sagebrush and used it as fuel, too." There was no running water. Water had to be drawn from the well outside. The weather, too, was not gentle. Tomita remembers that in deepest winter it was so cold in the house that "you could hear the eggs in the cupboard in the kitchen cracking" and "the place where the sheet was turned down under our chins at night got covered with frost from our breath." When summer came roaring in, "it was scorching hot with a temperature of more than 100 degrees," and at night the Tomitas would have to "spread a blanket under the peach tree" to sleep on.

Tomita helped her husband with the farming on the Yakama Indian Reservation, where he had leased land to grow hay. But in 1921, the year she arrived, and again in 1923, Washington passed stricter anti-alien land laws, which anti-Japanese agitators pressured the Department of Interior to apply to the Yakama Indian Reservation. The Yakama Indian Agency thus was forced to stop issuing leases to Japanese issei, since the new anti-alien land laws prohibited not only the ownership of land but the renting, sharecropping, and issuance of leases to those who had not in good faith registered their intent to become citizens. Inasmuch as the Japanese were denied naturalization rights by U.S. law strictly on a racial basis, they could not in good faith register their intent to become citizens. Thus they were ineligible to lease land either in Washington or on the reservation. The Tomitas lost their lease rights to their farm on the Yakama Indian Reservation.

Luckily, Tomita's husband was an accomplished agriculturist, and a white nursery owner quickly hired him as a foreman for his nursery in Satus. Tomita served as cook for the laborers working under her husband. She remembers having to cook in shifts in her small house, first serving the work crew, then her own family. It was in Satus that her first child was born.

For Tomita, Satus was an even more remote, isolated area of Washington than Wapato had been. She had to walk five miles to see another Japanese face. Isolated as she was she took solace by writing tanka for herself, recording her life and thoughts.

Issei pioneer women often lived in very isolated regions of Washington. Tomita conveyed in a poem the loneliness and monotony of this life, in which the only way to distinguish one day from another might be the sun's rising and setting (*Hokubei hyakunen zakura*, p. 519):

Neighbors are five miles far away
Many days without seeing anyone
Today, too, without seeing anyone
The sun sets

Tei Tomita *(courtesy Kay Hashimoto)*

This isolated life was common to most pioneer women of the West, as was exposure to the harshness of nature. The houses built by the pioneers with their own hands were not proof against the elements. Tomita's poems speak eloquently of this ceaseless intrusion of nature (p. 519):

Yakima Valley
The spring storm raging
Even in the house
A cloud of sand
Sifts in

The Yakima Valley was a desert that with water and sweat could be made to bloom. They worked the land, transforming desert and sagebrush into fertile fields of alfalfa, onions, tomatoes, beans, and melons. But hard work did not ensure success. In another poem, Tomita expresses her realistic assessment of the immigrants' struggle to cultivate the land (p. 519):

Sagebrush desert to fertile plain
A transformation, I hear,
But when the windy season comes
There's no transforming the sandstorm

The persistent sand was a constant reminder of the desert that could reclaim the newly fertile land at any moment, and of the tenuous hold on success that the Japanese as aliens had on the leased land. At any moment the whirling sandstorm could engulf them and return the fertile plain to sagebrush desert.

Tomita's poems evoke not only the grit of desert sand in the newly developed Yakima Valley, but also the severe desert heat (p. 539):

As we busily pick beans
Even the breeze stirring
The weeds at our feet
Feels hot

Perseverance in the face of adversity characterized the early issei women. This spirit was taught to the children, who worked in the fields with their parents. Tomita writes (p. 539):

"Soon the heat will be gone"
While picking beans
I encourage my children
And myself

In encouraging her children to persevere in adversity, Tomita strengthened herself to persevere for her children.

Tomita's poems offer a key to her motivations for enduring and continuing to tame and cultivate the burning frontier. Her use of the symbolism of grafted cherry trees, particularly, makes clear the way she viewed her place in this new land (p. 539):

Carefully grafting
Young cherry trees
I believe in the certainty
They will bud
In the coming spring

The cherry blossom is a Japanese symbol not only of spring but of Japan and the Japanese people themselves. In the grafting of cherry trees, Tomita sees the grafting of the Japanese immigrant onto the root stock of America, where the graft will continue to grow and become a permanent part. The importance of this symbolism is again underscored in her choice of the title "Tsugiki" (a graft or grafted tree) for her section of the issei poetry anthology *Renia no yuki.* She views not only her past work in the nursery as grafting but perhaps also her own self.

In the poem above she expresses her belief in a coming spring when the grafted tree will bud and grow, just as the hopes and dreams of the immigrant Japanese will be fulfilled. The centrality of this hope of a coming spring is expressed in another poem (*Hokubei hyakunen zakura,* p. 539):

Whirls of storming winter
I tolerate
Believing in spring
To come again

By believing in the certainty that the grafted tree will bloom in its new environment, the winter of travails can be endured. Perhaps, though, the blossoms will be the next generation, not Tomita's own. Meanwhile the grafting process is an arduous one, as another poem indicates (*Renia no yuki,* p. 248):

Grafting cherry saplings
Along long furrows
The August sun
Burns on our back

In 1929 the Tomitas moved to Sunnydale, near Seattle, where Seattle-Tacoma International Airport (Sea-Tac) now sprawls. There, they started their own nursery. Moving to more populous Sunnydale meant that Tomita was able to have many Japanese families as neighbors for the first time in America. It also meant the further development of her poetry writing, for she heard of a tanka club in Seattle, and joined the group in 1939. Although

Tomita family in 1941 *(courtesy Kay Hashimoto)*

she was not able to attend the monthly meetings, she would each month send new poems for criticism. Many of her poems were sent on to Japan for publication. But in Sunnydale, misfortunes and hardships continued, with the loss of the youngest daughter of the Tomitas' five children and the impact of the Great Depression. Tomita became a Christian during the Sunnydale years, and many of her later poems reflect her new faith.

The small economic gains made by the Tomitas were wiped out by the outbreak of war between the motherland and the adopted land in December 1941. Since they were denied naturalization rights, all Japanese immigrants were aliens, now enemy aliens. Furthermore, even their U.S.-born children were considered suspect. The old anti-Japanese agitation was rekindled, and this time succeeded in perpetrating one of the most massive violations of civil rights in American legal history. With no formal charges of any wrongdoing, more than 110,000 issei and their U.S. citizen children were removed from their homes on the West Coast to incarceration in concentration camps. They were not to be allowed to return to their homes until 1945. Although most Seattle Japanese were interned in Minidoka in Idaho, those in the outlying areas of Seattle, like the Tomitas, were interned in Tule Lake, California, in 1942. In late 1943 they were moved to Heart Mountain in Wyoming, where, ironically, Tomita was reunited with Japanese from the Yakima Valley, her first home in America.[5]

Immediately after the bombing of Pearl Harbor, many rumors circulated in the Japanese community that military men were searching all Japanese homes for any incriminating evidence that would link them with Japan. Later, there was talk about something fearsome called "camp." Under this pressure, Tomita gathered up her precious poetry manuscripts, took them to the fields, and burned them all, fearing that the private thoughts recorded in her tanka might be twisted into something harmful to her family. Being forced to burn her poems remains one of the most painful memories of the war for Tomita. Much of the poetic record of her life was wiped out.

But despite the destruction of the manuscripts, not all the poems were lost. Many of the burned tanka remained etched in Tomita's mind, to be recalled in later years. Easily committed to memory, poetry has often been the device of oral tradition's preservation of preliterate history, passed on from one generation to the next.

When war broke out between Japan and the United States in December 1941, it looked as though spring would not come, even for the next generation. The war years were difficult ones for the issei women. After years of struggling, the little they had gained was wrenched from them overnight. Forced by the government to leave the land they had pioneered, they were imprisoned in even more isolated and desolate regions of America than they could ever have imagined. The internment camps were located in remote desert lands. Yet even here, surrounded by barbed wire, the creative spirit of the issei inmates persisted. The creative arts in the camps found expression in forms ranging from polished sagebrush roots to accomplished poetry. Many issei learned to write Japanese poetry for the first time in camp, and continued to write even after they had left the camps.[6]

At Heart Mountain, Tomita, with other issei, attended lectures and classes in poetry to while away the seemingly endless years of internment. Tomita began to keep a journal of her class lectures, as well as of her poems—a fresh book to replace the volumes she had burned. Her book of poems shows the changes she made from one draft to another, to final form. In poetry many issei found the solace Tomita noted in a poem written in 1943, at Tule Lake internment camp (*Renia no yuki,* p. 243):

Within the iron stockade
Always composing poems
From the sorrows of war
A little consolation

As she had done in the desert of Yakima, Tomita turned to poetry to comfort herself in her troubles. But, as always, her poems also reflected hope. In the midst of the sorrow and uncertainty of imprisonment in Tule Lake, in January 1943 she could still write (p. 243):

In the war concentration camp
The New Year's Day's sun rises
Look up at the light
Which breaks up the darkness of night

New Year's Day meant the hope of a new start, the hope that the darkness of the past year might be pierced by the light of freedom. But freedom did not come quickly. The war continued. Tomita's poems written in 1944 reflect the inner turmoil experienced by the issei caught by a war between the country of birth and the adopted country which had not accepted them as its own (p. 243):

I read the war news
Today again
My heart clouds
And my thoughts are frozen

When the war finally ended, in 1945, the Tomitas were living in Minnesota, having secured a work release earlier in the year. The war that had torn them from their homes and made prisoners of them had ended, but the war's end was bittersweet news (p. 243):

Among whites jubilantly shouting
"The war is over"
My husband and I
Cried throughout the night

Japan was defeated, horrifying atomic bombs had been dropped, and Japanese Americans had at last been released from the camps in which they had been held for years without any justification. Joy and relief at the end of the grief and hardships of the war combined with the sadness of war's aftermath and destruction and the uncertain future. Tomita worried over the fate of her family in Japan and their mutual concern over her fate in America (p. 243):

> For the first time in five years
> Letters are permitted to the home country
> Today I only write
> "We're safe"

The link with family in the home country was reestablished. The silence brought by war ended with the simple message, "We're safe."

They were safe. They had survived another hardship, but now they once again had to start from scratch. She wrote (p. 244):

> Returning home from the iron stockade
> Five years ago
> Reconstructing our lives
> Is no small thing even now

Her poem reflects the cold reality for Japanese Americans that even after returning from the concentration camps they still faced a long struggle to rebuild their lives. But although it was indeed not a "small thing," Tomita did reconstruct her life. Because of the internment, the Tomitas had not only lost their nursery business but had no capital to invest in another venture. Tomita took the only wage job available to her. She became a garment worker in Seattle. This job opened new worlds for her.

Sewing alongside other immigrant women in Seattle, Tomita gained closer contact and better understanding of women from other ethnic groups. The poems written while she was a seamstress reflect a growing awareness of the commonality of experience and emotions she shared with her coworkers. In one poem she writes (p. 243):

> A German woman and I
> Sewing together
> Sharing the same feelings
> Speaking of the war destruction
> In each of our home countries

Although they came from two countries separated by thousands of miles and by different cultural traditions, here in the workplace the two women shared their wartime experiences and became one.

While her prewar poems dealt mainly with herself or her family, Tomita's poems were now enlivened with observations of other people. In contrast to the isolation of her former rural life, her urban workplace offered a microcosm of the multiethnic, multicultural American society of which she was a part. In a series of more narrative poems, Tomita observed some conflict between white and black workers, but in general her poems suggested a sisterhood among the women workers that cut across ethnic lines.

Tomita's poems bring to life the variety of women she worked with, among them a black woman who had such a fine voice that when she sang, her voice rose clear and strong above the roar of the sewing machines, and a Filipino woman who seemed very cheerful and carefree, and who had learned a little Japanese that helped her communicate with Tomita. Tomita savored and valued these experiences (p. 245):

> For many years
> Mixed among the workers of different races
> I sew
> I'm used to it
> Such life is enjoyable

Tomita's growing appreciation of interaction with other ethnic groups is further demonstrated in a series of poems about her Italian neighbors. The first in the series notes the presence in her neighborhood of many Italians, most of them farmers who worked very diligently. She admired their industry, which made her feel an affinity with them. In the next poem she again took up this theme (p. 246):

> In their hard work
> Italians are like we Japanese
> Daughters and wives, too
> Work all day in the fields

It was in their shared history of the hard work of farming that Tomita found a commonality of experience with these European immigrants. And the feelings were mutual, it seems, for in the next poems we see that at least one of the Italian neighbors had become a friend. Beyond sharing hard work and vegetables with his Japanese neighbors, he shared the immigrant experience of separation from the land of one's birth (p. 247):

Mutually shared feelings
This Italian
Speaking fervently about
His homeland

In the postwar period we see Tomita's poems reflecting not only a more urban, multiethnic awareness but also a more global viewpoint. Fully understanding the terrible costs of war, Tomita is well aware of the world events that may lead to a war for which her children would have to pay the high price (p. 250):

My son is still young
I daily pray
For eternal peace
In this violent world

In particular, she has become ardently opposed to the nuclear arms race, devoting a whole series of poems to this subject. News of the Bikini Island nuclear test victims moves her to write (p. 251):

Reading of the condition
Of Bikini patients
Incurable disease
The power of science
Is rather a curse

She notes that Japan is a leader in the nuclear disarmament movement (p. 252):

A country that experienced
The death ash
Japan's accusing voice
Voice of desperation

In another poem in the series, Tomita observes that a ban on nuclear bombs has already been written with the blood of Japan, the only country to suffer an atomic bombing. But she notes, sadly (p. 252):

Regardless of the earnest prayers
Of the suffering country
Nuclear bombs
Are steadily produced

After decades of hard work, Tomita was finally able to realize her dream of owning a home. Her joy in the fulfillment of the dream is recorded in a series of poems (p. 249):

I enjoyed drawing pictures
Of my desired house
The long held dream
Became a reality

The dream became a reality just when they had virtually given up hope of achieving it in their generation (p. 249):

The dream I passed
On to my children
How many years!
The house is finished

But this joy at a dream finally fulfilled in America was also to be dashed. Her Sunnydale home was directly north of Seattle-Tacoma International Airport. Soon the roar of the airplanes shook her house (p. 245):

The runways are to be expanded,
I hear,
The roaring sound
Is drawing closer to me

The airport expanded, she wrote, despite the complaints and puzzlement of the surrounding people. Its expansion changed the environment (p. 246):

Farms and houses, too
Before I'm aware
I see their shadows no more
The runways are being built expansively

As houses and farms disappeared, the people disappeared. The Port of Seattle responded to the complaints of noise and low-flying jets by removing the people who complained. It acquired by eminent domain the property of people like Tomita to form a buffer zone around Seattle-Tacoma International. In 1967, Tomita was once again forced to relocate. More fortunate than some, she and her husband were able to move in with her daughter's family in Seattle.

The realization of the passing of time is very much part of the later writings of Tomita. Reflecting on the decades of pioneering that have flown past, she writes (p. 251):

Long ago are the days
I helped my husband
Cultivate the raw land
And raised our children
We two have grown old

Another poem continues the theme of old age (p. 251):

My husband
Reading with bifocals
So many decades of struggles
Engraved deeply
In the wrinkles on his face

Thoughts rise of the unfulfilled aspirations of youth. For Tomita those memories are of dashed hopes of continuing her studies. In a series of poems she recalls these hopes of scholarship, symbolized in a treasured box given to her as a graduation prize (p. 247):

As a lifetime memory
Placed in a suitcase with love and care
For thirty years
A lacquer calligraphy box

She remembers the words that accompanied the prize—words admonishing her to continue to train her mind and soul. But since coming to America (p. 247):

Too busy were
Thirty years of life
In a foreign country
Never used the brush and ink

There had never been time for her formal studies. She had written her tanka in isolation in the fields of Yakima. Even after moving to the Seattle area, though she had been able to join a tanka club, she had not been able to attend the monthly meetings, because the nursery had required her constant care.

Her life, she said in an interview, could be summed up in one word, *isogashii*—busy, a life filled always with things she had to do.[7] As for thoughts of the luxury of studies (p. 247):

Never to return are the days
When I put my heart and soul
In my studies only
I grow old in a foreign country

Although her aspirations may have had to be set aside in the grafting process of settling in America, there was always the belief in the fulfillment of dreams for the next generation, when the grafted tree would bloom and bear fruit. The struggles were well worth the pain for Tomita, if her children could fulfill their own dreams and aspirations. Tomita reveled in the fact that her children had not been adversely affected by the family's hard life (p. 246):

My daughter has
A rainbow-like dream
Cheerful as she is
The poverty of me her mother
Hasn't stained her life

Memories of the poverty of much of her life in America, with repeated setbacks, led her to write (*Hokubei hyakunen zakura*, p. 173):

When winter comes
I wonder what it was
That enabled me to endure
Heartrending sorrows

It had been for her children that she worked, and it was the hope of their spring that sustained her through her winter of struggles and sorrows. In her poems, she celebrates the triumphs of her children as they go off to college, get married, and start new, exciting jobs. Her poems reveal a conviction on her part that her children will not suffer the trials and tribulations she endured (*Renia no yuki,* p. 250):

My son's start in life
Like a clear morning
Without a single cloud
Limitless blue sky of hope

Her struggles have not adversely affected the lives of her children, but rather seem to have ensured their future. She could write hopefully in 1968:

The centennial of
The Japanese immigrants in America
Our next generation
With a great future before them[8]

Fifteen years later Tomita looks back on her more than six decades of life experiences in America and concludes:

The bitter ordeals I have suffered
One after another
As I remember
Now without sorrow
Filled with grace[9]

Tomita's most recent poems reflect a continuation of her thanksgiving that her grandchildren, too, are enjoying the spring out of the travails of her winters. In a series of poems in the summer of 1983 she writes of her trip to the East Coast to attend her granddaughter's graduation from Sarah Lawrence. With commencement comes a new flowering for the third-generation *tsugiki*, and a celebration uniting the generations. The ties that bind the generations together appear strong, as her grandchildren make efforts to communicate with their grandmother in Japanese:

From my granddaughter in New York
A letter in Japanese

As I read it
Tears of joy overflow[10]

Whatever their literary merits, the poems presented in this essay provide valuable information and insight into the life of Teiko Tomita. Each poem is a diary entry relating a significant event or thought in her life. Often a series of poems gives a full account of a particular incident in her life. Even more than a diary, the poems reveal the inner thoughts and emotions of the author. The tanka critic Hideko Matsui, in an article in *Cho-on,* the Japanese poetry magazine to which the Seattle tanka club sent their selected poetry for publication, believes that although poems such as Tomita's in *Renia no yuki* have a simple, classical, moving quality about them, their importance is mainly that they relate the immigrants' history in the traditional form of the Japanese tanka.[11] In fact, both the historical value and the literary merit of issei poetry deserve a great deal of further discussion.[12]

Recognition of the value of issei poetry as a vehicle for understanding the Japanese American experience in America has led to the publication of anthologies of translated poems written by the issei. One such anthology is *Poets Behind Barbed Wire,*[13] which contains Japanese short poems, haiku, and tanka written by Hawaii issei interned during World War II. The editors of the anthology note that "in view of the scarcity of writing paper, these short poems, being less cumbersome than long diaries, were ideal forms for the internees' expression of their pent-up emotions." They further point out that "it also perpetuates the Japanese tradition of expressing their innermost emotions through short poems instead of prose." The editors believe that the short poems express the issei internment experience far better and more explicitly than prose written on the experience.[14] Indeed, one of these poets behind barbed wire scribbled hundreds of poems on the only two sheets of paper he was able to take with him from detention to internment camps.

For Tomita and a great many issei, poetry was a means of recording their lives for posterity, as well as an artistic release of their emotions. They wrote their tanka as poetic expressions of their lives and thoughts. In writing their tanka they were conscious of their role in recording their history—a history they believed would not be included in general histories about American immigrants. Another issei woman poet, Keiko Teshirogi, wrote:

Not recorded in immigrant history
Your struggles are inscribed
In the depths of my heart alone[15]

As it was for Tomita, the cherry tree was a common issei symbol of Japan and the Japanese. Teshirogi also composed a tanka similar to those of Tomita, speaking of the issei as cherry trees making the adaptation to the American continent from their roots in the island environment of Japan:

A cherry tree
That cannot adapt itself to a continent
Is small
And without taking on autumn colors
Its leaves fall[16]

Despite great hardships, the issei immigrants did indeed adapt to their new environment. For some, like Tomita, poetic expression helped to make that adaptation more endurable. Their poetry, in turn, helps us to grasp the history of that adaptation and survival.

Teiko Tomita's life as presented in this essay provides an outline generally representative of the issei woman's rather harsh life in Washington State. Although the early Japanese immigrants to Washington were predominantly young, single men, women began to enter the state in large numbers after the so-called gentlemen's agreement in 1907–1908, which restricted the further immigration of Japanese male laborers to the United States. Like Tomita, most women who came were wives of settled immigrants. Many were "picture brides" whose marriages had been arranged by their families through the exchange of pictures with Japanese male immigrants living in Washington. After 1921, because the Japanese government did not issue passports to picture brides, most grooms, like Tomita's husband, traveled to Japan to marry, and brought their wives back with them. In 1924, Congress passed a new immigration and naturalization act that prohibited the immigration of "aliens ineligible to citizenship," a category the U.S. Supreme Court had created in its 1922 Ozawa decision and 1923 Thind decision, ruling that Mongolians as a racial group and people from India were not eligible for naturalization. Thus no new immigrants from Japan, male or female, arrived after 1924. Still, because the Japanese males had been able to send for wives from 1908 to 1924, there occurred a dramatic increase in the numbers of women of Japanese ethnicity in Washington.[17]

The Japanese women who came between 1910 and 1924 played a crucial role in the growth of a Japanese American community in Washington. The summoning of wives like Tomita reinforced the commitment to permanent residency in America more than economic stakes in farms and businesses. There was a settled family life with the coming of wives, and an emergence of Japanese American family units with the dramatic increase in American-born children between 1900 and 1930. With the birth of the second generation, there was a transformation from immigrant society to permanent settlers, as issei began to focus and identify their own futures in terms of the future of their children in America. Entry of women into Japanese immigrant society was an integral part of the process by which Japanese immigrant society sank its roots into American soil. The arrival of women guaranteed that a community with a family life could be established in America. The Japanese community developed a family orientation around schools, churches, clubs, and associations. The women brought both community and Japanese culture with them. Often highly educated, like Tomita, they preserved such values as love of learning and an appreciation of the arts.

Tomita's lifetime of work in the Yakima Valley, Sunnydale, and Seattle underscores the fact that Japanese pioneer women were not only wives and mothers but also workers. Their labor was indispensable in the operation of farms, small businesses, and labor camps, as well as in family enterprises, such as small shops and tiny farms. Japanese women played a vital economic role in the new land.

The majority of Japanese women initially lived in rural areas, helping their husbands till the soil as farmers. Japanese agriculturalists were especially prominent in Washington. In urban areas, women entered small businesses operated by their husbands, such as laundries, markets, restaurants, and boardinghouses, or they became domestic servants, seamstresses, and cannery workers. Labor camps that provided laborers for railroads, lumber camps, and mills were often run by issei men. Many issei women worked in these labor camps. As Tomita did in her Yakima years, the women cooked for the large group of workers employed by their husbands.

Japanese women performed tasks essential to the maintenance of the family by earning income, rearing children, preparing meals, shopping, and tending the sick. Because of their essential role in running the family and their valuable economic role, the women enjoyed greater power in decision making for the family than did their counterparts in Japan. Moreover, in the pioneer setting the issei women were free of the traditional control of the mother-in-law, another factor that greatly enlarged their influence in the family.

In the 1930s the power of issei wives in the family increased, as the men aged. Many of the issei men in the 1930s were over fifty-five. As the men aged, their wives—on the average ten years younger—took on increased economic responsibilities, and made more of the important decisions. The women thus became increasingly the focal point of the Japanese American family.

Issei women did not have an easy time making a home in Washington.

The most sustained and serious difficulty they faced was anti-Japanese sentiment. As we have seen, Japanese were denied naturalization on the basis of race, and so were condemned to remain aliens in their adopted land. In Washington, their status as "aliens ineligible to citizenship" made it possible to restrict their economic opportunities severely through a series of anti-alien land laws. The culmination of these anti-Japanese policies came with World War II, when thousands of Washington Japanese—aliens and U.S. citizens alike—were removed to concentration camps.

After the war, the issei pioneers, now nearing retirement age, had to begin their lives over again. Like Tomita, many issei women, whose assets and capital had been taken from them by the internment, went to work in garment factories or into domestic service. Tomita's postwar urban life also reflects a general shift of Japanese Americans after the war to urban residences and occupations.

In the postwar years, hard work once more bore fruit—though not as great a harvest as might have been possible, given more hospitable conditions. The children of the pioneers, the nisei, married and had children of their own. A third generation was born. The issei women looked back on their years of struggle, and saw in their grandchildren the fulfillment of their young hopes when they first came to America. They believed the *tsugiki* to be strong and firmly rooted in its adopted land. The children and the grandchildren, the second and third generation branches of the *tsugiki*, are blooming in the spring that has finally come. Tomita can write in May 1983:

The seeds I planted
Sprout and grow up
Even in this very old body
Joy overflows[18]

Through the struggles of Tomita and other issei pioneer women, the history of Washington State has been enriched.

NOTES

1. In the 1920, 1930, and 1940 censuses, women of Japanese ethnicity were the most numerous nonwhite women in Washington State, making up almost half of the nonwhite female population, including Native American women. See U.S. Bureau of the Census, *Sixteenth Census of the United States* (1940), vol. 2: *Population 2: Characteristics of the Population* (Washington, D.C.: U.S. Government Printing Office, 1943), pt. 7: Utah-Wyoming, p. 304.

2. The best English source of information on issei women in Washington is Kazuo Ito, *Issei: A History of Japanese Immigrants in North America*, trans. Shinichiro Nakamura and Jean S. Gerard (Seattle: Executive Committee for Publication, Japanese Community Service, 1973). This is a translation of Ito's *Hokubei hyakunen zakura* (North American Hundred Years Cherries) (Tokyo: Hokubei hyakunen zakura jikko iinkai, 1969), which contains written statements and poetry by issei women recalling their lives in the Pacific Northwest.

3. The biographical information is drawn from an interview with Teiko Tomita, Seattle, Washington, July 26, 1983.

4. Mihara Senryu et al., *Renia no yuki* (Snow of Rainier) (Kamakura, Japan: Choonsha, 1956), p. 249. This anthology contains the best published collection of Tomita's poems. Some of the earlier poems have annotations that give the date of writing. Other poems can be dated by their content, since Tomita wrote her poems contemporaneously with the events about which she wrote. The best source of her more recent poems is the Seattle newspaper *Hokubei Hochi,* in which her poems appeared monthly.

The English translations of Tomita's tanka that appear in this chapter do not fully convey, of course, the poetic beauty, rhythm, and nuances of the original. I have made an attempt to remain as close to the original Japanese meaning of the tanka as possible, though I was not able at this time to render the translation into an English poetic equivalent, if that is ever possible. We can hope that in the near future better translations will allow the reader to understand and appreciate more fully the poetic beauty of these poems.

5. See Frank F. Chuman, *The Bamboo People: The Law and Japanese-Americans* (Del Mar, Calif.: Publisher's Inc., 1976), for information on restrictive laws; for information on the internment of Japanese Americans, see such works as Commission on Wartime Relocation and Internment of Civilians, *Personal Justice Denied* (Washington, D.C., 1983); Roger Daniels, *Concentration Camps: North America* (Malabar, Fla.: Robert E. Krieger Publishing Co., 1981); Peter Irons, *Justice at War* (New York: Oxford University Press, 1983); and Michi Weglyn, *Years of Infamy* (New York: William Morrow, 1976).

6. Interview with Toshiko Toku, Seattle, Washington, July 25, 1983. Toku learned to write *senryu,* Japanese satirical poems, in an internment camp during World War II and continues to write to the present.

7. Interview with Teiko Tomita, Seattle, Washington, July 26, 1983.

8. Kazuo Ito, *Zoku hokubei hyakunen zakura* (North American Hundred Years Cherries, Supplement) (Tokyo: Hokubei hyakunen zakura jikko iinkai, 1972).

9. "Shiatoru tankakai," *Hokubei Hochi* (Seattle), May 25, 1983, p. 7.

10. Ibid., Oct. 12, 1983, p. 5.

11. Hideko Matsui, "Renia no yuki no igi" (Significance of *Renia no yuki*), *Cho-on* 42, no. 6 (1956): 27–28.

12. For a discussion of how local American settings, history, and culture have affected the creation of an issei poetry, see Stephen H. Sumida, "Localism in Asian American Literature and Culture of Hawaii and the West Coast," *Hawaii Literary Arts Council Newsletter* 71 (August-September 1983): n.p. The essay was originally delivered in this form at the Asian Studies on the Pacific Coast Conference, University of Alaska at Fairbanks, June 1983. Issei poetry calls for literary evaluation in terms of the poetry's own issei contexts.

13. Keiho Soga, Taisanboku Mori, Sojin Takei, and Muin Ozaki, *Poets Behind Barbed Wire,* ed. and trans. Jiro Nakano and Kay Nakano (Honolulu: Bamboo Ridge Press, 1983).

14. Ibid., p. vii.

15. Mihara, *Renia no yuki,* p. 239.

16. Ibid., p. 240.

17. U.S. Census (1940), p. 304. In 1900 there were 185 Japanese women in Washington, including 21 born in the United States; in 1910 there were 1,688, with 347 being U.S. born. But in 1920, after a decade of immigration of wives and picture brides, there were 6,065 women of Japanese ethnicity, with 2,117 U.S. born. From 1920 until 1940, women of Japanese ethnicity composed the largest group of nonwhite women in Washington State. In 1920, women of Japanese ethnicity numbered 6,065 out of 13,836 nonwhite women in Washington. In 1930, out of 16,744 nonwhite women in Washington, there were 7,637 women of Japanese ethnicity, including 4,308 U.S. born. And in 1940, out of 15,975 nonwhite women, there were 6,532 women of Japanese ethnicity, including 4,234 U.S. born. The numbers of issei women actually fell between 1920 and 1940 because of increasing legal restrictions that greatly limited the issei's economic opportunities, forcing them to seek better opportunities in other states.

18. "Shiatoru tankakai," *Hokubei Hochi,* June 8, 1983, p. 7.

SUGGESTIONS FOR FURTHER READING

RESEARCH

Andrews, Mildred. *Seattle Women: A Legacy of Community Development, a Pictorial History, 1851–1920.* Seattle: Seattle–King County YWCA, 1984.

_____. *Woman's Place: A Guide to Seattle and King County History.* Seattle: Gemil Press, 1994.

Blair, Karen J. *Northwest Women: An Annotated Bibliography of Sources on the History of Oregon and Washington Women, 1787–1970.* Pullman: Washington State University Press, 1997.

Jameson, Elizabeth, and Susan Armitage, eds. *Writing the Range: Race, Class, and Culture in the Women's West.* Norman: University of Oklahoma Press, 1997.

Schwantes, Carlos. *The Pacific Northwest: An Interpretive History.* Lincoln: University of Nebraska Press, 1996.

Ward, Jean, and Elaine A. Maveety, eds. *Pacific Northwest Women, 1815–1915: Lives, Memories, and Writings.* Corvallis: Oregon State University Press, 1995.

POLITICS AND LAW

Ault, Nelson A. "'The Earnest Ladies': The Walla Walla Women's Club and the Equal Suffrage League of 1886–1889." *Pacific Northwest Quarterly* 42 (April 1951): 123–37.

del Mar, David Peterson. *What Trouble I Have Seen: A History of Violence Against Wives.* Cambridge: Harvard University Press, 1996.

Duniway, Abigail Scott. *Path Breaking: An Autobiographical History of the Equal Suffrage Movement in Pacific Coast States.* Portland: James, Kerns and Abbott Company, 1914.

Edwards, G. Thomas. *Sowing Good Seeds: The Northwest Suffrage Campaigns of Susan B. Anthony.* Portland: Oregon Historical Society Press, 1990.

Haarsager, Sandra. *Bertha Knight Landes of Seattle: Big-City Mayor.* Norman: University of Oklahoma Press, 1994.

Horner, Patricia Voeller. "May Arkwright Hutton: Suffragist and Politician," pp. 25–42 in Karen J. Blair, ed., *Women in Pacific Northwest History: An Anthology.* Seattle: University of Washington Press, 1988. First edition.

Larson, T. A. "The Woman Suffrage Movement in Washington." *Pacific Northwest Quarterly* 67 (April 1976): 49–62.

Montgomery, James W. *Liberated Woman: A Life of May Arkwright Hutton.* Spokane: Gingko Publishers, 1974.

Moynihan, Ruth Barnes. *Rebel for Rights: Abigail Scott Duniway.* New Haven: Yale University Press, 1983.

Pearce, Stella E. "Suffrage in the Pacific Northwest: Old Oregon and Washington." *Washington Historical Quarterly* 3 (April 1912): 106–14.

Sheeran, Marte Jo. "The Woman Suffrage Issue in Washington." Master's thesis, University of Washington, 1977.

Smith, Helen Krebs. *Presumptuous Dreamers.* Lake Oswego, Ore.: Smith, Smith, and Smith Publishing Company, 1974.

Strong, Anna Louise. *I Change Worlds: The Remaking of an American.* New York: H. Holt and Company, 1935. Reprint, Seattle: Seal Press, 1979.

Watkins, Marilyn P. "Political Activism and Community-Building Among Alliance and Grange Women in Western Washington, 1892–1925." *Agricultural History* 67 (Spring 1993): 197–213.

WORK

Additon, Lucia H. Faxon. *Twenty Eventful Years of the Oregon Woman's Christian Temperance Union, 1880–1900.* Portland: Gottshall Printing Company, 1904.

Anderson, Karen. *Wartime Women: Sex Roles, Family Relations, and the Status of Women During World War II.* Westport, Conn.: Greenwood Press, 1981.

Bagley, Clarence B., ed. *Early Catholic Missions in Old Oregon.* Vol. 2. Seattle: Lowman and Hanford Company, 1932.

Clark, Ella E., and Margot Edmonds. *Sacagawea of the Lewis and Clark Expedition.* Berkeley: University of California Press, 1979.

Daugherty, James. *Marcus and Narcissa Whitman, Pioneers of Oregon.* New York: Viking Press, 1953.

Dembo, Jonathan. *An Historical Bibliography of Washington State Labor and Laboring Classes.* Seattle: Dembo, 1978.

Douthit, Mary Osborn. *The Souvenir of Western Women.* Portland: Anderson and Duniway Company, 1905.

Drury, Clifford M. *Elkanah and Mary Walker, Pioneers Among the Spokanes.* Caldwell, Idaho: Caxton Printers, Ltd., 1940.

Frank, Dana. *Purchasing Power: Consumer Organizing, Gender, and the Seattle Labor Movement, 1919–1929.* New York: Cambridge University Press, 1994.

Glenn, Evelyn Nakano. "The Dialectics of Wage Work: Japanese-American Women and Domestic Service, 1905–1940." *Feminist Studies* 6 (Fall 1980): 432–71.

Halvorsen, Helen Olson, and Lorraine Fletcher. "Nineteenth Century Midwife: Some Recollections." *Oregon Historical Quarterly* 70 (March 1969): 39–49.

Hazard, Joseph Taylor. *Pioneer Teachers of Washington.* Seattle: Retired Teachers Association, 1955.

Kesselman, Amy. *Fleeting Opportunities: Women Shipyard Workers in Portland and Vancouver During World War II and Reconversion.* Albany: State University of New York Press, 1990.

Koslosky, Nancy. "A Filipino Nurse in the Thirties: An Interview with Maria Abastilla Beltran." *Backbone* 3 (1981): 28–32.

Miller, Helen Markley. *Woman Doctor of the West.* New York: Julian Mesner, Inc., 1960.

Turner, Russell M. *The First Forty-Five Years: A History of Cooperative Extension in Washington State.* Extension Miscellaneous Publication 55. Pullman: Washington State University, Institute of Agricultural Services, 1961.

West, Leoti L. *The Wide Northwest: As Seen By a Pioneer Teacher.* Spokane: Shaw and Borden Company, 1927.

Williams, Jacqueline. *Wagon Wheel Kitchens: Food on the Oregon Trail.* Lawrence: University of Kansas Press, 1993.

Woloch, Nancy. *Muller v. Oregon: A Brief History with Documents.* Boston: St. Martin's Press, 1996.

RACE AND ETHNICITY

Armitage, Susan. "Everyday Encounters: Indians and the White Women in the Palouse." *Pacific Northwest Forum* 7 (Summer-Fall 1982): 27–30.

Barnhart, Edward N. *Japanese-American Evacuation and Resettlement: Catalog of Material in the General Library.* Berkeley: University of California General Library, 1958.

Bingham, Robert D. "Swedish-Americans in Washington State: A Bibliography of Publications." *Swedish Pioneer Historical Quarterly* 25 (April 1974): 133–40.

Blee, Kathleen M. *Women of the Klan: Racism and Gender in the 1920's.* New York: Oxford University Press, 1991.

Davidson, Sue. "Aki Kato Kurose: Portrait of an Activist." *Frontiers* 7 (1983): 91–97.

Davis, Lenwood G. *The Black Woman in American Society.* Boston: G. K. Hall and Company, 1975.

Edson, Christopher H. *Chinese in Eastern Oregon, 1860–1890.* San Francisco: R and E Research Association, 1974.

Haeberlin, Hermann, and Erna Gunther. *The Indians of Puget Sound.* Seattle: University of Washington Press, 1930.

Horn, Juana Raquel Royster. "The Academic and Extra Curricular Undergraduate Experiences of Three Black Women at the University of Washington, 1935–1941." Ph.D. dissertation, University of Washington, 1980.

Jeffrey, Julie Roy. *Converting the West: A Biography of Narcissa Whitman.* Norman: University of Oklahoma Press, 1991.

Mumford, Esther Hall. "Group Portrait: My Mother, My Grandmother, and I." *Backbone* 3 (1981): 33–37.

_____. *Seven Stars and Orion: Reflections of the Past.* Seattle: Ananse Press, 1986.

Sone, Monica. *Nisei Daughter.* 1953. Seattle: University of Washington Press, 1979.

Sunoo, Sonia S. "Korean Women Pioneers of the Pacific Northwest." *Oregon Historical Quarterly* 79 (Spring 1978): 51–63.

Van Kirk, Sylvia. *Many Tender Ties: Women in Fur-Trade Society, 1670–1870.* Norman: University of Oklahoma Press, 1983.

THE ARTS

Armstrong, Nancy Cameron. "Quilts of the Gulf War, Desert Storm—Participation or Protest?" *Uncoverings 1992.* San Francisco, Calif.: American Quilt Study Group, 1992.

Campbell, Esther W. *Bagpipes in the Woodwind Section: A History of the Seattle Symphony and the Women's Association.* Seattle: Symphony Women's Association, 1978.

Cross, Mary Bywater. *Quilts and Women of the Mormon Migrations: Treasures of Transitions.* Nashville, Tenn.: Rutledge Hill Press, 1997.

_____. "Reflections on an Oregon Quilt Contest." *Bits and Pieces: Textile Traditions.* Lewisburg, Pa.: Oral Traditions Project, 1991.

_____.*Treasures in the Trunk: Quilts of the Oregon Trail.* Nashville: Rutledge Hill Press, 1993.

Cunningham, Imogen. *After Ninety.* Seattle: University of Washington Press, 1977.

DiBiase, Linda Popp. "Culture at 'The End of the Line': The Arts in Seattle, 1914–1983." Master's thesis, California State University at Los Angeles, 1984.

Dodds, Anita Galvan. "Women and Their Role in the Early Art of Seattle." Master's thesis, University of Washington, 1981.

Elberson, Stanley Denton. "The History of the Tacoma Little Theater, 1918–1932." Master's thesis, University of Utah, 1961.

Fields, Ronald. *Abby Williams Hill and the Lure of the West.* Tacoma: Washington State Historical Society, 1989.

Grant, Howard F. *The Story of Seattle's Early Theaters.* Seattle: University of Washington Bookstore, 1934.

Gunther, Erna. *Art in the Life of the Northwest Coast Indians.* Seattle: Superior Publishing Company, 1966.

Halper, Vicki. "Northwestern Exposure," pp. 107–30 in Patricia Trenton, ed., *Independent Spirits: Women Painters of the American West, 1890–1945.* Los Angeles: Gene Autry Museum of Western Heritage, in association with Berkeley: University of California Press, 1995.

Hoffman, Elizabeth. "The Murder Quilt: A Multimethod Investigation." *Uncoverings 1996.* San Francisco, Calif.: American Quilt Study Group, 1996.

Miller, Kristin. "Innovative Group Quiltmaking in an Isolated Coastal Community in British Columbia, Canada: Out of the Mainstream." *Uncoverings 1993.* San Francisco, Calif.: American Quilt Study Group, 1994.

Mills, Hazel E., ed. *Who's Who Among Pacific Northwest Authors.* Salem, Ore.: Pacific Northwest Library Association, 1957.

"Patterns and Passages: Quilts as an Expression of Human Experience." Exhibition catalog. Tacoma: Washington State Capital Museum, Cheney Cowles Museum/Eastern Washington Historical Society, 1994.

Pollard, Lancaster. "A Checklist of Washington Authors." *Pacific Northwest Review* 3 (January 1940): 3–96.

_____. "A Checklist of Washington Authors: Additions and Corrections." *Pacific Northwest Quarterly* 35 (July 1944): 233–66.

Powers, Alfred. *History of Oregon Literature.* Portland: Metropolitan Press, 1935.

Queener-Shaw, Janice. "Fidelity to Nature: Puget Sound Pioneer Artists, 1870–1915." Seattle: Museum of History and Industry, November 1986.

Reynolds, Helen Louise. "Ella Higginson, Northwest Author." Master's thesis, University of Washington, 1941.

Roher, Mary Katherine. *A History of Seattle's Stock Companies from Their Beginnings to 1934*. Seattle: University of Washington Press, 1945.

Rowley, Nancy J. "Red Cross Quilts for the Great War." *Uncoverings 1982*. San Francisco, Calif.: American Quilt Study Group, 1983.

Schlick, Mary Dodds. *Columbia River Basketry: Gift of the Ancestors, Gift of the Earth*. Seattle: University of Washington Press, 1994.

Twelker, Nancyann. *Women and Their Quilts: A Washington State Centennial Tribute*. Bothell, Wash.: That Patchwork Place, 1988.

CONTRIBUTORS

LILLIAN ACKERMAN received a Ph.D. in anthropology from Washington State University in 1982 and is an associate professor at that institution. She has edited Women and Power in Native North America (1995, with Laura F. Klein) and A Song to the Creator: Traditional Arts of Native American Women of the Plateau (1996). She has also written a book-length ethnographic overview of the Colville Reservation for the National Park Service. Her field research has included studies of the Tlingit Indians, the Yup'ik Eskimos, the Plateau Indians, and primarily the Colville Indian Reservation. She has published articles mainly on gender but also on clan organization.

SUSAN H. ARMITAGE, professor of history at Washington State University, holds a Ph.D. in history from the London School of Economics and Political Science. She is the author of a number of articles on western women, and the co-editor (with Elizabeth Jameson) of *The Women's West*, published by the University of Oklahoma Press in 1986. Her essay for this collection was delivered at the Annual Pettyjohn Symposium in 1998 at Washington State University.

KAREN J. BLAIR is a professor of history and department chair at Central Washington University in Ellensburg, Washington. She has published *The Clubwoman as Feminist: True Womanhood Redefined, 1868–1914* (1980); *The Torchbearers: Women and Their Amateur Arts Associations in America, 1890–1930* (1994); *Northwest Women: An Annotated Bibliography of Sources on the History of Oregon and Washington Women, 1787–1970* (1997); and *The*

History of American Women's Voluntary Organizations, 1810–1960: A Guide to Sources (1988). Her first edition of this collection was published in 1989. She is currently working on a guide to researching men's and women's clubs.

MARY BYWATER CROSS is a quilt historian and quilt artist living in Portland, Oregon. Her major focus of study has used documented quilts as visual records of women's experiences. She has written *Treasures in the Trunk: Quilts of the Oregon Trail* (1993) and *Quilts and Women of the Mormon Migrations: Treasures of Transition* (1997); both books examine the lives of previously unknown women who traveled west to establish themselves and their families. She is currently working on research projects related to quilts made by and for Methodists and quilts made of woolen cloth.

DAVID PETERSON DEL MAR of Portland, Oregon, is the author of *What Trouble I Have Seen: A History of Violence Against Wives* (1996) and articles in the *Journal of Interdisciplinary History, Journal of American Ethnic History, Journal of Family Violence, Ethnohistory,* and *Environmental History.* He is currently writing a history tentatively entitled "Violence and Power: An Intimate History."

JERRY GARCÍA is an assistant professor of history and Latina/o Studies at Iowa State University. He received his Ph.D. in history at Washington State University. He is preparing a manuscript on a Mexican community in Washington State and is co-authoring an article on the development of Chicano communities in the Columbia Basin. Presently he is conducting research on braceros in Washington and Mexican immigration to the state of Iowa.

MAURINE W. GREENWALD is an associate professor of history at the University of Pittsburgh. She is the author of *Women, War, and Work: The Impact of World War I on Women Workers in the United States* (1980) and co-editor of *Pittsburgh Surveyed: Social Science and Social Reform in the Early Twentieth Century* (1996). She is writing a book on the centrality of gender as a category of historical analysis for understanding the economics, politics, and culture of the United States from 1950 to 2000.

LAUREN KESSLER has a Ph.D. in communications history from the University of Washington (1980). She is currently director of the graduate program in literary nonfiction and a professor in the School of Journalism at the University of Oregon. She has written *Full Court Press* (1997) and *Stubborn Twig* (1993), works of literary nonfiction, as well as *The Dissident Press: Alternative Journalism in American History, Uncovering the News: The*

Journalist's Search for Information (1984, with Duncan McDonald), and *When Words Collide: A Journalist's Guide to Grammar and Style* (1992, with Duncan McDonald).

RUTH BARNES MOYNIHAN, who earned her Ph.D. from Yale University in 1979, is the author of *Rebel for Rights: Abigail Scott Duniway* (1983). She is the co-editor of *So Much to Be Done: Women Settlers on the Mining and Ranching Frontier* (2d edition, 1998), and *Second to None: A Documentary History of American Women from the 16th Century to the Present,* vols. 1 and 2 (1994). Now retired from teaching, she is a historical consultant and writer, specializing in the history of women. She lives and works in northeastern Connecticut.

GAIL NOMURA has a Ph.D. in history from the University of Hawaii. She is an assistant professor in the Department of American Ethnic Studies at the University of Washington. She is a past president of the Association for Asian American Studies. She has co-edited two anthologies, *Frontiers of Asian American Studies* (1989) and *Bearing Dreams, Shaping Visions: Asian Pacific American Perspectives* (1993), and has published numerous chapters and articles on the history of Asian Americans. She is completing a book manuscript, "Contested Terrain: Asian Americans on the Yakama Indian Reservation," and working on a history of Japanese Americans in the Midwest.

DORIS H. PIEROTH, an independent historian in Seattle, has a Ph.D. in history from the University of Washington. She is currently working on a study of women who taught in the Seattle School District between the two world wars. She is the author of *Their Day in the Sun: Women of the 1932 Olympics,* a work of sport history published by the University of Washington Press in 1996. Her article on Mayor Landes won the Washington State Historical Society's Charles M. Gates Memorial Award "for the most scholarly contribution to the *Pacific Northwest Quarterly* in the year 1984."

KAREN BECK SKOLD earned a Ph.D. in sociology from the University of Oregon in 1981. She taught classes in women's studies and sociology at the University of Oregon, San Diego State University, and San Jose State University. She was an independent scholar affiliated with the Institute for Research on Women and Gender at Stanford University for eight years, then worked for the city of Sunnyvale, California, helping to implement its child-care policy. Currently she uses her teaching and writing skills as a community volunteer.

SYLVIA VAN KIRK earned her Ph.D. at the University of London. She is a professor of Canadian history and women's studies at the University of Toronto. Best known for her monograph *Many Tender Ties: Women in Fur Trade Society, 1670–1870* (1983), she is the author of numerous articles on fur trade social history and the role of women in various western frontiers.

INDEX

Boldface numerals indicate illustrations.